AMERICAN WINDSOR FURNITURE

Specialized Forms

AMERICAN WINDSOR FURNITURE

Specialized Forms

NANCY GOYNE EVANS

HUDSON HILLS PRESS · NEW YORK
in association with
The Henry Francis du Pont Winterthur Museum

Photography funded in part by the National Endowment for the Humanities.

FIRST EDITION

© 1997 by The Henry Francis du Pont Winterthur Museum, Inc.

PUBLISHED IN THE UNITED STATES BY HUDSON HILLS PRESS, INC.,
SUITE 1308, 230 FIFTH AVENUE, NEW YORK, NY 10001-7704.

Distributed in the United States, its territories and possessions, and Canada by National Book Network.
Distributed in the United Kingdom, Eire, and Europe by Art Books International Ltd.
Distributed in Australia by Peribo PTY Limited.
Distributed in New Zealand by Nationwide Book Distributors Ltd.
Exclusive representation in China by Cassidy and Associates, Inc.

EDITOR AND PUBLISHER: PAUL ANBINDER

ASSISTANT EDITOR: FAYE CHIU

CONTENT EDITOR: GERALD W. R. WARD

COPY EDITOR: LYS ANN SHORE

PROOFREADER: LYDIA EDWARDS

INDEXER: KARLA J. KNIGHT

PRODUCTION MANAGER: SUSAN RANDOLPH

DESIGNER: HOWARD I. GRALLA

COMPOSITION: ANGELA TAORMINA

MANUFACTURED IN JAPAN BY TOPPAN PRINTING COMPANY.

Library of Congress Cataloguing-in-Publication Data

Evans, Nancy Goyne.
    American Windsor furniture : specialized forms / Nancy Goyne Evans. — 1st ed.
        p.   cm.
    Includes bibliographical references and index.
    ISBN 1-55595-064-7 (alk. paper)
    1. Furniture—United States—History—18th century.   2. Furniture—United
States—History—19th century.   3. Decoration and ornament—United States—
Windsor style.   I. Henry Francis du Pont Winterthur Museum.
NK2406.E9   1997
749.214—dc21   97-15401
                                                                                CIP

FRONTISPIECE:
High, shaped-tablet Windsor rocking chair, Josiah Prescott Wilder,
New Ipswich, N.H., ca. 1837–40 (see fig 1-50).

This book is dedicated to my mother, Lucille Johnston Goyne

Contents

Foreword

As a student in the Winterthur Program in Early American Culture, I was led on a journey of discovery and amazement through the Winterthur period rooms by former director Charles Montgomery and the curators of Winterthur. I recall the thrill of seeing many of the rooms for the first time, but one that stands out in my memory is the Court. There, facades from four eighteenth- and early nineteenth-century buildings were installed in what had formerly been an indoor squash court. The facades are magnificent and the architectural setting thrilling (still), but what I recall most vividly is the collection of Windsor chairs and settees displayed there. Today the Court contains several dozen Windsors, most of them chairs, but six are rare settees with four to twelve turned legs. Each is extraordinary, and the grouping is overwhelming. An eight-legged settee from the central Pennsylvania–Maryland border region (fig. 1-76) remains my favorite piece of Windsor furniture in the entire museum.

This late eighteenth-century settee, a tour de force of the turner's art, is a symphony of brilliant craftsmanship. Each of the twenty-nine spindles and two arm supports is boldly turned, as are the eight legs and stretchers. The assembly is dramatic, with each opposing pair of spindles set at a different angle, the angles increasing as they move toward the ends of the arms. The rake of the legs complements that of the upper structure, and the maker carved bold knuckles at the ends of the arms. It is a piece that cries out to me to sit in it—but I have steadfastly resisted its siren call. Instead, it remains a magnificent sculpture in wood that continues to delight me every time I visit the Court.

American Windsor Furniture: Specialized Forms draws upon Nancy Goyne Evans's career-long examination of literally hundreds of specialized Windsor furnishings. A companion to *American Windsor Chairs,* this volume explores the rarer and more unusual Windsor objects, such as children's furniture, miniatures, rocking chairs, writing-arm chairs, settees, stools, and many other forms. Because these distinctive furniture items were most often custom-made for individual use, they provide insight into the daily lives of early Americans—how they worked, played, and even thought.

Furniture connoisseurs will appreciate the thorough approach that continues from *American Windsor Chairs* to the study of specialized forms of Windsor furniture in this volume. *American Windsor Furniture: Specialized Forms* is an indispensable reference for all collectors, scholars, and lovers of American decorative arts. It is a distinguished complement to the triumphant *American Windsor Chairs,* and I am confident that both volumes will become classics.

DWIGHT P. LANMON, *Director*
Henry Francis du Pont Winterthur Museum

Preface and Acknowledgments

American Windsor Furniture: Specialized Forms is an integral extension of the author's comprehensive study of stick-and-socket framed plank-seat furniture, *American Windsor Chairs.* It draws upon the author's study and examination of several hundred pieces of specialized Windsor furniture and is based on the same types of primary and secondary materials used in *American Windsor Chairs.* The sources include manuscripts and public records, published journals and commentary of the period, and modern furniture studies centering on the craftsman. Organization is by form, then by region and pattern chronology. The craftsman's interaction with his environment is once again an important focus. Whenever possible, period terminology is used to describe chairmaking products and practices.

Figure numbers printed in boldface within the text identify principal references to the illustrations. Figures not in boldface are cross-references. Identification of the right and left sides of a chair or other furniture form in the illustrations corresponds to the viewer's right and left. The exception, noted in the text as appropriate, is the writing-arm Windsor, with its writing surface positioned for use by a right-handed or, rarely, a left-handed sitter.

Details of furniture parts and makers' identifications accompany some of the primary illustrations in this volume. The captions provide further information about brands on documented chairs, when photographic details are not included. Letter formats are given as closely as possible but do not distinguish between two sizes of uppercase letters.

Wood identification is by visual inspection, except when microanalysis is specified. Measurements — height, width, and depth — have been taken at points of greatest dimension.

Assistance in the creation and production of this book has come from many sources — colleagues, students, independent researchers, collectors, and dealers. In particular, I recognize Carol and Roy Allen, the late William S. Bowers, Marian and the late Oliver Deming, Florence and George Dittmar, Helen and Edward Flanagan, Marilyn and James Flowers, John R. Grabb, Charles A. Hammond, Judy and John Hasler, Wendell Hilt (via Charles F. Montgomery), Joan and Victor Johnson, Helen and Steven Kellogg, John T. Kirk, Joseph A. McFalls, Wayne Pratt, the late Joseph K. Ott, the late Charles S. Parsons, Thomas Phelan, Thomas B. Rentschler, Carrie and Ray Ruggles, Susan B. Swan, Page Talbott, Elizabeth and Edward Wallace, Marilyn M. White, and Elwood S. Wilkins.

The cooperation of staff in other institutions is gratefully acknowledged. I especially thank the following institutions: Chester County Historical Society, West Chester, Pennsylvania; Connecticut Historical Society, Hartford; Historic Deerfield, Deerfield, Massachusetts; Hitchcock Museum, Riverton, Connecticut; Independence National Historical Park, Philadelphia, Pennsylvania; James Mitchell Varnum House and Museum, East Greenwich, Rhode Island; Jeremiah Lee Mansion, Marblehead,

Massachusetts; Metropolitan Museum of Art, New York City; Museum of Early Southern Decorative Arts, Winston-Salem, North Carolina; Newport Historical Society, Newport, Rhode Island; New York State Historical Association, Cooperstown; Old Sturbridge Village, Sturbridge, Massachusetts; Museum of Art, Rhode Island School of Design, Providence; Scotland Historical Society, Scotland, Connecticut; Shelburne Museum, Shelburne, Vermont; Stratford Historical Society, Stratford, Connecticut; Woodstock Historical Society, Woodstock, Vermont; Worcester Historical Museum, Worcester, Massachusetts; Yale University Art Gallery, New Haven, Connecticut; Historical Society of York County, York, Pennsylvania.

Special thanks are due to a group of people who have been involved in the production of this volume. George Fistrovich, Winterthur photographer, created most of the excellent photographic images. As copy editor, Lys Ann Shore refined the text and accompaniments to their present crisp, lucid state. Susan Randolph in the Winterthur publications office guided the manuscript through the publication process, and at each stage of manuscript development, the word processing staff at Winterthur provided able assistance.

NANCY GOYNE EVANS
Hockessin, Delaware

Introduction

American Windsor Furniture: Specialized Forms is a companion volume to *American Windsor Chairs,* which chronicles this branch of the furniture-making industry from the 1740s to the mid nineteenth century, by geographic region. The present volume is organized along similar lines and uses the same cultural, economic, and technological framework. Examination of each type of specialized form begins with a brief historical review, followed by a discussion of the form in its regional contexts, starting with Pennsylvania and/or Philadelphia and moving on to New York and New England. Discussion of the South, Midwest, and Canada follows, as appropriate. Standard Windsor seating—the armchair and especially the side chair—was produced in quantity and formed the backbone of the Windsor industry. Specialized Windsor furniture, however, was "bespoke," or ordered, and was considerably less common. Hundreds of side chairs and armchairs were sold for each specialized form produced by a chairmaker.

Patterns in specialized Windsor furniture parallel those of standard Windsor seating, with modifications as required to suit the function of the form. Several patterns are rare in specialized furniture because of the structural requirements of the form or the need for cost-effective construction. The discussion takes note of stylistic features common to particular regions, variations within regions, relationships between regions, and the modification of features over time. Regional characteristics are more fully discussed and illustrated in *American Windsor Chairs.* Stylistic influences on specialized Windsor design are discussed, as appropriate. The principal sources of influence were English Windsor furniture, American vernacular and formal furniture, and neoclassical design and ornament derived from price books, design books, and contemporary furniture in the neoclassical taste. The child's Windsor cradle, for example, is a clever adaptation of a board-framed furniture form to Windsor construction.

This study also illuminates the mechanics of specialized forms. Constructing a writing arm, for instance, required alterations to standard designs for arm rails and seats, and chairmakers chose one of several methods to install a drawer beneath the arm or seat. For rocking chairs, they used three basic techniques for attaching rockers to the bottoms of chair legs to permit forward and backward motion. Each of these different techniques dictated the design of the lower part of the legs. The sweeping three-piece, S-scroll seat of the Boston rocking chair, although more a stylistic feature than a mechanical one, assisted in the smooth performance of these large chairs while enhancing the comfort of the sitter.

The ingenuity of convertible furniture designs and their developers is seen in a patent drawing and description of a cradle-chair by S. S. May and in the two illustrations of an example made to the specifications of the patent (figs. 1-61, 1-62). The settee-cradle represents a simplification of the same principle of converting a rocking seat to a rocking bed (figs. 1-94, 2-71). Wheels added to the Windsor transformed standard furniture into mobile chairs for invalids (fig. 1-66), wagons for children (fig. 2-59), or horsedrawn vehicles (fig. 3-38).

Documentation of the ownership and use of specialized Windsor forms provides still another dimension to the study of this class of furniture. The range extends from professional men to craftsmen, from children to invalids. Private households were common settings for specialized Windsor furniture, but selected forms, such as the settee, rocking chair, and stool, proved equally suitable for use in public houses and institutions. Several forms, the settee in particular, made up a small segment of the waterborne trade in Windsor furniture, especially the trade to the coastal South and the islands of the Caribbean.

Initially, settees and children's furniture were the most popular specialized forms of Windsor furniture in terms of general sales. During the 1820s the Windsor rocking chair, which had been introduced in the 1790s, took the market by storm. Almost overnight it became a fixture in households across the country. The writing-arm chair was considerably less popular because of its size and function, but even so it was fairly common from its introduction in the postrevolutionary period. Simple stick stools were produced in several sizes and large quantities. They were inexpensive and received hard use, so comparatively few have survived.

The fabrication of spinning wheels and reels, implements crucial to the self-sufficiency of many households during the eighteenth and early nineteenth centuries, contributed measurably to the income of the turner-chairmakers, particularly those in rural and frontier areas. By contrast, stands and tables of true Windsor construction, with the legs socketed directly into the top, were never common. Production is difficult to track because the form remains unidentified in contemporary records. Also on the fringes of mainstream production were commode chairs, seats for invalids, and seating for use in vehicles. The following chapters discuss in detail specialized Windsors for adults, Windsor furniture for children, and miscellaneous stick forms.

Color Plates

Pl. 1 Child's high-back Windsor armchair, Rhode Island, 1785–1800. (See fig. 2-1.) An old alligatored surface comprising multiple layers of paint and resin dating from the late eighteenth to the late nineteenth century.

Pl. 2 Child's sack-back Windsor armchair, New York, 1785–95. (See fig. 2-5.) An old chipped surface exposing several layers of paint and resin dating from the nineteenth century.

Pl. 3 Detail of lower left end of figure 1-73. A yellow-ocher and speckled brown varnish surface dating from the late nineteenth century. Older coats of dark paint are visible at small chipped spots.

Pl. 4 Boston (Windsor) rocking chair, New England, 1845–55. Materials and dimensions unknown. (Hitchcock Museum, Riverton, Conn.: Photo, Winterthur.) Original rosewood-grained surface paint with daubed and striped seat top and stenciled decoration on crest and seat front.

Pl. 5   Detail of crest of figure 1-49. Original rosewood-grained surface paint with handpainted and stenciled decoration.

Pl. 6   Detail of crest of figure 1-50. Original surface paint and restrained decoration, including gilt star in each end of tablet scroll.

Pl. 7   Detail of crest of high, crown-top Windsor rocking chair, Massachusetts or northeastern New England, 1830–40. White pine (seat); H. 43⅝″, (seat) 15⁵⁄₁₆″, W. (crest) 22¾″, (arms) 21⅜″, (seat) 19⅛″, D. (seat) 18¾″. (Dr. and Mrs. J. Goodman collection: Photo, Winterthur.) Original surface paint with handpainted and stenciled decoration.

Pl. 8   Detail of crest of high, crown-top Windsor rocking chair, probably eastern Massachusetts, 1830–40. White pine (seat); H. 44⅜″, (seat) 14¼″, W. (crest) 22⅝″, (arms) 21″, (seat) 19⅝″, D. (seat) 18¼″. (Steven and Helen Kellogg collection: Photo, Winterthur.) Original surface paint with handpainted and stenciled decoration. A design alternative to the crest in plate 7.

Pl. 9   Detail of crest of figure 1-53. Original surface paint and decoration.

Pl. 10 Detail of upper back of figure 1-55.
Original surface paint and decoration.

Pl. 11 Detail of crest of figure 1-56. Original
surface paint with handpainted and stenciled
decoration.

Pl. 12 Detail of upper back of figure 1-57.
Original surface paint and decoration.

Pl. 13 Detail of crests of tablet-top Windsor
rocking chair with top extension, Elisha
Trowbridge, Portland, Maine, 1822 (dated).
White pine (seat); H. 41¼″, (seat) 15¼″,
W. (primary crest) 21½″, (arms) 21″, (seat)
20¼″, D. (seat) 18¼″. (Private collection: Photo,
Winterthur.) Original surface paint and decora-
tion. The decoration is the same as that in figure
1-59, a rocking chair from the Portland shop of
Hudson and Brooks.

Pl. 14 Detail of upper back of slat-back Windsor rocking chair, Portland, Maine, 1820–30. White pine (seat); H. 32¼″, (seat) 15″, W. (crest) 19⅜″, (arms) 21¾″, (seat) 18¾″, D. (seat) 17″. (Maine Historical Society, Wadsworth-Longfellow House, Portland: Photo, Winterthur.) Original surface paint and decoration. The slat back was an alternative construction to the tablet-framed crest of plate 13.

Pl. 15 Detail of crest of figure 1-69. Original surface paint and stenciled decoration.

Pl. 16 Detail of left end of figure 1-97. Original surface paint and decoration.

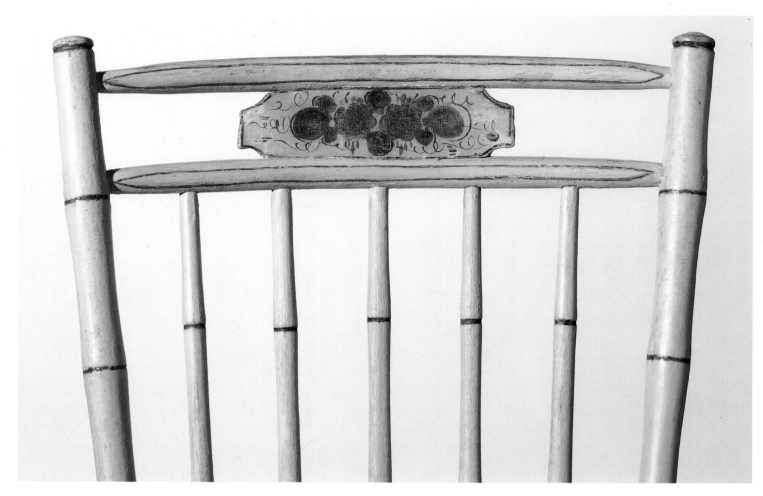

Pl. 17 Detail of upper back of figure 2-31. Paint and decoration partially original. Pale yellow, or "straw" color, was the ideal choice for the simulated-bamboo Windsor; dark-painted grooves heightened the effect. Flowers and fruits were the most popular decorative motifs for the Windsor crest during the early decades of the nineteenth century.

Pl. 18   Detail of back of figure 2-35. Original surface paint and decoration.

Pl. 19   Detail of back of figure 2-36. Original surface paint and decoration.

Pl. 20 Detail of crest of figure 2-41. Original surface paint and decoration.

Pl. 21 Detail of crest of figure 2-42. Original surface paint and handpainted and stenciled decoration.

Pl. 22 *Portrait of a Family*, attributed to Jacob Maentel, York, Pa., ca. 1825. Watercolor on paper; H. 17½″, W. 23″. (Winterthur 57.1123.) The family seating forms a suite of Windsor furniture.

Pl. 23 Youth's slat-back Windsor rocking chair, northeastern New York state, Vermont, or southeastern New Hampshire, 1835–40. Basswood (seat, microanalysis); H. 31½", (seat) 14⅜", W. (crest) 16¾", (seat) 16", D. (seat) 16⅜". (Hitchcock Museum, Riverton, Conn.: Photo, Winterthur.) Original surface paint and decoration.

Pl. 24 Detail of crest of figure 2-45. Original surface paint and decoration.

Pl. 25   Child's rocking horse with Windsor chair, New England or New York, 1860–85. H. 13½", (seat) 8³⁄₁₆", L. (rockers) 31¾", W. (rockers) 11¹⁄₁₆". (Stratford Historical Society, Stratford, Conn.: Photo, Winterthur.) Original surface paint and decoration with painted trompe l'oeil canework seat, painted cloth ears, and leather rein.

Pl. 26   Miniature tablet-top Windsor side chairs, eastern Pennsylvania or Maryland, *(left to right)* 1810–30 and 1820–40. Yellow poplar (seat) with maple and yellow poplar, and yellow poplar (seat) with maple, ash, and yellow poplar (microanalysis, both); H. 9⅝", 8¹³⁄₁₆", (seat) 4⅜", 4³⁄₁₆", W. (crest) 7", 6⅛", (seat) 5½", D. (seat) 5¾", 5¹⁵⁄₁₆". (Winterthur 59.983, 61.1776.) Original surface paint and decoration; (right) left front leg varies in profile from others but the paint is similar.

Pl. 27   Miniature or doll's tablet-top Windsor side chair, south-central Pennsylvania or Maryland, 1830–50. Yellow poplar (seat); H. 17", (seat) 7³⁄₁₆", W. (seat) 8", D. (seat) 7⅞". (Florence and George Dittmar collection: Photo, Winterthur.) Original surface paint and decoration. This chair is too small to seat a child properly and too large to truly qualify as a miniature. It likely served best to seat a doll.

Pl. 28 Miniature low-back Windsor armchair, northern New England, including Massachusetts, 1850–70. White pine (seat) with beech, birch, and red oak (microanalysis); H. 9⅞″, (seat) 5⅞″, w. (arms) 6¹¹⁄₁₆″, (seat) 6⅜″, D. (seat) 6⅝″. (Winterthur 64.1318.) Original surface paint and decoration.

Pl. 29 Miniature balloon-back Windsor side chair, Pennsylvania, 1870–95, possibly 1891, as penciled on bottom. Yellow poplar (seat); H. 12⅜″, (seat) 5¹⁵⁄₁₆″, w. (seat) 6⅜″, D. (seat) 6⅜″. (Richard S. and Rosemarie B. Machmer collection: Photo, Winterthur.) Original surface paint and decoration.

Pl. 30 Detail of top surface of figure 3-7. Original surface paint and decoration.

Production of Specialized Adult Furniture

The Writing-Arm Chair

INTRODUCTION

The earliest seat described as a "writing chair" may have been a roundabout chair. This low-back form with a flat rail supported on three leg extensions and a seat set diamondwise was convenient for use at a fall-front desk; the broad, flat arms provided an elbow rest. Both John Gaines II and his son Thomas Gaines of Ipswich, Massachusetts, made "writing" chairs. John produced one for 15s. in 1736; Thomas sold one priced at 24s. to Daniel Appleton, Esq., in 1743. Both chairs likely were framed to receive upholstery, since the cost was much too high for common rush seating. Like many "inventions," the development of a Windsor armchair with a flat surface for writing may have been a chance thing. The first use of this form in America dates to the postwar years in Philadelphia, despite the claim that one example was made in 1763. The idea of converting a chair to a desk or writing table appears to have come to America directly from England. Robert W. Symonds identified a specially constructed joiner's writing chair made there between 1766 and 1768, probably for use at St. James's Palace. Although the writing arrangement differs from that in the American Windsor, all the necessary features are present: a board, drawer, and candle arm. The form was described as "a Walnuttree Writing Chair with a Compass [horseshoe] Front & cross Stretchers, a desk behind & drawer under the Desk for Papers. A Drawer with an Ink and Sand Bottle to turn out under one Elbow and a Supporter for a Candlestick under an other."[1]

A few chairs of similar function had already been constructed in Philadelphia by an emigrant craftsman from England. J. Stogdell Stokes, a pioneer collector of Windsor furniture, cited an entry from a local family journal, said to date to the spring of 1763, that mentioned seasonal country retreats furnished with "tables and chairs that do not meet approval," that is, furnishings which were unfashionable:

I noticed in A__'s home the large chairs, one of commodious seat having a bracket with a drawer underneath in which one can keep quills and sand, the bracket is useful to hold our account books and other papers and enable us to quote from the books those things that need our attention. My inquiry... is that they were made by one Richmonde on Sassafras Street, a joiner of much repute who has come out from the motherland.... Ordered the chairs.... Am so pleased shall not take them to country.

The craftsman Richmonde has never been located in Philadelphia records, suggesting that the name was misinterpreted. Furthermore, there is no evidence that Windsor construction was used. Richmonde probably adapted a joined chair for writing purposes.[2]

The earliest known writing-arm Windsor from Philadelphia is a heavily restored, high-back chair in the study collection at the Winterthur Museum that recalls prerevolutionary work. Fixed to the seat bottom is the craftsmen's original printed label, now defaced, darkened, cracked, and almost illegible. A second, handwritten label placed under the drawer in the writing arm further identifies the shop, the original owner, and the line of descent: "This chair is to be fixed so I am copying the name paper as best I can as it has become very mutilated and hard to read as follows. 'All kinds of Windsor chairs made and sold by Gilbert and Robert Gaw at 18 North Front twelve doors above Mulberry street Philada.' This chair belonged to Uncle Joshiah [*sic*] Newbold and was handed down from his family. Martha Wetherill, 1891, Phila. Chalkly Hall."

The repair work was extensive, comprising four new legs in the ball-foot style, two outer writing-leaf posts supported on the original seat projections, a writing leaf and box (containing the original drawer), and the outer pad of the left arm. The Gaw brothers were actually located at 88 Front Street beginning with their directory listing of 1793 and possibly earlier. The construction of this chair coincides with John Letchworth's fabrication of another "writing chair" of unknown pattern for Jonathan Williams, a "gentleman." The substantial charge of 30*s.* for this special chair was equivalent to five days' wages for an average Philadelphia woodworker. Another Philadelphia writing chair was shipped to Richmond, Virginia, in 1798 on board the sloop *Experiment*.[3]

The products of at least three other Philadelphia writing-chair makers were in the market in the 1790s. Lawrence Allwine shipped three dozen chairs and "Two Writing ditto" to Norfolk, Virginia, on February 4, 1795. Anthony Steel is known by three low-back chairs (fig. 1-1), two branded, the third unmarked. The turnings of all three interrelate but vary subtly. The illustrated example is the only one with a horizontally scrolled arm; the other two have carved knuckle grips. A bow-front drawer under each writing leaf fits into a three-sided case. The case bottom, which sockets the three supports, is nailed to the sides, and the sides are nailed to the leaf from the top surface. The drawer, also of nailed construction, is unusual in retaining the original interior fittings. Two long and two short partitions, beveled at the top, are slotted into either the drawer sides or each other at the inner end and form several compartments to hold writing materials. Adjacent to this unit is a sizable area for storing papers or account books. Steel's brand, an "A" followed by a diamond-shaped pellet and the surname, is clearly visible inside the drawer bottom and is stamped again beneath the seat. Scraped paper remnants in the drawer may be part of an original chairmaker's label or the remains of a later handwritten note. The seat-front profile, rising to a low center pommel and terminating at the left in a long, boat-shaped projection — one of two extensions — seems to be characteristic of Steel's writing chairs, since all three planks are the same. The drawer boxes follow one of two arrangements. The one in the illustrated chair is rotated outward; the drawer, which slides through, never had any pulls. The boxes in the other chairs are nearly aligned with the seat front. The reason for the shift in position in one of those chairs is the addition of a second small drawer that opens from the front and rides on cleats beneath the primary drawer case. When closed, the small drawer tucks neatly between the two turned front supports and butts against the third one. The same chair also has a broad, shallow drawer suspended on cleats beneath the seat.[4]

Stokes identified what he thought was the earliest Windsor with a writing surface dating from 1763 and originating in the shop of the mysterious Richmonde (fig. 1-2). In reality, the chair is a product of the 1790s and represents the hand of a master craftsman of the caliber of John B. Ackley. Two high-back writing chairs branded by Ackley are close in form to the one illustrated. The profiles of the bamboowork and the scored short spindles are slightly different. Otherwise, the three chairs appear identical, from the carved crests, lamb's-tongue rail ends, scrolled arms, and cleat-hung drawers to the broad seats with a single tongue to support the leaf. Although the shield-shaped plank

Fig. 1-1 Low-back Windsor writing-arm chair and detail of drawer, Anthony Steel (brand "A·STEEL"), Philadelphia, 1790–1800. Yellow poplar (seat) with maple, chestnut, and yellow poplar (microanalysis); H. (arms) 31¹⁄₁₆″, (seat) 13¹³⁄₁₆″, W. (seat) 25″, D. (seat) 16³⁄₁₆″, (leaf) 22½″ by 17″. (Winterthur 64.1924.)

is unusual in a writing Windsor, it is employed successfully here. Bamboowork was first introduced in Philadelphia about the mid 1780s.[5]

Writing-arm Windsors of the 1790s from New York and Philadelphia differ substantially. New York chairs are undocumented, although some may have once possessed labels. A distinctive feature of more than half the number known is the modest or pronounced tilt of the back rail and writing surface, which permits the sitter to recline somewhat when writing (fig. **1-3**). Almost all known New York writing chairs have a bold, carved terminal in the left arm and full rounded turnings. The uncarved but moderately curved crest is common to most examples, while the "high" backs are lower than those usually found in tall chairs. In the manner of Philadelphia work, lap joints connect the heavy back rail and the arms. The first long spindle behind the knuckle arm passes through both pieces of wood, and a wooden pin between the first

Fig. 1-2 High-back Windsor writing-arm chair,
Philadelphia, 1790–1800. Yellow poplar (seat)
and other woods. (Former collection J. Stogdell
Stokes.)

Fig. 1-3 High-back Windsor writing-arm chair,
New York, 1790–1800. Yellow poplar (seat) with
maple, hickory, yellow poplar, and white pine
(microanalysis); H. 37⁷⁄₁₆″, (seat) 16¾″, w. (crest)
15⅞″, (seat) 24″, D. (seat) 16¹⁵⁄₁₆″, (leaf) 26⅛″ by
18½″; right stretcher probably old replacement,
writing-arm repairs. (Winterthur 59.1963.)

and second long sticks further reinforces the joint. The illustrated chair has been
repaired in the writing arm, although its integrity is intact. The cleats suspending the
drawer beneath the leaf were replaced within the past century, but the presence of a lip
at the top of the long drawer edges confirms this as the original type of attachment. A
drawer stop was once fixed beneath the leaf near the outside edge. Farther back on the
outside, a small, pivoting shelf once swung outward, balanced catercorner by a candle
slide dovetailed beneath the leaf; the slot is clearly visible adjacent to the front of the
drawer. The left side stretcher (the right as viewed) may be an old replacement; it
appears to be missing the original coat of green paint.

By chance, it is possible to identify the probable repairer. Inscribed in pencil under
the seat is the legend: "March 15 1855 / John Jelliff Newark / 301 Broad st." John Jelliff
was a well-known cabinetmaker of Newark, New Jersey. The mid-nineteenth-century
date appears consistent with the paint chronology found on the suspect stretcher.
Other repairs probably are later, since they bear only one or two paint layers. The writing surface itself was painted only twice, but for good reason. Numerous tack holes
around the edge indicate that it was covered originally with a material such as leather
or baize to provide a resilient surface for writing with a quill pen. Obviously, the original or a later covering was still intact when Jelliff owned the chair. Because the board
was covered at the time of construction, it was never painted. A second chair, which is
almost a mate, still has a leather-covered leaf, although the material probably is a late
nineteenth-century replacement. That chair, too, has a Newark history; it once belonged
to Judge Elisha Boudinot of that city.

TRACY FAMILY AND RELATED WORK

Interest in the writing chair also blossomed in New England in the late 1700s. Felix
Huntington of Norwich, Connecticut, constructed six writing chairs at *20s.* apiece,
which he delivered to the brig *Polly* in March 1789 for a voyage to Demerara (British
Guiana). At the same time he deposited for shipment three dozen green Windsors, case

Fig. 1-4 High-back Windsor writing-arm chair, attributed to Ebenezer Tracy, Sr., Lisbon Township, New London County, Conn., 1790–1803. Sycamore (seat) with birch, oak, maple, and white pine (microanalysis); H. 45⅞", (seat) 15¹³⁄₁₆", W. (crest) 18¾", (seat) 24⁵⁄₁₆", D. (seat) 18⅛", (leaf) 26½" by 18¾". (Winterthur 55.15.2.)

furniture, and a stuffed easy chair. Whether Huntington's writing chairs were Windsors or roundabouts is impossible to say, since the price is correct for either. Other area craftsmen were producing the specialized Windsor at about this date. A "Writing Chair" destined for Boston, which was shipped in 1794 from the coastal port of New London, a few miles down the Thames River from Norwich, was almost certainly of Windsor construction. Boston was a cabinetmaking center well able to meet local demands for roundabout chairs, but Windsor-chair making was still relatively new in the area. Members of the Tracy family had the Windsor business well in hand in the neighborhood of Norwich. Ebenezer Tracy, Sr., patriarch of the family, owned a "Writing Chair & cushing" valued at $4 when he died in 1803. The records of his son-in-law and former apprentice, Amos Denison Allen of South Windham, list a pertinent item under the date August 11, 1797: "1 Writeing Ch 1 draw[er] only." Reverend Elijah Waterman paid Allen 24s. (about $4). Other references follow in the same volume: a "writing Chr compleat" for 26s. in September 1797 and similarly priced chairs in 1798 and 1801, and a "Writing Chair 2 In[ches] higher than Common 2 draws, lock on lower draw @ 27/″ in December 1801.[6]

Writing chairs known from the shops of Tracy family members include high-back (fig. 1-4) and low-back patterns (figs. 1-6, 1-7); some examples are marked with the name brand of Ebenezer, Sr. A greater number are undocumented, although they exhibit unmistakable Tracy characteristics. Ebenezer's earliest tall writing chairs have crests with upturned, compass-scribed terminals comparable to those in his earliest high-crested chairs. Other shared features are also similar, except for the seats and arm supports. Tracy writing-chair backs have either five or six long spindles; the latter design is more successful. Most of the later tall Tracy writing chairs, which form a sizable group, can be dated firmly in the 1790s, based upon the chronology of family design. Except for the crest, features were fairly standard. Two top pieces succeeded the compass-volute crest, one with a moderate to pronounced scroll-end hook and another with full rounded scrolls (fig. 1-4). The former group, which probably was introduced first, contains both the largest number of examples and most of the known documented

Fig. 1-5 Staircase balustrade, Ebenezer Tracy, Sr., house, Lisbon Township, New London County, Conn., ca. 1769–72. (Photo, Winterthur.)

chairs. The body of unmarked work probably represents three Tracy chairmakers—Ebenezer, Sr., his son Elijah of Lisbon, and Amos D. Allen of South Windham.[7]

The Tracy tall writing chair is a composite of several influences (fig. 1-4). The base structure derives from Ebenezer's early high-back and sack-back work, which features the same tipped stretchers, large crowned spools, and flared-neck baluster turnings. All elements have their roots in early Connecticut turnery. The seat front with its hollow pommel follows that in Tracy's early compass-scroll, high-back chair, which in turn was inspired by English design. With the addition of the writing arm, modification was necessary. To compensate visually for the projecting tongues socketing the leaf supports, the chairmaker recessed the opposite front corner so that the contoured central section breaks forward in the manner of joined seating dating from the early federal period. Following typical regional practice, the legs do not pierce the plank top and there is no groove on the inside of the spindle platform. The scroll-end arm is a common pattern in Rhode Island and Philadelphia Windsor-chair making; the profile is adapted from the roundabout chair. The lap-joint construction of the back corners follows Philadelphia practice. Similar influence is present in the arm supports. Comparison with an early tall chair made by Francis Trumble shows a sequence of shapes so close in form and proportion that a relationship is undeniable. Tracy used this pattern only in his writing chairs.[8]

Still other impulses were critical in Ebenezer Tracy's development of roundwork for his chairs. At his Lisbon house, built about 1770, the craftsman turned the front staircase banisters (fig. 1-5) to a pattern that incorporates a short, squat turning near the base; thin wafers in the upper neck ring and crown; and long, swelled balusters through the body. Similar elements appear in early Connecticut turned seating. The compressed baluster near the base of the banister was used in two of Tracy's three writing chairs (figs. 1-4, 1-7). The longer balusters of the staircase are related to the arm posts of Tracy's small writing chair (fig. 1-6). The influence of the long turning can also be seen in the back posts of the family fan-back side chair in concert with the neck ring. The ring was also used in the long, arm-post balusters of at least one low-back, D-seat writing chair.[9]

The specialized features of the tall writing group are about the same from chair to chair (fig. 1-4). The writing surface is a large oval board. In the illustrated example, a small wedge inserted at a later date at the outside back raises the leaf slightly and tilts it inward. The storage assembly under the leaf, which is original, consists of cleats, a drawer stop, and a dovetailed container with a flush, nailed bottom. Operation of the drawer invites comparison with the previous New York chair, since instead of having lips at the top edges to ride on the cleats, each side is grooved to run on a narrow projection, or tongue, protruding from the base of each cleat. Another set of cleats, nailed crosswise to the drawer bottom, once accommodated a candle slide whose forward cleat end extended below the candle board to create both a stop and a fingerhold. Many Tracy chairs originally had a slide, but at least half are missing today, and for good reason. The boards have two deep slots cut on the inside end. When the entire unit is closed, the slots permit the slide to bypass the two forward posts (and adjacent spindles), effectively locking the drawer until the slide is pulled out. Doubtless, many a user found this a troublesome arrangement and soon dispensed with the slide.

Many tall chairs support a second dovetailed drawer of varying depth beneath the seat; nailed stops prevent their pushing through. The large box in the present chair bears a late nineteenth-century inked inscription: "PAINTED BY E. E. White Rutland Vt. Nov 19 1897." When acquired for the Winterthur collection many years ago, the chair had a badly flaking coat of dark paint, probably the one referred to here. Seat edges, drawer fronts, arm rail, and crest were penciled in a contrasting light color. A somewhat crude leaf stencil ornamented the inside face of the back rail; the date "1780" was centered in the crest, with a square cross in each scroll end. The seat front projection is eliminated in some tall Tracy writing chairs, and less than half have only a single seat tongue and two leaf supports. Most branded examples fall into this category. Four chairs from a group of six branded examples have a broken "Y" at the end of the Tracy

Fig. 1-6 Low-back Windsor writing-arm chair, attributed to Tracy family, Lisbon Township, New London County, Conn., 1790–1803. Buttonwood (seat) with maple and oak (micro-analysis); H. (arms) 30⅛", (seat) 16½", W. (seat) 21¾", D. (seat) 17⅛"; drawer missing under leaf. (Former collection Winterthur 67.668.)

surname, pinpointing the beginning of production as the early 1790s. Another marked chair is said to be inscribed "1797, Norwich, Ct." within the writing-leaf drawer.[10]

Within the sizable group of low-back writing chairs attributable to the Tracys, there are three significant seat variations. Several chairs have D-shaped planks of the general type found in figure 1-1, with flat sides and a thick front surface substituted for rounded edges. The turnings are distinctive as well. The principal balusters of the arm supports have elongated, slim bodies, and at times the thin disk under the squat baluster is missing (fig. 1-4). One leg profile resembles that in Ebenezer Tracy's fan, bow, and continuous-bow chairs. The spool turning is compressed and spreading; the baluster is elongated through the neck though still flared at the top. All chairs noted in this subgroup have a drawer under the writing leaf. One rides on cleats via a groove in the side panels, while the others are cased within a box.[11]

The chairs in another low-back writing group (fig. **1-6**) are framed with the oval plank common to Ebenezer Tracy's sack-back Windsor. These chairs have only one seat projection socketing an outer writing-arm support, although the illustrated example has two heavy supports on the seat proper under the leaf. The sack-back chair provided the arm-post pattern; the baluster narrows at the base and the lower element forms an inverted bulb, sometimes of carrot shape. The illustrated supports are exceedingly well turned and stylish, echoing the bold swells of the spindles. Beneath the seat, standard writing-chair elements hold sway, although the baluster turning varies in its vigor. The illustrated baluster is not as bold in concept as some in the group or those illustrated in other writing Windsors by the Tracy family. Two chairs have background histories. The example pictured—one of two low-back writing chairs from the New London, Connecticut, estate of Senator Frank B. Brandegee—was purchased in 1925 by Henry Francis du Pont (the other was bought by Stokes). The chairs once stood in the law office of Brandegee's father Augustus, who presumably acquired them from a Judge Goddard with whom he had studied law. Another chair, owned by the New London County Historical Society, is said to have belonged to Colonel Oliver Smith of nearby Stonington.

The members of the third and largest group of Tracy low-back writing chairs are framed in the manner of a high-back chair (fig. **1-7**). In most cases the individual parts

Fig. 1-7 Low-back Windsor writing-arm chair and detail of brand, Ebenezer Tracy, Sr., Lisbon Township, New London County, Conn. H. (arms) 31″, (seat) 15⅜″, W. (seat) 24¼″, D. (seat) 18⅜″, (leaf) 26¾″ by 18½″. (E. and E. Wallace collection: Photo, Winterthur.)

of the high and low patterns are interchangeable. Often the turnings are less bold than those illustrated, and only a few chairs are documented. A Windsor in the collection of Colonial Williamsburg was branded by Ebenezer Tracy under the seat. Figure 1-7 is stamped by the maker in the same location and again on the seat top immediately in front of the center back spindles. The iron that created the impressions was in its original state when struck on this chair. By the time Tracy marked the Williamsburg Windsor, however, the brand had sustained damage. A drawer — probably of the large size found in the tall writing chair, judging by the position of the surviving cleats — was once suspended from the seat. A small, rectangular hole on the seat bottom near the front indicates that the drawer had a lock. The bottom of the small drawer under the writing leaf is chisel-marked "II." Similar marks, or numbers, have been found on other writing chairs. The marks probably matched chairs to their correct fitted parts in the final stages of framing, when several chairs were in process at the same time. The candle slide under the small drawer has had its front cleat repaired or replaced; originally, the ends would have been flush with those of the board sides. Once again, the slide acts as a locking mechanism for the drawer when both are closed. The leather cover of the writing leaf, secured by ornamental nails, probably was added in the late nineteenth century, although such treatment could have been part of the original board surface. At the chair back, heavy lap joints securing the arms and rail are pinned three times, top and bottom. Not all back rails rise in a small hump like this one; some are flatter. Frequently, spindle holes are drilled through the heavy rail, permitting the short sticks to pierce the top surface, although this practice is not typical of low-back construction in general. Close examination of several Tracy examples, including the present chair, reveals that the spindle tips carry all the paint layers found on the rest of the chair, confirming the originality of the construction. Within this group there is an overwhelming dominance of double, as opposed to single, seat projections to accommodate the writing-arm supports.[12]

The Tracy craftsmen had imitators in New London County and probably across the border in Rhode Island as well. Unidentified workmen copied particular elements closely while improvising on others. A leaf chair in this category is illustrated in figure **1-8.** Analysis of the design begins with the pronounced hook-end crest, which duplicates the top piece in fan-back side chairs and tall writing chairs made by Elijah

Fig. 1-8 High-back Windsor writing-arm chair, Connecticut–Rhode Island border region, 1790–1800. Butternut (seat) with maple, oak, and white pine (microanalysis); H. 46½", (seat) 16¼", W. (crest) 18", (seat) 23⅝"; D. (seat) 17⅞", (leaf) 25¼" by 18¼"; drawers not original to chair. (Winterthur 65.3030.)

Tracy, eldest son of Ebenezer Tracy, Sr. Arm-support turnings are those illustrated in figures 1-4 and 1-7, although they are not executed as flamboyantly; a few Tracy turnings are also restrained in character. An unusual detail is the extra, wafer-thin disk between the short baluster and the tapered base of the two outside writing-arm supports, which slightly increases the post length. The seat, patterned generally after the large Tracy plank, breaks forward differently across the front; the prominent pommel ridge, inspired by Rhode Island design, has a pinched quality. At the back, behind the spindles, a barely visible seam marks the place where a narrow piece was added to the original plank to increase the depth. Although Tracy influence is apparent in the upper part of the legs, the sharply tapered feet follow a Rhode Island pattern. The ends of all three stretchers are terminated by rounded, Tracy-style tips, although the center brace is a later replacement. The paint chronology of the drawers also differs from that of the original parts; however, the boxes have been in place a long time.[13]

OTHER EIGHTEENTH-CENTURY NEW ENGLAND CHAIRS

Two high-back chairs that resemble each other, one illustrated in figure **1-9,** serve to identify the northern coastal Connecticut style as interpreted in the writing chair. The pictured chair belonged to Reverend Frederick W. Hotchkiss, pastor of the Congregational Church of Old Saybrook from 1783 to 1844. Both writing chairs are close in pattern to a tall armchair with a family history in adjacent Lyme, Connecticut, where it is said to have been owned by William Noyes (1760–1834). The dominant feature of the chairs is the crest with its full-blown, rounded terminals, a distinctive characteristic of this region. The turnings and the squared oval plank of canted side profile and double front sweep are also comparable to work from this area, although the fancy side stretchers are an unexpected embellishment. Following a construction practice found in many northeastern Connecticut chairs, the leg tips do not pierce the seat top. One feature absent from the second writing Windsor is the small, cuplike extension poised delicately at the front seat corner beneath the writing arm. The double posts of the second chair are both anchored in the seat proper. The two writing leaves, how-

Fig. 1-9 High-back Windsor writing-arm chair and detail of arm terminal, northern coastal Connecticut, 1790–1800. Yellow poplar (seat); H. 41⅜″, (seat) 17″, W. (crest) 18⁷⁄₁₆″, (seat) 20⅝″, D. (seat) 16″, (leaf) 30⅛″ by 17¾″; tip broken off back extension of writing arm. (Old Saybrook Historical Society, Saybrook, Conn.: Photo, Winterthur.)

Fig. 1-10 High-back Windsor writing-arm chair and detail of incised inscription, Rhode Island, ca. 1800–1808. White pine (seat) with maple, oak, and other woods; H. 43¼″, (seat) 18″, W. (crest) 23″, (seat) 26¼″, D. (seat) 16¼″, (leaf) 22⅞″ by 17¾″. (Watson House, University of Rhode Island, Kingston: Photo, Winterthur.)

ever, appear identical. The illustrated board probably once had a small wooden tip at the back completely surrounding the first long spindle and duplicating that in the second chair, but it is now missing. Numerous nail holes around the leaf edge indicate that it was once covered. Such treatment would have been part of the original construction because nails anchoring the support cleats for the writing drawer penetrate the board top and are clinched over. The capable craftsman who produced this chair would have avoided that crude finishing technique if he had intended to leave the surface exposed. The drawer has a crosswise compartment at one end and pushes through for dual access. The opposite arm ends in a slim oxbow rest that duplicates those in the other chairs.[14]

A second tall example extends the range of the writing chair to Rhode Island and introduces the slim, stylish, bamboo-turned support (fig. 1-10). Closely associated with work of this area are the uncarved scroll-end crest and the serpentine arm pad. The oval plank, with its sharply defined edges, is related to several regional examples, although the pommel has already disappeared from the front, as was common at the end of the eighteenth century. The oval seat projection supporting the writing arm seems less of an afterthought here than in figure 1-9; its bold shape and size are well balanced by the strong upward thrust of the writing assembly. The verticality introduced in the tall spindles and attenuated bamboowork effectively contrasts with the simple round shapes of the horizontal features. Together the two have a sculptural impact. The forward-oriented writing-leaf drawer is lipped to glide on cleats; its small brass pull of flared profile may be original to the construction. Incised in fluid script on the outside bottom is the name of an owner, "W Magoun / 11." Regional censuses, however, have failed to yield candidates before 1840.[15]

Rounded profiles dominate the backs of two groups of writing chairs from southern New England. Examples of the first group have exceptionally bold features (fig. 1-11). The core of this group includes four sack-back writing Windsors, a sack-back armchair, and two bow-back side chairs. Other examples fringe the group. The illustrated chair exhibits the salient features associated with the primary body of work: a

low, squat arch above a heavy back rail, spindles of exaggerated bulbous form, and highly stylized turnings. Three pieces of wood make up the Rhode Island–style rail: arms that meet at the center back in a short lap joint and a capping piece. The long spindles, which pass through both wood layers and the center joint, help to secure the construction. The writing leaf, supported on a chair arm, abuts the rail capping piece between the bow end and the first long spindle. Large, dowellike pins secure the joint. Under the leaf, the arm ends in a rounded, fanlike terminal socketing the short spindles and three turned supports. The drawer is lipped at the long sides to ride on cleats. All roundwork is socketed inside the plank. Where the seat front of figure 1-11 is rounded, the forward edges in the other chairs are squared and centered by a pinched pommel. The bold turnings dominate the design. Those under the arms reproduce a Tracy sequence of elements but redefine the profile with swelled elements of larger size and collars in place of the flare above and below the baluster. Similar shapes are present in the legs, down to the heavy feet that exhibit strong Rhode Island influence. A bow-back side chair with related, though not identical, turnings and the same pencil-slim spindles marked by pronounced swells is branded on the seat bottom "ISAAC P SIMMS." A search of regional census records located a man of this name and initial in Preston, Connecticut, in 1850 — clearly a later owner. The area, however, which is near Lisbon and the Rhode Island border, is correct for the features. The writing chair itself has a history of ownership in Pomfret, a town about twenty-five miles north of Norwich.

Chairs in the second sack-back writing group are more strongly associated in feature with Rhode Island craftsmanship. The full, slightly bulging bow curve and clustered long spindles, sometimes straight, sometimes arced, dominate the form. The five writing-arm chairs that share these characteristics are only loosely related, though three are by the same hand. The illustrated chair, converted at a later date for writing purposes, is further aligned with Rhode Island chairmaking in having an oval seat of flat-chamfered edge, balusters of angular profile, and an arm terminal of rounded pad and wavy side piece (fig. 1-12). A second chair, in the Museum of Fine Arts, Boston, supports a large leaf on three posts, two of which anchor in a broad rectangular projection

Fig. 1-11 Sack-back Windsor writing-arm chair, Connecticut–Rhode Island border region, 1795–1805. H. 41⅞", (seat) 19½", W. (seat) 23", D. (seat) 17¾", (leaf) 25" by 17½". (Judy and John Hasler collection: Photo, Winterthur.)

Fig. 1-12 Sack-back Windsor writing-arm chair, Rhode Island, 1790–1800 (arm conversion later). Chestnut (seat) with maple, oak, and other woods; H. 40⅝", (seat) 16⅞", W. (seat) 20⅛", D. (seat) 14¾", (leaf) 18⅝" by 13¼". (Steven and Helen Kellogg collection: Photo, Winterthur.)

Fig. 1-13 High-back Windsor writing-arm chair, area of New Haven, ca. 1798–1805. Basswood (seat, microanalysis); H. 45⅛", (seat) 16⅜". (Mabel Brady Garvan Collection, Yale University Art Gallery, New Haven.)

at the plank side. The turnings are comparable, but the feet taper more sharply. In three other chairs loosely associated with this group, the seat is the distinguishing feature. Basically an oval, it is rounded at the sitter's left but is squared to a point under the writing leaf. There, in addition to an arm support, two spindles are set in a V at the front. The writing leaf terminates in a long point at the back, which caps the arm rail and is pierced by the bow end. The legs of one chair are bamboo-turned with double grooves above the foot in the fashion of eastern Connecticut, indicating that the craftsman had knowledge of work done by the Tracy family, Beriah Green, and others working in the border region.[16]

Conversions of standard Windsors to writing chairs during the lifetime of the original owner or shortly thereafter are not unknown. In figure 1-12 the eighteenth-century–style oval leaf, smaller than usual because the chair is only of standard size, lies directly atop the original finished arm. Three wedged, spindle-size pins, or dowels, extending in a line from the back of the leaf toward the center, hold the two parts together. The leaf is neatly executed, suggesting that the two crude, angled, spindlelike bracing sticks before and behind the turned post are still later additions to provide better support. Despite appearances, both sticks slant at about a forty-five-degree angle. Two early high-back chairs from the Philadelphia area were also later converted for writing purposes. One has a movable oval leaf that fits over the original arm, where it is secured in place as needed by a wrought-iron wing nut. The second chair sustained some destruction of the original arm in the conversion; a drawer was added beneath the leaf.[17]

A large group of tab-crested chairs with tall backs originated in the vicinity of New Haven and the inland communities to the northwest (fig. **1-13**). The design is adapted from standard seating developed in the mid 1780s. In the group, which includes a dozen or more examples, an oval plank substitutes for the shield seat of the standard armchair to better integrate the outsize, tab-shaped projection accommodating the leaf supports. Seat edges still exhibit the flat-chamfered profile visible in the standard chair, a feature showing direct Rhode Island influence. The broad period of pattern production is indicated in the turnings. Some chairs are in the full baluster style; others are transitional, with bamboo turnings above the plank and baluster turnings below. One chair is completely bamboo-turned. Falling into the first group is a chair said to have belonged to Reverend Joseph Bellamy (d. 1790) of the First Church of Bethlehem, north of Woodbury. Chairs in the full bamboo style probably date no earlier than about 1800. Another point of design focuses on the writing leaf. In most, if not all, of these large boards, the oval sweep is modified by noticeably squared curves. The reason is apparent in two chairs with drawers, for these large, broad boxes open toward the front. Typically, all leaf supports are of spindle form with a slight swell through the length compatible with that of the other sticks. Before 1930, the illustrated chair was owned in Guilford and Bridgeport.[18]

Documents from the late eighteenth century also place the Windsor writing form in the Hartford area, although no examples have yet been identified. In an advertisement of September 4, 1800, John Wadsworth informed the public that his stock of Windsor furniture included "Settees and Writing Chairs . . . in the newest fashions," although this was not the city's first introduction to the specialized form. A decade earlier, in October 1790, Jacob Norton had made a writing chair for Thomas Lloyd, Jr., at a cost of 12s. (about $2). By that time Dr. Mason Fitch Cogswell (1761–1830) had settled in the city, where a year later Ralph Earl painted the physician seated in his low-back writing chair, his medical library at one elbow, his faithful dog at the other (fig. **1-14**). Cogswell acquired the chair from the local shop of Stacy Stackhouse through an exchange of services. The writing leaf, covered with dark leather, exhibits a late eighteenth-century technique of securing a finishing strip around the board edge with widely spaced ornamental nails. An alternative practice of closely nailing the covering was still current a century later, as illustrated in figure 1-7. Below the nails is a deep, slightly ruffled skirt, presumably of leather. This rare ornament of the writing chair precludes the use of a drawer beneath the leaf. Cogswell, a gifted surgeon and founder of the Hartford Asylum for the Deaf and Dumb, was a prominent figure in medical circles. He first set up his medical practice in New York City in 1783 and some years later was appointed guardian to Ralph Earl when the artist was released from debtor's prison.[19]

Chairs fitted for writing purposes formed a small part of Solomon Sibley's furniture production at Auburn (formerly Ward), Massachusetts, around 1800. Each of three such chairs constructed in 1799 cost $2; Sibley sold another writing chair to Simeon Stockwell in 1802 for $2.66. Stockwell also purchased three dining side chairs and an armchair en suite, probably in the bow-back pattern. When cabinetmaker Samuel Davison of Plainfield, Hampshire County, exchanged services in 1804 with chairmaker Stephen Parson(s), he acquired in the transaction two writing chairs, one valued at 17s. (almost $3), the other at 24s. ($4). The cabinetmaker seems to have retained one chair and passed on the higher-priced seat to a customer. Earlier evidence of the writing chair in Massachusetts centers in the eastern part of the state. On February 18, 1791, Samuel Jones Tucke sold "1 Riting Chair" at his Salem shop. A writing chair valued at 15s. was part of the Nantucket estate of Oliver Spencer in 1794.[20]

Perhaps Samuel Jones Tucke was responsible for constructing the rare high-back Boston writing chair in the Winterthur collection (fig. **1-15**), although there were a dozen or more chairmakers at work in the city in the early 1790s. The chair is a rare example of its kind. The turned features and uncommon carved crest relate closely to contemporary Boston work. Construction of the heavy back rail, which is rounded on the front surface and flat on the back, follows Philadelphia and Connecticut practice (fig. 1-1); the arms slip under the one-piece back rail to form lap joints at either corner. The left arm (when seated) is fashioned in the traditional outward-curved flat scroll of the corner chair adapted by Windsor-chair makers for sawed-rail construction. Under the oval writing leaf, an open-ended box with the base butted to the sides contains a drawer that slides through, the bowed end out. Some compartment dividers still remain. Shallow cleats under the box probably once supported a candle slide that extended forward. The D-shaped pine seat with its rounded sides and two projections

Fig. 1-15 High-back Windsor writing-arm chair, Boston, ca. 1790–98. White pine (seat) with birch, oak, ash, and white pine (microanalysis); H. 45⅝″, (seat) 17″, W. (crest) 23″, (seat) 25″, D. (seat) 17¼″, (leaf) 23½″ by 16¼″; writing box perhaps once fitted with a candle slide. (Winterthur 58.3270.)

is close in form to a Philadelphia plank (fig. 1-1). Below the seat, crisp, shapely supports are turned in the classic Boston manner of the 1790s. The reel-type disks of the medial stretcher are light in feeling and well spaced beyond the central swell, suggesting a date early in the decade.[21]

Among other late eighteenth-century writing chairs, Windsors of lighter construction—namely, the bow-back, continuous-bow, and fan-back patterns—generally are less successful in their adaptation to this form. A large writing leaf, and especially one with a drawer, creates an imbalance in delicate structures. Chairs scaled up in size to counter this deficiency usually are awkward. In conversions made at a later date, the arms were jerry-rigged as the imagination dictated.

NINETEENTH-CENTURY CHAIRS

In a major design shift dating to about 1800, round and serpentine Windsor profiles gave way to highly linear, square-back styles. The earliest pattern was the Philadelphia wavy-crest chair, which had back posts and top piece flattened on the face, beaded, and linked in one continuous visual unit. The McKims, Andrew and Robert, of Richmond, Virginia, produced at least two writing chairs directly influenced by this short-lived design (fig. 1-16). The illustrated example is documented by a label dated May 31, 1802. The other, undocumented chair is slightly earlier; it has baluster-type supports under the arms and spindles without grooves, stylistic characteristics associated with the McKims' early standard production. As found in the best contemporary work, the scroll arm of the illustrated chair continues the detailing of the back post, having a bead at the top edges. The front terminal is more fully developed than that of the early McKim writing chair, and the beaded detailing is repeated on the edges of the writing leaf and seat. The new leaf shape of the early nineteenth century was a long, rounded rectangular board, usually with a drawer. Here, the yellow pine drawer is dovetailed and fitted at the squared outer end with three small compartments; the partitions and frame are fitted together with V-shaped slots in the manner of Anthony Steel's

Fig. 1-16 Square-back Windsor writing-arm chair and detail of label, Andrew and Robert McKim, Richmond, Va., 1802. Yellow poplar (seat) with maple and other woods; H. 38¼", (seat) 18", W. (crest) 21⁵⁄₁₆", (seat) 24⅜", D. (seat) 18", (leaf) 29¾" by 18½". (Museum of Early Southern Decorative Arts, Winston-Salem, N.C.: Photo, Winterthur.)

Philadelphia chair (fig. 1-1). Arms tenon through the back posts in wedged rectangular projections. The seat fronts in the McKims' chairs are unusual. The forward break is a departure from Philadelphia design; the influence may have originated in New London County, Connecticut (figs. 1-4, 1-7, 1-8). Shipping records point to commercial contacts between the two areas. In 1795 the schooner *Metomkin* from New London carried three boxes of cabinetwork to Richmond. Later records show the Norfolk entry of the schooner *Industry* from the same port on July 15, 1803, carrying five boxes of furniture and forty-two chairs. Clearly, it was possible for New England influence to have shaped the McKims' writing-chair pattern during the period in question. Somewhere there probably was also direct knowledge of contemporary classical design, which introduced a similar forward break in the seat frame of the formal federal chair. The McKims seem to have favored substantial leg splay, both in these chairs and in the rest of their work.[22]

Another writing chair of slightly varied pattern was almost certainly made in Richmond and possibly in the McKim shop. The same scroll arm, leg splay, and forward break in the seat front are present. The back posts are heavy tapered sticks shaped like spindles, with a large, ball-type bulge halfway down the length to accommodate the arm joint. The crest piece is a narrow slat with rounded upper corners that caps the sticks and overhangs the ends slightly. The chair was consigned to auction in 1930 by a descendant and namesake of William Wirt, U.S. attorney general under President Monroe. Inside the drawer under the leaf is a notarized affidavit attesting to the chair's descent from the attorney general, who indeed had the opportunity to make such a purchase in Richmond. Wirt (1772–1834) studied law as a young man and spent his early career in Albemarle County. He moved to Richmond in 1799, remaining there until appointed a district chancellor in 1802, which necessitated his removal to Williamsburg. Wirt took up residence in Norfolk early in 1804 but two years later returned to Richmond. Further evidence of his ownership of a writing chair is found in a letter directed to his brother-in-law on October 9, 1806: "Your letter has been lying ever since in the drawer of my writing chair awaiting for an interval of leisure to answer it."[23]

Elsewhere in Virginia, there is evidence of the growing popularity of the writing Windsor. At Petersburg Archer Brown offered the chair in 1805 along with other specialized Windsor forms. Another local Windsor-chair maker, Joel Brown, expanded upon common terminology the following year by offering "10 Secretary Chairs."

Staunton chairmaker Jacob Kurtz retailed writing chairs and spinning wheels in 1804. During the next decade James Beck constructed Windsor chairs of "different colours" at his cabinet shop in Fredericksburg and produced settees, children's chairs, and writing chairs to suit. The 1813 Charles City County estate of the Honorable John Tyler itemizes two and one-half dozen Windsors and a writing chair. Across the Appalachians James S. Bridges, who made chairs in Knoxville, Tennessee, in 1819, offered the "Righting Chear" as part of his production.[24]

From the standpoints of aesthetics and comfort, the most successful designs for square-back writing chairs were those with heavy frames or tall backs. A Philadelphia chair of the latter type branded by Anthony Steel probably dates between 1810 and the chairmaker's death in 1817 (fig. 1-17). The design is an unusual combination of eighteenth-century, contemporary nineteenth-century, and innovative elements. The arm balusters are close in form to turnings used earlier by Steel (fig. 1-1); the slender, shapely bamboowork is the best of its type for the period of construction. The outward-scrolling knuckle arm balances the curves of the writing leaf, whose oval form is a holdover from the eighteenth century. The small drawer is fitted with compartments. The D-shaped seat was characteristic of the large writing chair until well into the nineteenth century. The outstanding feature here is the crest, a design that combines the double-rod scheme with a shaped tablet borrowed from fancy chairmaking to form a highly original profile. The centered medallion is an inverted, modified shell. The same form is seen in small brass drawer pulls. In a second chair of this pattern at the Philadelphia Museum of Art, the medallion and top piece are slightly varied in profile, and the arm supports, like the legs, are bamboo-turned. Philadelphia writing chairs "just received and for sale by R. W. Otis" at Charleston, South Carolina, in 1816 could well have been of this pattern.[25]

Three writing chairs were valued at a substantial $18 when appraisers surveyed the Anthony Steel shop in 1817. They probably were of the pattern illustrated, with bamboo posts substituted under the arms. Steel's inventory included thousands of chair parts, some destined for writing-chair use, including the "creased" sticks, feet, "chair stumps" (arm posts), and "arm chair stretchers." In central Pennsylvania Gilbert Burnett of Harrisburg supplied customers along the Susquehanna River with writing chairs at least from November 1812, when he advertised from his "factory" on Front Street near the Swan Tavern. Joseph Jones offered writing chairs in 1819, within two years of opening for business at the seat of Chester County, and continued advertising this form into the 1820s. In western Pennsylvania George Landon first billed an Erie customer for a writing chair in 1817 and made several more sales in the 1820s.[26]

A rare, documented Baltimore writing-arm chair bears the stenciled "label" of Jacob Daley (fig. 1-18). Although Daley began working shortly after the turn of the century, the chair could date as late as 1820. The pattern is a composite of Windsor and fancy designs. The arm, viewed in profile, is nothing more than the top piece of a rod-back chair swelled to receive a spindle and "peaked" at the tip in a stylish flair. Typically, the short and long posts are stout. The close-fitting crest is adapted from Baltimore fancy seating. This chair, like contemporary Maryland and Pennsylvania work, has a seat rounded noticeably at the front. Stenciled under both the plank and the writing leaf is the maker's identification: "JACOB DALEY / Fancy Chair Factory / Mkt Street Bridge / BALTIMORE." Both the seat and writing board once had drawers. The short spindles and heavy supports under the leaf pierce the top surface and are wedged. To provide structural balance in a chair of this size, some Baltimore craftsmen and imitators shifted the right leg socket (when seated) to the seat projection beneath the leaf. What the chair gains in strength, however, it loses in aesthetics. When viewed from the front, the plank appears to be hanging in space. The front stretcher is extra long.[27]

Chairs of shallow-tablet pattern appear to have been popular in the Baltimore area, and copies and variations were produced in regions that came within the sphere of Baltimore influence. The more successful designs employ a forward-scroll arm and have normal leg supports at the front. One chair with a massive writing arm has an

Fig. 1-17   High, shaped-slat Windsor writing-arm chair, Anthony Steel (brand "A·STEEL"), Philadelphia, ca. 1810–17. Yellow poplar (seat); H. 46⅜", (seat) 17⅝", w. (crest) 23⅜", (seat) 28 1/16", D. (seat) 17 1/16", (leaf) 27⅜" by 17". (New York State Historical Association, Cooperstown, N.Y.: Photo, Winterthur.)

Fig. 1-18   Tablet-top Windsor writing-arm chair and detail of stencil, Jacob Daley, Baltimore, ca. 1807–20. H. 33⅞", (seat) 17⅞", w. (crest) 18⅞", (seat) 20", D. (seat) 16¼", (leaf) 25⅛" by 15⅜"; drawers missing. (James C. Sorber collection: Photo, Winterthur.)

additional, long leg under the leaf that is tied into the chair base with stretchers linked front and back. Another variation has a higher back, and some chairs are fitted with arrow-type spindles. In time, chairmakers made the tablet crest larger.

Evidence of a nineteenth-century New England writing chair centers in the southern part of the region around 1820. Levi Stillman of New Haven made a "leaf chair" for Phineas B. Wilcox in 1819 and charged him $3.50. Wilcox bought another Windsor at the same time and paid for the two with a secondhand chair and cash. Stillman recorded another "leaf" chair sold in 1822. At Canterbury, Connecticut, in 1811 Thomas Safford constructed a $2.50 writing chair for Dr. Rufus Johnson. Dr. Samuel Lee, who died in 1815 at neighboring Windham, owned many Windsor chairs, including one for writing; he was a customer of Amos Denison Allen. At least two purchases can be identified by comparing Lee's inventory with Allen's accounts: namely, a "Green Rocking Chair" and "6 Yellow dining Chairs" purchased in 1798 and 1800, respectively. Lee's writing chair may have been acquired after the period of Allen's existing accounts, or it may have been the "1 armed chr high top" purchased in 1797 and still valued at $1.50 in 1815. The 1812 inventory of Seth Wells of Boston attests to the continuing use of the writing chair in Massachusetts.[28]

The 1820s and 1830s show much the same kind of activity. The range broadened, although the writing chair seems to have remained uncommon in northern New England. A rare reference is found in the 1873 estate records of chairmaker Josiah Prescott Wilder of New Ipswich, New Hampshire, who was an entrepreneur in the 1830s. Another writing chair stood in the Litchfield, Connecticut, furniture shop of Silas E. Cheney in 1821. In 1819 and 1820 Cheney had sold similar chairs to town residents: a Mrs. Taylor purchased one fitted with a drawer, and Betsey Collins, who operated a school for girls, acquired a "Chair with arm to write on & rockers." By 1825 a chair owned by New York attorney Theodosius Bailey had been relegated to the front room, third story, although local interest in the commodity remained. A principal focus of this interest was the export trade. In January 1835 the furniture-making firm of Meeks and Sons ordered a dozen writing chairs from chairmaker-painter Benjamin W.

Branson at a cost of $4.50 apiece. The Meeks family enterprise extended to the South and Midwest. Across New York Bay in Newark, David Alling's records throw considerable light on the writing-chair business. The earliest account dates to November 14, 1836, when Alling made repairs to a writing chair owned by C. R. Groves, Esq. Alling's workmen painted the chair "Anew ornamenting & covering [the] leaf with velvet" at a charge of $3. Work for another customer the following year involved either replacing or adding a leaf to a used chair at a charge of $1.75. Account entries for writing chairs constructed in 1837 and 1838 identify one with "2 drawers & leaf covered" and another with "covered cushions, locks on drawers." An entry for December 6, 1838, titled simply "Writing Chair," provides dimensions for constructing a writing arm: "leaf 2 . . 9 by 1 . . 10 wide – hight of leaf on back pillar 11½ to top – D[itt]o of leaf at nearest point to arm 11½ – space between arm & leaf 13 to 14 inches."[29]

At the death in 1827 of one-time Windsor-chair maker John B. Ackley of Philadelphia, appraisers noted that his household was furnished with a writing chair. When David Wilson — whose brick house still stands on the navigable Appoquinimink in neighboring Odessa, Delaware — was forced to assign personal property to meet financial obligations in 1829, he sold painted furniture from his household at auction. The selection included fancy and Windsor chairs, a child's highchair, three rocking chairs and a cushion, and a writing chair. In the coastal South specialized seating was available from both local artisans and retailers of imported goods. Across the Appalachians at Wythe Court House (Wytheville) in Virginia, cabinetmakers Thomas J. Moyers and Fleming K. Rich repaired and altered specialized seating as necessary. They made "a draw and arm" for Mrs. Sanders's chair in 1835. A decade later William Culverhouse, who had just commenced the Windsor trade at Charlotte, North Carolina, advised potential customers that specialized forms, such as settees and writing chairs, were "made to order, . . . on short notice."[30]

Midwestern activity was increasing by the 1820s. B. Dodd offered "*Gentlemen's Writing* CHAIRS" at Nashville in 1824. Furniture dealers Thompson and Drennen provided competition in 1831 by importing standard and specialized furniture from manufacturers in Cincinnati. At Rising Sun, Indiana, not far from the "Queen City," William H. Mapes pursued business aggressively. In a lengthy advertisement of September 1838 he offered a comprehensive selection of merchandise, including the writing chair. He assured patrons that his workmen and materials were of the best quality and solicited repair work. At Indianapolis Joseph Stretcher offered "Large Writing Chairs" at his centrally located chair factory near the post and newspaper offices.[31]

Two last groups of writing-arm chairs warrant attention. The first includes chairs identified by their high backs and two or three cross slats (fig. 1-19). Most examples have features associated with Middle Atlantic chairmaking, although a plain example is inscribed under the seat "Capt. Ganno Providence, R. I." The pattern is generally described in contemporary records as a "triple back" chair. Another Windsor, one of large, ungainly size with a generous flat, rectangular seat and a four-slat back, is said to have been owned by the governor of New York in the 1820s. The underarm, arrow-spindle profile is a type associated with New York work, although the delicacy of the sticks is out of keeping with the rest of the chair.[32]

Writing chairs exhibiting mixed features of Middle Atlantic origin are frequently highly ornamented (fig. 1-19). The tall backs are often set at a cant with little or no backward bend to the cylindrical or shaved-face posts. The geographic range extends from the central Pennsylvania–Maryland border westward as far as Ohio and Kentucky. Most left arms are of generous size and scroll forward; a few have a flat, outward scroll. The writing leaf is either an oval or a long rounded rectangle; sometimes it has a drawer. Seat planks show variation in outline from the squared oval or rounded square to the Pennsylvania–New York shovel shape (figs. 2-35, 2-36). A projection, or tongue, usually extends from the side supporting the leaf. The backs and arm assemblies feature one of several spindle profiles, beginning with the tapered cylindrical stick. One unusual example, possibly of Kentucky origin, has New York–inspired Cumberland spindles in

Fig. 1-19 High, slat-back Windsor writing-arm chair, probably western Pennsylvania, 1835–55. H. 48¼″. (Private collection: Photo, Winterthur.)

the lower back (fig. 2-39) and tab-top arrow spindles above (fig. 1-19, beneath arm). The legs are the moderately stout Baltimore bamboo supports of figure 1-18.[33]

The presence of strong Middle Atlantic influence in western chairs is explained in several ways. First, migrating families often carried household possessions with them, while other chairwork arrived disassembled or in pattern form. Designs were also transported in the heads of migrating workmen for production in a new location. The opening of the Erie Canal and the growth of steam-powered navigation accelerated the process of dissemination. New York influence generally is less obvious than that of Pennsylvania and Maryland, although the front legs in figure 1-19 and in other chairs reflect direct New York influence in the heavy, inverted-carrot-and-ring forms at the top. Another chair has a ball fret in the back, a rare feature in Pennsylvania and Maryland work. Prominent elements that derive from Baltimore or Pennsylvania work include slat-type and diamond-centered front stretchers and leg tops of beehive form (figs. 1-96, 1-98). Some chairs have a Baltimore-type extended leg at the front (fig. 1-18). The underarm, tab-top arrow spindles of figure 1-19 derive basically from Maryland work, although the feature was used occasionally in New York. The chair is also rare in having a drawer beneath the seat. The painted surfaces and decoration appear to be renewed or retouched. The chair has a western Pennsylvania history in Mount Pleasant Township, Washington County.

The latest groups of writing-arm Windsors recorded here include New England chairs constructed with moderately low, broad backs. A few have roll tops, cross slats, and half-length spindles, features popular in the 1830s. Boston influence can be seen in chairs with broad astragal- or arc-ended crests above long, tapered spindles (fig. 2-42). A Canadian example of the latter type made by George Cole (d. 1859) of Nova Scotia has narrow, arrowlike spindles of unusual form below the top piece. Chairs of a late, bulky, low-back style form a larger group (fig. 2-43). The heavy single arm and raised back rail balance the massive oval or long rectangular writing leaf. Short, stocky, ball-turned spindles and fancy front legs are the rule.

Writing-arm Windsors have retained a closer association with their place of origin through records or tradition than perhaps any other antique seating. This may be explained in part by the substantial initial cost of the chair. Also, its size, form, and function were considered something of a novelty. Many original owners were men of position, wealth, or stature in their communities, and some achieved national prominence. Members of the clergy constitute the largest group associated with the writing chair; undoubtedly, some found it a comfortable seat for writing sermons. The Windsor that belonged to Reverend Frederick W. Hotchkiss of Old Saybrook, Connecticut, is illustrated in figure 1-9.[34]

Doctors (fig. 1-14) were the second most numerous group of known writing-chair owners. A leaf chair was the choice of Connecticut physicians who resided in Litchfield, Hartford, Old Lyme, and Canterbury. Dr. Samuel Lee of Windham probably bought his chair from Amos Denison Allen. Other writing chairs are notable because their owners were men of letters, public servants, or political figures. A chair of early nineteenth-century date is said to have belonged to the poet Henry Wadsworth Longfellow. As mentioned earlier, William Wirt of Virginia, attorney general under President Monroe, purchased a writing chair in Richmond, probably at the McKims' shop. Charles Mason, Iowa's first chief justice, owned a tablet-top writing chair with short arrow spindles in the lower back. The best known of all writing-arm Windsors is the large swivel-seat, high-back Philadelphia chair at the American Philosophical Society, Philadelphia, which was made to Thomas Jefferson's specifications. The writing leaf was actually a later addition, the work probably done at Monticello.[35]

The Rocking Chair

BACKGROUND AND DEVELOPMENT

Esther Stevens Fraser (later Brazer) and Walter A. Dyer produced the pioneering studies of the American rocking chair. Fraser documented the first appearance of the form to 1774, and her chance discovery of a reference to Benjamin Franklin's mechanical "fan" chair with rockers, dating a few years later, suggested a possible inventor. Later contributions have pushed back the date by several decades and demonstrated that Franklin's genius played no part in developing this specialized form.[36]

Fraser and Dyer were the first to identify the inspirational role of the cradle in the development of the rocker. More recently Ellen and Bert Denker have offered thoughtful insights. They found that the word *cradle* was part of the English language before A.D. 1000 and that cradles supported on rockers appeared in illuminated manuscripts by the fifteenth century. The soothing benefits of gentle motion were recognized as a boon to child care. Chairs, which were relatively uncommon before the development of the cane-chair industry during the reign of Charles II (1660–85), were perhaps first fitted with rockers in the early eighteenth century. Various authors have suggested Lancashire as the origin of the feature, although without documentation. On January 28, 1749, the Lancaster firm of Gillows billed a customer for "a *new* Rocking Chair," implying that the form was neither uncommon nor unknown. More than a century later, in 1851, a Londoner viewing a display of American chairs at the Great Exhibition suggested that the rocking form had been transplanted "from Lancashire to the New England States" and was then being "reimported as a curiosity." The Lancashire fashion for rocking chairs, he said, had died out half a century earlier and current use did "not find much favour . . . except in nurseries."[37]

The two earliest references to the rocking chair in America date to 1742. Solomon Fussell, a chairmaker of Philadelphia, debited the account of Thomas Robinson by 6s. for "one Nurse Chair with Rockers" on January 26. The same year a rocking chair was itemized in the Chester County, Pennsylvania, estate of William Templin. The routine nature of both references indicates that the rocking chair was not an unfamiliar form and had already been in use for a decade or longer. Four years after his first recorded sale of a rocking chair, Fussell sold similar seating for 4s. to 6s. The price indicates that the chairs had rush bottoms and three or four back slats. Though often unpretentious, the rocking chair was not restricted to back rooms. William Buckley's rocking chair stood in his Philadelphia parlor at his death in 1759, although the "old" rush-bottom and cane-back family chairs had been banished to the second bedchamber.[38]

If indeed the Delaware Valley was the first American home of the rocking chair, diffusion beyond southeastern Pennsylvania occurred by the 1750s. Isaiah Tiffany, a furniture maker and general storekeeper of Lebanon and Norwich, Connecticut, recorded the sales of a "small" chair "with rockers" to two Norwich customers in 1756 and 1757. Tiffany's terms "small" and "little" appear to refer to children's seating. At 2s.6d. apiece, the children's rockers had simple slat backs. The wood probably was stained, since Tiffany recorded the sale of another small "colour'd" chair priced at 2s.2d. The difference of 4d. probably represents the cost of making and applying the rockers. The accounts of a Leicester, Massachusetts, craftsman describe "a Chare frame with Rockers." Robert Crage (Craig) supplied the seating in 1758 to a local customer for just 2s. In Rhode Island Nathaniel Heath of the town of Warren and William Barker of Providence recorded six sales of rocking chairs between 1768 and 1777. Heath charged from 2s.6d. to 4s. for his product. Barker's debits include a charge to the prominent Brown family for mending and "Colloring rocking chare for Nicholas."[39]

References to rocking chairs are more frequent in the postrevolutionary period. "Two Roking Chairs" and six Windsors made up part of William Newton's household furnishings sent from Baltimore to Alexandria, Virginia, in 1792 on board the sloop *Jaby*. In New England the Proud brothers' Providence accounts record the sale of seven rockers between 1790 and 1800 and further describe four of the chairs as little, "grate," banister-back, and low. Samuel Williams, owner of a sawmill at Saybrook, Connecticut, obtained a rocking chair valued at 9s.6d. by exchange in July 1796. At Windham, Amos Denison Allen, a kinsman of the Tracys, recorded both rush- and wooden-bottom chairs, types that are representative of family production as a whole. Allen constructed no fewer than twenty-eight rocking chairs between September 1796 and January 1803. Evidence from northern New England points to modest production around 1800 by James Chase of Gilmanton and Jacob Merrill, Jr., of Plymouth in central New Hampshire. One chair made by Merrill in 1797 was "Coloured Red."[40]

Along with the construction of new rocking chairs came the alteration of old seating. There is evidence for this as early as the 1760s, but undoubtedly craftsmen undertook such work even earlier. Conversions were simple enough to carry out, although at times the resulting product was awkward in appearance. The earliest references to "putting rockers on a chair" are those found by Reverend Clair F. Luther in the Hadley, Massachusetts, accounts of cabinetmaker Eliakim Smith. Luther cited three entries recorded between 1762 and 1764. A Chester County, Pennsylvania, reference of 1766 follows. William Barker of Providence bottomed a customer's chair and added rockers in 1774. The Proud family undertook the first of a series of rocker conversions at their cabinet shop in Providence the same year, adding "a Paire of Rockers" to a chair owned by metalworker Samuel Hamlin. Across Long Island Sound, Nathan Topping Cook of Bridgehampton charged each of two customers 1s.6d. "to Put Rocars on a Chair" in 1799. In later decades there follow hundreds of references, as the great era of rocking-chair production began.[41]

Motion in a chair was not limited to rockers, as Edward Jarvis of Concord, Massachusetts, recalled. Speaking of the early nineteenth-century rush-bottom chair, he described how "some people rocked in these throwing themselves forward on the front legs & backward on the rear legs, coming down on either with a great jar or noise." Children were fond of engaging in this activity, but most adults would have found little comfort and ease in the practice compared to rocking in the conventional manner, and in the bargain they would have gained only a broken chair, or at least a ruined chair seat.[42]

The slow adoption of the rocking chair in prerevolutionary American life can best be explained in terms of its original function as a seat to meet the needs of the elderly, infirm, and ailing. This explains, too, why in 1759 appraisers found William Buckley's rocking chair in the parlor of his Philadelphia home rather than in a bedroom. In the parlor he could rock in comfort while chatting with family and friends in his declining years. A bedroom was the repository of two rocking chairs in the Salem, Massachusetts, household of merchant Elias Hasket Derby before 1800. Another eighteenth-century refuge of "ease" was the overstuffed easy chair, although its expensive upholstery was well beyond many people's pocketbooks. The eventual acceptance of the rocking chair as a common substitute is suggested by chairmakers' advertisements, which list an "easy" chair among the painted seating.[43]

The rocking chair is almost unknown in American portraits and genre scenes dating before 1800, a circumstance that changed gradually in the early nineteenth century. More often than not, the subjects depicted are advanced in years. Especially helpful in this regard is a sketch with commentary made in 1853 by Lewis Miller of York, Pennsylvania, during a trip to Virginia (fig. 1-20). Miller is seated left of the hearth in the Roanoke County home of Mr. McClanaham. An excited youngster identifies the gentleman in the rocking chair as his grandfather: "O—grandpa what *a big Egg* I found." An excerpt from the "Reminiscences" of Mrs. Elizabeth Calder Rock paints a similar picture. The author described Christmas eve festivities at Cherry Valley, New York, in 1835: "After the feast . . . dancing to violin music began. The merriment went on till midnight, my dear old Grandmother enjoying it all from her rocking-chair in the corner." In contemporary reminiscences from Bay of Quinte, Ontario, Canniff Haight recalled the use of "the spacious rocking-chair for old women." Allen Holcomb's New Lisbon, New York, accounts offer parallel evidence in crediting a workman for "puting on Rockers on widow jacksons Chair" in 1817. Occasionally, the young also had need of a rocking chair, as explained in 1815 by Harriet Manigault, a Philadelphia resident, when commenting on the delicate health of her sister Emma: "Yesterday morning we took a ride with her of two hours length, & bought her a famous rocking chair with arms, & a high back for her to lean her head on. This rocking chair is merely to give her exercise."[44]

Nineteenth-century paintings and drawings also depict rocking furniture padded for comfort and protection from drafts with cushions, cases, and sundry draped coverings. Only on occasion do documents suggest that such accouterments were part of eighteenth-century rocking furniture, although the widespread use of fabric accessories in nineteenth-century seating strongly suggests an earlier precedent. One unusual inventory entry dating from 1802 refers to a "linned & Stuf'd rocking Chair" among the household furnishings of Hale Hilton at Beverly, Massachusetts. In 1808 the Proud brothers of Providence supplied a "Grate Chair with Rocker[s] for Stufing" to a local customer. Henry W. Miller, a chair manufacturer of Worcester, sold a "Rocking Chair Lin'd with Hair Cloth" to an area resident two decades later. Cushions formed the more common "padding" of the rocking chair. Sarah Anna Emery of Newburyport described how in the late 1790s when "Aunt Betsey wished to embroider cushions for her rockers" she visited Miss Betty Bradstreet who "was celebrated for designing patterns for such work." Maria Foster Brown, writing about her family home in Athens, Ohio, as it was furnished several decades later, noted the presence of Windsor furniture in the "best room" and "one large rocking-chair with the most beautiful cushion on it."[45]

Two paintings by Asahel Powers dating to the 1830s depict women in "covered" chairs. Although the chairs have been described as upholstered, they actually appear to be "draped" rocking chairs, in view of the loose, sacklike appearance of the coverings. Both Powers and his sitters favored this seating form. The same treatment may be referred to in the estate records of Providence chairmaker Samuel Proud, whose kitchen contained "1 Rocking chair & Cover" in 1835. Two chairs of similar description stood in the "West Room," which was furnished for sitting and sleeping. Another kind of drapery, a partial cloth secured with ties, covers the back of a large Boston rocking chair supporting the seated figure of William Sidney Mount's elderly mother (fig. 1-21), drawn by the artist in 1841. Earlier, a simple cloth to exclude drafts draped the back of Barzillai Hudson's continuous-bow armchair at his Hartford home. A posthumous portrait of the Providence merchant Moses Brown, dating to 1856–57, pictures the city's

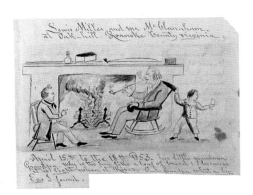

Fig. 1-20 Lewis Miller, *Mr. McClanaham in Rocking Chair.* From *Sketchbook of Landscapes in the State of Virginia,* Roanoke County, Va., 1853. Ink and watercolor on paper; H. 3½″, w. 6½″ (image). (Abby Aldrich Rockefeller Folk Art Center, Williamsburg, Va., gift of Dr. and Mrs. Richard M. Kain.)

benefactor in his early Pennsylvania high-back Windsor draped with gathered cloth in the fashion of the day. Another chair covering took the form of a multilayered length of cloth neatly folded over the crest and possibly anchored at the upper back with strings. The remaining fabric extended down the face of the back onto and over the seat. Such draping appears to have been a widespread practice, since both Pennsylvania and New England paintings illustrate the technique. It also helps explain the survival of some seating with painted surfaces almost intact (fig. 1-44). Two-sided slip cases that cover the entire chair back, with allowances for the arms, are also illustrated in contemporary paintings.[46]

By the second quarter of the nineteenth century, the rocking chair was a household fixture, even a national institution. There is scarcely an inventory that does not list at least one such chair. The business records of both major and minor shops speak clearly of the economic importance of the rocking chair. English visitors took note of its universal use. Not everyone approved of the rocking chair, however. Comments by two authors, both published in 1838, show the range of personal opinion. James Frewin, a builder, found it "a compliment to give the stranger the rocking-chair as a seat; and when there is more than one kind in the home, the stranger is always presented with the best." Harriet Martineau, on the other hand, considered rocking a disagreeable practice. "How this lazy and ungraceful indulgence ever became general," she commented, "I cannot imagine; but the nation seems so wedded to it, that I see little chance of its being forsaken." A note published a few years later at Middlebury, Vermont, sums up the attraction of the rocking chair in referring to it as a "wooden narcotic."[47]

NURSE, OR NURSING, CHAIRS

Development of the rocking side chair—often called a nurse, nursing, or sewing chair—paralleled that of the rocking armchair. Initially, the nurse chair was framed without rockers, although some seats may have been built low to the ground for convenience in handling an infant. Some late eighteenth- and nineteenth-century references to "low" chairs may describe this kind of seating. (Today low, rockerless seats are frequently referred to as slipper chairs.) A "Low Chair & Cushion" was in the Boston household of the Honorable Andrew Oliver at his death in 1774, and Daniel and Samuel Proud of Providence made "a Low Chair with Rocker" on several occasions at the turn of the century. An early reference to the "nursing chair" in the Philadelphia area is found in the 1717 Chichester inventory of William Flowers. Analysis of more than a dozen entries in Solomon Fussell's Philadelphia accounts provides a relatively clear picture of the usual appearance of this type of chair in the 1740s and later. The craftsman described backs of five or six slats and showed a cost comparable to that of the stationary side chair. The seats were woven of rush. On two occasions Fussell recorded a "Nurse Chair with Rockers," indicating that the curved pieces of wood were not yet a distinguishing characteristic. What, then, constituted a nurse chair? Only the shortened legs remain as a distinctive feature. Fussell further noted several surface finishes. One chair was left in the wood or, in his words, "white"; another was brown, and a third, black. The latter two probably were painted rather than stained. The craftsman mentioned two other nursing-chair groups—one "flowered," the other having cabriole legs. According to recent scholarship, the flowered chairs appear to have been constructed of figured wood, probably curled maple. A chair priced at 10s., twice the cost of most others, had "Crookt feet," or simple cabriole front legs. Fussell made the chair to order for Benjamin Franklin. Several decades later, in 1774, the New Haven household of Christopher Kilby, a merchant-farmer, contained a nursing chair. In the same period merchant Moses Brown of Providence acquired a nursing chair to meet the needs of his young family.[48]

The choice of rockers versus plain feet was still open when purchasing a nursing chair at the turn of the century. George G. Channing of Newport (b. ca. 1789) demonstrated the use of the nurse chair without rockers when as a young single man he "managed" the fretful baby of a young mother who was a fellow packet-ship passenger. He had witnessed the procedure many times in his youth. Locating one of those "peculiar 'high chair[s]', in which babies, held on the nurses' shoulders, were soothed to sleep," he imitated "those vibratory motions (by which the nurse tried to supply the place of rockers to the chair)" while at the same time "gently patting the little one's back, and singing one of [his] *chromatic* tunes." The baby "began to yield, by a sort of whine," whereupon Channing placed the child across his knees and passed his hands down its spine until finally "the little sobbing creature subsided into a heavenly calm" and was removed to the cabin.[49]

References to the nurse chair remain rare during the early 1800s. Thomas Boynton's Vermont accounts contain an entry in May 1813 for "2 nurse rocking chairs." Activity had picked up by the late 1820s when Andrew L. Haskell of Dover, New Hampshire, offered nurse chairs and a line of "New-York & Boston Fancy & common Chairs." Other accounts provide insights into the form and feature of the chairs. William Hancock of Boston sold a *fancy* nurse chair in 1828; Jabez Hatch, an auctioneer, followed shortly with similar seating. The fact that rocking and nursing chairs are mentioned together in furniture notices suggests there *were* differences. At Killingly, Connecticut, in 1835, William Rawson's 92¢ nurse rocking chair was just under half the price of his large $2 rocking chair purchased by the same customer. A Brooklyn, New York, notice itemizes "Nurse Chairs of Different kinds." Peter Peirce of Templeton, Worcester County, Massachusetts, made "dark colored" nurse rocking chairs; Philemon Robbins of Hartford offered chair stock painted yellow or tea color. Jacob Felton constructed similar seating with scrolled backs at Fitzwilliam, New Hampshire. In 1835 wooden-bottom nurse chairs were valued at $1.50 by the appraisers of Parrott and Hubbell's manufactory in Bridgeport, Connecticut. Small stocks of nurse seating stood in other New England shops during the 1830s. Gilson Brown had a dozen chairs on hand at Sterling, Massachusetts. The Taunton estate of Isaac Washburn contained twenty-eight nurse chairs with and without rockers. In 1834 Edmund M. Brown of Portsmouth, New Hampshire, advertised the nurse chair as "a very convenient article in sickness."[50]

SEWING CHAIRS

Like the nurse seat, the sewing chair generally was armless to permit the sitter freedom of movement, and at times it also had short legs. A view of the grounds at Stowe, Buckinghamshire, probably drawn by Jacques Rigaud about 1733–34, pictures a seated woman at her needlework in the portico of the house. The lady supports her feet on a low stool or footrest; the side chair appears to be of standard size and form. References to chairs specifically intended for sewing are not found, or are found only rarely, before the early nineteenth century. Even an 1807 notice for a Charleston, South Carolina, store omits the word *sewing*. Instead, the proprietor advertised the sale of Philadelphia "Low Chairs for Ladies to work on." The earliest direct reference to a sewing chair dates to 1810, although the wording of William Buttre's New York advertisement indicates that the "article" was not entirely new: "A large assortment of . . . Black, White, Brown, Coquelico, Gold and Fancy Chairs, Settees, Conversation, Elbow, Rocking, Sewing, Windsor, and Children's Chairs of every description, and on the most moderate terms."[51]

The Caleb Chambers household in rural London Grove, Chester County, Pennsylvania, contained a sewing chair in 1813. Between that date and 1818 Thomas Boynton of Windsor, Vermont, sold more than a dozen such seats priced from $1 to $1.50; one with rockers cost $1.83. *Large* and *small* are other descriptive words applied to sewing chairs. David Alling of Newark, New Jersey, recorded a good production. Some of his chairs were fitted with rockers, and a few had fancy spindles; other styles were identified as "bamboo" or "Windsor." The craftsman provided further information in his painting credits. Moses Lyon ornamented chairs to simulate satinwood in

1815–16 and striped a group that was framed with slat backs. A large shipment of seating sent to New Orleans in 1820 contained a pair of sewing chairs painted in imitation rosewood and touched with gilt on the slats. During the 1830s Alling occasionally constructed sewing chairs from fine wood, such as curled maple. As a special order, he made a figured maple sewing chair of "second size . . . cane seat . . . with scroll arms & foot board." The footrest took the place of the low stool that women often used with the sewing chair. Two additional account entries reveal that the critical feature was the seat, which appears to have been scaled up in size. On November 28, 1840, Alling paid Adam Stumpf $4.50 for making "sewing Chr seats." Five months earlier the entrepreneur had sold a special order of thirteen cane-bottom "roll top" chairs described as having "sewing size" seats.[52]

Silas Cheney produced sewing chairs in Litchfield, Connecticut, during the 1810s. Business was not quite as brisk as in New Jersey, but the presence in town of Miss Sarah Pierce's female academy stimulated a market for this furniture. On several occasions local householders bought two chairs at a time. The seats may have been intended for a mother and daughter; more likely the purchaser had two daughters attending the academy. Even incomplete student lists show numerous instances of sisters enrolled together. Philadelphia appraisers who compiled an inventory of Anthony Steel's shop in 1817 counted no fewer than fifty-six sewing chairs on the premises, along with other seating and chair stock in proportion.[53]

Through the 1820s and 1830s scattered records from New Hampshire to Baltimore to Indiana describe an escalating production of the sewing chair. Several documents yield particular data about this form of chair. Allen Holcomb of New Lisbon, Otsego County, New York, debited a customer in 1822 for a bent-back sewing chair with rockers. An unidentified cabinetmaker in Salem, Massachusetts, made a high-back chair in the following decade. Chairs of curled maple and imitation curled maple (painted) are listed in craft inventories of 1835. Many sewing chairs were of Windsor construction. In fact, wood-seat chairs are more numerous than any other type in Philemon Robbins's Hartford records, although flag-seat examples were also made. Special sewing chairs purchased at this establishment included several in the "Grecian" style and one with a scroll seat. There is no indication that the scroll-seat chair had rockers; the reference may identify a flat plank with a front roll only. The "raised" or "Boston" seats cited at midcentury in the daybooks of Chauncey Strong of Otsego County, New York, were three-piece wooden bottoms with a roll at the front and a raised section at the back. A good indication of the sewing chair's popularity among early nineteenth-century American women of the more leisured classes is the remark made by Mrs. Frances Trollope in 1831: "As to what they do . . . it is not very easy to say; but I believe they clear-starch a little, and iron a little, and sit in a rocking-chair, and sew a great deal."[54]

THE WINDSOR ROCKING CHAIR

The Emerging Form — Influences and Early Work
The tall, slat-back, rush-bottom rocking chair of the eighteenth century exerted strong influence on the first Windsor rockers, which appeared in the market just before 1800. The rush-bottom examples pictured in figure 1-22 illuminate the vernacular tradition and illustrate two of the three construction techniques in rocker attachment. The traditional Pennsylvania chair (left), a type developed in Philadelphia early in the century, remained in common production in southeastern rural Pennsylvania until almost 1800. This example was recovered in Bucks County. The four-slat rocking chair (right) is part of the Dominy furniture-making tradition of eastern Long Island, although it was strongly influenced by chairmaking as practiced north of Long Island Sound in coastal Connecticut and Rhode Island. Members of the Tracy family and other Windsor craftsmen of the Norwich area similarly employed bold, rounded stretcher tips (fig. 2-4). The same profile served as a model for Nathaniel Dominy V's inverted bud-shaped feet. Other Dominy features have parallels in Windsor work, such as the spool-centered front

Fig. 1-22 Rush-bottom rocking chairs, one by Nathaniel Dominy V (*right*), *(left to right)* Delaware Valley and East Hampton, N.Y., 1760–1800 and 1795–1800. Maple, hickory, and oak (microanalysis, both); H. 47½″ (*left*), 36⅛″. (Winterthur 70.198, 57.34.3.)

stretcher and the extended cones forming the bases of the arm supports. Anchoring the long extensions are Windsor-style side stretchers. The Dominy scroll arms, without blocks, reflect another feature of contemporary Windsor design (fig. 2-10).[55]

The rocker construction of the slat-back chairs illustrates two methods of attachment. Probably the earliest is the foot slotted in the center to receive the curved rocker. Pins secure the joint. Both the turned work and sawed work here are particularly well conceived. The ornamental rocker tips also serve as stops. The construction of the second chair, which sinks the feet *into the rockers,* requires broader strips of wood. The blunt-tipped rocker design, which minimizes the front and back extensions, also decreases movement. Because of considerable wear to the rockers, it is possible to examine the basic construction. Feet tips have been turned to small round tenons that deeply penetrate the curved sticks of wood.

Toward the end of the 1790s members of the Tracy family of Connecticut designed and constructed some of the earliest Windsor rocking chairs in America. Their action stimulated some interest in the form within the Rhode Island border region. The shop accounts of Amos Denison Allen, son-in-law and former apprentice to the family patriarch, Ebenezer Tracy, Sr., shed light on family craft practice at this time. Between September 1796 and January 1803, Allen constructed twenty-eight rocking chairs of various types. One was a slat-back chair, which ranged in price from 6*s.* to 8*s.* ($1 to $1.33); at least one example received a coat of brown paint. Allen referred to two other rocking styles as "winsor" and "fancy," the former produced from 1797 to 1799 and the latter in 1801–2. *Fancy* was the area term for the continuous-bow chair; the word *winsor* identifies a sack-back chair with rockers. A few undocumented examples have been located. The turnings in figure 1-23 suggest the hand of Ebenezer Tracy; the short, bulging leg baluster almost duplicates that in a standard sack-back chair branded by him. The support length is compressed slightly to accommodate the new base feature. The rockers, which could be original, are an adaptation of the pattern illustrated in the Pennsylvania slat-back chair (fig. 1-22, left). Wooden pins inside and out secure the curved members to the feet. Between the seat and the bow the design is fairly standard,

Fig. 1-23 Sack-back Windsor rocking chair with top extension, attributed to Ebenezer Tracy, Sr., Lisbon Township, New London County, Conn., ca. 1795–1803. Chestnut (seat) with maple and other woods; H. 40⅝″, (seat) 13⅜″, W. (crest) 19⅞″, (arms) 24¾″, (seat) 21½″, D. (seat) 17⅜″. (Mrs. Reid Johnson collection: Photo, Winterthur.)

except for its large size. The chestnut plank is greater by two inches in depth and width than the usual sack-back seat. The chairmaker defined the spindle platform with a groove, an unusual feature in Tracy work; the legs socket within the plank, as expected. Above the bow Tracy introduced a fan-back crest that forms a head rest reduced in breadth by 1½ to 2 inches. The chair back probably duplicates one that Allen referred to in his accounts as a "winsor high top" priced at 12*s.*, or $2. A rocking chair is listed in Ebenezer Tracy's household inventory, although it is not further described.[56]

At least two rocking chairs of the "fancy," or continuous-bow, type made by the Tracy family are known. One is unmarked, while the other bears the second stamp used by Elijah Tracy. Both chairs are bamboo-turned. The grooved areas of the legs swell more than usual, and the turnings are again reduced in length. The supports resemble those of figure 1-25 from the upper groove down; the craftsman used an H-plan stretcher assembly similar to that in the sack-back rocker. One "fancy" chair has an extension above the continuous bow; the profile is identical to that illustrated in figure 1-23. An unusual feature in the eight-spindle back is the long stick at either end marked by two grooves, one centered in the nodule and the other near the top. These are the only grooved spindles. Amos Denison Allen charged either 12*s.* or 13*s.* for rocking chairs of this pattern. In one account dated 1801 he recorded the sale of a *fancy* rocking Windsor "2½ Ins higher than Common." The increased height probably refers to the back arch rather than an extension piece.[57]

About the time the Tracys introduced their rocking chair, Ansel Goodrich of Northampton, Massachusetts, placed his first advertisement in the local newspaper. Rocking chairs were among the forms he offered in 1795. One labeled example and another without documentation have baluster turnings (fig. **1-24**). Individual features conform to other identified work by Goodrich: the crest; the long, low spindle swell; the flat, wavy-edge arm pads; the well-contoured oval seats; the turned profiles; and the slim stretchers. The rocker pattern and fastening illustrates the third technique used

Fig. 1-24 High-back Windsor rocking chair, attributed to Ansel Goodrich, Northampton, Mass., ca. 1795–1803. H. 41½", (seat) 16¹⁄₁₆", W. (crest) 20¼", (arms) 21⅜", (seat) 20¼", D. (seat) 20⁵⁄₁₆". (Woodstock Historical Society, Woodstock, Vt.: Photo, Winterthur.)

Fig. 1-25 High-back Windsor rocking chair, southeastern Connecticut, 1800–1810. White pine (seat) with maple and other woods; H. 40¼", (seat) 13¾", W. (crest) 24⅛", (arms) 23⅛", (seat) 21¼", D. (seat) 16¼". (Private collection: Photo, Winterthur.)

for attachment. Right-angled rabbets cut into the outside faces of the feet receive the curved boards, which form flat peaks at the feet, separated by a long hollow; delicate tips terminate the front and back. Altogether the design is one of lightness and movement. Above the rockers the exterior surfaces of the feet have been flattened. The similarity of the rockers and their attachment in both chairs helps to confirm the originality of the parts. This particular technique permitted the chairmaker to use standard legs from stock when he received a rocking-chair order. The proportions and diameters are the same, so the craftsman needed only to saw and shave the bottoms of the feet to make the conversion. Goodrich's own household contained a rocking chair at his death in 1803. A group of bamboo-turned, high-back rocking chairs from Vermont shares several characteristics with the Northhampton work. Crests and arm pads are similar in profile, and the bamboowork of the legs relates to the supports in a Goodrich side chair; however, the seats are considerably less modeled.[58]

Another high-back chair, as generous in breadth as the Tracy rocker, has an eastern Connecticut–Rhode Island crest of a type seldom encountered (fig. **1-25**). The slim projecting tips turn upward in a profile seen occasionally in fan-back border chairs. The short, bulbous, bamboo-style legs relate to those in two continuous-bow rocking chairs by the Tracy family, one branded by Elijah Tracy. Here, the chairmaker has connected the legs with modified box-style bamboo stretchers rather than an H-plan brace. The arm pads are less vigorous than Tracy work in their outward thrust and side curve, although they are related. The rockers appear original, and they certainly approximate the type first used in this chair. Nails driven from the outside hold them fast to the feet. The profile is a modification of that found in the Tracy sack-back rocking chair (fig. 1-23). In size and height the chair recalls its roots in slat-back seating. Several entries for fan-back chairs with rockers in James Chase's Gilmanton, New Hampshire, accounts of the early 1800s appear to refer to chairs of this general pattern; the price was a substantial $2.[59]

A high-back chair with an unusual, though original, understructure exhibits strong Rhode Island characteristics (fig. **1-26**). The high collars above the club, or bottlelike,

lower legs are reminiscent of other rare patterns of this area. Although the chairmaker rounded the bottoms of the heavy feet in the lathe, it was necessary to cut the rear legs when fitting the rockers into the sawed slots to compensate for the front lift and to provide the proper seat slope. Wooden pins hold the rocking structure in place. Above the seat other features are linked to Rhode Island work. The extra-embellished outer back spindles are a variation of others known in the region. Angular, hooklike crest terminals are found in both eastern Connecticut and Rhode Island chairs. Except for their smaller size, these bear a strong resemblance to a pattern used by members of the Tracy family near Norwich. The flat arms are rounded at the ends in circular pads, which continue into large side pieces to form double-scalloped profiles. Of note is the back design of the one-piece arm rail. A small simulated "tongue," subtly executed, marks the point at either bend where the wood thickens. The design places extra structural strength in an area weakened by nine closely spaced holes drilled to accommodate the long spindles.[60]

One of the few rocking Windsor *side chairs* of this early period is illustrated in figure **1-27**; it qualifies as a nurse chair. Like figure 1-26, the legs were ended in the lathe. The double scoring and bamboowork above the capsule-shaped feet are highly suggestive of the Tracy family style. Thick, canted-edge seats, though uncommon in eastern Connecticut, are present in some side chairs; the crest profile also has its counterparts. The slim bamboo posts, formed of thin segments and nodules, relate to the spindles in an armchair from this area. The rockers probably are a restoration; they appear large for the design in spite of the heavy seat. A small, square-back armchair offered at auction in recent years has legs of similar form slotted up the center and fitted with rockers related to those in the Goodrich chair (fig. 1-24), a style that seems more appropriate. Thomas West, a chairmaker in New London, Connecticut, offered both large and small rocking chairs for sale in 1810. He boasted a seating stock that afforded "a greater variety than can be found at any other place in this County." In the same general area both green- and yellow-painted rocking chairs are enumerated in early nineteenth-century documents.[61]

Fig. 1-26 High-back Windsor rocking chair, Rhode Island, 1795–1805. H. 44¾", (seat) 18", W. (crest) 24⅛", (arms) 25⅜", (seat) 21⅛", D. (seat) 16½"; paint and decoration not original. (Hitchcock Museum, Riverton, Conn.: Photo, Winterthur.)

Fig. 1-27 Fan-back Windsor rocking side chair, southeastern Connecticut, 1800–1810. Rockers replaced. (Former collection J. Stogdell Stokes.)

Early Nineteenth-Century Patterns

A group of rocking chairs with distinctive triple backs and characteristics that suggest a late eighteenth-century date originated in the Champlain Valley of Vermont, where they are now identified as "Burlington" or "Shelburne" rockers (fig. **1-28**). Two features—the medial stretcher and the crest—belie a construction date earlier than 1815; in fact, two of three known crest patterns suggest that the chairs were produced as late as 1825–35. Tradition states that the maker was a man named Saxton from Shelburne. Records show the presence of members of that family in the town but offer little information as to their occupations aside from farming. Only the inventory of George Saxton, who died in 1872, gives evidence of a mechanical trade, in the form of a bench and unspecified tools. Saxton owned several vehicles, ranging from buggies to wagons, suggesting that he could have been a wheelwright. George was a son of Horace Saxton (d. 1848, age sixty-nine) and grandson of Frederick Saxton. Local histories relate that Frederick was an early settler of Burlington, where he resided from about 1785 until about 1792 when he removed to Shelburne; he drowned there in 1796. In 1867 grandson George still lived on the family homestead near Comstock's Point.[62]

The Shelburne rocker is far from being a standard chair. It represents a late eighteenth-century form altered significantly by an innovative provincial craftsman and embellished with selected elements of later date. The stylistic roots of the fully developed Shelburne rocker lie in the sack-back chair; the angular frame of the second back tier substitutes for the broad-arched bow. The transition is illuminated in a sack-back rocking chair that is similar to the one illustrated, with the substitution of an arched back. The crest in the arched-back chair is a plain rectangular slat supported on seven extended spindles, a top piece not current in the region until at least the 1810s. The same top appears on two angular-frame chairs, one of which is in the Shelburne Museum. Stylistically, the rectangular crest is probably the earliest of the three known profiles. The other two are variations of a single shape, consisting of a high, rounded, loaf-shaped board with a low arch across the top and bottom—a profile associated with the late 1820s at the earliest. Some boards are notched twice along the lower edge, as illustrated. At first inspection this crest appears to be a replacement, since it retains only the last of many coats of paint found on the other chair parts. Upon close examination, however, it is possible to identify the top piece as the lower remnant of an original loaf-shaped board that has lost about two-thirds of its height. When restored long ago, the fragment apparently was cleaned of old paint in the reshaping process. The medium-high end spindles in the second back tier are integral to the corner joint construction. After the sticks pierce the heavy, arced rail supports, they continue upward to the top surface of the rail itself, forming tenons that hold all the parts together. A wedge in each tenon tightens the joints. At the lower ends the curved rail supports pierce the arm in round tenons secured by pins inserted from the outside rail.

Two arm styles appear in the Shelburne rocker. One is a flat, rounded pad with a wavy side extension—a restrained version of the Tracy arm (fig. 1-23). The other is a short knuckle terminal, or scroll, the lower half made from a carved and applied block of wood; the side piece is broad and short. Figure 1-28 once had arm terminals of this type, but they have been mutilated over the years and the carved blocks lost. Two pieces of wood form the broad oval basswood seats of most chairs in this group. Applied to the front of the principal plank is a narrow section of wood held fast by two large, square wooden pins visible at the front edge near each leg. The reason for this construction is unclear. Perhaps the chairmaker in his limited production made do with stock on hand or what was readily available. Seat depth from the back through the front addition is 14 inches. Beneath the plank, the H-plan stretcher system again suggests eighteenth-century styling; however, use of a bold, ornamental medallion is absent even in Boston work until almost 1810. This one is three-sided. The rockers, like the crest, have only one coat of paint. They could be replacements, but the bottoms are well worn and the pattern is identical to others in the group. There is ample evidence in the form of nuts and bolts and old nail holes to indicate that the rockers have been

Fig. 1-28 Triple-back Windsor rocking chair, Champlain Valley of Vermont, 1825–35. Basswood (seat) with maple, beech, hickory, and ash (microanalysis); H. 37⅜″, (seat) 15″, W. (top crest) 13⅞″, (arms) 22½″, (seat) 20⅝″, D. (seat) 15¾″; rockers may be old replacements, crest modified. (Winterthur 64.1923.)

removed and remounted at least once, at which time they could have been cleaned of old paint. The rocker attachment is the same as that used by Ansel Goodrich, and indeed the basic rocker patterns are similar. Some chairs, including this example, still show evidence of the original lower leg treatment. Visible at the inside front is the chamfer that lightens and "finishes" the joint. This small flat area retains traces of every paint coat applied to the chair. The rear legs are now worn flat.

In the early nineteenth century chairmakers began to focus their attention on the Windsor rocking chair as production furniture. There was greater demand for conversion of older household seating, often rush-bottomed, to the rocking form. Craftsmen also repaired and refurbished chairs brought to the shop for the addition of rockers. Certain tasks were common: "to put on rockers & painting and bottoming 1 Chair," "to a pair rockers . . . & 2 rounds," and the inevitable "to a new Rocker on a rocking Chair." Shop language was flexible, so the Proud brothers of Providence could record that they "rockerd" eight chairs for fellow chairmaker Christian M. Nestell in 1821.[63]

Craftsmen's records provide insights into the nature of rocking-chair production, although the vast majority of references are general and do not specify chair types. Joseph Griswold of Buckland, Massachusetts, recorded "a winsor chair with rockers" in 1801. Other Windsor rocking chairs are identified by association, such as the "9 Green windsor, 1 Rocking, 1 little ditto" in the New York City household of William Ryder or the "4 dining chairs at 6/6 each & a rocking chair" purchased in 1809 at Titus Preston's shop in Wallingford, Connecticut. The number of chairs that made up a set varied with customers' needs. Reuben Loomis of Suffield, Connecticut, supplied widow Lydia Warner with "six chairs & a rocking chair" in 1816; the firm of Barlow and Curtis Rose bought "twelve chairs & one rocking chair" five years later. In 1802 Nathan Luther, a chairmaker of Salem, Massachusetts, sold to Captain Barton a large suite of "bamboo" seating furniture, consisting of twelve side chairs, an armchair, and a rocking chair. Once introduced, bamboo Windsor work became very popular. An invoice of Salem furniture shipped on board the schooner *Madocawando* sailing for North Carolina in 1812 lists four rocking bamboo chairs. The previous year chairmaker Isaac Stone made "Fallback" (bent-back) bamboo side chairs with rocking armchairs

Fig. 1-29 High, square-back Windsor rocking chair (one of a pair), attributed to James Chapman Tuttle, Salem, Mass., 1800–1810. White pine (seat, microanalysis) with maple and other woods; H. 38³⁄₁₆″, (seat) 15⅜″, w. (crest) 22¼″, (arms) 22⅜″, (seat) 18¼″, D. (seat) 17¾″. (Historic Deerfield, Inc., Deerfield, Mass.: Photo, Winterthur.)

Fig. 1-30 High, slat-back Windsor rocking chair, Zadock Hutchins, Jr. (brand "Z.HUCHENS"), Killingly or Pomfret, Conn., ca. 1814–20. Maple and other woods; H. 38⅜″, (seat) 14½″, w. (crest) 21¾″, (arms) 19⅞″, D. (seat) 17⅞″; left rocker replaced. (The late Carroll G. Alton Means collection: Photo, Winterthur.)

to match for storekeeper Ebenezer Fox. Two terms encountered occasionally in reference to the rocking chair, *high top* and *high back,* identify tall Windsors, the first having an extension above the crest.[64]

A bamboo rocking Windsor that qualifies as a high-back chair (fig. **1-29**), although it is only of medium height (fig. 1-32), is one of a pair. The plank shape and vigorous bamboowork compare favorably with the production of James Chapman Tuttle of Salem, Massachusetts, so that an attribution to that shop seems warranted. The chairmaker has included a turned detail that is not present in his side chairs — nodular bamboowork in the upper cross rod, or bow. Spindles, posts, and arm supports are all coordinated in profile. The arms conform in curve and shape to those in an unmarked, bow-back armchair attributed to Tuttle, allowing for a necessary increase in size. The punchwork rosettes in the scroll faces appear to be contemporary. Balancing the strong horizontal lines of the arms are rockers designed with particular sensitivity to detail. The top edges are subtly chamfered between the front and back legs, and comparable modeling continues forward to the tips. The chamfers peak, inside and out, at small flattened areas where the legs attach. Wooden pins inserted from both rocker faces firmly secure the rectangular tenons of the leg tips within the mortise holes of the rockers. The arms and posts are similarly pinned. Windsor bamboowork from Boston likely was comparable, although probably less nodular. Chairmaker William Seaver of Boston made rocking chairs in 1804, as indicated in a schedule of shop property.[65]

Most square-back, double-bow rocking chairs made in the early nineteenth century are taller than the Tuttle chairs. Some have scroll arms, while others have turned rests. Rocker design and attachment are variable. Medium-tall chairs are more common in the single-bow style; many have contoured backs, suggesting a date closer to 1810 than 1800. Extensions above the bow are common. The early Wilder craftsmen of New Ipswich, New Hampshire, made single-bow rocking chairs; Samuel Gragg of Boston branded a contoured chair. A chair with a high top, or extension, bears the Connecticut stamp of Stephen Tracy. The extension crest is a narrow, rectangular slat. The squared, angular, shield-shaped plank is a larger version of a contemporary Tracy seat for a side

Fig. 1-31 High, slat-back Windsor rocking chair, New York, 1810–20. H. 39″, (seat) 14⅜″, w. (crest) 18¼″, (arms) 22⅞″, (seat) 20″, D. (seat) 17⅜″; rockers may be replaced. (James Mitchell Varnum House and Museum, East Greenwich, R.I.: Photo, Winterthur.)

chair. Distinctive bamboowork is marked by nodules at the grooves, with outsize swells in the back posts anchoring the slim, forward-scroll arms. The support structure below the seat is comparable to that in a continuous-bow rocker made by Elijah Tracy. The rockers, which anchor turned leg tips, resemble those used in the Ebenezer Tracy sack-back rocker (fig. 1-23), modified by front tips that draw to a point.[66]

A large group of single- and double-bow rocking chairs has backs of standard arm-chair height. Some backs are straight, others bent, and many have extension tops. Scroll and turned arms cap short posts or project beyond them, while some curve horizontally in a wide arc. The support structures include both box and H-style stretchers; the rocker attachments include all types. Some chairs were made originally as rocking chairs, while others are conversions. A bent-back, double-bow chair branded by Amos Hagget of Charlestown, Massachusetts, has unusual features. The slim, rodlike arms dip slightly from back to front. Between the double bows of the upper back are three groups of three short rods; the center rod in each group is an extension of the long spindles.

The accounts of Thomas Boynton of Windsor, Vermont, contain several references to broad-top rocking chairs in 1815. These appear to describe the crest illustrated in figure 1-30. Still other entries identify the bent-back rocking form. The illustrated Windsor is a product of the rural Connecticut shop of Zadock Hutchins (b. 1793). Although the chair is as current as Boynton's work in some features — namely the crest, back posts, and arms — it is out of date in others. Undoubtedly constructed early in Hutchins's career, the chair reflects influences still current during the craftsman's training period. Thompson, the place of his birth, is close to Killingly and Pomfret, communities where Hutchins practiced his craft. All three towns are within twenty-five miles of Lisbon Township where members of the Tracy family continued working into the early nineteenth century. In profile and general proportions, Hutchins's chair legs duplicate those in bamboo rocking chairs made by Stephen Tracy. The comparison extends to the thickened spindles. For the rockers Hutchins chose a current design that is a modification of the pattern pictured in figure 1-24. Another feature of Hutchins's work appears rooted in New York design: the profile of the disk-and-baluster medial

stretcher is a scaled-up version of the "Cumberland" spindle first used in New York work before 1810. The Newark, New Jersey, accounts of David Alling associate the pattern with both sticks and "front rounds" (stretchers) shortly after 1800. By the time Hutchins constructed the rocking chair, shaved arms of the type he chose were also current in New York. New York influence may also explain Hutchins's use of an old-fashioned, H-plan bracing system below the seat. The rocking chair was owned in the Crosby family of Thompson, where Zadock's father resided until he died in 1835, having outlived his son by five years. At Zadock's death, his household contained two rockers; three "small rocking chairs" in the shop were valued at $2.25.[67]

What appears to be the New York counterpart of Hutchins's tall rocking chair is illustrated in figure 1-31. The primary regional features are the Cumberland spindles, which are slimmer versions of Hutchins's medial stretcher, and the shapely front brace composed of arrowlike elements flanking an oval medallion with small spurs at the four corners. The roots of this stretcher design lie in Baltimore fancy work. Other points of similarity with mainstream New York Windsors can be noted in the seat modeling and the silhouettes of the arms, the bamboowork, and the stout, tapered profile of the lower back posts. The rockers may be replacements, although they are of the same pattern as those of a related tall rocker in the same collection.[68]

The Genesis of the Boston Rocking Chair

Even in its heyday the tall, contoured-back chair with a scrolled seat and distinctive crest was known as a "Boston rocker." Its design (fig. 1-42) sprang from two roots, one domestic, the other foreign. Traditional American rush-bottom chairs of the eighteenth century with slats, banisters, or splats provided the model for the tall back; European furniture designs in the neoclassical, or "antique," taste supplied the seat and back curves. The eighteenth-century rush-bottom chair, the first American seat to be fitted with rockers as part of its original construction, first influenced development of the Windsor rocker in the 1790s. Just after 1800, square, straight-back Windsor framing supplied the model for an updated plank-seat rocker (fig. 1-32) with a high back that

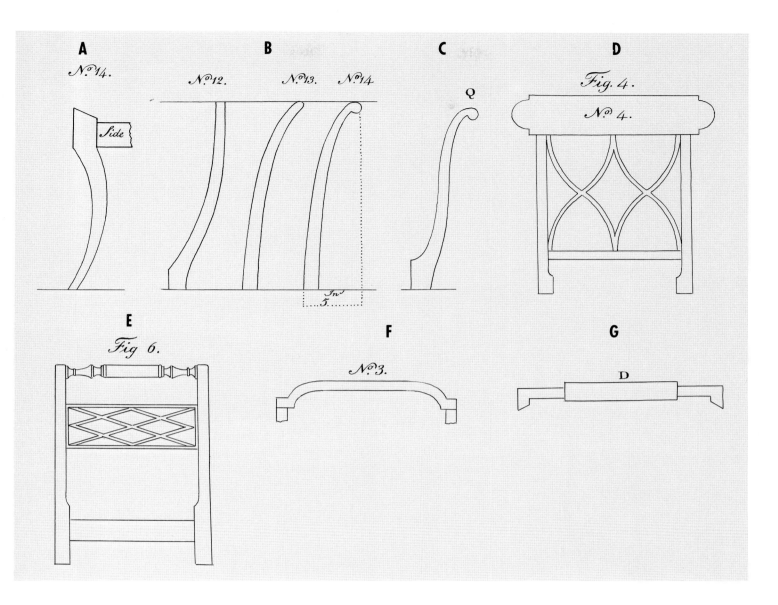

A   B   C   D

E   F   G

provided a comfortable support for the head. A progression of tall patterns followed, culminating in the "Boston" rocker. During its stylistic evolution, the tall Windsor acquired the "Grecian" curves that became a trademark of early nineteenth-century production.

Grecian design originated in mid eighteenth-century Europe. Architectural discoveries at Herculaneum and Pompeii, near Naples, and Napoleon's Egyptian campaign of 1798 sparked an interest in classical civilizations. Architectural publications by Giovanni Battista Piranesi (1769, 1778 in English) and Robert and James Adam (1773) circulated designs in the new classical taste. Work by the architect-designer Henry Holland for the prince of Wales (later George IV) and his circle in the 1780s and later emphasized still closer adaptations of decorative detail. Broad disseminaton of the classical style came through the works of George Hepplewhite (*Guide,* 1788) and Thomas Sheraton (*Drawing Book,* 1791–94).[69]

The Grecian chair as defined in the 1802 *London Chair-Makers' and Carvers' Book of Prices for Workmanship* has hollow, or concave, legs and a comparable back reversing direction at the top to form an S-shaped profile from crest to seat. The crest is framed on the posts as a tablet or between the uprights as a slat or cylindrical roll (fig. **1-33** A,C,D,E). The price book was reissued in 1807 and was followed by a supplement in 1808, in which variations on the basic Grecian theme are called "Egyptian" and "Trafalgar" chairs. Two important English design books also date from this period:

Fig. 1-33 Designs for chair parts. From the *London Chair-Makers' and Carvers' Book of Prices for Workmanship* (London, 1802), details from chairmakers' pls. 2–5 and carvers' pls. 1, 2. (Photo, The Magazine *Antiques.*)

Fig. 1-34 Fancy bentwood side chair and detail of brand, Samuel Gragg, Boston, ca. 1809–12. Birch, oak, and beech (microanalysis); H. 34⅜″, W. 18″, D. 25⅛″; pale yellow ground with shades of brown, black, green, and bronze. (Winterthur 61.321.)

Fig. 1-35 Design for a parlor chair. From George Smith, *A Collection of Designs for Household Furniture* (London, 1808), pl. 40. (Winterthur Library.)

Thomas Hope's *Household Furniture and Interior Decoration* (1807) and George Smith's *Collection of Designs for Household Furniture and Interior Design* (1808). Hope, a wealthy traveler, collector, and amateur architect, designed the interior settings and furnishings for his London house in Duchess Street in an exotic Greco-Roman-Egyptian style. These interiors, shown in his book, "set his stamp on English Regency furniture." Smith's engravings did more than Hope's to popularize the antique style and to circulate suitable models for cabinetmakers to copy or adapt.[70]

These developments pointed out a new direction in American popular chairmaking, which led eventually to the Boston rocker. On August 31, 1808, the U.S. Patent Office granted Samuel Gragg of Boston the exclusive right to manufacture an "elastic chair," a painted, bentwood form known today in several dozen examples (fig. 1-34). Gragg's design is daring and imaginative, exploiting to the limit "the plastic qualities of wood." The Grecian-style curves, as illustrated by George Smith (fig. 1-35) and others, were achieved by steaming and bending rather than sawing the wood. There are several variations of Gragg's basic design. He used two crest patterns, the more common of which is the "roller" top with turned ends framed between scrolling back posts and centering a small projecting tablet, as illustrated. The second pattern features a slat. Chair construction takes two forms. Either the back stiles continue forward and down to form the seat rails and front legs in one continuous sweep, with Grecian saber legs at the back, as pictured, or the construction terminates the bend at the seat front, at which point screws secure tapered cylindrical legs to the frame. The fancy patterns of the front legs include one terminating in tiny carved and painted hoofs similar to those in figure 1-35, a plate engraved for Smith in 1805. Smith's plates may have had limited circulation as prints before publication in the bound volume of 1808. The book itself probably was still on press when Gragg was designing his elastic chair.[71]

How did Gragg obtain first-hand knowledge of high-style chair design only then current in London and the technology for bending wood to a degree previously unknown in chairmaking? Nothing in his background indicates that he possessed particular inventive genius or unusual mechanical skill. Yet the idea and even the model for the elastic chair must have been well in hand when, early in 1808, Gragg terminated a four-year partnership with William Hutchins and moved to the "Furniture Warehouse, near the bottom of the Mall" in the newly developed south end of Boston. Cabinetmaker Thomas Seymour had operated the warehouse complex for the manufacture and commission sale of furniture since December 1804 and served as

Fig. 1-36 Settee, Boston, ca. 1805. Mahogany, birch, and maple (microanalysis); H. 42½″, W. 81″, D. 22¼″. (Winterthur 57.683.)

agent to the tenants. In renting a warehouse shop Gragg settled himself at a center of the furniture trade. Clearly, the chairmaker had access to English designs. He may have seen some of Smith's plates before their publication in book form, but more likely he consulted the London price book of 1802 or the reprint of 1807. In all probability a copy of this work was in the possession of Thomas Seymour or his father John. They were English-born craftsmen who emigrated to America in 1785 and soon served a sophisticated clientele that included Elizabeth Derby (West), daughter of the wealthy merchant Elias Hasket Derby. Either directly or through a Boston merchant, the Seymours would have maintained close ties with English suppliers, and in the normal course of business they would have learned of current developments in London furniture-making circles.[72]

The 1802 price book was well known in Boston. A large mahogany settee (fig. 1-36), which forms part of a suite of Boston seating furniture long ascribed (without documentation) to the Seymours, is linked to the price book by several features: the saber legs (fig. 1-33A); the back stiles, called "sweep scrolls" in the price book, whose profile is repeated at the front of each arm (fig. 1-33B); the open loop back, called a "double gothic splat" in the price book (fig. 1-33D); and the crest, made up of a central tablet flanked by trumpet-shaped turnings (fig. 1-33E). All of these features except the looped back appear in modified form in Gragg's elastic chair. His back stiles actually follow the related pattern of figure 1-33C in their forward sweep to form the seat rails. Gragg's painted peacock-feather decoration on the face of the central slat is present in other furniture from the Boston area, including a group of oval-back fancy chairs with upholstered seats made by an unknown craftsman for the Derby family. Paralleling Gragg's elastic-chair production was architect-designer Benjamin Henry Latrobe's work in 1809 for the Madison drawing room in the President's House (White House). Latrobe's designs for painted seating furniture commissioned from the Finlays of Baltimore betray their immediate debt to Hope's *Household Furniture and Interior Decoration*, published just two years earlier. American furniture designers did, indeed, have access to current developments in the English furniture market.[73]

Gragg learned wood-bending technique during a training period that began in the late 1780s when round-back Windsors came into fashion. Mastering the compound bends of the continuous-bow chair—its arched back in one plane, the arms in another—would have provided him with the necessary foundation for his later bentwood work. The brand "S.Gragg / Boston" identifies several square-back, double-rod

Fig. 1-38 High, shaped-tablet Windsor rocking chair, possibly Samuel Gragg, Boston, ca. 1812–20. H. 44¼″, (seat) 14⅝″, W. (crest) 20⅜″, (arms) 22¾″, (seat) 19⅜″, D. (seat) 17¾″; pale blue-green ground (old and possibly original) with dark green and shades of pink-rose. (Private collection: Photo, Winterthur.)

Fig. 1-37 Slat-back Windsor side chair (one of a pair), attributed to Samuel Gragg, Boston, ca. 1809–14. White pine (seat), birch (microanalysis), and other woods; H. 33″, (seat) 18″, W. (crest) 19⅜″, (seat) 17⅛″, D. (seat) 16¼″. (Private collection: Photo, Winterthur.)

Windsors dating to the early 1800s. The same brand, usually accompanied by the word "PATENT," appears under some elastic-chair seats.

In the annals of American chairmaking, Gragg's elastic chair is an extraordinary achievement. Curiously, it seems to have gained little contemporary recognition. Perhaps even then, as now, it was found to be a fragile chair subject to cracks and breaks in the individual bent parts. Gragg probably did not merchandise his new furniture before May 10, 1809, when he placed an advertisement in the *Columbian Centinel*:

Elegant Patent Chairs & Settees . . . Samuel Gragg, the Patentee . . . has now ready for sale, at his Shop . . . Patent CHAIRS and SETTEES, with elastic backs and bottoms, made in a new, elegant and superior style, and of the best materials; those Chairs and Settees are very strong, light and airy and afford the most comfortable and agreeable seats for drawing-rooms, parlors, halls and other apartments. They can be furnished in sets of any number and of any degree of elegance in ornamental painting and gilding and at a very reasonable price.

In the same notice Gragg reminded the public that he stocked "Bamboo, Fancy, and common Chairs and Settees." The term *bamboo* identifies both rush- and wooden-bottom seating whose turned work simulates the particular character of the tropical plant (fig. 1-29). After 1800 the word *common* frequently identified production-type Windsor furniture rather than the cheap rush-bottom chair of the eighteenth century.[74]

With the elastic-chair design in hand, Gragg appears to have introduced the S-curve profile to the posts and spindles of a small group of standard-size Windsor chairs (fig. 1-37). The narrow slat was the fashionable crest around 1810. At the seat back the chairmaker wisely increased the diameter of the sticks to provide extra strength in the area most subject to body pressure. The shaped seat, bamboo turnings, and fancy front stretcher with a tablet all reflect the finest period work. In a second group of contoured-back chairs attributed to him, Gragg introduced a stepped-tablet crest, shaved back posts, and a plain, bamboo-turned front stretcher. In the next bold step the back was extended and rockers were added, thus creating the tall "easy" chair of figure 1-38. The stepped top is a duplicate of that in the second group of Gragg Windsors. There is

Fig. 1-39 High, tablet-top Windsor rocking chair, Boston, 1820–25. White pine (seat); H. 43¼″, (seat) 15½″, W. (crest) 22⅛″, (arms) 21⅞″, (seat) 19⅞″, D. (seat) 18½″; golden mustard yellow ground with black, dark bronze, silver, green, and gray. (Marblehead Historical Society, Marblehead, Mass.: Photo, Winterthur.)

Fig. 1-40 *Girl in Blue Dress,* possibly William Bartoll, eastern Massachusetts or southern New Hampshire, ca. 1835. Oil on canvas; H. 26″, W. 22″. (Photo, Skinner, Inc.)

little doubt about the Boston origin of this chair, which was found in neighboring Brockton. The high-style prototype for the crest, already on the Boston market for about a decade, was a composite of two patterns from the London price book of 1802 (fig. 1-33 F,G). The stepped-tablet crest was widely imitated throughout Massachusetts and northern New England.[75]

The seat in the tall rocking Windsor chair (fig. 1-38) compares well with planks in Gragg's standard-size Windsors; the arm and support profiles reflect other Boston work. The rocker pattern, typical of work produced between 1810 and 1830, is that used by Zadock Hutchins (fig. 1-30); the rockers are attached by the slotted-leg method. The sinuous curves from seat to crest extend the contour first introduced in the elastic chair. By 1820 tall, contoured Windsor rockers were in production at Boston, as shown by the extensive 1819 inventory of cabinetmaker Benjamin Bass. Item number 490 lists "78 Sticks, 29 Cornerposts, 59 legs, 45 Stretchers & Pillars for high back Rocking Chairs."[76]

The high, contoured-back rocking chair (fig. 1-38) inspired many New England variations on its design before emerging as the Boston rocker. Chairmakers introduced new crests, reshaped seats, and modified bamboowork. In a rare variant of the illustrated stepped-tablet crest, long horizontal ogee curves flank a short central projection. Several versions of a rectangular tablet appeared on the market during the 1820s and later. One pattern has a small hollow at each corner (fig. **1-39**). A chair of almost identical form and decoration has a Boston history. The rocker pattern, attachment method, and arm profile are the same as found in the tall, stepped-tablet rocking chair (fig. 1-38). The legs, now stouter, have a definite triangularity in the upper segment. In a related chair depicted in a painting of a young girl dressed in blue (fig. **1-40**), a hollow-cornered crest is similarly embellished with painted panels. The unidentified likeness appears to be from the brush of William Bartoll of Marblehead (b. 1812).

With the introduction of the crown-top crest (fig. **1-41**), the Boston rocker was close to assuming its definitive form. The new design achieved popularity toward the end of the 1820s and spread rapidly throughout New England and New York State. There seems little doubt that the pattern was influenced directly or indirectly by

Fig. 1-41 High, crown-top Windsor rocking chair, Maine, probably area of Farmington, 1830–40. H. 45⅝″, (seat) 15¾″, w. (crest) 23¹/₁₆″, (arms) 24¾″, (seat) 19⅞″, D. (seat) 18⅜″; bright yellow ground with black, white, dark green, and silver-gray. (Steven and Helen Kellogg collection: Photo, Winterthur.)

Fig. 1-42 Boston (Windsor) rocking chair, Massachusetts or northeastern New England, 1830–40. White pine (seat); H. 44¾″, (seat) 16½″, w. (crest) 26⅞″, (arms) 26⅛″, (seat) 23⅛″, D. (seat) 19¼″; dark brown and dark brick red grained ground with yellow, gilt, gold, and bronze. (Henry Ford Museum and Greenfield Village, Dearborn, Mich.)

designs from George Smith's *Cabinet-Maker and Upholsterer's Guide* (London, 1826). The first adaptations probably appeared in formal chairs constructed of fine woods. These were followed by figured-maple and painted fancy chairs with cane and rush seats. Chester Johnson of Albany, New York, who received a patent in 1827 for the design of an improved convertible rush-bottom sofa, used a crest of early crown pattern. In western Connecticut, Lambert Hitchcock constructed fancy and Windsor chairs with crown tops before 1832. The names of at least four other New England chairmakers are associated with the crown-top rocker through documented work, one of them being Amos Denison Allen (fig. 1-52). In central New York State Allen Holcomb produced Windsor side chairs with crown tops. References to wood-seat chairs with this crest often turn up in Connecticut records of the 1830s. The illustrated rocking chair, recovered in the area of Farmington, Maine, is one of only a few crown-tops to use round-tenon construction in the rocker attachment.[77]

The crown top and contoured back are two of the three essential features that define the Boston rocking chair (fig. **1-42**). The third and most distinctive element is the large, three-piece "scrolled" seat. Its immediate design source is easily identified by comparing the profile to the scroll ends of contemporary upholstered Grecian couches and sofas or to the back of Gragg's elastic chair (fig. 1-34). To counterbalance the heavy seat and tall back, craftsmen introduced thick, fancy-turned front legs. Suppliers of chair parts, such as the Wilders of New Ipswich, New Hampshire, regularly differentiated in their accounts between "Rocking Chr Front Legs" and "d[itt]o Back." One customer for "chair stuff" was the firm of Calvin R. Wilder (a brother) and Edwin Stewart of "64 Gold St N. York."[78]

Throughout the early development of the Boston rocker, furniture makers and the public knew the form by several names. Some terms focus on size, although such words as *large* and *tall* are too general to identify the Boston pattern in records; other references note the presence of a "scroll seat." In 1832 Luke Houghton, a cabinetmaker of Barre, Massachusetts, credited a Templeton chairmaker with a "rased Seat Rocking Chair." This is the earliest known use of this term. A few years later a Windsor,

Vermont, chairmaker advertised raised-seat rocking chairs. When chairmaker Peter Peirce of Templeton, Massachusetts, died in 1836, his shop stock included "large raised seat rocking" and "common rocking" chairs. With a 25¢ price difference between them, the entries appear to identify the general types shown in figures 1-42 and 1-41, respectively. Chairmakers in Fitzwilliam and New Ipswich, New Hampshire, used similar terms. It is not coincidental that so many references come from the periphery of Boston. If chairmaking accounts were available for the metropolitan area, they likely would identify the city as a major production center of the Boston rocker.[79]

On October 20, 1830, Richard Wright, a Washington, D.C., merchant, referred in an advertisement to "those much admired high back Boston-made Rocking Chairs." In another notice, on November 25, 1831, he described "scroll seat high back Rocking Chairs" just received from Boston. The term "Boston Rocking Chair" was used in a New York City estate inventory taken in 1833; another citation dates to the following year. Other early references appear throughout the northeast and Middle Atlantic states, but none has been discovered for Boston itself. Even a systematic search of Suffolk County, Massachusetts, inventories recorded between 1828 and 1834 has failed to uncover use of the word *Boston* in describing a rocking chair or any other seating furniture. The rapid dissemination of the Boston form is demonstrated in the geographic scope of references dating from 1834 to the mid 1840s, which range from Trenton, New Jersey, to Portage, Ohio, and from Utica, New York, to Philadelphia.[80]

A few documents provide greater insight into the manufacture of this article. James C. Helme, a furniture craftsman of Luzerne County, Pennsylvania, prepared a manuscript book of prices for constructing cabinetware and chairs in August 1838. Under a section headed "Prices for making Rocking Chairs," his entry for Boston-style chairs reveals something of the mechanical operations involved: "Making Boston Rocking Chairs, & getting out and bending Stuff, and sawing top, arms, & Rockers." Labor and materials were $2. Making a raised, or scroll, seat involved piecing a flat section of plank with a short, thick, curved section, or rise, at the back and applying a full or half-size roll to the front. Some wooden-bottom seating employed a front roll before the addition of a balancing back curve was common. Comprehensive records kept at Hartford, Connecticut, by chair merchant Philemon Robbins between 1833 and 1836 describe an elegant Boston rocking chair, priced between $17 and $20, as "Large" or "first rate." It was constructed of mahogany, some surfaces were further embellished with "rich gilt," and the seats could be stuffed. The top price represented half the cost of a mahogany dressing bureau.[81]

The American rocking chair appears to have been common in all settings. Almost every inventory of the 1830s or 1840s lists this form at least once. New York cabinetmaker Michael Allison owned an elegant "Boston rocker (in red moreen)," and an "old" Boston rocker stood on the piazza of another city home. A rocker had its place in a Philadelphia bedroom filled with rich green and gold "French style" furniture, and a "Boston Rockin Chare" stood in a New Jersey dining room furnished with a mahogany table and sage green chairs. Clearly, the form served both many needs and the needs of many people. A pair of watercolor portraits of James and Lydia Bixby by J. A. Davis pictures James seated in a roll-top fancy chair and Lydia in a Boston rocker (fig. 1-43). Davis painted the couple in November 1845 when they had been married less than a year and were living in Webster, Massachusetts, where James was a millhand. The furniture represents part of a set of household furnishings typical of the period.[82]

A note of irony in the tale of the early Boston rocker is present in the New Hampshire accounts of Jacob Felton, a Fitzwilliam chairmaker who sold both chair parts and framed chairs, with and without paint, to private customers and woodworking craftsmen in a broad area covering southern New Hampshire, northern Worcester County, and Boston. On more than one occasion, as recorded in 1836, Felton conveyed to George L. Miller, an ornamental painter of Boston, chairs to be finished for retail or wholesale on Miller's own account. Some chairs carted to Boston for this purpose were raised-seat, or Boston, rocking chairs.[83]

Fig. 1-43 J. A. Davis, *Lydia Goddard Bixby* (b. 1825), Webster, Mass., 1845. Watercolor on paper; H. 9½″, w. 7⅞″. (Russell Ward Nadeau collection: Photo, Winterthur.)

Later Development of the Boston Rocking Chair

A large, Boston-style rocker produced in limited quantity during the 1840s and later features a front seat scroll that forms a deep skirt (fig. 1-44). The chair's sheer mass commands attention, and the painted decoration of known examples is striking. The breadth and depth of the skirt are balanced by large forward-scroll arms finished in the natural wood and a large crown piece. Turned elements can be compared to those in the earlier Boston rocker. One chair is documented to the Hitchcocksville, Connecticut, factory of Thomas Nelson Hodges, who appears to have commenced business about 1843 when he purchased a building on the Farmington River turnpike road. The crest follows the pattern shown in figure 1-42; the decoration is a waterscape with a steamboat painted in a naïve style. The remaining chairs, including the one illustrated, are distinctly different, varying in crown profile, flaring skirt, and painted decoration. Starting with the basic crown pattern of figure 1-52, the center top of each crest rises in a secondary scroll as seen in the backboards of contemporary painted washstands and dressing tables and as delineated in a crest piece in Smith's *Guide*. Minor variation in one crest introduces two long, shallow hollows on the top surface. Other differences may be noted in the painted decoration, although the hand of the same decorator or a close associate is evident. The panel vignette in figure 1-44 contains a horse and hunter; in another example, a waterscape with a bridge fills most of the board. Gilded leaves of the same style cap the crest shoulders, and banded decoration along the top and bottom edges follows a similar pattern. The turned and painted decoration of the front legs and stretchers is complementary. The skirt decoration of the illustrated chair, featuring a landscape with ruins, is the only example that survives. The subject suggests considerable influence from sources such as European prints or English transfer-ornamented ceramics. The use of gilt is lavish and would have added a premium to the original cost.[84]

Fig. 1-44 Boston (Windsor) rocking chair, western New England or New York State, 1840–50. Mahogany (arms) and other woods; H. 41½″, (seat) 15⅝″, W. (crest) 25¾″, (arms) 25¼″, (seat) 21¼″, D. (seat) 21½″; pale peach ground with cinnamon, shades of brown, black, green, and gilt. (Hitchcock Museum, Riverton, Conn.: Photo, Winterthur.)

Fig. 1-45 Boston (Windsor) rocking chair and detail of crest, William Page Eaton, ornamenter ("W.P.EATON." painted within decoration), area of New Boston, N.H., 1865–75. White pine (seat); H. 40¾", (seat) 15⅛", W. (crest) 22¾", (arms) 21⅞", (seat) 19¾", D. (seat) 19"; black ground and black and dark red grained seat with silver-gold touched in blue-green and pink. (Marblehead Historical Society, Marblehead, Mass.: Photo, Winterthur.)

By the early 1840s rocking chairs in the Boston market featured a large tablet crest rounded along the outside edges (fig. 1-45). Small lunettes cut along the bottom are the usual embellishment. Occasionally the hollows form triangles, ogee arches, or fanciful S-scrolls. Tablet ends frequently push out at the top to form a loaf-shaped profile, and the lower corners may flare slightly (pl. 4). Cylindrical sticks are the usual back supports, but occasionally ball or flat (arrow) spindles are present. The sticks are straight or slightly hollow, but they lack the earlier full back contour. Leg turnings generally follow a ball-and-multiple-ring pattern, although some New England examples retain a late bamboo-style support with a sharply tapered upper section (fig. 1-39). Pennsylvania seating may employ the cylindrical leg common to that area (fig. 2-34). Generally, the turnings under the scroll arms are compatible with those of the legs. In post–Civil War design, some arms roll over at the front and cap the supports, as illustrated. Later in the century, the back posts, arms, and supports are often made of one continuous bent piece of wood, although the styling is comparable to that shown. Caned panels and scroll feet appeared even before midcentury. An innovation that introduced greater comfort was the padded and covered spring, or sprung, seat, which was in the market before 1830. Several spring-seat rocking chairs with stuffed backs bear the Boston label (1829–33) of William Hancock; Dorr and Allen, city auctioneers, offered haircloth-covered examples in 1829. Edward Bulkley of New Haven featured spring-seat rocking chairs in a March 1830 notice. Charles H. White marketed this form at Philadelphia in 1832, and the next year furniture warerooms in Providence and Washington, D.C., offered the new product.[85]

Further crest variation was introduced even before the Civil War. Most patterns retain the prevailing curved-end form. One has reverse scalloping along the lower edge, while another introduces a long serpentine curve in the same area. Sometimes a centered, shallow tablet projects from the top or bottom edge. By the last quarter of the century a large, solid or pierced, vertical splat of baluster form often took the place of spindles to provide the back support. Two distinctive back variants are found in Pennsylvania work with Boston-style seats; both appeared first in standard seating. One top is a shouldered tablet supported on long spindles and posts, although this

Fig. 1-46 High, shaped-tablet Windsor rocking chair, Worcester County, Mass., 1815–25. White pine (seat); H. 41″, (seat) 15½″, W. (crest) 18⅜″, (arms) 21¾″, (seat) 17¾″, D. (seat) 16⅝″; repair at left end of crest. (Worcester Historical Museum, Worcester, Mass.: Photo, Winterthur.)

Fig. 1-47 High, shaped-tablet Windsor rocking chair, Worcester County, Mass., 1820–30. White pine (seat); H. 40¼″, (seat) 16″, W. (crest) 19″, (arms) 19½″, (seat) 18¾″, D. (seat) 17¾″; paint not original. (Mr. and Mrs. R. F. Meisberger collection: Photo, Winterthur.)

crest is actually more common to the tall rocking side chair with a flat plank (fig. 1-56). The later balloon-back chair (pl. 29) almost always has a raised, or scroll, seat united with a vertical splat of variable profile.[86]

Crest pieces of the mid nineteenth century and later usually are stenciled or, less frequently, hand painted in naturalistic floral designs; the latter were especially popular with Pennsylvania consumers and chairmakers. Among stenciled ornament, fruit, curled leaves, and floral motifs are the most common (pl. 4). William Page Eaton, who decorated the chair illustrated in figure 1-45, often included birds in his stenciled patterns. His printed name appears as part of the crest design at the right. Sometimes floral motifs flank central panels containing small scenes; occasionally views cover the entire crest. Of these, waterscapes with or without sailing vessels and landscapes with buildings appear most frequently. Specialized subjects include a steamship copied from a contemporary print, a train of cars pulled by a locomotive, a political campaign theme, and patriotic motifs. The armchair is the most common form of Boston rocking chair. Armless seating, such as the "Sewing Chair Boston Seat" mentioned in the Laurens, New York, accounts of Chauncey Strong in 1849, is considerably less common. Boston chairs for children had limited production (fig. 2-46).[87]

Other Tall, Contoured Patterns

Contemporary with the tall, stepped-tablet rocking chair of the 1810s (fig. 1-38) are two variants of the general pattern, one that alters the profile of the tablet, the other altering the back structure. The first, probably from Worcester County, has one of the most handsome crests in this general group (fig. **1-46**). The profile may have been inspired directly by the crest in Samuel Gragg's bentwood chair (fig. 1-34). The basic structure, with its contoured back, scroll arms, and beveled-edge seat, adheres closely to the Boston models. Some arm posts are slimmer versions of the Boston support, while others have a small top swelling, as shown. The pierced "closepin" slots in the front stretcher duplicate those in a Worcester County side chair of identical crest. The side chair and several rockers of this pattern have traditions of ownership in western

Fig. 1-48 Shaped-tablet Windsor rocking chair with top extension, attributed to Joseph Wilder, probably New Ipswich, N.H., 1815–25. White pine (seat, microanalysis) with maple and other woods; H. 44″, (seat) 15″, W. (primary crest) 20″, (arms) 21⅜″, (seat) 19″, D. (seat) 17″; reddish brown ground with dark green and white. (Private collection: Photo, Winterthur.)

Worcester County. Through the fancy stretcher, the chairs also interrelate with work from the northern part of the county. Two tall rocking chairs of "fancy" back have plain bamboo-turned front stretchers but retain the same scrolled crest (fig. 1-47). One has a single, slim cross slat with pierced ends separated from the crest by four medium-length arrow spindles; the lower spindles are plain. As illustrated, the second chair has two pierced cross slats separated by three small shield- or urn-shaped medallions. The arrow spindles, top and bottom, are similar; their appearance has been modified by elongating the body or adding a slim neck at the top. The small medallions are close in size and shape to ornaments in a northern Worcester County side chair with a crest of arched-slat form (fig. 2-56). The slotted rocker attachment of figure 1-47 is common to the group; generally the rocker pattern is stepped, front and back. The fancy-back chairs of this group may have had a long commercial life, for Philemon Robbins's Hartford accounts of 1835 credit Sullivan Hill of Spencer, Massachusetts, with the delivery of "25 [common] R[ocking] chair with urns." The reference is to Windsor seating, and the pattern may have been that shown.[88]

The second variant is a Windsor rocker of standard height with a high crest extension (fig. 1-48). Occasional references to these chairs are found, such as Thomas Boynton's sale of a "high top rocking chair" at Windsor, Vermont, in 1815. Extensions first appeared before 1800 in Windsor seating framed with and without rockers. Amos Denison Allen of Windham, Connecticut, recorded the construction of a "Rockind ... winsor high top" in 1797. That chair would have had a round back with a straight extension formed of continuous spindles similar to an example attributed to Ebenezer Tracy (fig. 1-23). Early nineteenth-century design added a "high top" to the square-back rocking chair only a few years before Boynton made his account-book entry. The typical extension piece, framed with or without continuous back spindles, curves forward above a low, bent back, here capped by a stepped-tablet crest. The overall effect of the backward and forward bends is that of a tall, contoured back. From a design viewpoint, the best high-top chairs are those with double crests that correspond in profile. While some extensions anchor in the rail so as to align the short spindles with those

Fig. 1-49 High, tablet-top Windsor rocking chair, eastern Massachusetts or southern New Hampshire, 1825–35. White pine (seat); H. 43¼″, (seat) 15⅜″, W. (crest) 22½″, (arms) 21¾″, (seat) 18⅝″, D. (seat) 17¼″; dark brown and dark brick red grained ground with white, yellow, orange-brown, bronze, and black; left armpost and spindle replaced. (Mr. and Mrs. Oliver Wolcott Deming collection: Photo, Winterthur.)

Fig. 1-50 High, shaped-tablet Windsor rocking chair, Josiah Prescott Wilder (brand "J.P.WILDER/WARRANTED"), New Ipswich, N.H., ca. 1837–40. White pine (seat) with maple, birch, beech, and mahogany (arms, microanalysis); H. 43″, (seat) 15⅜″, W. (crest) 22″, (arms) 22½″, (seat) 19¾″, D. (seat) 18⅜″; deep straw-color ground with black, wine red, and gilt. (Winterthur 80.9.)

below, others are set above the voids. The delicate leaf decoration on the top piece, crest, and rockers of figure 1-48 further integrates the design. The low arch under each crest is a subtle feature of Boston origin, as interpreted by a New Hampshire chairmaker. Back extensions on square-back chairs are not limited to the stepped-tablet pattern (figs. 1-58, 1-59).[89]

During the early 1820s the first in a series of rectangular tablet-top chairs appeared in the consumer market. Like other tall chairs framed with tablets, they have contoured backs. By contrast, slat-framed rocking chairs generally have straight or bent backs. Early rectangular tops are straight-edged with either square or hollow corners (fig. 1-39); the boards are wedge-shaped in section. The crest that followed is slightly arched across the top and bottom (fig. **1-49,** pl. 5). The prototype exists in fancy cane- and rush-bottom seating. The seat, now oval rather than shield-shaped, is less rounded at the side and back edges than formerly; the forward surfaces are flattened, then sharply canted. Moderately thick legs show a definite triangularity in the upper segment. That characteristic, noted in another rectangular-tablet chair (fig. 1-39), became prominent in the Boston rocking chair (fig. 1-42). Most, but not all, rockers fit into slotted legs in the manner illustrated. In this example the leg tips are nicely chamfered. The chair is close in design to one bearing the label of Minot Carter, a member of the Wilder clan of New Ipswich, New Hampshire, although the proportions and the profiles of the legs and scroll arms differ. Members of the New Hampshire Wilder family knew and were influenced by Boston chairwork. Peter, the father, and Joseph, the eldest son, worked in the city early in the century before establishing a chair factory at New Ipswich between 1807 and 1810. The arch in the Wilders' tablet top became more pronounced after about 1835.

A chair with a modified crown-top crest marked by angular ends (figs. 1-50, 1-51) was in the marketplace by 1830. The design drew on several sources. One was the true, or scroll-end, crown pattern under contemporary development (figs. 1-41, 1-42), while others were designs of longer standing, such as the round-top slat of Boston and Worcester County production (fig. 2-56) and the stepped tablet (fig. 1-38). The devel-

Fig. 1-51 High, shaped-tablet Windsor rocking chair, Maine, ca. 1828–40. H. 43″, (seat) 17″, W. (crest) 21½″, (arms) 21¼″, (seat) 18½″, D. (seat) 17⅛″; dark brown and dark brick red grained ground with white, yellow, and dark colors. (Mr. and Mrs. Oliver Wolcott Deming collection: Photo, Winterthur.)

opment area was southeastern New Hampshire and southern and central Maine. As either a tablet or a slat, the crest enhances both rocking chairs and standard seating. In its mature form the profile is anything but static. In general, the New Hampshire pattern is curvilinear, while Maine work is more angular. At present, members of the Wilder family are the only New Hampshire chairmakers who can be associated with the pattern through documented examples. Minot Carter, a Wilder brother-in-law, branded rocking chairs of standard height, framing the ribbon-end crest as a slat. A tall chair of this pattern with an extension piece illustrates an 1830 directory notice of Stephen Toppan, showing that the design was current at the start of the decade. Josiah Prescott Wilder, who framed the crownlike crest on the post tops, flared the central tablet and attached a small scroll along the back edge (fig. **1-50,** pl. 6). Undoubtedly, centerpieces designed in this manner were modeled after Boston scroll-top chairs of the 1820s. The Boston crest, in turn, was developed from Baltimore fancy prototypes. Unmarked chairs with overall features relating to Wilder's documented work indicate that he also made tablets without the back scroll. The seat of the chairmaker's tall rocker is a duplicate of the plank in figure 1-49, although the stout legs are closer in size to those of a rocking chair made in Boston (fig. 1-39). The triangular profile of these supports is more extreme than formerly, and the lower tips are chamfered, as are those of many rocking chairs made in the 1820s and 1830s (figs. 1-48, 1-49). The arm posts are those first seen in Boston work several decades earlier (fig. 1-38). As in the 1790s, chairmakers often chose a fine cabinet wood, such as mahogany, to form the arms in top-of-the-line seating. Figure 1-50 has relatively restrained decoration, which relies for effect upon penciling and banding in black and wine red on a straw-colored ground (darkened now to a mustard color).[90]

Crown tops in Maine chairs show greater variety of profile (fig. **1-51**). Generally, the outer tips are larger, sometimes almost square, and the arches deeper and higher. A plain tablet is more common than the scrolled centerpiece. Most chairs have plain, tapered spindles of contoured profile. An occasional straight-back, ball-spindle rocker is fitted with a broad cross slat just below the top piece. The crests are framed as slats in a

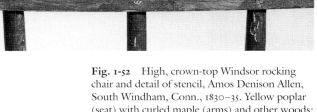

small group of flat-spindle chairs. Figure 1-51 represents a limited fancy production, at best. The ancestry of the small shield-shaped medallions may possibly be traced through New Hampshire to Windsor work of Worcester County, Massachusetts (fig. 1-47), rather than directly to a high-style prototype. The chairmaker has retained the New Hampshire plank but selected a slimmer leg that is rounded slightly at the base. The rockers echo curves found in the crest and arms. A mottled brown and red ground is overpainted in the crest with original dark fruit and leaf decoration accented here and there with white and yellow.

Two craftsmen whose names are associated with the tall crown-top rocking chair of Maine are Samuel White of Exeter and Benjamin Newman of Gloucester, Massachusetts. Newman worked in Portland in the early 1820s and possibly later. In addition to the tall chairs, there is a group of low rockers framed with bold crowns, large arrow spindles, and extension tops supported on plain sticks. Most extensions form a high contour; one rare example is supported on arrow spindles.

The crown-top tablet used by Lambert Hitchcock in his Connecticut production of tall, flat-seated rocking chairs is a duplicate of that in figure 1-52 and a variant of plate 7. The profile is a hollow-cornered rectangle rather than the trapezoid of the popular crest variant illustrated in figure 1-41 and plate 8. Figure **1-52** is documented to the shop of Amos Denison Allen of South Windham, Connecticut. Aside from the similiar crest, Allen's chair differs from Hitchcock's in several ways. Allen chose a tenoned rather than a slotted leg for the rocker attachment. His long, slim back posts are plain, while Hitchcock selected fancy-turned back supports and sometimes added ring turnings to the arm posts and front legs. Although Allen used curled maple for the chair arms, the original finish appears to have been paint. Yellow penciling and striping contrast with the dark brown and red grained ground, and stenciled decoration highlights the crest. Sunbursts, rosettes, or roundels are the usual motifs in crown scrolls. Floral forms or fruit compositions usually fill the panel (pls. 7, 8). Perhaps consciously following Hitchcock's practice in western Connecticut, Allen stenciled his name in gold on the crown back: "ALLEN. WINDHAM. CT."[91]

An unusual variant crown dominates a chair made in north-central Vermont in the 1830s (fig. 1-53, pl. 9). Otherwise the design is more or less standard. The rockers with their stepped front tips are out of date by a decade or so (figs. 1-39, 1-46), but the legs are typical for the 1830s, even though the chairmaker dispensed with creases and substituted painted rings. The plank, shaped with flat-chamfered forward edges, is common to northern New England production. A ball-and-ring-turned front stretcher was introduced to the rocking chair when the Boston pattern entered the market in the early 1830s. The interest of this chair lies in the crest, which is highly individual in profile and decoration (pl. 9). The ground color of the chair is light mustard yellow with contrasting gray-green banding. Medium reddish brown spongework covers the seat top and arms and fills the crest roundels. Black and orange-red paint helps define the random leaf decoration of the panel. If not for a lengthy inscription on the seat bottom by the last family owner, it would be impossible to pinpoint the rural origin of this chair beyond what is indicated in the plank shape. That owner identified it as the "wedding chair" of her great-grandmother Mahala Willson, who was married in Barre, near Montpelier, on November 3, 1833. It is unlikely that Mahala's husband, "Thos I[?] Willson," whose name is inscribed in red chalk on the wood, was the maker, since his estate inventory contains only farming tools. It does list two rocking chairs and half a dozen "dining" chairs. Willson lived in Barre about the time the chair was made, as confirmed in the 1840 census.[92]

Nowhere in the terminology of the tall, contoured-back, plank-seat rocking chair is there reference to the name "Salem rocker." Contemporary documents generally refer to this form instead as a high-back rocking chair, while more specific references describe "crown"-top or "tablet"-top seating. The idea of a Salem rocker appears to have sprung into existence in the late nineteenth or early twentieth century. It is a misnomer, because Boston gave birth to the form and production covered a wide geographical area.

High and Low, Straight- and Bent-Back Patterns

The tall, straight-back chair is a closer adaptation of its rush-bottom ancestor than any other plank-seat form fitted for rocking (fig. 1-54). Although the illustrated example is of relatively late date, the basic form changed little during the decades following 1820. The seat of John Swint's branded chair made in Lancaster, Pennsylvania, is thinner than earlier planks and forms a rectangle rather than the usual oval outline. Introduced to the posts and legs are multiple ring turnings in place of creases simulating bamboo. Otherwise, the slats, scroll arms, and flat spindles are little changed from earlier work executed in Pennsylvania and New England. James Helme of Plymouth, Luzerne County, Pennsylvania, did not specifically name the tall rocker in his 1838 list of "Prices for making Rocking Chairs," but he did include plank-seat chairs with multiple "bows" (slats) and ball spindles, and upon occasion identified "Scroll arms." The upper bow, or slat, in the tall, straight chair back varies from a plain board to one with deeply hollowed upper corners, a projecting rectangular tablet, or a high flat arch. Sometimes arrow spindles extend from seat to crest; the profiles are of pointed spatulate, diamond, or inverted spear form.[93]

A Windsor rocker whose design is a successful combination of outdated and current features has a relatively rare, tall bent back (fig. 1-55, pl. 10). In contrast, the low rocker with a back bend is relatively common (fig. 1-48). The chair under discussion relates to Zadock Hutchins's tall slat-crested rocker from Connecticut (fig. 1-30), both in general form and in the design of its arms and legs. Further similarities with Connecticut–Rhode Island border work may be noted in comparing the legs of the illustrated chair with figure 1-25 and the seat front with figure 2-3. To date only a rocking chair at Old Sturbridge Village can be identified as originating in the same shop. That chair, like the present one, has a fancy back, although the pattern is different and at first inspection appears unrelated. Five similarly shaped short, flat spindles fill the lower back below a narrow cross slat. Above the cross piece, four long, flat spindles are positioned over the voids between the short sticks. Crowning all is a hollow-cornered

Fig. 1-53 High, modified crown-top Windsor rocking chair, Thomas Willson, owner (red chalk and pencil inscriptions), area of Barre, Vt., ca. 1833. H. 39½", (seat) 16", W. (crest) 22⅝", (arms) 20⅞", (seat) 18½", D. (seat) 17¼"; medium light mustard yellow ground with medium gray-green, sponged reddish brown, orange-red, and black. (Steven and Helen Kellogg collection: Photo, Winterthur.)

tablet crest of the type found in Boston and northern New England (fig. 1-39). Beyond lower backs of similar design, the chairs share four other highly individual features: a squared oval plank with blunt, canted edges and a prominent point at the center front; bulbous bamboo legs socketing stretchers at a swelled area heavily scored by two grooves; flat-topped arms scored on the underside near the outer tips; and thin, collar-like turnings in the back posts just above the arms. The rocker patterns are also similar, with a shallow arch on the lower back surface complementing the curved tips.[94]

What is to be made of two tall chairs whose stylistic attributes link them with specific areas in both southern and northern New England? The answer may lie in the population shift that was under way in the early nineteenth century. New England witnessed a substantial migration from the southern regions to the lightly settled northern areas beginning in the 1780s. If the particular mixture of old- and new-fashioned work in the chairs is any criterion, the transplanted Windsor craftsman probably left southern New England and headed north and west in the decade between 1810 and 1820, taking with him a knowledge of eighteenth-century plank and stretcher design.

The last family owner of the Old Sturbridge Village chair was a resident of Glastonbury, Connecticut, located on the Connecticut River below Hartford. The chair in figure 1-55 was recovered in the area of Brattleboro, Vermont, also on the Connecticut River. Seemingly native to the area between the two locations is a small group of chairs that appear to be related. In the Connecticut Valley Historical Society in Springfield, Massachusetts, is a tall rocking chair with long, slim arrow spindles socketed into a slat-type crest; the back posts are accented by short, swelled, collared cylinders at arm level. At the Porter-Phelps-Huntington House in Hadley, a low, slat-top rocking chair with H-plan stretchers and swelled bamboo legs has turned arms with equally unusual bulbous tips. A tall rocking chair with long, flat spindles, offered in the antiques market north of Hadley, has arms and a support structure similar to those in the Hadley chair. The chairmaker in question probably worked in the Connecticut Valley, somewhere between Northampton and southern Vermont, in a region that was also subject to strong influence from chairmaking centers in Worcester County, Massachusetts, and Cheshire and Hillsborough counties, New Hampshire.[95]

The roundels centered between the cross sticks of the Connecticut Valley rocking chair simulate the beads, or balls, of fancy chairs constructed during the 1810s and 1820s. Their large size is dictated by the extra height of the chair back. That height also was a factor in introducing a collar to the tall posts. Structural strength was critical in the area drilled to receive the arms, yet to continue increasing the post diameter above that point would have resulted in an ungainly design. The collar permitted a reduction in diameter comparable to post size at the base, and the taper could begin anew. The painted ornament in yellow with dark green and red on a muted light green ground introduces stylized foliate and floral forms to the back and legs. On the Old Sturbridge Village rocker, a naïvely rendered village scene spreads across the tablet top, and penciled geometric patterns accent posts and spindles in the upper back.

Rounding out the tall group is a Pennsylvania rocking chair of a type generally made without arms (fig. 1-56). The crest design grew out of the rounded-end Windsor tablet introduced about 1835. Charles Riley of Philadelphia stenciled his name on the bottom of a large rocking armchair of the early type before his death in 1842. Shoulders humped as illustrated probably appeared in the market about 1840. The posts generally are plain. Arms, when present, are scrolled forward; the legs usually are ring-turned. The flat planks are serpentine at the sides; the fronts roll forward and terminate abruptly or flatten in a blunt edge, as shown. In later examples cross slats or broad, vertical, baluster-shaped splats replace the spindles. The crests usually feature floral decoration, either stenciled or later handpainted in naturalistic colors. The illustrated chair, which is painted chocolate brown, has a stenciled floral composition of light color accented in pink, green, and tan and enclosed within a bronze-gilt, chainlike border (pl. 11).

Three bent-back rocking armchairs of standard height selected from a variety of patterns suggest the design range available to the consumer in the 1820s and later (figs. 1-57, 1-58, 1-59). The chairs demonstrate how individual elements were combined or modified to produce different effects. The first rocker in the group is a chair from Chester County, Pennsylvania, documented by a seat-bottom label to the West Chester shop of Joseph Jones (fig. 1-57). The plain, slat-style crest, flat spindles, and banded

Fig. 1-56 High, rounded-tablet Windsor rocking side chair, Pennsylvania, 1845–60. Yellow poplar (seat, microanalysis); H. 37⅛″, (seat) 14½″, W. (crest) 21⅞″, (seat) 16½″, D. (seat) 16¼″; chocolate brown ground with yellow, bronze, pinks, greens, and tans. (James Buchanan Foundation for the Preservation of Wheatland, Lancaster, Pa.: Photo, Winterthur.)

Fig. 1-57 Slat-back Windsor rocking chair and detail of label, Joseph Jones, West Chester, Pa., 1825–30. Yellow poplar (seat); H. 31″, (seat) 16¾″, W. (crest) 19″, (arms) 20⅛″, (seat) 19⅛″, D. (seat) 17¾″; medium light mustard yellow ground with orange-brown, black, and bronze shaded in dark green. (Mr. and Mrs. Robert Townshend Trump collection: Photo, Winterthur.)

JOSEPH JONES,
FANCY & WINDSOR
CHAIR MAKER,
Nearly opposite the Academy,
WEST-CHESTER.

Fig. 1-58 Slat-back Windsor rocking chair with top extension, Vermont, 1820–30. H. 33¼", (seat) 15½", W. (primary crest) 21½", (arms) 21¼", (seat) 17⅞", D. (seat) 18¼"; black ground with bright yellow, medium green, white, bronze, and gold. (Woodstock Historical Society, Woodstock, Vt.: Photo, Winterthur.)

turnings were introduced in the late 1810s. New features in the transitional Philadelphia market of the 1820s were heavy scroll arms mounted vertically or horizontally and the slim, hollow-cornered medallion of the front stretcher, introduced from Baltimore. The chair seat is a composite of two patterns known previously: the serpentine front is from one, the wavy sides are from the other. The thick, bamboo-turned legs are a holdover from the 1810s. They are attached to the broad, platformlike rockers with rectangular tenons pinned from the outside. The attachment method and chamfered rocker tops are reminiscent of earlier practice (fig. 1-29). Similar platforms appear in the felloes of some wagon wheels to socket the spokes. The painted straw-colored surfaces covered with varnish have darkened to a mustard yellow. The black penciling and orange-brown striping harmonize with the bronze-colored cornucopias and leaves of the crest, which are further shaded in dark green and accented with black (pl. 12).

The second chair in this group is a rocker of extreme back bend and unusually low extension top, which probably originated in Vermont (fig. **1-58**). Another chair of this crest with neither a history nor original paint sold at auction in the 1970s. Asahel Powers, who painted in Windsor County in the 1830s, pictured several sitters in chairs with unusually short extensions above the crest. Another point supporting a Vermont origin centers in the turned chair legs whose long top segment of hollow profile is distinctive. The shape is unlike standard production from eastern Massachusetts, Maine, or New Hampshire. Unusual in Windsor decoration are the crest rosettes. General ornament of the same kind adorns the tops of a set of Windsor side chairs owned for several generations by a Woodstock family. The most distinctive feature of the chair is the pierced crest, probably inspired by work from Massachusetts and New Hampshire. A fitting complement to the fancy back is the small front stretcher tablet. Original rockers rabbet into the outside leg surfaces, held fast by countersunk screws covered with a composition material. In the other chair of this pattern, the rockers join the legs at an inside rabbet.[96]

The third chair of this low-back group is documented to the contemporary shop of Hudson and Brooks in Portland, Maine (fig. **1-59**). Both pattern and decoration are virtually identical to documented work by Elisha Trowbridge of the same city (pl. 13).

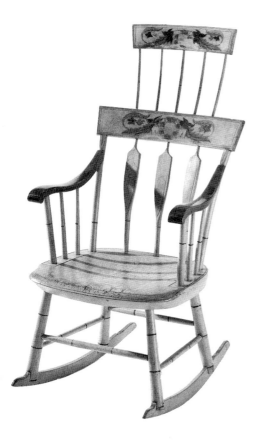

Fig. 1-59 Tablet-top Windsor rocking chair with top extension and detail of label, John B. Hudson and John L. Brooks, Portland, Me., ca. 1820–23. White pine (seat) with maple and mahogany (arms); H. 44¾", (seat) 15⅜", W. (primary crest) 20⅝", (arms) 20½", (seat) 19¼", D. (seat) 18¼"; pale mustard ground with black, orange-bronze, dark green, and light gray. (Metropolitan Museum of Art, New York, gift of Mr. and Mrs. Arnold B. Skromme: Photo, Winterthur.)

The Trowbridge rocker forms a suite with six side chairs. Compared to the rocker, the side chairs stand an entire crest-depth higher. In Portland the plain rectangular board served either as a tablet, as shown, or as a slat-type crest (pl. 14). Forward-scroll arms in the tablet-top chair are generally longer at the back and mounted higher on the posts than in slat-back construction (fig. 1-58). The rockers in figure 1-59 fit into short slots that pierce flat-bottom legs. Broad, high-bodied arrow spindles are distinctive of local production, and the three-grape pendant, barely visible on each flat face, is also a local trademark. Yellow-painted surfaces contrast with dark arms and ornament.[97]

A late nineteenth-century alternative to cutting the leg bottoms of old chairs for conversion to rocking was the addition of a pair of patented coil springs to the front legs, permitting a sort of bouncing motion (fig. **1-60**). Several eighteenth-century sack-back Windsors are so fitted, and at least two spring patterns are involved, with a minor difference in the method of attachment. In the illustrated example leg tips socket into cups mounted at the tops of steel coils. The second apparatus employs inverted, saucer-like disks attached to the feet. The spread of this device is shown in its presence on chairs of both Pennsylvania and Rhode Island origin. The Rhode Island features illustrated in figure 1-60 include tall, straight spindles bunched together through the center back, large blocked bow tips, generous knobs in the medial stretcher, and long feet with pointed toes. The knuckle arms of considerable length and breadth are a modification of those in a Connecticut–Rhode Island border chair. Another example of the use of coil-type rockers in the late nineteenth century is a painting signed and dated by Louis Betts in 1893, which depicts an old man seated in a Windsor armchair fitted with similar springs.[98]

Fig. 1-60 Sack-back Windsor armchair and detail of patented coil springs, Connecticut–Rhode Island border region, 1785–1800 and (springs) 1875–1900. H. (with springs) 36⅝", (seat) 18⅞", W. (arms) 23⅜", (seat) 20⅛", D. (seat) 15⅝". (Private collection: Photo, Winterthur.)

Special-Purpose Seating

CRADLE-CHAIRS

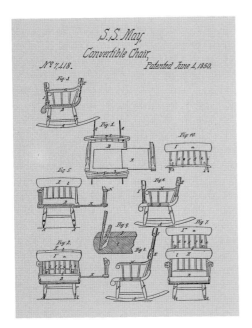

Fig. 1-61 Samuel S. May, patent for convertible chair. U.S. Patent Office, Washington, D.C., No. 7,418, June 4, 1850.

"Be it known that I, SAMUEL S. MAY, of Sterling, in the county of Worcester and State of Massachusetts, have invented [an] Improved Nursery-Chair, which I term the 'Cradle-Chair'" (fig. **1-61**). The U.S. Patent Office was created on April 10, 1790, but an identification system was begun only in 1836. Samuel May's cradle-chair was numbered 7,418 in that system under the date of June 4, 1850 (fig. **1-62**). Interest in the "mechanical" possibilities of furniture grew during the second quarter of the nineteenth century. The cradle-chair, known in at least six examples, is representative of the innovative attitude current in the seating industry. May appears to have both manufactured the cradle-chair and transferred the rights of manufacture to others. One chair is stenciled with his name and patent date under the seat. An unmarked example has been ascribed by its owner, the Farrar-Mansur House of Weston, Vermont, to one Edward Hatch of Wardsboro, Vermont. The 1850 census places a man of that name about fifty-five miles north in Bethel. A third chair, at the Sheldon Art Museum in Middlebury, bears an explicit label on the seat bottom: "PATENT / NURSERY CHAIR, / MANUFACTURED BY / N. PEARSON, / MASS. / Patented by S. S. May, June 4th, 1850." Among qualifying names in the 1850 Massachusetts census are two N. Pearsons in Essex County and one in Middlesex County. Two other cradle-chairs are unmarked and lack histories, but on the sixth example the patent identification is prominently displayed on a cross piece in the upper back (fig. 1-62). Otherwise, the chair is unmarked, so the actual maker remains unidentified. The crest is shaped in a rounded-end profile first introduced in the late 1820s but modified to the illustrated silhouette during the 1840s. The decoration contrasts a village scene and an exotic subject, an unusual juxtaposition of motifs that may be explained by the chair's use as a sample. This is even more plausible because the present owner acquired the chair with a second top piece.[99]

Lambert Hitchcock of Unionville, Connecticut, may be among those who manufactured May's patented cradle-chair. An item for two "cradle rocking" chairs in the

Fig. 1-62 Patented "Cradle-Chair," Samuel S. May, patentee, Sterling, Mass., 1850–55. H. (closed) 41¾", (open) 31⅛", (seat) 15", W. (primary crest) 22¾", (arms) 22¾", (seat closed) 21⅝", D. (seat) 18"; black and reddish brown grained ground (upper back only) with light and bronze gold. (Hitchcock Museum, Riverton, Conn.: Photo, Winterthur.)

inventory of commercial property compiled at his death in 1852 may have relevance. May's pattern, however, was not the only one in force at the time, since the specification states clearly in later paragraphs that May merely contributed to the improvement of the cradle-chair. May's innovation was twofold. First, he introduced a removable back piece to serve either as a "lolling chair" top when the seat was closed or as a front guard when the chair was open and functioning as a cradle. Second, he permanently fixed the moving arm to the sliding seat frame so as to provide a "foot guard" for an infant placed in the "cradle." There are minor differences between the patent drawing and the actual chair. As illustrated (fig. 1-62), the cradle-chair has cross stretchers, front and back, and fancy-turned front legs. The crest rail of the lower back is an inset slat rather than a tablet, and a slim cross piece takes the place of spindles in the upper back.

The construction of the chair is not complicated. The loaf-shaped crest rests on rabbets cut into the upper post faces where it is held by screws inserted from the back, as can be seen in the "open" view. Pointed lower tips insert into metal collars in the back posts above the lower slat or into sockets provided in the seat front. Figures 9 and 7 in the patent drawing illustrate what the inventor called "spring catches," which were inserted into the seat and back sockets to provide tighter joints. The lower back posts anchor in a two-piece rise at the seat back. The fixed right arm (the left as viewed) is held fast to the back post by a screw inserted from the rear. A hook and eye secure the movable arm to the second post when in the closed position. The floor of the "slide" is framed (one lap joint is visible at the front corner), and thin nailed boards form the bottom. Stretchers, front and back, are mounted in an X pattern, each upper end shaped in the form of a small foot that butts against the frame. Pins fasten the rockers to the legs.

INVALID CHAIRS

The care and "equipage" of invalids are mentioned in an early nineteenth-century source. In writing from New York to his daughter Eliza at New Orleans on October 19, 1817, John Pintard described a family visit to Burlington, New Jersey:

I had the pleasure of finding Cousin Bradford expecting us and her father so much improved in his health as to be able to bear his weight suff'y to descend & dine with us below. He looks like one of the old patriarchs & at night, seated in a very peculiar rocking Chair (so constructed as to be elevated or depressed so as to lie level or to sit upright as may suit the comfort of the patient) with his family & domestics on their knees whilst in an almost erect attitude, he offers up his prayers.

An earlier seat, which shared at least the back feature with the New Jersey chair, was in the Chester County, Pennsylvania, home of William Moore in 1783. Appraisers described it as "One Arm Chair with Iron Racks to fall back." Cabinetmaker Thomas Burling probably referred to a similar contrivance four years later when offering New Yorkers "Bed chairs for the sick . . . to let," noting that such conveniences were "much wanted in this city." Not all accommodation for invalids was as elaborate as these examples. In many families an ordinary chair sufficed. The increasing use of rockers on seating by the late eighteenth century proved a boon, since for a modest expenditure a new or altered chair provided both comfort and the benefits of backward and forward motion. Before the general use of the Windsor rocking chair, some families acquired a stationary "easy" chair of similar construction to meet special needs. This was a seat of tall, inclined back to support the head and ease the body. Such a chair is mentioned in a letter written in 1804 by George White of Ballston Spa, New York, to his employer Nicholas Low of New York City during the building and furnishing of Low's Sans Souci Hotel in the upstate community: "I have a sample of Alvords chair making, by an easey Chamber Chair he has made for me, the Chair & price does credit to the maker. I have desired him to make a Dozn: for the accomodation of the Sick in the different Houses here, they are much wanted." Pads, cushions, and drapery rendered

Fig. 1-63 High-back Windsor "easy" chair, New York, 1790–1800. Yellow poplar (seat) with maple and oak; H. 44½", (seat) 17⅜", w. (crest) 25", (arms) 27⅛", (seat) 23¼", D. (seat) 18". (Private collection: Photo, Winterthur.)

the unyielding wooden surfaces more comfortable. A basic earmark of New York eighteenth-century production is seen in the bulbous, baluster-style turnings of the illustrated example (fig. **1-63**). Behind the small arm pads are tiny pointed projections of the kind usually found in fully developed, continuous-bow chairs made in that city (fig. 2-6).[100]

Other Windsors provide more obvious evidence of their use in accommodating the weak and ailing. An eighteenth-century Massachusetts sack-back chair of extra breadth and depth is marked by numerous tackholes around the seat and on the upper structure where upholstery and padding once covered wooden surfaces that appear never to have been painted. A chair in the Philadelphia Museum of Art constructed about 1800 in a high sack-back style has small, winglike projections, consisting of short, arched bows and sticks, attached to the forward face of the main bow at either side, providing a suitable structure to receive padding or drapery. A nineteenth-century alteration to a square-back side chair introduced rockers to the legs and padded covers to the seat and back; the telltale nailholes securing the covers are clearly visible. Thomas Sheraton in his *Cabinet Dictionary* (1803) illustrated and described a framed barrel-back "tub easy chair, stuffed all over, and . . . intended for sick persons, being both easy and warm." He further noted that "the side wings coming quite forward keep out the cold air, which may be totally excluded from the person asleep, by laying some kind of covering over the whole chair."[101]

The many references to arrangements to accommodate the sick and elderly show that this was a concern in many American households. Of a general nature is Solomon Sibley's 1822 record of "making Chair for old Lady" at Auburn, Massachusetts. More explicit in purpose, though not identified in appearance or feature, are the three chairs "for sickness" constructed by Luke Houghton of Barre, Massachusetts, in 1829–30, which sold for either $2.75 or $3. John Martin priced "Sick" chairs at about $4.50 in his New York shop a few years later. Other chairs for the sick are recorded in Philadelphia, rural Pennsylvania, and Vermont. There may have been little difference in concept between these "sick" chairs and the "Gout Chair" belonging to loyalist Nicholas

Fig. 1-64 High-back Windsor "easy" chair, probably Vermont, 1810–30. H. 39″, (seat) 15½″, W. (crest) 25¾″, (arms) 23¼″, (seat) 21⅜″, D. (seat) 15⅞″. (Shelburne Museum, Shelburne, Vt.: Photo, Winterthur.)

Fig. 1-65 High-back Windsor "easy" chair, Vermont, 1830–45. Oak throughout; H. 41⅜″, (seat) 15½″, W. (top crest) 30½″, (arms) 23⅛″, (seat) 15⅞″, D. (seat) 15″; surfaces probably never painted. (Shelburne Museum, Shelburne, Vt.: Photo, Winterthur.)

Lechmere, which was confiscated at Newport in 1779. In extreme cases of infirmity it was sometimes necessary to confine the invalid in a "large cradle for sickness" fitted with a "bed," pillows, and quilts. Examples of these outsize boxes on rockers are still part of several New England institutional collections.[102]

Two chairs of extraordinary appearance and concept, both probably of Vermont origin, show the further development of special seating (figs. 1-64, 1-65). Each has a superstructure to accommodate a draped fabric. In practice the drapery created a kind of "settle" chair that protected the sitter from drafts, as described by Thomas Sheraton. When the chair was placed near the hearth or stove, the drapery helped capture and retain warm air from the heat source. Since there are no visible tackholes in the wood, the coverings must have been removable. Figure 1-64 is the earlier of the two chairs, and the wide sweep of its arms suggests a northern New England origin (figs. 1-84, 1-92). From the standpoint of balance, the present rockers, rabbeted to the outside leg surfaces and held fast with screws, appear original. In any event, they have been in place a long time and are covered with the same crazed paint found on other parts of the chair. Vertical members, top and bottom, mirror one another in profile. The heavy top rail, formed by bending, rests upon posts turned with round tenons at the tips. Old metal straps on the rear surface repair corner cracks. The curved, square arms are scratch beaded along the upper edges in the manner of a bow face, and the tenoned ends butt against flattened areas on the uprights. A low, vertical projection, or nub, near each arm front is just visible at the left. Forward of this point there is sufficient space to have accommodated a strap, cord, or rod to secure the sitter from the danger of a forward fall.

Figure 1-65 is constructed entirely of oak, including the two round-headed pins in the face of the tablet-style crest. The surfaces probably were never painted, and all the roundwork appears to have been executed by hand with shaving tools. Aside from the peculiarity of the "turnings," the spoonlike arms are the most unusual feature of the basic chair. The squared seat and tablet top permit the chair to be dated within the second quarter of the nineteenth century, and the bold, oval-centered front stretcher suggests a Vermont origin (figs. 1-28, 1-92). Inspiration from eighteenth-century Windsor work of southeastern New England is indicated in several round members, a circumstance to be expected in an area settled in part from that region. Leg tops are reminiscent of chairs made by Elisha Swan of Stonington, Connecticut, and the feet emulate Rhode Island or border patterns. In the forward posts of the superstructure, the inverted, flaring baluster at the center again duplicates profiles that appear in southeastern New England work. In plan the seating piece is actually two structures: a chair, and a shell built around it and secured at various points. The outer shell has a top rail, which in concept resembles that of figure 1-64 and in pattern approximates one found in a Vermont rocking chair. The short spindles and cross rods lend structural strength. The large wooden pins in the chair crest pierce through the long back posts of the shell, and each is secured by a long, wedge-shaped cut nail. The lower tips of the same posts pierce a large cylindrical roll below the seat back and interlock on the inside of the rear chair stretcher. The same heavy cylinder anchors the long front posts of the shell.[103]

The chair on wheels represented one of the most expensive seating forms for invalids and also one of the most cumbersome. Its primary function of mobility was limited, even under the best conditions. In American society, where multilevel houses were the rule, spacious gardens few, roads and walkways anything but convenient, and ramps nonexistent, such conveyances were the province of the few whose pocketbooks could support their whims. The wheelchair had a long history in Europe, however, before it was used in America. Louis XIV was conveyed through the grounds at Versailles in a platform chair with wheels before his death in 1715. One of Jacques Rigaud's views drawn in 1733–34 in the gardens at Stowe, Buckinghamshire, shows both a man and a woman being wheeled about in Windsor chairs mounted on mobile platforms pushed by attendants. A 1765 Staffordshire inventory of the household of Leak Oakover, Esq., at Oakover describes a "mahogany Chair for the Gout upon Wheels" in the "Passage by the Stair Case." The tradecards of chairmakers working in and around London in the late eighteenth century frequently represent a wheelchair among the small cuts surrounding the text; the principal use of the chair is described in its identification as a "Garden Machine."[104]

The first American reference to a wheeled invalid chair may date from January 7, 1751, when Thomas Elfe, a cabinetmaker of Charleston, South Carolina, advertised "All kinds of Machine Chairs . . . stuffed and covered for sickly or weak people." In this case, the word *machine* probably should be interpreted as "mechanical." Philadelphia residents were introduced to the wheelchair in 1785, if not earlier, when William Long, "Cabinet-Maker and Carver from London," advertised several specialty items. According to his statement about the "Go-Chair," it was intended "for the ease and comfort of those, who by gout or rheumatic pains, are deprived of the use of their limbs, as they can move themselves from room to room, on one floor, without the assistance of a servant, with ease and expedition; if they want to take the air in their garden, there it will be found useful—This chair has been highly approved by the Royal Society in London, and by many of the first physicians in Europe." In 1788 Long had another, seemingly improved "machine" on hand "in which . . . a person having only a slight use of one hand, may conduct himself . . . where he pleases." Long's second notice was followed in 1796 by a Boston announcement of the sale of "an elegant Rolling Chair for a sick person." Another mobile seat for invalid use was described in the early nineteenth century as "an easy chair with wheels." Owned by Mrs. Jane Villepontoux of Savannah, Georgia, whose household also contained half a dozen yew chairs, the conveyance likely was of English origin.[105]

The American wheelchair illustrated in figure **1-66** is one of at least five known Windsors with wheels, none dating before the 1820s. The wooden surfaces bear their original mustard yellow paint and black penciling, and the flat, blunt-tipped, serpentine arms have tackholes, giving evidence that they were once stuffed. The chair is of conventional Windsor construction and design, although the tall back posts scroll over at the top and are thick and blocked at arm level to ensure a sturdy joint. A wedge-

Fig. 1-66 High, slat-back, wheeled, invalid chair, Pennsylvania, 1825–40. Various woods and iron; H. 49⅛", (seat) 20¾", W. (crest) 19", (arms) 23⅜", (wheels) 28⅝", (seat) 19½", D. (seat) 17¾", (footrest) 19½" by 14½"; light mustard yellow ground with black. (Pennsylvania Farm Museum of Landis Valley, Lancaster, Pa.: Photo, Winterthur.)

shaped projection behind the round seat accommodates ironwork for the mechanical parts. Below the seat a normal, box-style stretcher system stabilizes the four block-tipped, cylindrical legs. The rectangular footboard tapers slightly from back to front and is reinforced in the same direction by cleats on the lower surface near both edges. The board hinges to the front leg blocks. Iron buckles mounted on the outer board edge and under each arm tip once secured adjustable leather straps to support the board. Two iron bars extend down from the seat back; one joins a U-shaped base rod bolted to the rear feet, the other attaches to a small rear wheel. The large wheels, with hubs and spokes of wood and rims of iron, are joined by an axle that is attached to the seat bottom with nuts and bolts at three points. The center connection is visible in the illustration. Those at either side mount a wooden block between the axle and seat to keep the bolts from driving up through the plank, suggesting the original treatment at the center.

Mechanical arrangements in other mobile chairs are similar to the one illustrated. Three chairs have backs of standard height with plain, inset, slat-type crests. One originated in Pennsylvania, the others in New England. The crest of the former is padded with brass-nailed leather, a treatment repeated on the arm tops. That chair and another have "straight," canted backs; the third has bent back posts and long, flat (arrow) spindles. The fifth chair in the group was either made in Boston or duplicates a Boston back of tall, contoured-spindle form with a head roll at the top. The arms are simple forward scrolls (fig. 1-41), and the seat is cushioned.

Mechanical chairs of all types came into their own during the second quarter of the nineteenth century, when these examples were made. A wheelchair of unknown description stood in a house in Chester County, Pennsylvania, in the 1840s. Within the same decade M. W. King, chairmaker on Broadway, New York City, manufactured a variety of seating to meet many needs, including those of the ailing and infirm. A notice of 1846 itemizes his stock as "Pivot Revolving Chairs, Recumbent Revolving Chairs, . . . Self Acting Extension Recumbent Chairs, Improved Invalid Wheel Chairs, and every variety of Mechanical Chairs, for comfort or convenience." A notice the same year by Abraham McDonough of Philadelphia suggests that it was not hard to obtain specialized seating in the large metropolitan centers of the day. McDonough warranted his "Chairs for invalids, so perfectly made that persons confined to their Chambers may move about at pleasure, without the least fatigue. —These chairs are unrivalled by any others." The Boston directory of 1860 announced that J. C. Hubbard pursued an active trade in specialized seating. His stock included "Invalid Locomotive Chairs" and "Invalid Tables." Custom work was available, as Hubbard noted: "Particular attention given to the manufacture of Invalid Chairs *to order.*"[106]

REVOLVING CHAIRS

In the 1840s chairmakers were beginning to show interest in a recently introduced form, the pivot revolving chair (fig. 1-67). M. W. King mentioned such chairs in his advertisement, quoted earlier, along with invalid chairs and other mechanical chairs. James Hazlet of Utica, New York, spoke of the form in 1843 as "newly invented," and John F. Barber of Wilmington, Delaware, offered the chair two years later. There were two revolving chairs in the "Front Ware Room" of James Renshaw's Phoenixville, Pennsylvania, furniture establishment when appraisers itemized his estate in 1857. The earliest such chairs may have had low backs, as shown in a small cut accompanying Hazlet's advertisement; a revival sack-back design was available by midcentury. Although several elements of the illustrated chair with a stool base recall eighteenth-century design — the arm posts, contoured seat, and leg turnings — more heavy-handed elements betray the chair's true vintage. The spindles and bow are almost twice the diameter of comparable eighteenth-century chair parts, and the arm rail is thick, with blunt terminals at the front. The pivoting mechanism is a sturdy one of the simplest design. About one-quarter of the distance down the swivel rod there is a small hole (see detail) for the insertion of a pin, which is positioned beneath the stool top. This small piece of metal firmly secures the two parts of the chair for use. An iron collar anchored by screws to the stool top prevents wear and tear on the pivot hole. The heavy front-to-back brace below the stool seat, which houses the tip of the pin, prevents undue movement or unexpected rocking when the chair is in use. It is interesting that in a period of major advances in technology, the chair-seat bottom was dressed with a hand plane. The broad, shallow, crosswise cuts are just visible in the detail.[107]

Originally the revolving chair seat rested flat on the stool base. A later owner added the wedge-shaped piece of wood that now secures the pivoting pin to the chair bottom, introducing a slight tilt from front to back. The heavy rectangular brace that rests on the high stretchers probably was replaced at the same time but appears to follow the original treatment and form. A low-back revolving chair made by S. S. Howe of South Gardner, Massachusetts, has a similar brace. The illustrated chair almost certainly was made in eastern Pennsylvania and likely in or near Bethlehem. The bow, seat, and vertical turnings are similar to those in two late sack-back chairs fitted with standard bases that originated in that community. Both the standard chairs are stenciled with the name and location of the manufacturer, along with the legend "GENUINE MORAVIAN CHAIR"; they date from the third quarter of the century. The present chair is more stylish in its turned detail and probably was made early in the period.

The revolving chair quickly became a merchantable commodity, and by the 1870s it was established as a permanent fixture in the business world. A trade sheet issued by the Sheboygan Manufacturing Company in 1876 illustrates 132 seating pieces, from the standard chair to the high stool. Nearly one-fourth of the items are revolving chairs. The Brooklyn Chair Company devoted ten pages to revolving-chair patterns in its 1887 catalogue. Nineteenth-century entrepreneurs were not the first to discover the convenience of a chair that turns in place. In the late eighteenth century two distinguished American statesmen owned large, upholstered bergère chairs that swiveled on framed circular, stoollike bases. George Washington referred to his seat as an "uncommon chair"; Thomas Jefferson fixed the name "Whirligig" to his. Apparently both men pur-

Fig. 1-67 Sack-back revolving office chair and detail of mechanism, eastern Pennsylvania, 1845–65. H. 33¾″, (stool) 13½″, W. (arms) 24½″, (seat) 21½″, D. (seat) 16⁵⁄₁₆″; central stretcher-brace restored. (Private collection: Photo, Winterthur.)

chased their chairs at the New York shop of Thomas Burling in 1790 when the federal government was located in that city. Earlier, Jefferson had acquired a Windsor chair of similar arrangement, presumably from a Philadelphia craftsman. The statesman and his chairmaker probably collaborated on the design of the mechanism, which is the same as that used in the Burling chairs: a central swivel rod accompanied by four spaced, sash-type pulleys inset near the outer perimeter of the base unit. Following these experimental efforts, the concept of revolving in a chair seems to have lain dormant—except for limited use in the piano, or music, stool—until commercial entrepreneurs of the 1840s seized upon the idea and reintroduced an improved mechanism. Probably before the close of the same decade, Shaker craftsmen developed a small revolving stool-chair for use in their craft shops and with the sewing table.[108]

CLOSE-STOOL CHAIRS

Modern sanitation facilities are taken for granted. The offensive odors of privies and necessary houses, chamber pots and night chairs were part of daily life until the twentieth century. From an early date a fitted cabinet for private bedroom convenience was available to householders of substantial means. This close-stool or close-stool chair was a boxlike affair, with or without a back and arms, that enclosed a chamber utensil. The form was already established by 1410 when a household accounting at Wye, Kent County, England, listed "2 close stoles." Two similar chairs are included in a 1601 inventory of Hardwick Hall, the residence of the countess of Shrewsbury (Bess of Hardwick) in Derbyshire. In the "Inner Room" beyond the countess's bedchamber was her richly embellished "Close stoole covered with blewe cloth stitcht with white, with red and black silk frenge." A smaller such chair, probably plain, stood in the same room for the use of her granddaughter, Lady Arabella. Nearby were three fresh "pewter basons," ensuring cleanly facilities. Lady Arabella's convenience may have more nearly resembled one described in an inventory of Hatfield Priory, Hertfordshire, in 1629 as "1 old leather closestoole chaire."[109]

Fig. 1-68 Low-back close-stool chair, area of Bethlehem, Pa., 1765–1800. Walnut throughout; H. 28¾", (seat) 18", W. (arms) 21¼", (seat) 20", (feet) 20¼", D. (seat) 17½"; surfaces probably never painted. (Mr. and Mrs. Joseph A. McFalls collection: Photo, Winterthur.)

The convenience and luxury of owning even a plain, unstuffed close-stool was transplanted from the Old World to the New probably with the earliest affluent settlers or officials to arrive. John Jones, a Philadelphia merchant with an estate valued at close to £1,600 at his death in 1708, counted among his seating furniture leather chairs, "old" cane chairs, and "1 Close Stoole Chaire and Pann," which appraisers valued at a substantial 25s. In the 1730s the lieutenant governor of Pennsylvania, Patrick Gordon, owned a "Necessary Chair" valued at £2, which was itemized with the bedsteads and bedding, indicating its location. The form continued in use at Philadelphia. A "Close Stoole & Earthen Pan belong'g to it" was part of widow Elizabeth Carter's household until her death in 1744. Solomon Fussell's furniture accounts show the repair of a close-stool in 1747 and the sale of another for 50s. to John Sims the same year. In all likelihood this was a mahogany chair in the Queen Anne style, since Fussell constructed other chairs for Sims at the same date from mahogany supplied by the merchant. In 1754 Francis Trumble, a cabinetmaker soon to expand into Windsor-chair making, offered a variety of furniture, including "close chairs," to the community. One patron bought a "Wallnut" close stool. Elsewhere in southeastern Pennsylvania, inventories place a "Close Stool and Pan" in the Chester household of Grace Lloyd in 1760 and a "Close Stool & pewter pot" in that of Joshua Hoopes at Westtown, Chester County, in 1769.[110]

The usual close-stool chair was a box having a hinged lid that covered a seat with a large hole in the center. Below, in a cabinet with an access door, was a ceramic pot or metal pan. More elaborate close-stool chairs were made in fine cabinet woods, with loose seats and deep skirts in the frame to conceal the pan.

An inventory of 1767 shows that the close-stool was in use in Virginia at Philip Ludwell's Green Spring on the banks of the James River. An inventory of the same year lists a close-stool at the residence of merchant William Jevon of Lancaster, Pennsylvania. By the eve of the Revolution the form was widely employed from Charleston, South Carolina, to Newburyport, Massachusetts. The name *close-stool* continued in use until well into the nineteenth century. During that period the quest for comfort and convenience extended to the painted chair. Chairmaker Henry W. Miller of Worcester, Massachusetts, provided a patron with a "Close Stool & cushion" in 1829. David

Alling, a fancy-chair and Windsor-chair maker of Newark, New Jersey, identified an "easy chair with cushions hole in seat" in his 1833 accounts. Three years later he made a special multipurpose seat at a cost of $10: "To large rock chr hole in seat cushioned with leather & making bck & seat cushions."[111]

Before 1820 another term describing the close-stool came into use, *night chair, night stool,* or *night cabinet.* The earliest reference located, though certainly not the first, dates to 1819 and is found in the accounts of Daniel and Samuel Proud of Providence. Abner Haven of Framingham, Massachusetts, used the term by 1822 and Increase Pote of Portland, Maine, by 1827. At midcentury still another term, "Reception chair & cover," appears several times in the Philadelphia inventory of Abraham McDonough.[112]

There was a modest production of close-stool chairs by Windsor craftsmen. The "2 large Chairs" priced at 37s.6d. each and sold by Gilbert Gaw to Mrs. Elizabeth Fisher of Philadelphia in 1799 probably had high backs. The special function of the furniture would go unrecognized, however, except for the next item in Gaw's bill: "2 pewter pans." The substantial price suggests that the chairs had one or more special features, such as mahogany arms and seat cushions. At Harrisburg on the Susquehanna several years later Joseph Robinson stocked a good general assortment of "ready made" chairs, some for specialized use, such as large and small rockers, "Close Chairs," and piano stools. Anthony Steel's Philadelphia estate of 1817 itemizes "3 close stool chairs unfinished," which suggests that there was a regular call for this item in Windsor construction by the early nineteenth century. A decade later Henry W. Miller, proprietor of a chair factory at Worcester, Massachusetts, credited a supplier with six close-stool chairs for which Miller paid 8s. (about $1.33) apiece. The chairs probably were unpainted. Close-stool chairs were part of the wide variety of seating furniture stocked by Thomas Walter Ward II at his general store in Pomfret, Connecticut, in the late 1830s. An annual inventory valued them at $2.33½ apiece, although that figure may reflect the cost rather than the sale price.[113]

Two close-stool chairs of plank-and-spindle construction illustrate work of the eighteenth and nineteenth centuries. The first is a walnut chair made in the late eighteenth century and recovered from the barn of a Moravian family near Bethlehem, Pennsylvania (fig. 1-68). The chair was just as likely made for service in the communal Moravian society at Bethlehem as for private family use. Possibly a unique piece of furniture, this close-stool chair combines the joiner's and turner's arts. The structure above the plank is based upon early Windsor design of southeastern Pennsylvania. The back rail is a variant of the usual regional construction, employing a capping piece above a three-piece arm rail with corner lap joints. A narrow chamfer at the top and bottom edges of the arms has its counterpart in other Pennsylvania seating. Posts and spindles pierce all rails and are wedged. The arm posts are swelled versions of the spindles, with a token cap and base; the ringed neck is sometimes found in early Windsor work and an occasional slat-back chair. At some point the post bases were set back; the circular pot cover once had a leather strap handle. Inside the cabinet the open segmental braces and all four top rails show that the box was once fitted with a large pan. Stiles and rails are framed in rabbeted mortise-and-tenon joints, the tenons pinned in place. Subtle embellishments include molded inside edges on the stiles and rails and tiny beads running the length of the four corner posts. The cylindrical feet are continuations of the same sticks of wood. Metal strips nailed to the lower corners are later additions to strengthen the joints. The cleats nailed under the seat serve both to reinforce the construction and to hold the seat in position when closed. The edges of these narrow boards are chamfered like those of the arms. The chair may have had a stain and varnish finish originally, but it appears never to have been painted.

A group of nineteenth-century close-stool chairs dating to around 1850 is represented by figure 1-69. Although there are subtle variations among the chairs, the basic form is consistent. Three chairs are documented, one each to the New Hampshire shops of J. P. Wilder of New Ipswich and David Clark of Peterborough, the third to the unidentified firm of V. and F. of Oxford, Massachusetts. A chair in the Worcester

Fig. 1-69 Rounded tablet-top close-stool chair, Worcester County, Mass., or southern New Hampshire, 1845–60. White pine (seat) with birch, maple, white pine, and basswood (microanalysis); H. 37¾", W. (arms) 23¹³⁄₁₆", D. 21³⁄₈"; black and brick red grained ground with white, yellow, gold, and bronze; commode lid restored (Winterthur 79.70.)

Historical Museum came from nearby Shrewsbury. Crest rails are rounded, except in the Wilder chair, which has a rectangular tablet top. Wilder's chair also is broader and lower in the back than the others. Supporting the forward-scroll arms at the front of the close-stool chairs are either bamboo posts or cylinders with ball or ring turnings. The large oval seats are depressed around the pot cover, permitting the lid to rest level with or slightly below the plank surface. Two fingerholes in the top of the lid afford easy access for use. With the addition of a cushion, the chair could be employed for normal seating, if desired. Most pot chambers, or boxes, open from the back, although the Wilder chair has a front access. All the chairs stand on short, stumpy cylindrical feet tapering slightly at the toe and braced with cylindrical box-style stretchers. A dark brown and red tortoiseshell rosewood ground is the most common painted surface. Light-colored penciling simulates grooves in the spindles and turned work. The box front usually is outlined as a rectangular panel and contains ornament; sometimes simple geometric patterns decorate the leg posts. The arms are either finished in the natural wood for contrast or painted to match the rest of the chair. The stenciled decoration in the crest of the illustrated chair is particularly well executed for the period (pl. 15).

BARBER CHAIRS

Seating designed for barbering purposes was not common before the early nineteenth century; until then, standard or improvised furniture sufficed. One early exception is recorded in the 1740 accounts of Thomas Gaines of Ipswich, Massachusetts, who sold Francis Cogswell, Esq., "a Barbers chairs" for 15s. Although the chair is not described further, it likely had a rush seat.[114]

In 1818, the woodworking Proud brothers of Providence, Rhode Island, sold a barber chair for the substantial sum of $2.75; the purchaser may have been a professional barber. A special seat made six years later was a simpler affair, priced at $1. At Erie, Pennsylvania, George Landon's barbering chair cost $2.50. He sold it to John C. Wallace on August 18, 1821, five days after the chairmaker had credited Rufus Clough with "irons for barber chair," a reference that provides insight into the construction. The irons likely were the fittings for a headrest and its supports. Two entries in David Alling's Newark, New Jersey, accounts dated 1837 and 1838 give more information. Peter Ennis purchased what appears to be the single most expensive chair recorded by Alling when he acquired for $14 a "cane seat & back curl maple Barber Chr." For another $2 he bought a "morocco seat cushion" for this substantial chair. The firm of Smith and Lippins acquired a barber chair from the Alling shop for $4 and four Windsors for an additional $4.50. Two low stools at 50¢ apiece probably were used to support a customer's feet when "in the chair." Across the bay in New York the firm of Calvin R. Wilder and Edwin Stewart anticipated a brisk trade in barber chairs. In the summer of 1841 they received from Calvin's brother Josiah Prescott Wilder of New Ipswich, New Hampshire, an order of more than 2,700 chair parts, among which were "50 Barber Chair Legs (Front)" and fifty back legs. The former were slightly more expensive, suggesting that the front legs had turned ornament, while the back supports were plain. A barber chair for personal use stood in the Philadelphia home of chairmaker Charles Riley before his death in 1842.[115]

Edward Hazen, the author of short essays illuminating the crafts, which were published in the 1830s and 1840s, described the barber's primary work as "taking off the beard." The usual requisites were "soft water, good soap, a brush, and a sharp razor." Hazen further observed, "Barbers have usually some regular customers, many of whom have a box of soap and a brush appropriated to their individual use." Two stages in the shaving process are illustrated by Lewis Miller of York, Pennsylvania, in his early nineteenth-century pictorial chronicle of community life (fig. 1-70). Barber Lewis Shive, when applying lather to the face of Daniel Dondele (also Dondle), played a practical joke on his customer: "Lewis Shive, Shaveing old daniel dondle, pushing his brush in his face and had cold watter—craying [crying] out Oh—I burnt you. daniel

Fig. 1-70 Lewis Miller, *Lewis Shive and Daniel Dondele* and *Jacob Nell, Barber,* York, Pa., drawn ca. 1810–25. Ink and watercolor on paper; *(left to right)* H. 2½″, 2¼″, w. 4⅜″, 2³⁄₁₆″. (Historical Society of York County, York, Pa.: Photo, Winterthur.)

Jumpet up from his cheer and rubing his face." Some years later Miller depicted barber Jacob Nell, straight razor in hand, shaving Nicklas Huber. Both barber chairs have back extensions to support the customer's head.[116]

A detailed picture of a typical shop interior in 1813 emerges from the inventory of John Nichols, who practiced barbering in New York City. Itemized among the contents of "the work Shop" is a variety of small equipment, such as razors, scissors, curling irons, hair and clothes brushes, a hone, and lamps. Other items identify major equipment or suggest shop procedure: "Nine towels home spoun & nine Dyaber [diaper towels] / one Shaving Box & brush / one wash hand Bason / one hand Looking Glass / two Shop Chairs / one rush D[itt]o / a Barbers Pole / three Signes / four Canary Birds & two Gages [cages]." The last entry is most singular, but Hazen supplied a historical focus: "When the practice of shaving off the beard was again revived in Europe, instrumental music was employed in the barber's shop, to amuse customers waiting their turn; but, at the present time, newspapers are furnished for this purpose." While not a band of musicians in the usual sense, the canaries appear to have been placed in the shop to amuse the customers.[117]

The inventory of barber William Taylor of Boston, made in 1832, expands upon the list of shop fixtures and accouterments. Engravings appear to have replaced canaries as an attraction. To heat the shop in winter and provide hot water for towels there was a "Stove and funnel [pipe]." Seating was more extensive than at the Nichols shop. Customers awaiting their turn in one of the two "Shaving chairs" were seated on other chairs or on one of the shop settees; one long seat had a cushion. Outside the shop stood, or hung, the traditional symbol of the trade, the red and white barber's pole, a reminder that until the eighteenth century barbers also practiced phlebotomy (blood letting). In 1825 the cost of "making a Barber Pole," as noted in the Providence shop records of Daniel and Samuel Proud, was about $1. Silas Cheney charged a like sum for a sign at Litchfield, Connecticut, in 1809 and priced a turned "urn" for the pole tip at 17¢.[118]

Supplementing the documentary and pictorial evidence are two surviving Windsors fitted as barber chairs (fig. 1-71). These seats, together with Lewis Miller's drawings, suggest the design range. Allowing for artistic license in Miller's portrayal of Shive, the barber's seat appears to be an eighteenth-century low-back chair with an extension, or headpiece, added to the heavy back rail. Barber Nell's chairs are recognizable as Baltimore-type, tablet-top chairs fashionable during the 1810s and later. The headpiece in the patron's chair probably is mounted on a lathlike metal support resembling that in figure 1-71. The surviving chairs are of late date, and each is supported on legs somewhat higher than usual, for the convenience of the barber. Obviously, the two were used in conjunction with a low or high stool (fig. 1-72). The primary features of figure 1-71—the rabbeted, arch-top crest, forward-scroll arms, and serpentine, roll-front seat—suggest a New England origin in Massachusetts or New Hampshire, although

Fig. 1-71 Tablet-top barber's chair, probably Massachusetts, New Hampshire, or New York State, 1835–45. H. (crest) 37¼″, (seat) 23¾″, w. (crest) 19¾″, (arms) 22½″, (seat) 19½″, D. (seat) 18⅜″, (headrest) 7⅝″ by 4¼″. (Henry Ford Museum and Greenfield Village, Dearborn, Mich.)

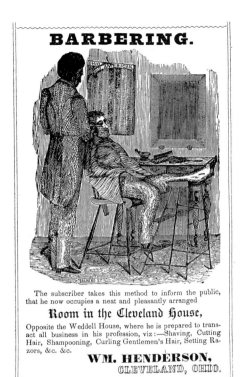

The subscriber takes this method to inform the public, that he now occupies a neat and pleasantly arranged

Room in the Cleveland House,

Opposite the Weddell House, where he is prepared to transact all business in his profession, viz:—Shaving, Cutting Hair, Shampooning, Curling Gentlemen's Hair, Setting Razors, &c. &c.

WM. HENDERSON,
CLEVELAND, OHIO.

Fig. 1-72 William Henderson's barber shop. From William Stephenson, comp., *Smead and Cowles' General Business Directory of the City of Cleveland for 1848–9* (Cleveland: Smead and Cowles, 1848), p. 155. (Photo, American Antiquarian Society, Worcester, Mass.)

the chair was acquired in 1929 in Chenango County, New York. The second chair has plain spindles, an inset slat, and plain, tapered, Pennsylvania-type legs with a ball turning near the top; it dates to about 1850. The extension piece in both chairs appears to work on the same principle. The headrest is fixed to a long support that passes through a slot in the seat back; the entire unit is raised or lowered to suit the customer, probably through the use of friction fittings. A similar arrangement is suggested in the tall-legged chair pictured in the interior of William Henderson's barbering room at Cleveland House in Ohio (fig. 1-72). The back brace for the headrest extends below the seat, and the plank is finished at the front with a scroll. Other utensils of the trade appear on the table in the background, and current newspapers hang on the wall.

By the date of Henderson's advertisement, the barbering room was a common service facility in American hotels. An 1842 inventory of the Baltimore Exchange Hotel lists a "Barber Shop" containing six chairs, two for shaving. During his American tour of 1853, the Englishman William Chambers found a "barber's apartment in every hotel" and commented on the luxury of "leaning back in a couch-like chair . . . the feet exalted on a velvet-covered rest." Even on board a Great Lakes steamer Chambers enjoyed similar accommodation. He described a scene not unlike Henderson's shop (fig. 1-72).[119]

Settees and Benches

INTRODUCTION

The terminology for the plank-bottom seat built to accommodate two or more persons is at best confusing. Words such as *settee, settle, bench,* and *couch* were all used at one time or another to describe this form, yet all these terms on occasion also referred to rush- or stuffed-bottom furniture, backless seats, and paneled or board-back furniture. Conspicuously absent from period terminology is the modern term *love seat,* often used today for the small two-seated settee.

The simple plank bench with stick legs acquired a back by the Renaissance. Curiously, the long Windsor does not seem to have evolved directly from this type of seat. Instead, the large Windsor form, which was new in the eighteenth century, was conceived as an expanded chair, complete with individual seat depressions worked on the plank surface (fig. 1-73, pl. 3). An inventory of the household possessions of William, Lord Byron, made at Newstead Abbey, Nottinghamshire, in 1736, itemizes "Single," "Double," and "Treble Windsor Chairs." The long seats were placed in the galleries in this transformed ecclesiastical structure. Other items include a "Long Settle" in the kitchen, probably of board-back construction, and a "Large Settee & Cushoon" in the Red Drawing Room, and ten chairs and two stools en suite "Covered wth Red Silk Damask," indicating that the furniture was framed and upholstered. Lieutenant governor Patrick Gordon brought similar seating with him to Philadelphia when he left London in the mid 1720s, although his settee and stools were covered in mohair. Gordon's five Windsor chairs may have been among his household baggage at the time.[120]

The expanded, plank-bottom chair was in use in America by 1754, when Jedidiah Snowden, cabinetmaker and Windsor-chair maker, billed merchant John Reynell £3 for "2 Double Windsor Chairs with Six feet & Stretchers answerable." Thomas Jervis of Moyamensing, Philadelphia County, may already have owned the pair of settees that were itemized a few years later in his inventory of 1761. By the early 1750s American chairmakers and merchants probably were familiar with imported settees of London construction having high or low backs. A London origin is suggested for the "Elegant Imported double chairs" offered for sale by J. A. Alexander of Annapolis, Maryland, in 1763. By then the Philadelphia product was already competing with the English seat. The first recorded use of the term *settee* for a Windsor product occurs at New York City on August 15, 1765, when Andrew Gautier, a retailer of Windsor furniture, advertised

Fig. 1-73 Small, low-back Windsor settee ("double chair"), Philadelphia, 1760–65. Yellow poplar (seat) with maple and oak (microanalysis); H. 30 1/16", (seat) 18 7/8", W. (arms) 53 3/4", (seat) 50 1/8", D. (seat) 16 3/4"; yellow ocher ground mottled with brown varnish over various paint coats, including the original light bluish green and gray primer. (Winterthur 82.116.)

"Settees, or double seated" Windsors, suitable for piazzas or gardens. The cut of the Philadelphia-style, high-back chair that accompanies the notice suggests that Gautier's merchandise either was imported from that city or made in the Philadelphia style by a local craftsman. Several months later, and again the following year, importers in Charleston, South Carolina, advertised similar Philadelphia merchandise. In 1774, at the death of Peter Manigault, planter and attorney of Charleston, appraisers itemized two "double" Windsor chairs among his possessions.[121]

PENNSYLVANIA REGIONAL WORK FROM 1750 TO 1800

The survival of a small group of Philadelphia "double chairs" permits a comprehensive study of their development (fig. 1-73). All examples have low backs. In fact, most surviving eighteenth-century settees have low backs, in direct contrast to the low-back chair, which is the rarest single-seat pattern. There is no evidence that American settees ever had slat-type arm supports comparable to those in the first Windsor chairs produced in Philadelphia. The earliest pattern features double-baluster, ring, and ball-centered medial stretchers bracing an understructure consisting of six ball-foot legs. Balusters are elongated. Plank surfaces have two depressions, each contoured to "saddle" form and centered with a front pommel in the manner of a single Windsor. The earliest planks have a small triangular depression near the center back between the "seats," although what purpose this served beyond ornamentation is unclear. Other features are the same as those found in the low-back chair: a plank with flat-chamfered edges, side and back; a spindle platform defined by a groove; a three-piece rail with flat-scrolled arms outlined by a scratch bead; and lap joints at the rear corners joining the arms and back rail. One settee has attenuated balusters in the arm supports like those in the earliest low-back chairs. Turnings in other settees have gradually swelled balusters similar to those in Windsor-chair legs. Back rails end in low, flattened, ogee-curved tongues above the fifth spindle from each arm post. In the next stage of development, the back rail was increased in height and length, first seen in a transitional example whose rail extends to the fourth spindle from each end. That double-chair has round-tipped medial stretchers and vigorously curved arms terminating in large, carved knuckle scrolls.[122]

The double-seated plank of the small settee remained through the next design change, which introduced medial stretchers swelled in the manner of side braces augmented by small flanking collars to compensate for the longer length of the central units (fig. 1-73, pl. 3). The triangular depression in the plank disappeared, and the back rail was increased in length to the point of the third spindle from either post. The rail is also slightly thicker, and the ends terminate more abruptly. The rail profile at the left end reveals a deep channel on the back surface similar to that in the low-back chair. The turnings in this example duplicate those in a tall chair of southeastern Pennsylvania origin. Visible surfaces are covered with a late nineteenth-century coat of mottled paint and varnish in shades of light brown over earlier paint layers that commence with Windsor green over a gray primer on the wood. In the last phase of design the double chair was converted to true settee form by eliminating the double-seated plank in favor of one with a continuous hollow between the posts. A small settee of this design in the Metropolitan Museum of Art, New York, is in other respects identical to the illustrated example. A tapered foot next replaced the ball terminal, and eventually that support gave way to the bamboo leg (fig. 1-75). Although the low-back settee reached a length that accommodates three or more persons, in American work only the two-seated size was made with individually contoured seats. Several Pennsylvania settees of longer length have ball feet. A few examples have eight supports, and at least one uses the Pennsylvania German dual-leg system (fig. 2-13). A ball-foot settee with ten legs and attenuated arm supports has a mahogany rail — a truly superb example. Reproductions — both new and old — have been made of the ball-foot, two-seated settee with individually contoured seating places.[123]

The "Windsor Settea" that Francis Trumble constructed for the Philadelphia firm of Levi Hollingsworth and Zebulon Rudolph in 1770 was probably two-seated, to judge by its cost of £1.13.0. Trumble made two others of comparable price the following year for General John Cadwalader, and a dozen "round top," or sack-back, chairs en suite priced at 15s. each. The cost of one settee was twice that of each chair, reaffirming its "double chair" size. Three years later, in 1774, Cadwalader purchased a "Grien Settee for Miss Nancy," his daughter, from William Cox, another leading city chairmaker. Again the 30s. price suggests that the seat was small. At the death that year of Lyford Lardner, a provincial officer and large landholder of Philadelphia County, appraisers itemized "8 Windsor chairs & a double d[itt]o" in the "Back Parlor" of Lardner's Somerset Farm near Fox Chase. Six chairs of similar construction stood in the front parlor. Also in 1774, businessman Uriah Woolman exported two Windsor settees and twenty-four round-top chairs to Charleston, South Carolina. It may have been increasing competition that induced Francis Trumble to advertise the following year in a lengthy notice itemizing formal and painted furniture and naming both Windsor chairs and settees.[124]

Several inventories dating to 1778 illustrate the occasional substitution of other terms for the word *settee* when itemizing household furniture of Windsor construction. Samuel Shoemaker's Philadelphia garret held a "Windsor Settle," its location and lack of value indicating that it was an old piece of furniture. With a value of £3, however, the front entry "Settle" accompanied by three Windsor chairs was relatively new. Outside the city, cooper John Roberts's Lower Merion township residence contained "1 couch and Windsor chair" in the southeast room, with similar chairs scattered in other areas. Of several rooms furnished with Windsors at Graeme Park near Horsham, one located downstairs held five chairs and a "settle." In the autumn of 1778, following the British evacuation of Philadelphia, the Pennsylvania Statehouse (now Independence Hall) was refurnished for the accommodation of various governmental bodies. The Supreme Executive Council paid John Pinkerton for two courtroom settees, and Francis Trumble constructed Windsor chairs to furnish several other areas.[125]

With the return of peace in the early 1780s the demand for painted furniture was on the rise, and Philadelphia craftsmen and merchants took the lead. There was a new generation of young consumers, and older householders, like Benjamin Betterton, who were ready to replace selected furnishings, such as the "old fashioned settee" in the upstairs back parlor, with the latest patterns in stylish new colors. At John Lambert's premature death in 1793, the shop stock included settee bows bent in readiness for use and one completed settee painted white. Meanwhile, in 1792 John Wire had furnished John Penn with chairs and settees, probably for use at Lansdowne, his estate across the Schuylkill in what is now west Fairmount Park. William Cox sold Windsor chairs and settees in the mid 1790s to General Henry Knox, a member of President Washington's cabinet. The export trade also took on new life. Settees sometimes accompanied sets of chairs destined for ports along the southern coast or in the Caribbean, although for each long seat shipped hundreds of chairs were exported. The trade gained momentum during the 1780s and continued at a fast pace during the 1790s, when settees were shipped to Norfolk, Richmond, Alexandria, and Cherrystone, Virginia; Charleston, South Carolina; and Savannah, Georgia. There were also named and unnamed ports in the islands, including Cape François and Port-au-Prince, Santo Domingo; Cape Nicola Mole, Haiti; and St. Croix, St. Thomas, Grenada, and Havana. One cargo with settees was landed at Surinam on the northeast coast of South America, and another was marketed in Funchal, the Madeiras, off the northwest coast of Africa. Some records include brief descriptions of the merchandise, such as the "Settees of six feet long" offered at Charleston by the ship *Clementina* or the "four Dozn of Green Chairs / four Sophas Ditto" shipped to Port-au-Prince on board the schooner *Polly*.[126]

Upon occasion it is possible to identify artisans who participated in the export trade. Francis Trumble sold 120 chairs and 2 settees to the merchant firm of Cox and Frazer on May 27, 1784, and received £73.10.0. for his labors. Taylor and King, partners in 1799 and 1800, fixed paper labels to their wooden seating, giving business particulars and soliciting "Orders from Captains of Vessels and others." Windsor chairs and settees shipped by Joseph Burden and William Cox on board the *South Carolina* and the *Maria* in 1796 were destined for the Charleston furniture market; Michael Murphy was part of the same trade.[127]

Evolution of the settee from the ball-foot support to the tapered foot to the bamboo-turned leg may be observed in Pennsylvania furniture of both urban and rural production. The settees illustrated in figures 1-74 and 1-75 exhibit subtle, though distinctive, characteristics of their German American heritage. Figure **1-74** is a judicious blending of the Philadelphia style with German mannerism and craft innovation. The treatment of the plank edges is transitional—not sharply flat and chamfered, yet not fully rounded. The pommels disappeared from the front edge when the seat ceased to be a double chair. The vertical turnings conform to Philadelphia work, but the craftsman's choice of ash for these parts indicates that he was located outside the city. The feet taper somewhat more than usual in Philadelphia Windsors, an influence that may spring from craft activity in the Pennsylvania-Maryland border region. Certainly, German design is indicated in the bold trumpet-shaped tips of the medial stretchers (fig. 1-76). This feature, common in the front stretchers of Delaware Valley rush-bottom chairs (fig. 1-22, left), was a profile adopted by the German chairmakers for their Windsors. An innovative feature is the bent rail whose thin, vertical blade imitates the heavy sawed back rail. The profile is simplified and lightened through use of the shave and the steambox. The flat arms terminate in pads of wavy outline, as developed in early Philadelphia Windsor work (fig. 2-21). Sometimes six-legged settees were "stretched" in length to accommodate three people, but the design is not nearly as successful as the small form illustrated.

Two small settees—one a transitional design, the other in the full bamboo style of the 1790s—are branded by Philadelphia chairmakers. The first, of low rectangular back with the slim rail lapped at the rear corners, has baluster posts and four bamboo-turned legs; it bears the stamp of John Letchworth. A six-legged, bamboo-style settee with a slim, low, curved rail, made by Anthony Steel, was formerly in the Arthur J. Sussel collection. The bamboo-style settee illustrated in figure **1-75** was made in rural Berks County, Pennsylvania. Although undocumented, it has turned parts resembling those

Fig. 1-74 Small, low-back Windsor settee, southeastern Pennsylvania, 1780–1800. Yellow poplar (seat) with ash and oak (microanalysis); H. 29½″, (seat) 18⅛″, w. (arms) 52⅝″, (seat) 51½″, D. (seat) 17¼″. (Winterthur 59.1627.)

Fig. 1-75 Small, low-back Windsor settee, Berks or Lebanon County, Pa., 1805–15. Yellow poplar (seat) with maple, hickory, and oak (microanalysis); H. 30⅜″, (seat) 17⅜″, w. (arms) 41½″, (seat) 40¼″, D. (seat) 17⅜″. (Winterthur 65.2832.)

in chairs marked by Jacob Fox of Tulpehocken Township and also turnings in a chair recovered in Jonestown near Lebanon. All probably are based on high-style Philadelphia bamboowork of the 1790s. In overall length the settee is shorter than figure 1-74 by about ten inches. Its small size, coupled with a bold rail, stylized turnings, and bulbous stretchers, makes a forceful visual statement. The chairmaker carefully flared the front seat corners in curves compatible with the arms, which attach to the back rail in typical Pennsylvania lap construction. The bold knuckles appear to be another trademark of the chairmaker: the side faces scroll in carved, crestlike volutes, while the knuckles have two scooped depressions on the top surface and a dimple centered in the front face in place of finely carved detail. Like figure 1-74, all the turnings above and below the plank coordinate perfectly. Bold stretcher profiles are a characteristic of Pennsylvania German work (figs. 1-77, 3-30).[128]

Two extraordinary low-back settees of great length and individual form relate significantly in detail to Windsor work from the Pennsylvania-Maryland border west of the Susquehanna (figs. 1-76, 1-77). The first, a tour de force of the turner's art, was recovered many years ago from a Frederick County, Maryland, estate in the Thurmont-Emmitsburg area (fig. 1-76). The rail is a modification of typical Pennsylvania construction. Knuckle-carved arms extend around the back corners to the point of the sixth spindle from either post, where they diagonally abut the lower half of the heavy back rail and form a short lap lock on the back face. The rounded crown of the back rail serves as an arm cap from the sixth spindle forward, but behind that point it forms one piece with the heavy rail. The precision drilling for the spindles begins with ninety-degree angles at the center back and gradually decreases to about seventy-three degrees at the rear corners. The manipulation of both angle and spindle length put the craftsman's mastery to the extreme test. The spindles themselves are the most elegant found in eighteenth-century Windsor-chair making, surpassing even the ornamental quality of Rhode Island and New York turned sticks (fig. 2-6). The front posts, which are thicker versions of the spindles, support well-carved, one-piece knuckle arms, pinned in place from inside the rail. The delicate flare of the front seat corners may interrelate

Fig. 1-76 Low-back Windsor settee, Frederick County, Md., 1795–1815. Yellow poplar (seat) with maple and yellow poplar (microanalysis); H. 32⅛", (seat) 19⅝", w. (arms) 81¾", (seat) 73¾", D. (seat) 21½". (Winterthur 59.1629.)

Fig. 1-77 Low-back Windsor settee, Frederick County, Md., and Pennsylvania border region, 1795–1810. Yellow poplar (seat) with ash, hickory, and yellow poplar (microanalysis); H. 32¾", (seat) 18¾", W. (arms) 96⅝", (seat) 95", D. (seat) 20"; lower half of right arm scroll restored. (Winterthur 59.1615.)

with a similar feature in a tall chair from southeastern Pennsylvania. Below the plank, turnings that are compatible with the spindles and posts are equally bold. These distinctive supports were inspired by the Philadelphia ball-foot leg, a turning that is also found in Pennsylvania German Windsors of southeastern Pennsylvania (fig. 2-17). A Frederick County side chair has turnings of compatible form through the cylinder unit. A familiar feature in figure 1-76 is the trumpetlike turning of the medial stretcher.[129]

A comparison can be made between the settee of figure 1-76 and a turned, raked-back, spindle bench with framed seat in the collection of Stratford Hall in Virginia. The product of a turner's shop, the bench has heavy front legs not unlike those illustrated but of more compressed form. A second turned bench of related form but with variant turnings is owned by the Baltimore Museum of Art. Both benches came from residences built in Montgomery County, Maryland, in the late eighteenth century. Even as late as about 1820 the bun-and-peg foot of this Windsor settee appeared on a fancy, rush-seated daybed of Maryland origin, as identified by its beehive-and-baluster stretchers that simulate profiles in the back posts and legs of Baltimore chairs in the classical style (fig. 2-35).[130]

Two unillustrated Windsor settees are closely related to figure 1-76. The same turnings and angles of bore define the spindles and posts, although the longer plank lengths reduce the dramatic impact of the styling. The arms of one end in flat, outward-scrolling terminals; those of the other are knuckle-carved. The plank edges of the first settee are flat-chamfered at the sides and back, similar to early Pennsylvania work; those in the knuckle-carved example are rounded, as illustrated. All medial stretchers have trumpet-style tips flanking another early Windsor feature: a double-baluster, spool-and-ring turning (fig. 2-17). The front-to-back stretchers are duplicates of a rare element in Philadelphia work, a centered barrel-shaped turning with molded ends. Although the leg turnings follow the general sequence illustrated, they differ in several ways: the foot is bulbous without a defined peg (fig. 3-30); the swelled cylinder is shorter; the spool has a flare like that of the arm supports; and the baluster is a larger version of the post and spindle balusters. This is the same shape found in the Baltimore Museum's turned and framed bench. The three Windsor settees appear to be products of the same shop, although they represent different periods in the chairmaker-turner's career. The example illustrated is the latest in the group.[131]

Fig. 1-78 Low-back Windsor settee, south-central Pennsylvania-Maryland border region, 1800–1815. Yellow poplar (seat) with hickory, maple, black walnut, and oak (microanalysis); H. 30¹³⁄₁₆″, (seat) 17¹⁄₁₆″, W. (arms) 85¼″, (seat) 83⅜″, D. (seat) 21⅝″; left arm support and outer and under pieces of left arm terminal restored. (Winterthur 59.1658.)

Completely different but equally outstanding is another settee from the Pennsylvania-Maryland border region, which includes among its merits ten legs (fig. **1-77**). The supports help establish the place of origin of the settee. The swelled foot, usually considered a New England feature, appears in two chairs that form part of a seating group recovered in and associated by family background with Frederick County, Maryland, adjacent to the Pennsylvania border. The short, squat balusters and the bulging elements just below the plank duplicate profiles found in a rocking chair in the group. A baluster of similar profile also forms the supports of a small, walnut stretcher-base table, one of a group with removable tops and Germanic joinery (common in the greater southeastern Pennsylvania region). A more typical feature associated with German Windsor work in America is the large centered swelling of the braces, an element noted earlier in the small Berks County settee (fig. 1-75). A characteristic of German work encountered here for the first time in a settee is the swelling near the ends of the front-to-back stretchers, a feature that often appears in the chair and other forms (fig. 3-30). Although the rail differs from standard Pennsylvania patterns, it is duplicated in other settees of Pennsylvania German origin. Critical changes have been introduced to the heavy back section, which no longer wraps around or even meets the corners, and to the slender arms, which elbow wide in a tight arc. The carved terminals are broadened and flare outward in the manner of figure 1-76. Arms and rail are united in the usual lap joints, and the thick back unit is channeled on the rear surface like a Pennsylvania low-back chair. Use of a short back rail may stem from the early double-chair design, since other midcentury features were incorporated into German American work of the 1780s and later.[132]

Widely angled arms and a short backrail are features of two settees of the same design at Winterthur (fig. **1-78**). One is supported on eight bamboo legs, the other on twelve. Settees with a dozen supports are rare. In its basic features figure 1-78 relates to Windsor work found in German settlements along the Pennsylvania-Maryland border. The arm rail exhibits significant differences in construction and detail from figure 1-77. The main unit is a thick, squared, bent rod that extends from one arm tip to the other. At the center back the rod is cased within a shell simulating a heavy back rail. The shell consists of a high capping piece resting on the top surface of the rod and a facing board, front and back. Together the three pieces of wood terminate at the ends in dec-

Fig. 1-79 Small, bow-back Windsor settee (one of a pair), John Letchworth (brand "I.LETCHWORTH"), Philadelphia, 1790–1800. Mahogany (arms); H. 36″, W. (seat) 40½″. (Independence National Historical Park, Philadelphia.)

orative detailing consisting of large quarter-rounds and modified ogee tongues. The sizable arm terminals are formed of two shaped pieces of wood pinned to the rail or to each other, one forming the outside pad, the other the scroll return under the knuckle. The short extension below the plank at each arm post is inexplicable, although the turning at the left end is a replacement along with the applied arm pieces. The right support is original and contains all paint layers found on other parts of the settee. Posts and spindles are comparable in silhouette, although the profile varies substantially from that of figure 1-76. The bulbous balusters in the smaller Winterthur settee are cut with a deep groove in the body. Both seat planks are finished at the side and back edges with a flat-chamfered surface, following early Philadelphia practice. Prototypes for the turnings are found in chairs made by Pennsylvania craftsmen.[133]

Pennsylvania baluster- and bamboo-turned low-back settees of more standard features are reasonably common. The usual number of legs is eight, although some settees have ten. The prominent Philadelphia chairmakers Joseph Henzey and Francis Trumble branded at least one example apiece. Another seat with eight legs bears the owner's stamp "C. CRESSON," probably identifying the merchant Caleb Cresson, Sr., who died in 1816. Cresson's household inventory itemizes a "settee" but without further description. Settees with bamboo-turned legs occasionally have baluster turnings under the arms; one was branded by Thomas Mason and another by Daniel Carteret, both Philadelphia chairmakers. There are more knuckle terminals than flat arms among this group.[134]

By the time chairmakers in the Philadelphia area updated the baluster-turned, low-back settee with bamboo legs in the 1790s, the "new fashioned" bow-back settee was equally popular (fig. **1-79**). Although of less sturdy construction than the low-back settee, the bow-back settee copied a prevailing chair style, making it more suitable as the long seat in suites of Windsor furniture. William Cox constructed oval-back (an alternative term) chairs and settees for General Henry Knox in 1795, on which white paint was contrasted with mahogany arms. The chairmaker's bill actually itemizes two settee sizes. Four priced at 90s. each and two at 45s. apiece identify eight- and six-legged examples, the latter probably similar to the illustrated settee, which coincidentally is one of a pair. John B. Ackley also constructed settees of bow-back pattern. One was painted yellow, fitted with mahogany arms, and stuffed in the seat to complement chairs of similar description ordered in 1796 by the local merchant Zacheus Collins for shipment to a southern customer. Presumably, Joseph Henzey's "Large High back Settee" made in 1791 for Stephen Girard also had a bow back, despite the conflicting terminology. Settees of true high-back form with a through rail, long spindles, and serpentine crest are virtually unknown. Henzey's bill to Girard also includes "Dining" chairs painted green, a term interchangeable in this period with the words *bow* and *oval* back.[135]

The small bow-back settee of the illustration was made by John Letchworth, a contemporary of Ackley and Henzey. Letchworth used mahogany for the arms as well as the segmental posts, although the same parts in other examples sometimes were made of less expensive woods that were "colored" and varnished to imitate mahogany or simply painted. The segmental post is less common than the turned bamboo post in bow-back settees, and occasionally even baluster posts are contrasted with bamboo-turned legs. Boston chairmakers made a few settees in this style. The bows nip in at the waist, and the segmental posts are of definite S curve; the bamboowork varies slightly from that of Philadelphia, having more pronounced swells and hollows. The Philadelphia settee follows usual local practice in armchair construction by employing a balloon curve. Other setteemakers represented by documented bow-back examples include Anthony Steel of Philadelphia and William McElroy of near Moorestown, New Jersey, across the Delaware River. Downriver at Wilmington, Delaware, Sampson Barnet advertised both chairs and settees.[136]

Unusual settees of bow-back form include a small Philadelphia group with bows bent to a long serpentine form, the rise at the center. One example has segmental arm posts, while another has small, undulating loops in place of arms and posts. A nine-foot, standard-bow settee from the Delaware Valley, formerly in the Winterthur collection, is framed with both baluster and bamboo turnings. An occasional settee has a deep seat or overstated bamboowork, and one small example was made without arms.[137]

NEW YORK WORK FROM THE REVOLUTION TO 1800

In New York, Andrew Gautier's advertisement for small "double seated" settees in the mid 1760s was followed in 1774 by that of Thomas Ash. Also in 1774 merchant John Aspinwall furnished his front entry with two "double Windsor Chairs," which perhaps balanced each other on opposite sides of the hall. Not long after, a "Large Settee" accompanied a "Large painted floar Cloath" in the entry of shopkeeper William Rhinelander's home. In the postwar years a flurry of activity took place among Windsor-settee makers. Jacob Vanderpool resettled in New York from Philadelphia, and the Ash brothers revived their prewar business. Timpson and Gillihen, also practicing cabinetmakers, advertised from their shop in Goldenhill in 1785. A year later Gabriel Leggett solicited the patronage of "Captains of vessels or other gentlemen" likely to purchase chairs and settees in quantity for venture or consignment. Indeed, Cornelius Schermerhorn, master of the brig *Rockahock,* carried New York Windsor chairs and settees to Savannah in 1786. Within three years similar furniture entered the port of Norfolk on the sloop *Katy,* and New York settees were in the Charleston, South Carolina, market by 1794. David Coutant, a craftsman of French Huguenot descent, pursued an active trade among members of the old Knickerbocker families. He painted a settee for John Beekman in 1793, the same year he had business dealings with an unidentified member of the Schermerhorn family. Earlier Coutant had refurbished chairs for Chancellor Robert R. Livingston. John DeWitt was particularly active during the late 1790s, advertising his japanned Windsor chairs and "Settees of any size," some specifically identified as garden seating.[138]

Settees advertised by John DeWitt between 1795 and 1799 included the sack-back pattern. An eight-legged, baluster-turned example bears his broadside-style label fixed

Fig. 1-80 Sack-back Windsor settee (en suite with chairs), John Always and Joseph Hampton (brand "ALWA[YS &] / H[A]M[T]O[N]"), New York, 1795–96. H. 36½″, (seat) 18⅜″, W. (arms) 81¾″, (seat) 78″, D. (seat) 19¼″. (Private collection.)

to the plank bottom. The text, a combination of DeWitt's several known advertisements, is followed by the printed date 1797. The full, oval baluster bodies flow into tapering necks in typical New York fashion (fig. 1-3); medial stretchers with centered swells flanked by caplike rings duplicate those in local chairs. The attachment of the bow and arm rail uses the partially exposed mortise common to New York sack-back chairs of the 1780s.

A second New York sack-back settee exhibits similarities and differences. The eight-legged seat bears the brand of John Always and James Hampton, who were partners only in 1795 and 1796 (fig. **1-80**). The legs are turned in the best New York tradition, while the long balusters of the posts are a variation of the usual profile. Pennsylvania influence is notable in the medial stretchers tipped with short balusters. A Philadelphia chair dating to about 1765 has identical terminals in the center brace, but whether the feature arrived in New York directly from the Delaware Valley or through Rhode Island design, which uses a similar brace, is unclear. In any event, the tips are a handsome addition and coordinate well with the bulbous leg elements. The plank edges of this settee and the DeWitt example retain just a hint of the flat-chamfered treatment characteristic of early Pennsylvania work and, undoubtedly, of prerevolutionary Windsor work from New York as well. The slight swell of the long spindles below rail level may reflect a similar influence. Arm terminals form small oval pads that duplicate the arms of the DeWitt settee. The bow treatment is unusual for a New York Windsor; the bent rod bulges in its end curves and slims at the tips in the manner of Rhode Island work.

Another long settee, this one of low back, relates to the Hampton and Always seat in the profiles of the plank, legs, and medial stretchers. The fancy stretcher tips are repeated in the front-to-back braces. The leg balusters, though long, seem slimmer than usual; those in the posts are comparable to the best New York work. If it were not for these full-swelled turnings, the profile and detail of the three-piece arm rail would identify the bench as a Pennsylvania product (fig. 1-73): flat scroll arms outlined by a scratch bead, lap joints at the back corners, and tonguelike tips terminating a heavy back rail.[139]

NEW ENGLAND WORK BEFORE 1800

Coastal locations account for most Windsor-chair making activity in Connecticut before the 1790s. The first evidence of settee production is found in a New Haven manifest of the brig *Rebecca,* which began a voyage to Martinique, West Indies, in December 1789 with two settees and a quantity of disassembled Windsor chairs on board. Thirteen months later the schooner *Union* left Fairfield bound for Saint Lucia carrying a substantial cargo, including 400 Windsor chairs and 7 settees. Meanwhile, inland craftsmen were beginning production. On November 9, 1790, William Chappel and Ebenezer B. White of Danbury advertised Windsor chairs and settees "on the most reasonable terms, and payment made easy." By June 1796 Connecticut had built a new statehouse at Hartford, and John Wadsworth was commissioned to supply twenty-five settees and other painted seating.[140]

In 1796 Ebenezer Tracy of Lisbon, New London County, had been constructing Windsor chairs for at least a dozen years on the homestead farm near Norwich. A well-documented settee attests to his occasional production of this form for the domestic market and provides insights into Yankee ingenuity (fig. 1-81). Stamped nine times under the seat is the maker's name "EB:TRACY," the large letters standing out against the striated ground of the chestnut plank, a wood favored in the region for Windsor planks. The design is distinctive in several respects. Beneath the plank the chairmaker divided four pairs of legs into two units with members set "chairwise." This support treatment is rare in eighteenth-century settees. Center legs commonly stand almost vertically, viewed from the front, with only the end supports raking outward. The seat is exaggerated at the front corners. The rounded projections probably were designed to increase structural strength in an area normally weakened by large holes drilled to accommodate the arm supports. Even in ordinary use, the force exerted upon the arms in Windsor seating frequently caused the short posts to break through the plank edges. Here, the chairmaker took precautions to prevent such an accident.

Fig. 1-81 Sack-back Windsor settee and detail of arm, Ebenezer Tracy, Sr. (brand "EB:TRACY"), Lisbon Township, New London County, Conn., ca. 1795–1803. Chestnut (seat) with maple and oak (microanalysis); H. 40⅜", (seat) 15⅝", W. (arms) 85⅛", (seat) 83⅛", D. (seat) 21⅜". (Winterthur 59.1662.)

The most individual feature of the settee appears in the upper back, where the chairmaker framed the long seat with a sawed top rail instead of a bent bow. Although the choice presented a problem with the end pieces, Tracy found a solution. Just as American pewterers improvised new metal forms from old molds, the woodworker modified his template for a tripod tea-table leg and created rail returns complete with "paw" feet. Although the design is not as aesthetically pleasing as it is interesting, it represents a unique solution to a construction problem and demonstrates the crafts-man's versatility. In structure, the rail returns and top piece form lap, or rabbet, joints at the upper back corners. Two or three heavy wooden pins penetrate both layers of wood and secure the joints. Other lap joints, secured by six pins, join the arms and heavy lower rail in the manner of Philadelphia construction. As is typical, the thick rail terminates behind each arm in a short ogee-shaped tongue. Two pieces of wood form each vigorously curved knuckle-arm scroll; the horizontal seam is visible at a point about midway from top to bottom. Internal pins and glue probably secure the applied, carved wood blocks to the arm pieces. Spindles shaped with a slight bulge in the lower half are typical of Tracy Windsors and those of other regional craftsmen, and so is the practice of socketing the legs inside the plank. Rather uncommon to the Tracy family's work, however, is the use of a groove to define the platform supporting the spindles and posts. The groove is now heavily coated with paint.

When Ebenezer Tracy fashioned this settee, he turned the posts and legs to profiles duplicating those in his large writing-arm chairs (figs. 1-4, 1-7). Full-bodied leg balus-ters with flaring necks are also found in sack-back chairs made by family members (fig. 2-4). The boldly stated medial and front-to-back braces are enlarged versions of Tracy's armchair stretchers with the addition of prominent, disklike rings to compen-sate for the extended lengths. Braces embellished with large disks are also present in Windsors of Rhode Island origin. The individual design and solid construction of the settee is typical of work documented and attributed to the Tracy group, which included five family members.[141]

Two low-back settees—one in the Museum of Fine Arts, Boston, and the other pri-vately owned—exhibit features similar to those in figure 1-81. The Boston Museum example has restored arms, but the original posts appear to have been patterned after supports in Tracy's sack-back chairs (fig. 1-23) rather than the design illustrated. The heavy back rail also terminates more abruptly. Beneath the plank the Boston example has less forceful turnings than those in the sack-back settee. The second low-back settee has turnings similar to those illustrated. The seats of both have rounded projections at the front corners. While all three settees are comparable in length, the second low-back seat has more spindles.[142]

Tracy influence extends to two other settees, one with a low back, the other with a sack back. The former *may* be a product of Ebenezer's eldest son, Elijah, or of Beriah Green, who probably worked in one of the Tracy shops during the 1790s. Features associated with local production are the bulbous spindles and the chestnut plank with-out a groove or through leg sockets. The slim necks and full bodies of the balusters relate closely to roundwork in Tracy family side chairs and continuous-bow armchairs. The second settee, which is at Historic Deerfield, was not made by a member of the Tracy group but clearly hails from the Connecticut–Rhode Island border region. The steamed and bent bow is relatively thick but slims to thin tips (fig. 1-23). The spindles are swelled, and the arm posts have the distinctive styling found in Tracy sack-back chairs (fig. 1-23). The flat-chamfered plank edges follow Rhode Island prototypes. Five pairs of legs rake forward or backward to an extraordinary degree, recalling in their turned profiles work of both the border region and New York City.[143]

The triple-bow settee is a rare pattern known in four examples, one with eight legs and three with ten (fig. **1-82**). Evidence favors an eastern Connecticut or Rhode Island provenance for this design. The heavy back rail of the illustrated example is made of genus *Populus,* a wood rarely used in Windsor construction. It is associated with several chairs from the Connecticut–Rhode Island border, as well as with case furniture. The

seat is ash, a relatively common material for Windsor turnings but unusual in the plank. A Rhode Island bow-back armchair with an ash seat is in the Yale University Art Gallery. A second triple-back settee at Winterthur (not illustrated) has a white pine seat, a material frequently associated with northern New England; however, Zadock Hutchins of Pomfret, Connecticut, and others in the area also used white pine for Windsor-chair seats.[144]

Inspiration for the triple-back Windsor probably sprang from a formal settee design with multiple chair backs linked to make a long seat. The multiple back is also found in English Windsor construction. The long, low arches of figure 1-82 and another example are slightly more successful aesthetically than the shorter, higher loops of the two remaining settees. Most of the turnings in the illustrated example are maple, although quite a few parts are red oak. This suggests that the craftsman used preturned parts or materials on hand, knowing that the surfaces would be covered with paint. The spindles, like the seat, are made of ash. The red oak bows have flat, beaded faces in the manner of bow-back rather than sack-back seating. Two other settees follow this plan, suggesting that the design dates to the 1790s, when bow-back Windsor seating was at the height of fashion and popularity.[145]

There is little written evidence of settee production in Rhode Island, but several long pieces of furniture are known to have been made in this trade-oriented region. Job Danforth of Providence, who occasionally exchanged services with the local woodworking Proud family, put a new top on a settee for Samuel Proud in 1792. Eleven years later the Proud brothers again recorded their work with this form, crediting William Colegrew "For Settee bows" on August 30, 1803. Newport shipping records of the early 1790s show that John and Stephen Cahoone, captains of the sloop *Aurora*, returned from many short voyages to New York City with chairs and settees of metropolitan manufacture as personal or venture cargo. Indeed, a great many Rhode Island chairs show New York influence in their turnings, and the continuous-bow armchair, which became a popular Rhode Island pattern, was developed in New York.[146]

Several small sack-back settees of individual character were made in Rhode Island. One example in the Henry Ford Museum and Greenfield Village has a double-scooped seat of early concept but postrevolutionary date. The seat depressions and conforming

Fig. 1-82 Triple, sack-back Windsor settee, eastern Connecticut or Rhode Island, 1790–1805. Ash (seat) with maple, oak, ash, and poplar (*Populus*) (microanalysis); H. 38″, (seat) 17¼″, W. (arms) 98½″, (seat) 95⅞″, D. (seat) 18¹⁄₁₆″; left arm, both back rail returns, and spindles at left end restored. (Winterthur 59.1528.)

Fig. 1-83 Small, sack-back Windsor settee
with top extension, Rhode Island–Connecticut
border, 1785–1800. Butternut (seat, microanalysis). (Metropolitan Museum of Art, New York.)

outline appear as two oval-bottomed, sack-back armchairs joined as one with a small,
arc-shaped piece filling the gap between the curves at the center front. Long slender
balusters, small compressed spools, and thick rings form the leg turnings. Round-tipped
medial stretchers that relate to Tracy family work (fig. 2-4) complete the design.[147]

Another two-seated Windsor of extraordinary design is illustrated in figure **1-83.**
The leg balusters are even longer than those of the Ford Museum settee, although the
profile is different: the long neck tapers directly into the body, and a short neck at the
base replaces a ring turning. The latter feature, though uncommon, appears in several
Rhode Island chairs. The full rounded, budlike turnings just below the seat are smaller
versions of the leg tops in an unusual triple-top fan-back chair from the border region.
The arm pads of wavy profile are a variant of those used by the Tracy family of New
London County, Connecticut, and chairmakers of the border region. The precisely
defined crest with uncarved volutes is an uncommon Rhode Island type (fig. 1-10). By
contrast, the pointed-end bow is fairly standard in area chairmaking. The identification
of the plank as butternut, a wood belonging to the walnut family, confirms the regional
features. Similar planks were used in several writing chairs made in eastern Connecticut
(figs. 1-6, 1-8).[148]

On April 13, 1786, Ebenezer Stone of Boston advertised "ROUND-TOP CHAIRS,
fan-back Garden-Chairs, Soffes, stuff-seat Chairs, and . . . a large Assortment of Dining-
Chairs, painted equally as well as those made at Philadelphia." His notice shows the
awakening interest in Windsor-chair making in the city's postwar furniture market. It
also hints at the difficulties local chairmakers experienced in merchandising their product in the face of mass importations from Philadelphia, still the undisputed production
center. Even as late as 1799 several vessels from the Delaware River deposited eleven
dozen Windsor side chairs, four armchairs, and two settees at Boston, but the tide was
turning. Boston craftsmen were taking the lead in their own market. Both documents
and objects testify to the increasing importance of the local trade during these forma-
tive years, and almost two dozen craftsmen can be accounted for in surviving records.

Fig. 1-84 Small, fan-back Windsor settee, Boston, 1795–1800. White pine (seat) with maple, ash, and oak (microanalysis); H. 36⅜″, (seat) 17⅝″, W. (crest) 33¾″, (arms) 38″, (seat) 36⅜″, D. (seat) 15¼″. (Winterthur 80.8.)

William Seaver, representative of the Boston chairmakers who left their personal stamp on the local product during the 1790s, advertised "Warranted WINDSOR CHAIRS, and GREEN SETTEES, of every denomination" in 1793. He followed that notice with another in 1796. By 1798 the clearance of the ship *Pattern* from Boston for Gonavies, Haiti, with Windsor chairs and settees shows modest export activity. Meanwhile, Windsor seating was being produced elsewhere in Massachusetts. Up the coast at Salem, James Chapman Tuttle began chairmaking in the "Philadelphia style" in 1796 in answer to customer demands for "Windsor Chairs and Settees." By 1795 Ansel Goodrich of Northampton in the Connecticut Valley was well into the production of Windsor chairs, settees, and rockers at his shop near the courthouse.[149]

Two small settees of delicate, distinctive form testify to the quality and originality of the Boston product in the 1790s. One is fashioned in the full baluster style, the other in a bamboo pattern. Neither is marked, but the characteristics are unmistakable. The baluster-turned settee pictured in figure **1-84** is a study in harmony and movement. There are strong vertical lines and gentle horizontal curves. Superb roundwork throughout ties the whole design together; from the full-swelled posts to the reel-turned stretchers, the Boston stamp is clearly visible (fig. 1-15). The edges of the expanded oval plank are gently rounded, and the crown is masterfully shaped and carved. The distinctive long feet, which may have grown out of the swelled-taper pattern, had only a short life in the Boston market of the late 1790s; similar supports appear on an equally unusual sitting stool (fig. 3-15). Although Philadelphia provided the impetus for Windsor production in Boston, Rhode Island supplied many of the basic design models. This is especially evident in turned work from Boston. In the illustrated example, it is also reflected in the sawed pattern of the arms with their circular pads and long, angular oxbow rail returns.

Almost identical arms and a plank of similar profile are features of a bamboo-turned settee (fig. **1-85**). The angular emphasis of the turned work is heightened by the pointed arch centered in the crest. Carved volutes of even bolder form than those of figure 1-84

Fig. 1-85 Small, fan-back Windsor settee, Boston, 1800–1805. White pine (seat, micro-analysis); H. 35⅞″, (seat) 15½″, W. (crest) 42½″, (arms) 49½″, (seat) 50″, D. (seat) 17¼″. (Former collection J. Stogdell Stokes.)

further attest to local skill. The pronounced, jointed bamboowork, especially that of the spindles with their flared bases and the legs, is comparable to turned elements originating in the shop of Seaver and Frost, as demonstrated in a branded cross-stretcher side chair and a labeled tall cradle (fig. 2-51). The scale of the bamboo pattern is increased in the settee posts, and the bottom flare of the spindles is replaced with a bulge. The medial stretcher swellings are only slightly bolder than those in a bow-back Boston armchair. Blocked cylinders, such as those centered in the front-to-back braces, appear now and again in Boston work throughout the 1790s (fig. 3-15). The loss of the lower part of the feet is unfortunate but understandable, since the seat is too big for most people to carry alone but light enough to be dragged across a surface, causing wear and tear on the legs.[150]

Somewhere in the vicinity of Boston, a chairmaker or owner stamped his name, "J. BALCH Jr.," on the white pine plank of a long, ten-legged settee related to figures 1-84 and 1-85. Although a Philadelphia origin has been suggested, the use of a pine plank negates such an attribution. The bamboo turnings below the seat are similar to those of figure 1-85; features above the plank show mixed influence. The crest imitates the sweep and form of that in figure 1-84, even to including a fine bead along the lower edge. The large, shell-like, carved volutes are somewhat varied; the segmental cut is exchanged for a continuous sweep of a type sometimes found in Rhode Island and Massachusetts chairs. The three baluster-turned posts of angular-oval profile resemble turned work produced in the Salem shop of James Chapman Tuttle. The spindles have a single grooved nodule below the center point. The chairmaker chose an arm pattern current in the Boston chair market of about 1800, a forward scroll supported on a segmental post in the Philadelphia style.[151]

SOUTHERN WORK BEFORE 1800

Little is known for certain about eighteenth-century production of settees in the South. A long, ten-legged, bow-back seat with a history of ownership in Mecklenburg County, Virginia, at Ivy Hill near Stovall has several features that are unusual enough to suggest it was made locally. The plank is yellow poplar, a material common in the Middle Atlantic region and southern New England but also found in southern work.

The flat-face bow has a bead only at the outside edge, a practice more common in rural than urban centers. The slim, sloping arms broaden slightly into knuckle-carved forward scrolls suggestive of figure 2-23, without the mannered undulations and exaggerated droop. The leg turnings have no obvious prototype. The collared baluster rests directly on a plain, inverted baluster forming a foot without an intervening collar or ring.[152]

Written records provide a somewhat better picture of the settee in the South before 1800. Philadelphia interests were already supplying the Baltimore market when the ship *Active* arrived there in 1784 with a cargo of fourteen chairs and one settee. But the picture was changing in 1791 when painter Chandless advertised a large assortment of Windsor seating from his shop on Cheapside Wharf: "Chairs, Settees, Garden Seats, etc. . . . Made and painted to particular directions." Presumably, Chandless employed a chairmaker or obtained his unpainted stock from a local source. Two Baltimore County inventories dating to 1793 and 1794 list Windsor chairs and a "Sopha" or a "Settee" en suite. Later in the decade a few Baltimore-made settees were shipped with Windsor chairs to the Caribbean.[153]

Philadelphia settees were also shipped to Virginia; for example, two were on board the sloop *Nancy* in 1785. Within a few years domestic activity had begun. Robert McKeen, of Dinwiddie southwest of Petersburg, advertised as a Windsor-chair and settee maker in 1793. Four years later David Ruth supplied Peyton Skipwith of Mecklenburg County on the North Carolina border with a substantial amount of Windsor furniture for use at his rural seat, Prestwould. The lot included three settees priced from 42s. to 48s., charges that indicate these long seats were large. Perhaps Ruth also supplied Ivy Hill. George Mason, who resided near the western community of Lexington, possessed "Two green winsor Setteas" at his death in the mid 1790s. Meanwhile, Vosburgh and Childs were introducing New York Windsor-seating styles to coastal Wilmington, North Carolina. From the stock of material in their shop near the wharf, they constructed "elegant settees of ten feet in length or under, suitable to either halls or piazzas." Charleston, South Carolina, was a particularly profitable market for northern furniture shippers. The brig *Friendship* arrived with seventeen dozen chairs and two settees in 1784. The traffic continued, and by 1798 local householders and merchants could choose from "an excellent Assortment of Yellow, Green, Mahogany, and Chocolate Colored CHAIRS and SETTEES." Humeston and Stafford were actively merchandising their own "Warranted Windsor Chairs and Green Settees" by that date.[154]

NINETEENTH-CENTURY STYLES THROUGH THE WAR OF 1812

With the nineteenth century came a marked change in basic Windsor design and a noticeable increase in output. Both developments extended to the production of specialized forms. Patterns with square backs prevailed until after midcentury. Philadelphia remained the center of the Windsor trade until the 1810s, when production at Baltimore, New York, and Boston-Salem achieved equal status. General activity was scattered over a much broader territory. The first nineteenth-century settee pattern in the market was one with a serpentine top rod meeting the posts at flaring, pointed corners, all the units having flat or crowned faces beaded at the edges. The design that first made a mark, however, was one with a simulated bamboo rod across the top bowed in a lateral curve (fig. 1-86). The illustrated example bears remnants of its original label, which is worth quoting in full from more complete copies, in view of the importance chairmakers attached to labels as merchandising tools: "ALL KINDS OF / Windsor Chairs and Settees, / MADE AND SOLD BY / GILBERT GAW, / No. 90 North Front, twelve doors above Mulberry or Arch St. / PHILADELPHIA: / WHERE Merchants, Masters of vessels, and others, / may be supplied at the shortest notice, at the / current prices for approved notes. / N.B. Orders from the West-Indies or any part of / the continent will be punctually attended to." Many craftsmen besides Gaw pasted labels on their products, but most of the labels disintegrated or fell off in time.[155]

Fig. 1-86 Square-back Windsor settee, Gilbert Gaw (label), Philadelphia, 1800–1805. Yellow poplar (seat) with maple, hickory, and oak (microanalysis); H. 33⅝″, (seat) 16″, W. (crest) 73⅛″, (arms) 75¼″, (seat) 76⅛″, D. (seat) 19⅝″. (Winterthur 77.116.)

In general, square-back designs are relatively straightforward, having fewer subtleties than earlier patterns. With the change in back shape came an alteration in the character of the turnings; uniform, four-section bamboowork replaced three-section bamboowork in the posts and legs. Delaware Valley bamboowork generally exhibits only minimal styling, although grooves were introduced to previously plain, tapered spindles. The bracing system was in transition for several years. The eighteenth-century-style, H-plan stretchers of figure 1-86 soon gave way to the all-bamboo box-stretcher system common to fancy seating. The flat, beaded-front plank is a contemporary pattern (fig. 2-31); other seats have rounded or chamfered edges. A subtlety likely to be overlooked is the gentle forward curve of the back corners, which modifies the angularity of the design. Alternative patterns introduce a post at the center back or divide the back into chair-width sections. In one multipost pattern, the horizontal rod is raised in height in the center. In another design variant, the seat plank curves in a gentle arc from end to end.[156]

Soon after the appearance of the square-back, single-bow (rod) settee, a long seating piece capped by two parallel bows was introduced (fig. 1-87). Sometimes the crest is further embellished with small medallions in one of several shapes, from squares and rectangles with hollow or canted corners to long ovals. The double-bow crest patterns constitute a larger group by far than the single-bow settees, although many design elements were similar: backs curved forward at the ends; backs divided by heavy posts into two, three, or four sections; rods varying in height from one section to another; scroll arms; and overall lengths ranging from double-seat to ten-legged size. New features included double-rod arms and bent back posts. One settee has four pairs of broadly spaced legs positioned chairwise. Other choices in the double-bow settees included a small oval medallion in the center-back spindle (fig. 1-87) or a long, slim rectangular medallion in *each* back spindle. Within the double-bow group are marked Philadelphia settees by Joseph Burden and Gilbert Gaw. Most bamboowork is stouter than in the single-bow style, and stretchers are mounted in box style. Bamboo arms usually project beyond the short front posts rather than cap them.

One of the most remarkable double-bow, square-back settees is a long, eight-legged example at the Yale University Art Gallery (fig. **1-87**). The undulating arms with their

Fig. 1-87 Square-back Windsor settee, region of Adams and Franklin counties, Pa., and Frederick County, Md., ca. 1810–18. Yellow poplar (seat) with oak and maple (microanalysis); H. 36″, (seat) 16⅛″, W. (seat) 75⅛″, D. (seat) 21¾″. (Mabel Brady Garvan Collection, Yale University Art Gallery, New Haven.)

carved, pendent scrolls identify the long seat as a product of the southern Pennsylvania/ Maryland border region, where a school of German American chairmaker-turners produced Windsor furniture of individual design. Turned work within this furniture group ranges from the full baluster to the full bamboo style. The grooved, bulbous turnings form a harmonizing counterrhythm to the movement of the arms and the elliptical medallions. Through careful placement of the medallions, the chairmaker has created a strong central focal point. The use of ornamental medallions probably sprang from the chairmaker's knowledge of Windsor fancywork of Philadelphia and Baltimore origin, either directly or through the work of other rural craftsmen. A settee with a single-rod top originated in the same area, if not the same shop. The arms and turnings of both are comparable. Across the back of the single-rod settee at arm level is a secondary cross rod spanning the distance between the two end posts and passing through two center supports. All the uprights are vigorously bamboo-turned and shaved flat on the face.[157]

Documents show a rise in the production of painted seating furniture at Philadelphia before the economic upheaval of the War of 1812. The household inventories of woodworkers Daniel Trotter (1800) and George Halberstadt (1812) make specific mention of Windsor settees. A cushion on Halberstadt's long seat boosted its value to $8. Commodore John Barry furnished Strawberry Hill, his country place near the Delaware River, with Windsor furniture. At his death in 1803 "14 new Winsor Chairs" were in the "best Parlour," and similar chairs and "a Green windsor sopha" were located elsewhere in the house. John Craig, proprietor of Andalusia on the Delaware in the early nineteenth century, provided a pair of Windsor settees to seat family and guests on the east piazza. Chairmakers may, however, have gained the greater part of their livelihood from an active local export trade. They targeted both domestic and foreign ports as markets for their work between 1800 and 1811, and the settee was part of that campaign.[158]

Philadelphia maritime records identify the shipment of several hundred settees to coastal and foreign destinations during these years. Eighty-two seating cargoes in the domestic trade contained 250 settees in all, nearly twice as many as were sent to foreign markets. Charleston was the port of entry in half the voyages; other landings were made in the South from Baltimore to Savannah to the gulf port of New Orleans. Thirty voyages to foreign ports accounted for 144 settees. The most popular markets were Havana and Saint Thomas. Stephen Girard, merchant king of Philadelphia and a pioneer in the South American trade, shipped black, coquelico (poppy color, or yellowish red), and cane-colored settees in suites of seating furniture to the southern continent. Philadelphia records of about 1810 place the retail price of a Windsor settee at $8 to $10, a sum that represented more than a week's pay for the average working man, who earned about $1 a day.[159]

Settees in the Philadelphia style furnished inland homes in the early years of the republic. For example, James Jackson in neighboring West Chester owned a "settee or long seat" before 1808. In central Pennsylvania, Philadelphia chairmaking met up with the Baltimore style. Gilbert Burnett, "late of Baltimore," was only one of several craftsmen who disseminated the Baltimore style at Harrisburg. Joseph Robinson of the same community stocked an "assortment of ready made Settees" to accommodate those who were refurbishing or going to housekeeping. At Carlisle beyond the Susquehanna, Edwin Mulhern and Moses Bullock had just formed a partnership in 1806 when Mulhern advertised their chair and settee work "in all the various branches and fashions now offered in Baltimore."[160]

The Windsor settee was popular in other Middle Atlantic regions as well. New York City documents provide insights into prewar activity. When John Karnes became insolvent in 1801, his assignees offered for sale "12 doz. finished windsor chairs and settees." William Challen in Greenwich Street had chairs and settees available for exportation, which he "carefully packed at the shortest notice." When Joseph Vail (Veal), a prosperous craftsman, died suddenly in 1805, plank and a quantity of "Turned Stuff" remained in his shop. The inventory included settee parts itemized as "Sopha" stretchers, bows, and seats. The value of each of two framed sofas was $4.66.[161]

Settees still furnished the entries of New York residences. One in the front hall of James Barron's merchant home was surrounded by nine green Windsor chairs, with four fire buckets for emergencies. With new colors and fancy ornament, the settee was moved into finer quarters, sometimes furnishing the best parlor. The fastidious householder occasionally went to considerable trouble to secure just the right pieces of furniture to fit special locations. Without long folding rules and tape measures, how were accurate measurements made? One solution is discussed in a letter written on July 23, 1803, by Reverend John Murray, founder of Universalism in America and a resident of Boston, to his friend William Palmer, a chairmaker of New York. Having previously acquired chairs from Palmer, probably fancy rush-bottom seating, Murray placed an order for additional chairs and several settees: "I inclose you a string for the settees — [from] the first knot to the second is the height — from the first to the third, is the lenght [*sic*] from one side of the window to the other, on the side next the window — from the first to the fourth, is the lenght of the *front,* you will make four of these as soon as you can, and the same as the Chairs to match them — and send them with the Chairs as soon as you can."[162]

William Buttre itemized the seating colors popular in New York in an 1810 advertisement: black, white, brown, and coquelico, with or without gold embellishments. Some of the same colors likely enhanced the surfaces of eight settees listed in the 1811 insolvency inventory of William Ash I. New York settees of this date competed with the Philadelphia product in markets such as Rhode Island, Virginia, Georgia, Cuba, Saint Croix, Saint Thomas, Guadaloupe, Martinique, and Haiti. G. and F. Penny of Savannah advertised on January 22, 1808, that the *Liverpool Packet* had just arrived from New York with "an assortment of handsome Fancy and Windsor Chairs, Sofas &c. which will be sold cheap for cash." Five years later Thomas Howard, a furniture maker and entrepreneur of Providence, Rhode Island, announced that Tunis and Nutman, chairmakers of Newark, New Jersey, near New York, had appointed him their "sole Agent" for the sale of "CHAIRS and SETTEES, of the first Quality" from their manufactory.[163]

In Connecticut, Captain Solomon Ingraham of Norwich, who made the first voyage to India from Connecticut in 1798 and died at Madras in 1805, furnished his Connecticut home with Windsor chairs and a settee. In 1805 a cargo of two settees and two hundred chairs cleared neighboring New London for Martinique. Within two years, Thomas and David S. West announced as partners in the chair and settee business in New London. Inland some few miles at Windham, the estate of Dr. Samuel Lee, a known customer of Amos Denison Allen, included a settee among the household Windsor seating in 1815. Although Allen's record book, dating from 1796 to 1803, does not mention this form, a shipping record of 1817 documents its production in his shop.[164]

Brisk activity marked the Boston-Salem furniture market in the early nineteenth century. Records contain the names of several prominent chairmakers. In 1802 Samuel Jones Tucke made a suite of fancy seating for Francis Dana that included a settee. Two years later a property schedule of William Seaver's shop made during a court suit located eleven settees and the bottom for another on the premises. Richard Austin of Salem constructed dozens of "Bamboo" style chairs and two settees in 1805–6 for the furniture-exporting enterprise organized by Elijah and Jacob Sanderson. A few years earlier the schooner *Patty* had left neighboring Beverly for Saint Lucia carrying a sideboard, three cases of tables, and a suite of chairs with a sofa, possibly all rush-bottomed. Out on Nantucket the Windsor settee was uncommon, and "Mariner" Jonathan Paddock may have imported his long seat. Its listing in his household inventory near an item for ten bow-back chairs perhaps describes its pattern.[165]

Records for northern New England are thin but indicate that Thomas Boynton continued to build an occasional settee after his removal from Boston to Windsor, Vermont. His accounts show that he supplied a $4 settee, probably with a wooden bottom, for use in the local meetinghouse in 1816; the same year a Montreal customer bought two long rush-bottom seats for $7 apiece. In neighboring New Hampshire Abel Wilder advertised settees at Keene in 1807, and Henry Beck made and sold settees at Portsmouth the following year. Canadian activity is indicated in a notice of Daniel Tiers, who worked at York (Toronto) in 1802 and advertised a full range of painted chairs with settees to suit. Jay Humeston, an emigrant from the American South to Halifax, Nova Scotia, informed sea captains that he could supply them with chairs and settees for the West Indies.[166]

Southern craftsmen still competed with importers. Between 1801 and 1809 Silas Cooper of Savannah bought a quantity of seating stock in the wood and applied the paint and ornament himself. By March 1810 he advertised New York settees received via the schooner *Edmund*. Virginia craftsmen challenged the import trade with some success, and settee production is recorded for Richmond, Petersburg, and Fredericksburg. Alexander Walker of Fredericksburg made long seats of "every description" in 1805 and undoubtedly coordinated the patterns with the chairs he produced in the "round"-back and "double and single square"-back styles. Walker found Baltimore seating serious competition. Indeed, the production of rush-, cane-, wood-, and stuffed-bottom painted seating was becoming a principal focus of the Baltimore furniture trade. The Finlay brothers, John and Hugh, offered "a number of sets of *new pattern* Rush and Windsor Chairs and Settees" in 1805. Francis Younker's notice of 1810 emphasizes top-of-the-line merchandise: "Private Families can always be supplied with *Chairs & Settees* of the most elegant taste and fashion." Wood-seat settees were only slightly cheaper imitations of the rush-seat patterns that began to set standards up and down the coast. Baltimore influence spread westward, as well, through southern Pennsylvania and into West Virginia, where regional seating bears many attributes of Maryland work. Chairmakers in the panhandle advertised settees along with chairs. At Winchester, Virginia, David Russell paid Isaac Smith $3.50 per seat to construct Windsor settees for shop resale.[167]

Modest activity is recorded in the Midwest. In December 1805 Hector Sanford, newly arrived in Chillicothe, Ohio, from Georgetown, District of Columbia, was pre-

Fig. 1-88 Small, shaped-tablet Windsor settee, Baltimore, ca. 1807–15. Yellow poplar (seat) with hickory, maple, and yellow poplar (microanalysis); H. 36⅛″, (seat) 18¾″, w. (crest) 39½″, (arms) 39⅞″, (seat) 39⅛″. (Winterthur 59.3627.)

pared to make settees; presumably the styles followed those of his round- and square-back chairs. The Windsor settee was available at the Cincinnati shop of Jacob Cotts in November 1803. David and Daniel Kautz and John H. Smith, also chairmakers in this river town, followed with similar merchandise in 1811; Jacob C. Roll's advertisements began in 1814. When William Challen removed from New York to Lexington, Kentucky, in 1809, he offered settees in the latest fashionable New York colors: black, white, brown, green, and coquelico. Charles McKarahan was active as a chairmaker and setteemaker a year later at Nashville, Tennessee.[168]

The distinctive ornamental quality of early nineteenth-century Baltimore painted furniture became a signature of the city's furniture trade and influenced design throughout the American industry. This is illustrated in two small settees of delicate form but bold detailing (figs. 1-88, 1-89). Both have tablet tops of distinctive profile, slim turnings, and planks featuring short projections along the front edge. The crest in the first, and smaller, settee (fig. **1-88**) is a variant of a now rare Baltimore pattern introduced before 1810. Substitution of a hollow-cornered tablet for a rounded arc at the center of each unit represents influence from other painted-seating patterns. The slim, rectangular spindle medallions coordinate with those of the front stretchers, visually linking the upper and lower structures. The decorative rectangle is a feature borrowed from fancy-chair making. Top-of-the-line Windsors from Philadelphia and Wilmington, Delaware, have similar spindles, and use of the feature extended as far north as Boston. The arm piece, which caps the short front post, is one of two constructions in general use. Settees of related design have three-section backs. Crest variations range from a small, single, centered tablet to a long, diminishing, stacked projection and a tablet with rounded ends. Chairs of related crest were produced in western Pennsylvania.[169]

The second settee appears to be slightly later in date (fig. **1-89**). Its principal feature, the crest, derives almost directly from the middle back ornament in a small group of high-style, fancy-painted Baltimore chairs and settees dating to the early 1810s (fig. **1-90**). One piece of furniture in that group, a four-back settee, is documented by the maker, Thomas Renshaw, and the ornamenter, John Barnhart. The elements of

Fig. 1-89 Small, fancy, shaped-tablet Windsor settee, Baltimore, ca. 1812–20. H. 36½", (seat) 18", W. (crest) 43", (seat) 41¾", D. (seat) 16¾"; medium yellow ground with dark green, rose, and polychrome landscapes. (Photo, Gary C. Cole.)

both the decoration and the construction are more sophisticated than those found in the Windsor, but there is no mistaking the close relationship. The small rounded buttons of the Windsor post tips appear in the fancy chair, although partially obscured by the arms. The feature is fairly common in Baltimore painted seating. Broad, stubby arrow spindles with wide tops, as shown, are not common, though occasionally present in chairs from the southern Pennsylvania border region. The hollow-corner detail is repeated in the front stretcher medallions. The design source again is fancy furniture. Comparable profiles form centered urns in the backs of other Baltimore seating. The stout posts supporting the projecting arms reflect Philadelphia work, while the slim, cylindrical legs grooved near the bottom to simulate a cuffed foot are a regular feature of Baltimore design. Although some painted Baltimore furniture may be assigned to Francis Guy, the artist, or John Barnhart, an ornamenter and sign painter, the present decoration is much too simplistic in its execution to be by either hand and probably represents the work of a general practitioner. Small landscape vignettes with buildings became popular on Baltimore painted furniture at the beginning of the century.[170]

Fig. 1-90 Fancy cane-seat armchair, possibly made by Thomas Renshaw and ornamented by John Barnhart, Baltimore, ca. 1812–15. Maple (microanalysis); H. 34½", W. 21", D. 17". (Winterthur 57.1058.)

Two small tablet-top settees from New England (figs. 1-91, 1-92) provide a striking contrast in their simplicity to the embellished Baltimore furniture. Although the northern crests represent one general pattern, they are remarkably different, demonstrating the flexibility of interpretation. Fig. **1-91** is the earlier of the two. Rockers were introduced to a small group of settees beginning with this pattern, although the feature was slightly more common among later styles. Dr. Joseph Moffit of Fayette County, Indiana, owned a settee with rockers valued at $5 in 1833; another long rocking seat was in the estate of Reverend Ambrose Edson at Somers, Connecticut, in 1836.[171]

The slim styling of the double top rails in the rocking settee relates to work associated with southern New Hampshire, although an old cardboard label tacked to the seat bottom appears to extend the area of manufacture to the Connecticut River valley in Massachusetts. The inscription in black ink reads: "Mrs. / L.T. Bardwell. / 11 Woodside Avenue. / Springfield. Mass." The basswood used for the seat strengthens the attribution. A chair of similar profile has been owned by a Keene, New Hampshire, family

Fig. 1-91 Small, shaped-tablet, rocking Windsor settee with top extension, Connecticut Valley in Massachusetts, southern Vermont, or southern New Hampshire, 1815–25. Basswood (seat) with beech, birch, ash, and oak (microanalysis); H. 47$\frac{9}{16}$", (seat) 16$\frac{1}{2}$", W. (primary crest) 37$\frac{5}{8}$", (arms) 40$\frac{1}{2}$", (seat) 38$\frac{3}{16}$", D. (seat) 17$\frac{13}{16}$"; paint and decoration old but not original; medium blue-gray-green ground with white. (Winterthur 53.155.34.)

Fig. 1-92 Small, shaped-tablet Windsor settee, probably Vermont, 1815–30. White pine (seat) with birch and oak (microanalysis); H. 31$\frac{5}{16}$", (seat) 16", W. (crest) 27$\frac{1}{2}$", (arms) 39", (seat) 39", D. (seat) 16$\frac{1}{8}$"; metal tip repairs to back legs. (Winterthur 67.1798.)

since the late nineteenth century. Another is depicted in a portrait by Asahel Powers, the sitter identified as a resident of Springfield, Vermont. Both towns are near the Connecticut River. Seat planks of the rounded front illustrated are found in both southern New Hampshire and the Connecticut Valley. The forward-scroll arms represent a delicate interpretation for the date. The long, slim rectangular medallion in the front stretcher is unusual in the way it is blocked. Rather than the stretcher tips emerging from the ends, the medallion is simply "grafted" onto the face of the long stick. The only paint on the wood is the delicate, leafy sprigged decoration in cream or white on a ground of medium blue-gray-green, now darkened to olive with the varnish overcoats. The paint is in excellent surface condition, although dry with age, and probably represents a refurbishing of the later nineteenth century. Even during the lifetime of an original owner it was not uncommon for painted furniture to be sent out one or more times for "cleaning" and repainting. Several New Hampshire and Vermont chairs have period decoration of related form. The rockers are original, although repaired; they are now held fast with screws.[172]

Characteristics of southern and northern New England are mixed in the second tablet-top settee (fig. 1-92). This piece of furniture was made by a craftsman who migrated to Vermont from Rhode Island or southeastern Massachusetts. Dominating the design are two outsized oval medallions in the front stretcher; their bold form interrelates with the embellished medial stretcher of figure 1-28. Both interpretations may represent exaggerated versions of a decorative device found in Boston chairmaking. The bamboo-style legs relate to work associated with James C. Tuttle of Salem, and the link with Boston is clearly seen in the narrow back and widely curved arms (fig. 1-84), now updated in the bamboo style. Although the chairmaker chose a seat atypical of Boston work, the thin forward edges and squared front corners are found in chairs from southeastern New England. One example was once owned in Providence; another was made by a chairmaker at neighboring Taunton. The style was current in eastern Connecticut as well.[173]

The crest of figure 1-92 has no exact prototype. The tablet projects higher than others of this general type, creating steep curves at the ends. This long seat and two bent-back chairs with tops of similar profile, though lower, may be the work of a single craftsman. One chair, now in the Ward House at Shrewsbury, Massachusetts, has a history of ownership by Thomas W. Ward, son of General Artemas Ward. The second chair, which is in the Bennington Museum, is said to have belonged to Parthenia Dewey (1783–1856), granddaughter of Reverend Jedidiah Dewey of Bennington. The seat is made of basswood, a common material for chair planks in the Connecticut River valley. A third chair with a top piece of close profile but little back bend bears the unidentified brand "N. DOLE" on the plank bottom. Another uncommon crest feature is the long, low arch along the bottom edge. This appears to represent influence from northern Worcester County, Massachusetts, where low-arched slats set between the posts have similar bottom profiles. A Nova Scotia chair of related top could have been influenced by the same southern New England sources. Several other variations of the stepped tablet exist.[174]

POSTWAR WORK THROUGH THE 1820S

There is widespread evidence of settee production following the War of 1812. In Philadelphia, both shop and estate records point to increasing activity. For example, Aaron Boughman's chairmaking establishment contained two finished settees, "93 Settee Sticks," and "1 Settee Bow" in 1813 (the term *bow* described either a rod or a slat). Anthony Steel's extensive shop inventory of 1817 contains many references to settee production. Of seven finished long seats, several were described as "Common." Five "bent back" settees were unfinished, probably requiring only paint and decoration. The inventory listed many settee parts, including 1,209 stretchers, of which 243 were plain, 272 were "creased" (grooved), 75 were flat (probably with a medallion), 400 were

Fig. 1-93 Shaped-slat Windsor settee, attributed to Samuel Moon, Fallsington, Bucks Co., Pa., ca. 1814–18. H. 36⅞″, (seat) 18¾″, W. (crest) 75¾″, (arms) 79½″, (seat) 78½″, D. (seat) 19¾″. (Mr. and Mrs. James Palmer Flowers collection: Photo, Winterthur.)

"short," and 219 were turned "with balls" at the center. The 225 feet (legs) were creased, and the 89 bows were already bent (probably laterally). Among the 36 settee "bottoms" were 9 of "small" size. In the household of chairmaker Thomas Millard, a settee formed a suite with eight Windsor chairs. Benjamin Love of Frankford owned both a "short" settee and two larger "Second hand" Windsor seats. North on the Delaware River at Fallsington, Bucks County, Samuel Moon constructed long settees in innovative designs echoing those of his chairs.[175]

Moon's settees, like his chairs, are distinctive (fig. 1-93). Here, the silhouette of the top ripples with greater movement than is possible within the confines of a chair back. Austere bamboowork forms an effective contrast that heightens the ornamental quality of the long, two-tiered spindles and scalloped crest. The crest pattern is drawn from several Moon chairs by combining the top profile of one and the bottom curves of others. A second Moon settee of similar size shows two changes: the front and rear stretchers are all socketed at the same height, and the crest follows a scalloped-panel pattern terminated by pierced ends forming double fingers. The back ends curve forward slightly in the Philadelphia manner (fig. 1-86). A two-seated, panel-end bench with a Windsor upper structure introduces single-tiered arrow spindles to a plain slat back set between bent posts. Tradition holds that Moon made it for a neighbor and that it was used in a wagon.[176]

The Philadelphia export trade flourished again in the postwar period, with most domestic shipments still going to southern ports. Several chairmakers handled consignments on their own account. Foreign trade with the West Indies remained strong, and there was occasional trade with South and Central America. During the early 1820s the merchant firm of J. H. Stevenson and Company conducted a brisk trade in the Golfo de Campeche at the southern extremity of the Gulf of Mexico. The destination mentioned most frequently in company records is the port of Alvarado, south of Vera Cruz, where Windsor chairs, settees, and cabinetware were landed along with general commodities.[177]

At Newark, New Jersey, David Alling continued to manufacture settees of several styles: bamboo, bronzed ball-back, and slat-back. The seating trade also flourished across the bay in New York City. Charles Fredericks, John K. Cowperthwaite, and

William Brown, Jr., were three craftsmen who supplied local and export markets with painted settees. City householders still found the Windsor settee convenient for the entry of their homes. In other situations, the settee provided seating at Lewis Bancel's school in Provost Street and at the "country" house of John C. Vanden Heuvel, Esq., at Bloomingdale. On Long Island, Carman Smith's newly established chair and settee manufactory at Huntington reflected the rising trade east of the city. Upstate, Albany was a particularly important center, both as an established community and as the eastern terminus of the Erie Canal. "Settees of all descriptions" were available in the chair shops lining State Street. Bates and Johnson also sold "Johnson's Patent Portable Settees" as early as 1819.[178]

Coastal New England chairmakers enjoyed the benefits of both local and regional markets. Henry Barney of Bridgeport was sufficiently encouraged to advertise "Fancy, Bamboo, and Windsor Settees, all of which will be warranted of the first quality." On October 25, 1817, Amos Denison Allen shipped forty-two chairs, two settees, and sixteen boxes of cabinet furniture from New London, consigned to his brother-in-law Frederick Tracy at Savannah, Georgia. In western Connecticut Silas Cheney had more calls for settee repairs than for new construction. Caning, painting, gilding, and ornamenting filled the usual needs of his customers. Along the Connecticut River in Massachusetts Daniel Munger of Greenfield boasted "Settees of every description." Low and Damon of Concord, New Hampshire, were equally prepared to produce painted seating, although they combined that business with house painting and ornamental painting. Canadian woodworker Chester Hatch had a successful chair and settee business at Kingston, Ontario; he expanded to a branch facility at Toronto by 1823. To encourage sales in an economy where specie was limited, Hatch willingly accepted produce in lieu of cash.[179]

Southern chairmakers in coastal locations still faced the challenges of the import trade in the postwar period, but local activity was on the rise. In 1822 Thomas Adams of Georgetown, District of Columbia, built two settees 4 feet in length for John Underwood at a cost of $12 each. John Lloyd of Alexandria paid freight on a 14-foot settee acquired in Philadelphia, although he probably could have purchased one just as well made at a local manufactory, such as that of N. Blasdell, who offered settees of "different qualities and prices." Like Blasdell, Hobday and Barnes of Richmond combined house painting and ornamental painting with the manufacture of painted furniture. They may have been the suppliers of Edmond Harrison's suite of eight chairs and a settee that in 1826 stood in the master bedroom/sitting-room at the Oaks, a plantation southwest of Richmond in Amelia County.[180]

Chairmaking establishments producing settees began to dot the interior parts of North Carolina in this period. Joel Brown, who moved south from Petersburg to Raleigh in 1816, manufactured chairs, settees, and cradles. Whenever possible he tried to employ a northern workman, thereby keeping abreast of current patterns and finishes in the style-setting commercial centers. At Salisbury in 1823, Grimes and Cooper constructed settees in patterns compatible with their Windsor and fancy chairs. To attract customers to the public sale of his business in October 1826, at which he offered chairs, settees, and bedsteads, William Culverhouse of Charlotte extended a credit of six months "with approved security." In coastal Charleston and Savannah, the import trade was still a substantial business. The Northern Warehouse in King Street, Charleston, offered Philadelphia Windsor chairs and settees of a "handsome pattern" in 1819. The dozen chairs and matching settee owned in 1828 by Savannah carpenter Isaiah Davenport were likely acquired from a similar source.[181]

Western seating markets expanded rapidly in the years following the war, with Cincinnati a major source of supply. Samuel Stibbs in a public notice of 1829 indicated that western design continued to be influenced from outside sources: "Settees of the latest, eastern improved FASHIONS." Downriver at Louisville, Kentucky, wareroom proprietors offered merchandise from Cincinnati, much as southern centers on the East Coast sold northern goods. Chairmaking partnerships were common and usually short-lived. At Nashville in 1823, Sherwood and Dodd, who manufactured a complete range of painted seating, including settees and children's chairs, were on the lookout for "a good WINDSOR CHAIR MAKER." The region attracted many workers from the East. S. Williams employed "several of the best workmen from . . . shops in New York and Philadelphia." James S. Bridges of Knoxville followed suit, adding craftsmen from Baltimore and Washington. Is it any wonder that a midwestern seating style has yet to be identified?[182]

Settees in the postwar market were of several patterns, some of which were uncommon. One unusual pattern was the roll-top crest, first available in the 1820s. A two-seated example made with rockers shares its basic form with figure 1-91. The earliest "Patent Portable Settee" constructed with a rush or fabric seat by Chester Johnson of Albany in 1819 probably had a crest of this style. The date provides a reference point for the introduction of the pattern. Some long, wooden-bottom settees with roll tops have three- and four-section backs. Production of the pattern continued into the 1830s, when features such as slat-type stretchers, fancy legs, and scroll-and-ball arms appeared. David Alling's Newark, New Jersey, accounts for 1837 record a "winsor roll top settee" priced at $10. Other settee patterns of limited production include the slat with pierced ends, the loaf-top slat (fig. 2-56), the hollow-cornered slat (fig. 2-44), and variations of the slat or tablet-top crest with one or more flat projections on the top surface and, perhaps, one at the center bottom (fig. 1-66). The tablet-style settee top with a scrolled lip at the upper back is rare (fig. 1-50, center section).[183]

The plain, slat-back settee was a popular basic form, although it was interpreted in many different ways. One specialized design with rockers often is fitted with a removable front gate of full or partial width, converting the seat to a cradle at will (fig. 1-94). The settee-cradle, as it was called during the period of manufacture, was available in several sizes, accommodating from two to four people as a settee. Allen Holcomb of New Lisbon, Otsego County, New York, produced this special form as early as 1821, according to his accounts. The rocking seat was more popular in the next decade; Samuel Church advertised the form at Toronto in 1836. In the Midwest William H. Mapes manufactured settee-cradles at Rising Sun, Indiana, in 1838, and a chairmaker in St. Louis, Missouri, produced the form in 1840. In Ipswich, New Hampshire, Josiah Prescott Wilder's production records list at least seventeen examples constructed during the 1840s. When the contents of Peter A. Willard's Worcester shop were offered at public sale in 1842, the prepared stock included "167 settee Cradle pillars," or posts. On the southeastern coast of Massachusetts at Barnstable, Calvin Stetson produced seventeen or more settee-cradles between 1843 and 1847; references describe one of dark color and another of painted or natural maple. At New London and Norwich, Connecticut, Erastus Jones and George W. Smith itemized settee-cradles in individual advertisements. The price ranged from $2 to $6, depending on such variables as size and decoration.[184]

The settee-cradle illustrated in figure 1-94 may have originated in New York State, as suggested by a typed label on the plank bottom, now brown with age: "For / Catharine S. Owens / In care of / Mrs. T. S. Rogers / 309 West Linden Street / Rome, New York." The unusual profile of the flat arms also seems related to furniture from New York State. Similar rests are found in several rush-bottom rocking chairs of tall, narrow back and roll-top crest that exhibit other features associated with New York work: a cross slat composed of Prince of Wales feathers; ornamental, arrow-tipped front stretchers; and short, swelled, lower-back spindles centered by multiple rings. The waferlike disks below the flattened spindle faces also have their counterparts in New York City Windsors. Similar grooving ornaments the back posts and flat-faced gate ends; the short posts supporting the arms, however, are noticeably plain. The explanation lies in the close proximity of the two sets of short posts when the gate is fitted into the holes at the plank front, effectively obscuring the underarm supports. The additional ornament could have proven distracting rather than harmonious. The blunt plank edges and slat-type stretchers suggest a date in the 1830s. The painted sur-

Fig. 1-94 Small Windsor "settee-cradle," probably New York state, 1830–45. H. 31¼", (seat) 13½", W. (crest) 37¼", (arms) 38", (seat) 36⅜", (gate) 35½", D. (seat) 13½"; medium straw yellow ground with medium green. (Steven and Helen Kellogg collection: Photo, Winterthur.)

face is a medium straw color with banded and leafy decoration in medium green. Rockers with original paint are attached with screws on the outside of the feet, although most other construction is socketed or slotted. Arms usually are forward scrolls; sometimes they are bamboo-turned cylinders. Some "convertibles" have gates formed of solid boards scrolled at one end.[185]

Scroll or bamboo arms are the norm in slat-back settees made without rockers in New England and the Middle Atlantic region. Spindle profiles are varied, and plank lengths extend from two to five seat widths. Some long settees have intermediate back posts. Several unusual examples, which curve forward at the back corners in the Philadelphia fashion (fig. 1-86), likely were made by Lawrence Allwine after his removal to Zanesville, Ohio. Most long seats have forward-scroll arms; beneath the plank, fancy-turned legs often are substituted for bamboo supports. Front stretchers sometimes are centered by long, slim medallions, and flat arms are introduced upon occasion. One exceptional settee with scroll arms has seven pairs of legs; it was made and remains at the Pleasant Hill Shaker site in Kentucky. The backs of several settees have ball spindles, and within this group are several examples with two pairs of legs set chairwise near each end. One eight-legged settee has delicate Cumberland spindles across the back (fig. 2-39), well-turned bamboo uprights and braces, and a plank shaped to shield form at the front corners. It appears to be of New York origin and is the earliest settee in this general group, possibly dating even before 1810.[186]

Slat-back settees of specialized form include a bench from the Berks County, Pennsylvania, shop of Samuel Lobach; it was built especially for the Salem United Church of Christ at Spangsville and designed to fit around the base of the pulpit in a part of the building erected in 1822. The seat forms an arc almost 10 feet long; the front is concave and the back is convex, except at the center, where there is a short half-circular indentation to accommodate the pulpit base. The back contains four posts with slats and spindles conforming to the plank contours. Eight pairs of legs support the structure. Another group of settees made to a fancy pattern has short spindles in the lower back, usually of arrow form. Above the spindles there frequently is a ball fret, replaced in one case by outsized roundels.

The slat-back settee remained in production during the 1830s, but the tablet-top crest design gradually became more prominent. This Baltimore style extended its influence to most centers up and down the coast. The New York accounts of chairmaker Benjamin W. Branson show the popularity of the Baltimore style. On August 29, 1835, Branson credited James Vanderbilt with painting and ornamenting "25 Doz Baltimore Chrs" at $3.50 per dozen. He sold the seating the same day for $7.25 a dozen to chairmakers Benjamin and Elijah Farrington, further describing it as "25 Dozn Baltimore backs [tablet crests] and legs of Chairs." Additional inspiration for the tablet top came from design books, such as George Smith's *Cabinet-Maker and Upholsterer's Guide* (London, 1826). Smith's designs appear to have influenced both the crown top of New England and the shouldered tablet of Pennsylvania and Maryland. Drawings prepared by John Hall for *The Cabinetmaker's Assistant* (Baltimore, 1840) recorded and further disseminated patterns already in the local market. Charles Riley's Philadelphia shop inventory of 1842 describes a full production of long seating. There were tablet-top "Baltimore" settees, "bent"-back long seats framed with slats between the posts, and a "strait Settee" that could have been framed either way. Riley's top-of-the-line seat had a "ball back." He offered a range of colors: imitation maple and rosewood, cane and "light" color, blossom (peach color), and dark olive. In neighboring Bucks and Montgomery counties, Lester Rich and Jacob Fillman both stocked "a large and diverse assortment of Fancy and Windsor Chairs, Settees, &c." South of Philadelphia at Chester a "sage colour" settee and cushion furnished the home of Elizabeth Yarnal.[187]

In 1837 James Helme of Plymouth, Luzerne County, Pennsylvania, recorded costs of settee construction in his manuscript "Book of Prices":

> For framing Common Settees, straight or bent
>   back, with scroll arms, getting out seat,
>   top slat, back and front Stretchers   1.25
> For do with Ball Back, two slats, getting out
>   stuff as above, and stumps for arms   2.00

The expense of ornamenting and varnishing a long seat was the same as that for "6 chairs of the same description," a figure that varied from 50¢ to 65¢. In Chester County Joseph Jones sold a settee to Major Benjamin Sharpless for $3.75 in 1842, described as drab with "bronz bands." Across the Delaware River at Salem, New Jersey, chairmaker William G. Beesley built straight- and bent-back settees during the late 1820s and early 1830s. Plain ones cost $5 and $6, respectively; special ornament sometimes added as much as another dollar to the price. When Beesley repainted a settee for a customer, he charged $2 or $2.50, depending upon the embellishment.[188]

Throughout the German-speaking regions of Pennsylvania, recorded activity identifies the "splendid assortment" of common, scroll, and ball-back settees that was available at Frederick Fox's stand in Penn Street, Reading, in 1845. John Schroder offered "SETTEES of various colors and qualities" at his shop in Lancaster opposite the Farmer's Bank, and John Swint did business near the National House and Schofield's Tavern, establishments that drew many customers, especially on market days. Along the Susquehanna George W. Boyd was an active setteemaker at Harrisburg. At Erie in northwestern Pennsylvania William E. Willis was well beyond Philadelphia and Baltimore competition, but he had the Buffalo market to contend with. He offered to meet Buffalo prices for chairs and settees with merchandise of equal quality.[189]

Eastward from Buffalo were pockets of similar activity. Settee makers A. and E. Brown relocated in Rochester about 1841 after conducting their cabinet and chair business in Schenectady for eight years. Cooperstown craftsman Miles Benjamin recorded the sale of a "Small Settee" for $5 in 1829. As usual, activity was brisk in New York City. Nathaniel S. Rose operated a well-stocked chair store in 1827, while fellow New Yorker Philip I. Arcularius, Jr., reached across the East River to tap the Brooklyn market. At neighboring Newark David Alling's business prospered during the 1830s, although it is not always possible to distinguish between fancy and Windsor production in his accounts. Repairs probably accounted for as much income as new work. Alling's workmen altered, repaired, and "rearmed" four settees for D. D. Chandler in April 1837 and repainted them yellow. The total cost was $8, or one dollar more than a new Windsor settee. Sometimes the old paint was sufficiently damaged that it was necessary to "clean off" all the surfaces, or at least the seat, before repainting and "striping"; at other times "tuching up and varnishing" were all that was required. The only long seating pattern identified by name in the Alling accounts is a "winsor roll top settee," which at $10 appears to have been a seating piece of consequence.[190]

During the second quarter of the nineteenth century, industrial expansion in New England led to a corresponding increase in population in many towns and villages. New private dwellings, boardinghouses, and public facilities created additional demand for durable, inexpensive furnishings. Painted furniture was acceptable, even fashionable. Daniel Proud's "North Parlour" at Providence contained a "wood settee" and a dozen chairs in 1833; the tea tray in the room may identify this as a "company" area. The "South Parlor" with its five chairs and settee furnished with a cushion may have been for general family use. In Hartford, Connecticut, chairmakers J. Pratt, Jr., and Son approached settee and chair sales aggressively, issuing a printed broadside in 1840 with the headline "STRANGER LOOK HERE." Massachusetts records indicate that Daniel Rogers of Gloucester bought a quantity of furniture at auction in Salem on April 7, 1829. A listing for five settees in the purchase account follows that for two large groups of chairs described as having "N York back[s]." The New Bedford chairmakers Samuel Bennett and George Piggott probably also produced New York–style painted furniture, as indicated in the documented chair of a competitor. The versatile partners stood ready to "manufacture any kind of Chairs, Settees, &c. to order" in 1832. At mid-century the firm of Merriam and Holden advertised on their billhead "CANE AND WOOD SEAT CHAIRS AND SETTEES, OF EVERY DESCRIPTION" at Westminster, Worcester County. They supplied a customer with thirty-four settees ranging in length from 4½ to 9 feet, surely for resale.[191]

Settee production also was increasing in northern New England. Dewey and Woodworth of Bennington, Vermont, offered settees in "the most fashionable modern style" in 1827. Henry F. Dewey's independent accounts of later date record the production of both fancy maple and plain wood-seat settees. On one occasion he credited Alvin Bates, a parts supplier, with "turning settee front roll," probably for the seat, suggesting that the settee was on rockers. Josiah P. Wilder of New Ipswich, New Hampshire, made Windsor settees in different lengths priced from $1.75 to $4. The 8-foot bench sold to innkeeper John Peabody in 1848 and priced at 3s. per foot commanded the top price of $4. The single settee in the farmhouse of Marshall Spring in Hiram, Maine, may have met several needs. Thirteen beds and "2 Doz. common dining Chairs" give some evidence of the family's size. At Toronto in 1836, Samuel Church offered chairs and settees for the "lowest possible prices" at his warehouse.[192]

In the South, Humberston Skipwith, proprietor of "Prestwould" in Mecklenberg County, obtained two settees in 1832 at Petersburg, Virginia, which he paid for in tobacco. The settees may have been of local rather than coastal origin. Two decades later, Washington G. Henning of Lewisburg, West Virginia, stockpiled seating furniture for disposal at auction, choosing a time when the local court was in session. A newcomer to the chair business, Henning produced more than 1,000 pieces of seating furniture, including 25 settees, for regional distribution as "samples" of his work.[193]

Isaac M. Lee's Cincinnati advertisements of the 1820s, which describe settees "for ease and elegance and durability" and offer "the latest and most improved fashions from the Eastward," show how eastern styles continued to influence the western market. Late in the following decade Nelson Talcott, a chairmaker in Portage County, Ohio, retailed a selection of settees described as cane-seated or wooden-bottomed, 5 or 6 feet in length, with or without rockers. Indiana chairmakers offered settees by

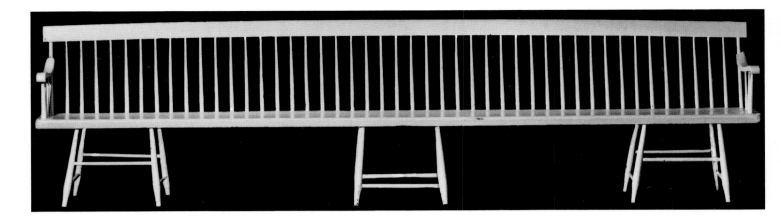

Fig. 1-95 Long, tablet-top Windsor settee, attributed to John N. White, Woodstock, Vt., 1840–50. H. 35⅛", (seat) 17¾", W. (crest) 143½", (arms) 143½", (seat) 144¼", D. (seat) 14½". (Woodstock Historical Society, Woodstock, Vt.: Photo, Winterthur.)

1829 when J. Jones of Vincennes exchanged all sizes for cash or produce. Retailers in Louisville, Kentucky, and Nashville, Tennessee, imported quantities of seating from Cincinnati. This did not deter Sherwood and Dodd of Nashville from offering settees of their own make. At Travellers' Rest, the local home of Judge Overton, the lone Windsor settee in the household may have been painted brown to match either a fancy or "common" set of Windsors.[194]

There is about as much variety in tablet-top settees as in the slat-back group. Crests are divided into rectangular and rounded profiles. Further variation is present in spindle pattern, arm design, and leg placement. One small group of rectangular-top settees is supported on legs set chairwise, a system with its roots in the late eighteenth century (fig. 1-81) but uncommon even in later years. The support system seems to have had no geographic bounds. One exponent was John N. White of Woodstock, Vermont, who worked during the 1830s and later (fig. **1-95**). Several dozen of his benches, varying in size from about 8 feet to 12 feet, furnished the local town hall and courthouse. Construction is straightforward. The tablet rests on the spindles and posts, the latter chamfered slightly at the top, front and back, to form a smooth joint with the board. The arms are attached to the back posts with a screw inserted from the rear. From a design standpoint, the most successful patterns are those with heavier end posts than illustrated and scroll arms that sweep up at the back to meet the tablet. The plank is of the simplest type, with flat edges on three sides and a rounded-chamfered front. The upper surface is without grooves to define the spindle area, and the legs socket inside the plank. The stretcher placement in the center unit of this settee is reversed from the end supports and also from the treatment common to other settees made by White, although there are no plugged holes or other indications of repairs. If the pattern is not original, the whole unit may have been rotated ninety degrees during early repair work.[195]

A majority of tablet-top settees are supported on late bamboo or "fancy" legs of conventional placement. More often than not, narrow slats form the front and back stretcher units. They are framed with mortise and tenon between pairs of legs (fig. 1-94) or nailed as a continuous unit across the front or back surfaces of the supports. The planks usually are almost flat with little shaping around the edges; an occasional seat has a scroll at the front and a rise at the back, like the Boston rocking chair (fig. 1-42). Back posts usually are straight, mounted at a slight backward cant; a few bend slightly at a carefully controlled angle. The rectangular top pieces usually are wedge-shaped in section, the greater depth at the base to accommodate sockets for the spindles and posts. Sometimes a small roll is applied to the upper back edge, and occasionally the face is contoured or crowned. Several arm styles are common to this group. One rail sweeps downward from the crest to the seat in a concave curve imitating Baltimore work. Examples have been found in such diverse locations as New Brunswick, Canada, and Cincinnati, Ohio. Another arm extends forward in a shallow curve and caps a plain, vase-shaped stump (fig. 1-45, related pattern). Two chairmakers

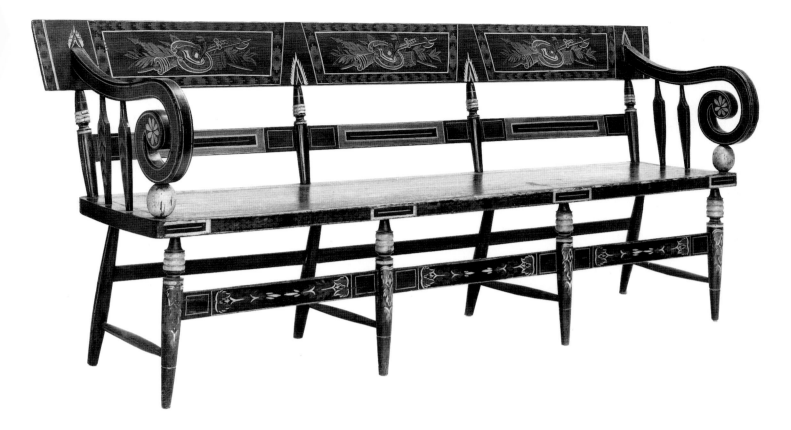

Fig. 1-96 Fancy, tablet-top Windsor settee
and detail of related decoration, Baltimore, 1835–
45. Yellow poplar (seat); H. 35⅛″, (seat) 18″,
W. (crest) 86½″, (arms) 77″, (seat) 78¼″, D. (seat)
17⅜″; dark brown grained ground with cream,
golden yellow, bronze, and dull gold. (Historical
Society of York County, York, Pa.: Photo,
Winterthur. Detail from stenciled mahogany sofa
in Maryland Historical Society, Baltimore.)

identified with this design are William O. Haskell and Son of Boston and Joseph
Bachelder and Son of West Waterville, Maine. This late pattern continued in production until the end of the century. In a variant style, the forward roll continues down to
the seat as one unit. One unusual long seat has five such arms anchored in spaced back
posts, creating four individual seating places along the plank. Another settee is fitted
with three spaced, right-handed writing leaves and a single scroll arm. Most tablet-top
settees have plain, tapered cylindrical spindles; a few have long sticks of arrow form,
including one documented to William Graham's shop in Wheeling, West Virginia.
Cross slats and half-length arrow or ball-centered spindles mark the backs of another
small group; ball frets at midback are uncommon. In a rare grain-painted settee at Old
Sturbridge Village, pairs of plain, long sticks alternate with four vertical, vase-shaped
splats, a pattern related to Walter Corey's work in Portland, Maine.[196]

Some Shaker-made settees, varying in size from two to about seven seat widths,
were constructed in the tablet pattern without arms. The plank edges are rounded and
the ends are shaped in vigorous ogee curves. Members of another notable group of
thirty rectangular-top settees forming a suite of furniture have ten legs and planks
curved in a slight arc. In their original setting at the Middlesex County Superior
Courthouse in Cambridge, Massachusetts, they formed long, curved rows of seating in
the courtroom gallery. All bear the stamp of John C. Hubbard of Boston, who supplied the long seats and chairs about 1848 when the courthouse was enlarged and ren-
ovated. The curved settees and an unrelated straight-bottom one from the same shop
have unusual braces. Cylindrical rods socketed lengthwise between the legs are faced
with a narrow slat nailed across the front and back.

Of extraordinary design, even for its late date, is a rectangular-tablet settee of
Baltimore origin whose features are bold, yet harmonious (fig. 1-96). The outsize tablet
top and prominent spiral arms draw the eye immediately to the form. The spirals are
duplicates of those in a pair of high-style, painted cane-seat armchairs in the Baltimore
Museum of Art framed with crest pieces similar to that illustrated in figure 1-98 but of
more delicate profile. Tenoned construction secures arms to balls and balls to seat; the
attachment of the upper arms to the tablet face is unusual. A similar arm profile was

first delineated in the *London Chair-Makers and Carvers' Book of Prices* for 1802, where it is called a "scroll elbow"; it was further refined in the 1811 supplement to the price book. By 1817 the scroll elbow had found its way into the New York book of prices. Instrumental in integrating the overall design of figure 1-96 are the turned back posts, which correspond in number, position, and form to the legs, and also the narrow slats at mid back and between the leg braces. The strong horizontal lines of the design—crest, slats, and seat—are held in check by the repeating verticals of the posts and legs and the forceful curves of the arms. The leg turnings are composites of several designs in the Baltimore chair market of the 1820s and 1830s.[197]

Almost as remarkable as the silhouette of figure 1-96 is the painted decoration of the settee, which features bronze-colored leafage on a streaked, dark brown ground with cream-colored banding and accents in golden yellow. The focal points of the decoration are the three military trophies centered in the leaf-bordered tablet panels. The pattern is a close copy in reverse of one found on a painted and upholstered, scroll-end Baltimore sofa. General inspiration for the motifs may come from Thomas Hope's *Household Furniture and Interior Decoration,* which illustrates a folding door ornamented with a related stylized shield and crossed weapons. Further uniting the upper and lower structures are the small painted rectangular panels of the mid slats, seat front, and stretchers.[198]

A settee with pristine decoration has an unusual roll top (fig. **1-97,** pl. 16). The long seating piece clearly shows the importance of ornament in the early nineteenth-century home and amplifies the splendor of a group of furniture all too often devoid of original embellishment. The decoration on a tan-gray ground is almost monochromatic. The grays of the primary scheme are accented with black and further enhanced by the dark olive green of the ring turnings, spindle balls, and slender, wispy leaves of the foliate compositions. Once again structural design is dominated by strong horizontals relieved by vigorous arm curves, here visually rolling up and over the crest to develop a low overall profile. The repetitive decoration, which relates significantly to southern Pennsylvania work, is another powerful integrating force. The front legs reflect turned work of the same area. Perhaps this is the "winsor roll top" pattern described by David Alling of Newark, New Jersey, in his accounts for 1837. Use of the heavy top roll springs from other furnishing forms, such as window drapery rods, capping pieces in upholstered sofa backs, and headboard tops in bedsteads. Increase Pote, a turner of Portland, Maine, turned both "headboard Rolls" and "Sopha Backs" for 25¢ apiece or less in 1827–28.[199]

By far the most common pattern among rounded-tablet settees is the Pennsylvania shouldered crest divided into three chair-back sections (fig. 2-36). Single cross slats and short ball spindles complete the basic structure. Most arms scroll forward, although the large ball-and-spiral elbow of Baltimore origin is substituted in several settees. One settee has a Boston-style scroll seat (fig. 1-42). Floral decoration predominates. One long seat bears the identifying stencil of Melchoir W. Burkhard, a manufacturer of Philadelphia, who is listed in city directories from 1839 to 1855. A settee of similar pattern appears in the background of Thomas Hovenden's *The Old Version* (1881), a painting depicting a middle-aged man and woman in their parlor reading the Bible. The sitters are identified as tollkeepers on the Conshohocken Pike outside Philadelphia. In a slightly later interpretation of the crest, three loaf-shaped sections are joined. One settee is branded by the Reading chairmaker Emanuel Ermentrout, who is listed in the 1850 census. Another group of two- and three-seat settees features a shouldered crest divided into two sections with one interior post. In a late version of the three-back, shouldered settee, vertical splats, most of them pierced, replace the spindles. One is marked by George Nees, who worked after 1850 in Manheim, Lancaster County, Pennsylvania.[200]

Settees of long, one-section, shouldered crest include two unusual groups. One pattern framed with Baltimore-style legs substitutes cylinder ends for arms. The cylinders form large elevated rolls imitating sofa bolsters, faced by and supported in figure-

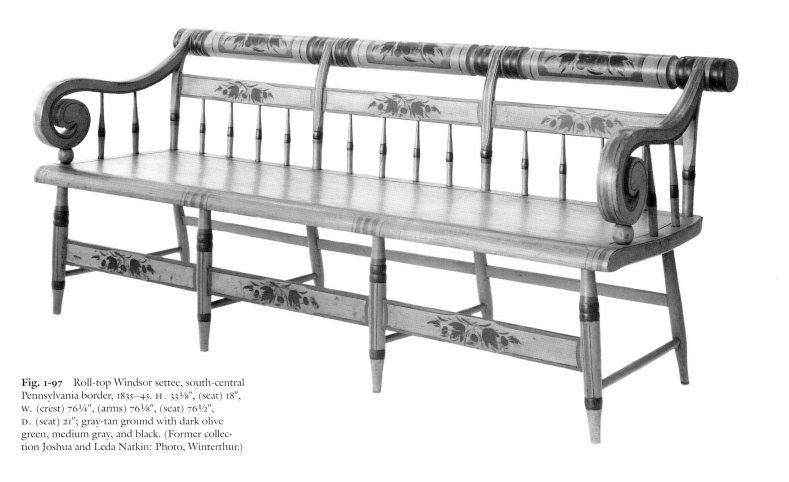

Fig. 1-97 Roll-top Windsor settee, south-central Pennsylvania border, 1835–45. H. 33⅛″, (seat) 18″, W. (crest) 76¼″, (arms) 76⅛″, (seat) 76½″, D. (seat) 21″; gray-tan ground with dark olive green, medium gray, and black. (Former collection Joshua and Leda Natkin: Photo, Winterthur.)

Fig. 1-98 Rounded tablet-top Windsor settee, George Boyd (stencil), Harrisburg, Pa., ca. 1838–42. H. 31⅝″, (seat) 15¼″, W. (crest) 83½″, (arms) 80″, (seat) 81″, D. (seat) 21¼″; pale mustard ground with deep bronze, reddish brown, black, and polychrome landscape. (Private collection.)

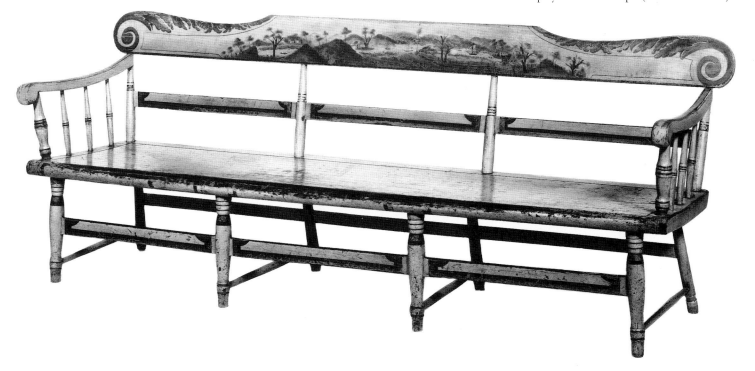

Production of Specialized Adult Furniture 133

eight panels. The cylinder backs butt against the shouldered ends of the crest. The second group comprises a small number of central Pennsylvania settees retaining original painted landscape scenes in the tablets (fig. 1-98). The illustrated example is the earliest type; the others have deeper tablets and scroll seats. Stenciled on the plank bottom is the name of George W. Boyd and a Front Street address in Harrisburg; by 1843 Boyd had moved to Second Street. The crest corresponds in profile to the first Philadelphia shouldered pattern, which was introduced about the mid 1830s. The use of Baltimore-style turnings and a grooved cuff in the back legs is another commentary on that city's influence on the inland regions of Maryland and central Pennsylvania. Harrisburg is only seventy miles north of Baltimore. The landscape, executed in naturalistic colors on a pale mustard ground, could depict a scene along the Susquehanna River, which was visible from the front door of the chairmaker's shop. Certainly, the body of water appears to be a river with its small islands and shallow-draft vessels; the hilly terrain is also typical of the area. Other embellishments are painted in colors of reddish brown and deep bronze with black penciling.

In summary, the production of specialized Windsor seating began in the 1750s, within a few years of the introduction of Windsor construction to the American furniture trade. Chairmakers produced the settee first. The writing chair and rocking chair followed at the end of the century. Specialized furniture was "bespoke" work, that is, made to order. Styles closely followed those of standard Windsor seating in pattern, structural elements, and decoration. Although specialized forms constitute a moderate body of furniture, their number is small compared to standard Windsor production.

During the eighteenth century, the Pennsylvania low-back style was the most common one for the settee. Low- and high-back styles proved the most suitable for the writing chair, with its massive arm structure. A high back or an extension headpiece added to a pattern of standard height were requirements of the rocking, or "easy," chair.

Square-back styles were fashionable after 1800. From the 1810s consumers chose between slat-back patterns (the crest framed between the back posts) and tablet-top patterns (the crest framed above the posts). The broad, flat surfaces of the slat and tablet proved suitable for the introduction of painted or stenciled ornament, an important feature of nineteenth-century design. Even within the confines of standard patterns, innovative chairmakers could find room for design initiative.

Notes

1. John Gaines II and Thomas Gaines, account book, 1712–62, Joseph Downs Collection of Manuscripts and Printed Ephemera, Winterthur Library (hereafter cited as DCM and WL); Catherine Naish, bill (probably for St. James's), ca. 1766–68, as transcribed in Robert Wemyss Symonds Collection, DCM.

2. J. Stogdell Stokes, "The American Windsor Chair," *Antiques* 9, no. 4 (April 1926): 225.

3. The Gaw chair is in the Winterthur Museum study collection, 83.138. John Letchworth, bill to Jonathan Williams, December 1792, private collection; bill illustrated in Nancy Goyne Evans, *American Windsor Chairs* (New York: Hudson Hills Press, 1996), fig. 3-52. Manifest of sloop *Experiment,* May 2, 1798, Philadelphia Outward Coastwise Entries, U.S. Customhouse Records, National Archives, Washington, D.C. (hereafter cited as NA).

4. Manifest of sloop *Brilliant,* February 4, 1795, Philadelphia Outward Coastwise and Foreign Entries, U.S. Customhouse Records, French Spoliation Claims, NA. The second branded Steel chair is in the Museum of Art, Rhode Island School of Design, Providence, and is illustrated in Charles Santore, *The Windsor Style in America,* vol. 1 (Philadelphia: Running Press, 1981), fig. 171.

5. Stokes, "American Windsor Chair," pp. 223–24, figs. 5, 6.

6. "Acct Sundries del'd & Labor on Brig Polly," March 1789, and invoice of cargo, March 31, 1789, Joseph Williams Papers, Mystic Seaport Museum, Mystic, Conn. (hereafter cited as MSM); manifest of sloop *Honor,* 1794 (probably April), New London, Conn., Outward Entries, U.S. Customhouse Records, French Spoliation Claims, NA; Ebenezer Tracy, Sr., estate records, 1803, Lisbon, Conn., Genealogical Section, Connecticut State Library, Hartford (hereafter cited as CSL); Amos Denison Allen, memorandum book, 1796–1803, Connecticut Historical Society, Hartford (hereafter cited as CHS).

7. Comparable Windsors are illustrated in Evans, *American Windsor Chairs,* figs. 6-96, 6-100 (earliest crest), fig. 6-103 (hook-end crest). The chronology of family design is described in chapter 6.

8. Comparable Windsors are illustrated in Evans, *American Windsor Chairs,* figs. 6-96, 6-98, 6-99 (high-back and sack-back chairs), 6-97 (English-type chair), 3-130 (joined federal-period chair), 3-6 (Trumble chair).

9. Tracy family fan-back side chairs are illustrated in Evans, *American Windsor Chairs,* figs. 6-103, 6-104.

10. Dating of Tracy chairs, based upon use of the broken branding iron, is described in Evans, *American Windsor Chairs,* chap. 6. The date-inscribed chair is illustrated in *Ross H. Maynard Collection,* November 6, 1926 (New York: Anderson Galleries, 1926), lot 144.

11. Tracy fan, bow, and continuous-bow chairs are illustrated in Evans, *American Windsor Chairs,* figs. 6-103, 6-107, 6-111.

12. The chair is illustrated in Ada R. Chase, "Ebenezer Tracy, Connecticut Chairmaker," *Antiques* 30, no. 6 (December 1936): 269, fig. 7. The seat drawer is missing in the illustration.

13. Wallace Nutting, *Furniture Treasury* (1928; reprint, New York: Macmillan, 1966), fig. 2622.

Henry Francis du Pont purchased this chair via an agent from the Frederick W. Ayer sale at the American Art Galleries, New York, May 1929.

14. Advertisement of J. B. Kerfoot, *Antiques* 9, no. 2 (February 1926): 122; and advertisement of Henry V. Weil, *Antiquarian* 14, no. 3 (March 1930): 90. Comparable Connecticut Windsors are illustrated in Evans, *American Windsor Chairs,* figs. 6-168, 6-169.

15. Comparable Windsors are illustrated in Evans, *American Windsor Chairs,* figs. 6-29 (crest), 6-40 (arm pads), 6-50 (plank).

16. The Boston Museum chair is illustrated in Richard H. Randall, Jr., *American Furniture in the Museum of Fine Arts, Boston* (Boston: Museum of Fine Arts, 1965), fig. 197. The bamboo chair with eastern Connecticut and Rhode Island characteristics has a tradition of ownership by Major General Ira Allen (1751–1814) of Vermont, brother of Ethan Allen. Perhaps the maker emigrated from Rhode Island to Vermont in midcareer. The chair is in the Bennington Museum, Bennington, Vt. Comparable Windsors are illustrated in Evans, *American Windsor Chairs,* figs. 6-42 (angular balusters), 6-40 (arm terminals), 6-109, 6-117 (bamboo turnings).

17. One converted writing-arm chair is illustrated in Nutting, *Furniture Treasury,* fig. 2625; the second converted chair is at the Monmouth County Historical Association, Freehold, N.J.

18. A comparable Windsor is illustrated in Evans, *American Windsor Chairs,* fig. 6-177. The Reverend Bellamy chair is illustrated in John F. Page, *Litchfield County Furniture* (Litchfield, Conn.: Litchfield Historical Society, 1969), fig. 66.

19. John Wadsworth, advertisement in *American Mercury* (Hartford, Conn.), September 4, 1800; Jacob Norton, bill to Thomas Lloyd, Jr., October 20, 1790, Phelps-Gorham Papers, New York State Library, Albany; Ephraim Orcutt Jameson, *The Cogswells in America* (Boston: A. Mudge and Son, 1884), pp. 244–45; Mason Fitch Cogswell, account book, 1789–91, CHS; Elizabeth Mankin Kornhauser, "Regional Landscapes in Connecticut River Valley Portraits, 1790–1810," *Antiques* 128, no. 5 (November 1985): 1014; and Kornhauser, "Ralph Earl as an Itinerant Artist: Pattern of Patronage," in *Itinerancy in New England and New York,* ed. Peter Benes, Dublin Seminar for New England Folklife: Annual Proceedings, 1984 (Boston: Boston University, 1986), pp. 176–79 (with thanks to Barry A. Greenlaw and Elizabeth M. Kornhauser).

20. Solomon Sibley, account book, 1793–1840, Old Sturbridge Village, Sturbridge, Mass. (hereafter cited as OSV); Samuel Davison, account book, 1795–1824, Historic Deerfield, Deerfield, Mass; Samuel J. Tuck, bill to Samuel Barton, February 18, 1791, Papers of Samuel and John Barton, Peabody Essex Museum, Salem, Mass. (hereafter cited as PEM).

21. Comparable Boston Windsors are illustrated in Evans, *American Windsor Chairs,* figs. 6-197, 6-198.

22. Comparable chairs are illustrated in Evans, *American Windsor Chairs,* figs. 3-112 (Philadelphia chair), 8-6, 8-7 (McKim chairs). Manifest of schooner *Metomkin,* December 5, 1795, New London, Conn., Outward Entries, U.S. Customhouse Records, French Spoliation Claims, NA; manifest of Schooner *Industry,* July 15, 1803, New London, Conn., Outward Coastwise Entries, U.S. Customhouse Records, Federal Archives and Records

Center, Waltham, Mass. (hereafter cited as FRC–Waltham).

23. William Wirt in *Dictionary of American Biography,* ed. Dumas Malone, vol. 20 (New York: Charles Scribner's Sons, 1936), pp. 418–21. Other information, including the quoted excerpt from Wirt's letter to his brother-in-law, is given in an affidavit accompanying the Wirt chair. The Wirt chair is now in the Davenport Collection at Williams College, Williamstown, Mass.

24. Archer Brown, advertisement in *Petersburg Republican* (Petersburg, Va.), January 22, 1805; Joel Brown, advertisement in *Petersburg Republican,* October 20, 1806; Jacob Kurtz, advertisement in *The Phenix* (Staunton, Va.), August 22, 1804; James Beck, advertisement in *Virginia Herald* (Fredericksburg), November 3, 1815; all in citation file, Museum of Early Southern Decorative Arts, Winston-Salem, N.C. (hereafter cited as MESDA). Tyler estate records, as quoted in *William and Mary Quarterly* 17, no. 4 (April 1909) (reprint, New York: Kraus Reprint Corp., 1966), pp. 231–35; James Bridges, advertisement in *Knoxville Register,* August 24, 1819, as quoted in Ellen Beasley, "Tennessee Cabinetmakers and Chairmakers through 1840," *Antiques* 100, no. 4 (October 1971): 613.

25. R. W. Otis, advertisement in *Courier* (Charleston, S.C.), June 8, 1816, citation file, MESDA.

26. Anthony Steel, estate records, 1817, Philadelphia Register of Wills. Gilbert Burnett, advertisement in *Pennsylvania Republican* (Harrisburg), November 3, 1812. Joseph Jones, advertisements in *Village Record* (West Chester, Pa.), February 3, 1819, November 7, 1821, and October 29, 1823; all as quoted in Margaret Berwind Schiffer, *Furniture and Its Makers of Chester County, Pennsylvania* (Philadelphia: University of Pennsylvania Press, 1966), p. 132. George Landon, account book, 1813–32, DCM.

27. Comparable Baltimore fancy chairs are illustrated in Evans, *American Windsor Chairs,* fig. 3-118. Chairs that have broad leg placement are illustrated in Edgar G. Miller, Jr., *American Antique Furniture,* vol. 1 (1937; reprint, New York: Dover, 1966), figs. 476–77.

28. Levi Stillman, account book, 1815–34, Sterling Memorial Library, Yale University, New Haven (hereafter cited as Yale); Thomas Safford, ledger, 1807–35, CSL; Dr. Samuel Lee, estate records, 1815, Windham, Conn., Genealogical Section, CSL; Allen, memorandum book; Seth Wells, inventory, [1812], Greenough Papers, Massachusetts Historical Society, Boston (hereafter cited as MHS).

29. Josiah P. Wilder, estate records, 1869–73, Hillsborough Co., N.H., Registry of Probate; Silas E. Cheney, estate records, 1821, Litchfield, Conn., Genealogical Section, CSL; Silas E. Cheney, day-book, 1813–21, Litchfield Historical Society, Litchfield, Conn. (hereafter cited as LHS; microfilm, DCM); Theodosius Bailey, inventory, 1829, DCM; Benjamin W. Branson, estate records, 1831–35, DCM; David Alling, account book, 1801–39, and daybook, 1836–54, New Jersey Historical Society, Newark (hereafter cited as NJHS; microfilm, DCM).

30. John B. Ackley, estate records, 1827, Philadelphia Register of Wills; David Wilson, assignment of household property, 1829, DCM; Thomas J. Moyers and Fleming K. Rich, account book, 1834–40, DCM; William Culverhouse, advertise-

ment in *Catawba Journal* (Charlotte, N.C.), February 8, 1825, as quoted in James H. Craig, *The Arts and Crafts in North Carolina, 1699–1840* (Winston-Salem, N.C.: Old Salem for the Museum of Early Southern Decorative Arts, 1965), p. 210.

31. B. Dodd, advertisement in *Nashville Gazette* (Nashville, Tenn.), May 7, 1824; and Thompson and Drennen, advertisement in *Nashville National Banner* (Nashville, Tenn.), January 31, 1831; both as quoted in Beasley, "Tennessee Cabinetmakers and Chairmakers," p. 614. William H. Mapes, advertisement in *Rising Sun Journal* (Rising Sun, Ind.), September 29, 1838; and Joseph I. Stretcher, advertisement in *Indiana Journal* (Indianapolis, Ind.), October 22, 1841; both as quoted in Betty Lawson Walters, *Furniture Makers of Indiana, 1793 to 1850* (Indianapolis: Indiana Historical Society, 1972), pp. 145, 202.

32. Advertisement of Richard T. French, *Antiques* 105, no. 5 (May 1974): 1048; John L. Scherer, *New York Furniture at the New York State Museum* (Alexandria, Va.: Highland House, 1984), fig. 57.

33. The New York–inspired chair is illustrated in *Kentucky Furniture* (Louisville: J. B. Speed Art Museum, 1974), fig. 17.

34. Other Connecticut clergymen who owned writing chairs were Richard B. Saltar, Lyman Beecher of Litchfield, Elijah Waterman of the Windham area, and Mr. Learned of Westminster. Reverend Dr. Samuel Hopkins of Newport, Rhode Island, owned a chair constructed in the Tracy family style. Other late eighteenth-century chairs are associated with a Congregational minister in Chesterfield, Mass., and Reverend Ezra Ripley of Concord, step-grandfather of Ralph Waldo Emerson. Reverend John Croes of Trinity Church in Swedesboro, New Jersey, owned an early Philadelphia high-back chair converted for writing purposes, while Archdeacon Nelles of Ontario, who translated the Anglican Book of Common Prayer into the Mohawk language, possessed a tall, contoured-back, crown-top rocking chair with a writing leaf. Deacon Joseph Safford of Bennington, Vermont, handed down a writing chair to his son, Lieutenant Colonel Samuel Safford. Reverend Mr. Waterman is cited in Allen, memorandum book.

35. The Scotland, Conn., physician, Dr. Johnson, is cited in Safford, ledger; Dr. Lee is possibly cited in Allen, memorandum book.

36. Esther Stevens Fraser, "The American Rocking-Chair," *Antiques* 13, no. 2 (February 1928): 115–18; Walter A. Dyer, "The Boston Rocker," *Antiques* 13, no. 5 (May 1928): 389–92; Walter A. Dyer and Esther Stevens Fraser, *The Rocking-Chair: An American Institution* (New York: Century Co., 1928).

37. Ellen Denker and Bert Denker, *The Rocking Chair Book* (New York: Mayflower Books, 1979), pp. 15–19. A cradle having semicircular end panels in place of rockers to permit rocking motion is pictured in Jacques de Longuyon's *Voeux du paon,* an illuminated manuscript dating to about 1350, now in the Glazier Collection, Pierpont Morgan Library, New York, and illustrated in Frances Gies and Joseph Gies, *Marriage and the Family in the Middle Ages* (New York: Harper and Row, 1987), p. 205. Benno M. Forman, *American Seating Furniture, 1630–1730* (New York: W. W. Norton, 1988), pp. 229–37; John Gloag, *A Short Dictionary of Furniture* (London: George Allen and Unwin, 1969),

p. 561; Gillow Papers, waste book, 1742–54, Westminster Library, London (hereafter cited as WL; microfilm, DCM); Great Exhibition commentary in "Clues and Footnotes," *Antiques* 115, no. 5 (May 1979): 1064.

38. Solomon Fussell, account book, 1738–48, Stephen Collins Papers, Library of Congress, Washington, D.C. (hereafter cited as LC; microfilm, DCM); Margaret B. Schiffer, *Chester County, Pennsylvania, Inventories, 1684–1850* (Exton, Pa.: Schiffer, 1974), p. 106; Nancy Goyne Evans, "Unsophisticated Furniture Made and Used in Philadelphia and Environs, ca. 1750–1800," in *Country Cabinetwork and Simple City Furniture,* ed. John D. Morse (Charlottesville: University Press of Virginia, 1969), pp. 169–70.

39. Isaiah Tiffany, account book, 1746–67, CHS; Robert Crage, ledger, 1757–81, OSV; Nathaniel Heath, account book, 1767–91, Rhode Island Historical Society, Providence (hereafter cited as RIHS); William Barker, account book, vol. 1, 1750–72, RIHS.

40. Manifest of sloop *Jaby,* June 23, 1792, Baltimore Outward Entries, U.S. Customhouse Records, French Spoliation Claims, NA; William, Daniel, and Samuel Proud, ledger, ca. 1770–1825, and daybook and ledger, 1810–34, RIHS; Samuel Williams, ledger, 1789–1810, MSM; Allen, memorandum book. James Chase, account book, 1797–1812; and Jacob Merrill, Jr., account book, 1784–1812; both in Charles S. Parsons, New Hampshire Notes, Visual Resources Collection, WL (hereafter cited as VRC).

41. Clair F. Luther, "Anent the Rocking-Chair," *Antiques* 13, no. 5 (May 1928): 409; Schiffer, *Furniture of Chester County,* p. 270; Barker, account book; Proud brothers, ledgers; Nathan Topping Cook, account book, 1792–1823, DCM.

42. Edward Jarvis, "Traditions and Reminiscences of Concord, Massachusetts, . . . 1779 to 1878," p. 143, Concord Free Public Library, Concord, Mass.

43. Elias Hasket Derby, estate records, 1799–1805, Essex Co., Mass., Registry of Probate.

44. "Clues and Footnotes," *Antiques* 104, no. 6 (December 1973): 1101; Haight, as quoted in Philip Shackleton, *The Furniture of Old Ontario* (Toronto: Macmillan, 1973), p. 25; Allen Holcomb, account book, 1809–28, Metropolitan Museum of Art, New York; Virginia Armentrout and James S. Armentrout, Jr., eds., *The Diary of Harriet Manigault, 1813–1816* (Philadelphia: Colonial Dames of America, 1976), p. 78.

45. Hale Hilton, estate records, 1802, Nathan Dane Papers, MHS; Proud brothers, ledgers; Henry W. Miller, account book, 1827–31, Worcester Historical Museum, Worcester, Mass; Sarah Anna Emery, *Reminiscences of a Nonagenarian* (Newburyport, Mass.: William H. Huse, 1879), p. 33; Brown quoted in Mary R. Beard, ed., *America through Women's Eyes* (New York: Greenwood Press, 1969), p. 92.

46. Nina Fletcher Little, *Asahel Powers, Painter of Vermont Faces* (Williamsburg, Va.: Colonial Williamsburg Foundation, 1973), figs. 2, 30; Samuel Proud, inventory, 1835, as quoted in William Mitchell Pillsbury, "The Providence Furniture-Making Trade, 1772–1834" (Master's thesis, University of Delaware, 1975), p. 120. The Hudson portrait is in the Connecticut Historical Society. The Heade portrait of Moses Brown is illustrated

in "Current and Coming," *Antiques* 120, no. 2 (August 1981): 262.

47. Frewin, as quoted in Gloag, *Short Dictionary,* p. 562; Harriet Martineau, *Retrospect of Western Travel,* vol. 1 (London: Saunders and Otley, 1838), p. 72; *Northern Galaxy* (Middlebury, Vt.), December 11, 1844, as quoted in Edith Gaines, "The Rocking Chair in America," *Antiques* 99, no. 2 (February 1971): 240.

48. Andrew Oliver, sale of personal estate, 1774, Hutchinson-Oliver Papers, MHS (photostat, DCM); Proud brothers, ledgers; Flowers reference in Schiffer, *Chester County Inventories,* p. 106; Fussell, account book. The term *flowered* is discussed in Benno M. Forman, "Delaware Valley 'Crookt Foot' and Splat-Back Chairs," *Winterthur Portfolio* 15, no. 1 (Spring 1980): 43–44. Christopher Kilby, inventory, 1774, as transcribed in Alice Hanson Jones, *American Colonial Wealth,* vol. 2 (New York: Arno Press, 1977), pp. 561–68; Brown reference in Barker, account book.

49. George G. Channing, *Early Recollections of Newport, R.I., from the Year 1793 to 1811* (Newport, R.I.: A. J. Ward and Charles E. Hammett, Jr., 1868), pp. 246–48.

50. Thomas Boynton, ledger, 1811–17, Dartmouth College, Hanover, N.H. (hereafter cited as DC; microfilm, DCM); Andrew L. Haskell, advertisement in *Dover Gazette* (Dover, N.H.), December 1, 1827, as transcribed in New Hampshire Notes, DCM; William Hancock, bill to Mrs. Dunlap, March 11, 1828, Andrew Dunlap Papers, PEM; *New-England Society's Semi-Annual Sale,* March 10, 1831 (Boston: J. H. Eastburn, 1831); William Rawson, account book, 1835–41, OSV; John T. Hildreth advertisement in *Brooklyn Directory, for 1835–36* (Brooklyn, N.Y.: Lewis Nichols, 1835), n.p.; Peter Peirce, estate records, 1836, Worcester Co., Mass., Registry of Probate; Philemon Robbins, account book, 1833–36, CHS; Jacob Felton, daybook, 1836–38, OSV; Parrott and Hubbell, insolvency records, 1835, Bridgeport, Conn., Genealogical Section, CSL; Gilson Brown, estate records, 1833–35, Worcester Co., Mass., Registry of Probate; Isaac Washburn, estate records, 1832, Bristol Co., Mass., Registry of Probate; Edmund M. Brown, 1834, source of advertisement not given, Charles S. Parsons, Wilder Family Notes, VRC.

51. The Rigaud view is illustrated in Peter Willis, *Charles Bridgeman and the English Landscape Garden,* Studies in Architecture, 17 (London: A. Zwemmer, 1978), fig. 129. Charleston notice in *Charleston Courier* (Charleston, S.C.), December 31, 1807; William Buttre, *Longworth's American Almanac, New-York Register, and City Directory* (New York: David Longworth, 1810), n.p.

52. Schiffer, *Chester County Inventories,* p. 107; Boynton, ledger, and Thomas Boynton, ledger, 1817–47, and invoice book, 1815–25, DC (microfilm, DCM); Alling, daybook, and David Alling, ledgers, 1803–53 and 1815–18, invoice book, 1819–20, and receipt books, 1824–42 and 1844–56, NJHS (microfilm, DCM).

53. Cheney, daybook, and Silas E. Cheney, ledgers, 1799–1817 and 1816–22, LHS (microfilm, DCM); Elizabeth C. Barney Buel, *Chronicles of a Pioneer School* (Cambridge, Mass.: University Press, 1903), appendix D (student lists); Anthony Steel, estate records.

54. Holcomb, account book; anonymous cabinetmaker, ledger, 1824–40, PEM; curled maple

chairs in Branson, estate records; painted maple chairs in Parrott and Hubbell, insolvency records; Robbins, account book; Chauncy Strong, daybook, 1842–52, New York State Historical Association, Cooperstown (hereafter cited as NYSHA); Frances M. Trollope, *Domestic Manners of the Americans*, vol. 2 (London: Whittaker, Treacher, 1832), p. 77.

55. Charles F. Hummel, *With Hammer in Hand* (Charlottesville: University Press of Virginia, 1968), pp. 248–52.

56. Allen, memorandum book; Ebenezer Tracy, Sr., estate records.

57. Allen, memorandum book.

58. Ansel Goodrich, advertisement in *Hampshire Gazette* (Northampton, Mass.), September 16, 1795 (reference courtesy of Susan B. Swan). A labeled Goodrich rocking chair is in the Henry Ford Museum and Greenfield Village, Dearborn, Mich. (hereafter cited as Ford Museum). Other examples of Goodrich's work are illustrated in Evans, *American Windsor Chairs*, figs. 6-243 to 6-246. Ansel Goodrich, estate records, 1803, Hampshire Co., Mass., Registry of Probate.

59. Chase, account book.

60. Comparable Windsors are illustrated in Evans, *American Windsor Chairs*, figs. 6-33 (embellished spindles), 6-103 (hooklike crest ends), 6-18 (arm terminals).

61. Comparable Windsors are illustrated in Evans, *American Windsor Chairs*, figs. 6-109 (Tracy bamboowork), 6-168 (seat edges), 6-117 (crest profile), 6-122 (spindles). Thomas West, advertisement in *Connecticut Gazette* (New London), February 10, 1810. Other rocking chairs are enumerated in Titus Preston, ledgers, 1795–1817 and 1811–42, Yale; and Isaac Treby, estate records, 1809, New London, Conn., Genealogical Section, CSL.

62. Saxton family, estate records, Chittendon Co., Vt., Registry of Probate; property records, Town Clerk's Office, Shelburne, Vt.; vital records, State of Vermont, Division of Vital Records, Montpelier. Abby Maria Hemenway, ed., *Vermont Historical Gazetteer*, vol. 1 (Burlington, Vt.: A. M. Hemenway, 1868–91), pp. 862, 870, 877. Another Frederick (d. 1828, age twenty-six) and a Horace B. (d. ca. 1854) were brothers of George. Nehemiah Saxton (d. 1851, age eighty) may have been an older son of Frederick of Burlington (his son was Alonzo F., d. 1857, age sixty). A Webb Saxton who married in Shelburne in 1801, cannot be placed in this assembled genealogy. Perhaps he was still another son of Frederick. A recent publication, Kenneth Joel Zogry, *The Best the Country Affords: Vermont Furniture, 1765–1850* (Bennington, Vt.: Bennington Museum, 1995), p. 74, further confirms the Champlain Valley origin of the "Shelburne" rocker in stating that chairs of this pattern "have been found in local houses since the 1920s" and in citing a similar reference in a scrapbook owned in the 1920s by a Burlington resident.

63. Solomon Cole, account book, 1794–1809 (Glastonbury, Conn., 1800), CHS; Proud brothers, ledger, 1770–1825 (1816); Holcomb, account book (1825).

64. Joseph Griswold, account book, 1798–1804, DCM; William Ryder, inventory, 1806, DCM; Preston, ledger, 1795–1817; Reuben Loomis, account book, 1793–1836, CHS; Nathan Luther, bill to Captain Barton, October 19, 1802, Barton Papers, PEM; invoice of furniture shipped on

schooner *Madocawando*, February 10, 1812, vol. 2, Papers of Elijah Sanderson, PEM; Isaac Stone, bill to Ebenezer Fox, November 28, 1811, Papers of Ebenezer Fox and Family, PEM; high-top rockers in Boynton, ledger, 1811–17 (1815); high-back rockers in Benjamin Bass, estate records, 1819, Suffolk Co., Mass., Registry of Probate (microfilm, DCM) (document brought to author's attention by Page Talbott).

65. Comparable Tuttle chairs are illustrated in Evans, *American Windsor Chairs*, figs. 7-43, 7-44, 6-220 (arms). David Tilden, lawsuit vs. William Seaver, 1804, Colonial Court Records, Social Law Library, Boston, Mass. (hereafter cited as SLL) (reference courtesy of Charles A. Hammond and John T. Kirk).

66. Comparable Tracy chairs are illustrated in Evans, *American Windsor Chairs*, figs. 7-7 (slat type, seat), 7-6 (bamboowork).

67. Boynton, ledger, 1811–17; Alling, account book. Comparable New York chairs are illustrated in Evans, *American Windsor Chairs*, figs. 5-34 (spindles), 5-45 (arms), 5-37 (stretcher system). Marvin Clayton Hutchins, comp., *Our Ancestral Heritage* (Hilton, N.Y.: privately printed, 1961), pp. 16, 26, 38 (reference courtesy of Carroll Alton Means); David Goodell, estate records, 1817–18, Pomfret, Conn., and sale of right of redemption of Pomfret real estate to Zadock Hutchins, Jr., Killingly, Conn., April 1818, Genealogical Section, CSL; Zadock Hutchins, Jr., estate records, 1830, Pomfret, Conn., Genealogical Section, CSL.

68. Comparable New York chairs are illustrated in Evans, *American Windsor Chairs*, figs. 5-34, 5-40.

69. Giovanni Battista Piranesi, *Diverse maniere d'adornare i cammini ed ogni altra parte degli edifici* (Rome, 1769); Robert Adam and James Adam, *The Works in Architecture* (London, 1773–86), vols. 1, 2; [George] Hepplewhite, *The Cabinet-Maker and Upholsterer's Guide* (London, 1788); Thomas Sheraton, *The Cabinet-Maker and Upholsterer's Drawing-Book* (London, 1791–94).

70. *The London Chair-Makers' and Carvers' Book of Prices for Workmanship* (London, 1802); *Supplement to the London Chair-Makers' and Carvers' Book of Prices for Workmanship* (London, 1808); Thomas Hope, *Household Furniture and Interior Decoration* (1807; reprint, New York: Dover, 1971), including introduction, p. x; George Smith, *A Collection of Designs for Household Furniture and Interior Decoration* (1808; reprint, New York: Praeger, 1970), including introduction.

71. M. D. Leggett, comp., *Subject-Matter Index of Patents for Inventions Issued by the United States Patent Office from 1790 to 1873, Inclusive* (Washington, D.C.: Government Printing Office, 1874), vol. 1, p. 473; Gragg design observation in Charles F. Montgomery, *American Furniture: The Federal Period* (New York: Viking Press, 1966), p. 469; Smith, *Designs for Household Furniture*, pl. 79.

72. Patricia E. Kane, "Samuel Gragg: His Bentwood Fancy Chairs," *Yale University Art Gallery Bulletin* 33, no. 2 (Autumn 1971): 26–37. The account gives Gragg's birth date as October 25, 1772, at Peterborough, N.H., and relates that the young man went to New York State at about age twenty-one, where he remained for several years. He had resettled in Boston by September 10, 1801, when he married Elizabeth Hopkinson. Gragg's earliest city directory listing (1803) gives a boardinghouse address but mentions no trade, suggesting that he

worked as a journeyman and had not yet entered into partnership with William Hutchins.

73. A painted, peacock-feather fancy chair is illustrated in Montgomery, *Federal Furniture*, fig. 17. Robert L. Raley, "Interior Designs by Benjamin Henry Latrobe for the President's House," *Antiques* 75, no. 6 (June 1959): 568–71.

74. Advertisement, as quoted in "Clues and Footnotes," *Antiques* 107, no. 5 (May 1975): 939.

75. A second contoured-back pattern attributed to Gragg is illustrated in Evans, *American Windsor Chairs*, fig. 7-36.

76. Bass, estate records.

77. Comparable designs from plate 199 in Smith's *Guide* are illustrated in Evans, *American Windsor Chairs*, fig. 4-21. The Johnson sofa is illustrated in Dean A. Fales, Jr., *American Painted Furniture, 1660–1880* (New York: E. P. Dutton, 1972), pp. 186–87. Documented Hitchcock crown-top chairs are illustrated in John Tarrant Kenney, *The Hitchcock Chair* (New York: Clarkson N. Potter, 1971), facing p. 148, pp. 173–75, 180, 194–96. Documented crown-top rockers are known by Amos Denison Allen of Windham, Conn., Joel Pratt, Jr., of Sterling, Mass., A. J. Stephenson of Sangerville, Maine, and a member of the Wilder family of New Ipswich, N.H.

78. A Boston Grecian couch is illustrated in Page Talbott, "Boston Empire Furniture, Part I," *Antiques* 107, no. 5 (May 1975): 881. Josiah Prescott Wilder, daybook and ledger, 1837–59, Wilder Family Notes, VRC.

79. Luke Houghton, ledger B, 1824–51, Barre Historical Society, Barre, Mass. (hereafter cited as Barre; microfilm, DCM); Peirce, estate records; Felton, daybook; Wilder, daybook and ledger.

80. Richard Wright, advertisements in *Daily National Intelligencer* (Washington, D.C.), October 20, 1830, and November 25, 1831, as excerpted in Denker, *Rocking Chair Book*, p. 57; Gerard Beekman, inventory, 1833, DCM.

81. James C. Helme, book of prices, 1838, DCM; Robbins, account book.

82. Michael Allison, inventory, 1855, DCM; James Kain, estate records, 1838, DCM; *Catalogue of Elegant Household Furniture*, September 25, 1834 (Philadelphia: C. J. Wolbert, 1834), DCM; Ebenezer P. Rose, estate records, 1834–36, NJSL.

83. Felton, daybook.

84. The Hodges chair is illustrated in Page, *Litchfield County Furniture*, fig. 76. Smith, *Guide*, pl. 119. The chair with the shallow hollows on the crest top is illustrated in Zilla Ryder Lea, ed., *The Ornamented Chair* (Rutland, Vt.: Charles E. Tuttle, 1960), p. 126, figs. 22, 22a. Another chair is illustrated in Howard Pain, *The Heritage of Country Furniture* (New York: Van Nostrand Reinhold, 1978), fig. 296.

85. *Catalogue of... Furniture*, August 28, 1829 (Boston: Dorr and Allen, 1829), DCM; Edward Bulkley, advertisement in *New Haven Palladium* (New Haven), March 30, 1830 (reference courtesy of Wendell Hilt); Charles H. White, bill to James J. Skerrett, January 26, 1832, Papers of James J. Skerrett, Historical Society of Pennsylvania, Philadelphia, Pa. (hereafter cited as HSP); Sacket and Branch, bill to Richard W. Greene, May 3, 1833, A. C. and R. W. Greene Collection, RIHS; Boteller and Donn, advertisement in *Daily National Intelligencer*, April 10, 1833, as quoted in Anne Castrodale Golovin, "Cabinetmakers and

Chairmakers of Washington, D.C., 1791–1840," *Antiques* 107, no. 5 (May 1975): 908.

86. Crest variants are illustrated in Lea, *Ornamented Chair*, p. 129, fig. 32; p. 133, figs. 42, 43, 45; p. 137, figs. 56, 57. A balloon-back Windsor with a splat is illustrated in Evans, *American Windsor Chairs*, fig. 3-149.

87. Several ornamented crest pieces are illustrated in Lea, *Ornamented Chair*, pp. 129–32. Strong, daybook.

88. Another fancy-back rocker is illustrated in Lea, *Ornamented Chair*, p. 122, fig. 14. A Worcester County side chair with a similarly pierced front stretcher is illustrated in Evans, *American Windsor Chairs*, fig. 7-55. Robbins, account book.

89. Boynton, ledger, 1811–17; Allen, memorandum book.

90. The illustrated Toppan notice is in *Dover Directory* (Dover, N.H.: Samuel C. Stevens, 1830), p. 94. A Boston scroll-top chair and a Baltimore prototype are illustrated in Evans, *American Windsor Chairs*, figs. 7-39, 4-18.

91. Hitchcock crown-top rockers are illustrated in Kenney, *Hitchcock Chair*, pp. 194–95.

92. Thomas Willson, estate records, 1891, Washington Co., Vt., Registry of Probate.

93. Helme, book of prices.

94. The Old Sturbridge Village chair is pictured in Henry J. Harlow, "Decorated New England Furniture," *Antiques* 116, no. 4 (October 1979): 862.

95. The Connecticut Valley Historical Society chair is pictured in Nutting, *Furniture Treasury*, fig. 2466.

96. The second chair of this pattern is illustrated in Samuel Pennington, Thomas M. Voss, and Lita Solis-Cohen, *Americana at Auction* (New York: Dutton, 1979), fig. 68, right. Similar low-back chair extensions are illustrated in Little, *Asahel Powers*, figs. 10, 15, 16. The Woodstock-owned chair is illustrated in Lea, *Ornamented Chair*, p. 71, fig. 12. Comparable Windsors with pierced crests are illustrated in Evans, *American Windsor Chairs*, figs. 7-35, 7-84.

97. Comparable Windsors are illustrated in Evans, *American Windsor Chairs*, figs. 7-108 (Trowbridge chair), 7-110 (broad spindles). Both examples have the pendent-grape decoration.

98. Comparable Windsors are illustrated in Evans, *American Windsor Chairs*, figs. 6-34, 6-36, 6-37 (Rhode Island chairs), 6-128 (border chair). The Betts painting is illustrated in an advertisement of the Litchfield Auction Gallery, *Antiques and the Arts Weekly* (Newtown, Conn.), August 29, 1986.

99. Samuel S. May, Specification of Letters Patent, No. 7,418, June 4, 1850, U.S. Patent Office, Washington, D.C.; Olive Crittenden Robinson, "A Convertible Boston Rocker," *American Collector* 11, no. 8 (September 1942): 12–13; Rodris Roth, "Nineteenth-Century American Patent Furniture," in *Innovative Furniture in America from 1800 to the Present*, ed. David A. Hanks (New York: Horizon Press, 1981), pp. 23–46.

100. Pintard letter quoted in Dorothy C. Barck, ed., *Letters from John Pintard to His Daughter… 1816–1833*, vol. 1 (New York: New-York Historical Society, 1940), p. 84; Schiffer, *Chester County Inventories*, p. 322; Thomas Burling, advertisement in *Daily Advertiser* (New York), March 16, 1787, as quoted in Rita Susswein Gottesman, comp., *The Arts and Crafts in New York, 1777–1799* (New York:

New-York Historical Society, 1954), p. 111; George White, letter to Nicholas Low, February 10, 1804, Nicholas Low Collection, LC.

101. The Massachusetts and Pennsylvania chairs are illustrated in Santore, *Windsor Style*, 1: figs. 115–16. The "wings" of the Pennsylvania chair may be an early alteration carried out at the time the legs were shortened at the cylinder bottoms. The square-back chair with the nailhole evidence is illustrated in Evans, *American Windsor Chairs*, fig. 7-34. Thomas Sheraton, *Cabinet Dictionary*, vol. 1 (1803; reprint, New York: Praeger, 1970), p. 20.

102. Sibley, account book; Luke Houghton, ledger A, 1816–27, Barre (microfilm, DCM); John Martin, inventory, 1834, DCM; Abraham McDonough, estate records, 1852, Philadelphia Register of Wills (microfilm, DCM); William C. Gildersleeve, account book, 1825–43, DCM; Schiffer, *Chester County Inventories*, pp. 105, 107; Boynton, ledger, 1817–47; Nicholas Lechmere, confiscated loyalist estate, 1779, Newport, R.I., Rhode Island State Archives, Providence, R.I. (photostat, DCM). The cradle is itemized in Elisha Hawley, estate records, 1843, Monroe, Conn., Genealogical Section, CSL.

103. Comparable Windsors are illustrated in Evans, *American Windsor Chairs*, figs. 6-166 (leg tops), 6-25, 6-122 (feet), 6-155 (posts).

104. Nancy Mitford, *The Sun King* (New York: Harper and Row, 1966), p. 140. The Rigaud view and a London tradecard are illustrated in Evans, *American Windsor Chairs*, figs. 1-11, 1-30. Leak Oakover, inventory, March 25, 1765, Chancery Masters' Exhibits, C-110, no. 163, Public Record Office, London (hereafter cited as PRO).

105. Thomas Elfe, advertisement in *South Carolina Gazette* (Charleston, S.C.), January 7, 1751; William Long, advertisement in *Pennsylvania Packet* (Philadelphia, Pa.), September 10, 1785; both as quoted in Alfred Coxe Prime, comp., *The Arts and Crafts in Philadelphia, Maryland, and South Carolina, 1721–1785* (Philadelphia: Walpole Society, 1929), pp. 166, 174–75. William Long, advertisements in *Pennsylvania Packet*, July 11, 1788, and February 15, 1794, as quoted in Alfred Coxe Prime, comp., *The Arts and Crafts in Philadelphia, Maryland, and South Carolina, 1786–1800* (Topsfield, Mass.: Walpole Society, 1932), pp. 188–89; Lewis Hayt, advertisement in *Boston Gazette* (Boston, Mass.), January 25, 1796; Mrs. Charlton M. Theus, *Savannah Furniture, 1735–1825* (n.p.: By the author, ca. 1967), p. 21.

106. Schiffer, *Chester County Inventories*, p. 135; M. W. King, advertisement in *J. F. Kimball and Co.'s Eastern, Western, and Southern Business Directory* (Cincinnati: J. F. Kimball, 1846), p. 31; Abraham McDonough, advertisement in *Mercantile Register or Business Man's Guide* (Philadelphia, 1846), p. 104; J. C. Hubbard, advertisement in *Boston Directory for… 1860* (Boston: Adams, Sampson, 1860), p. 80.

107. James Hazlet, advertisement in William Richards, comp., *Utica City Directory, for 1843–'44* (Utica, N.Y.: Roberts and Henry H. Curtis, 1843), p. 144; John F. Barber, advertisement in *Wilmington Directory for 1845* (Wilmington, Del.: Lewis Wilson, 1845), p. 100; James Renshaw, inventory, 1857, as transcribed in Schiffer, *Furniture of Chester County*, p. 205.

108. Broadside, Sheboygan Manufacturing Co., Sheboygan, Wis., 1876, Smithsonian Institution (photograph, VRC); *A Victorian Chair for All Seasons: A Facsimile of the Brooklyn Chair Company Catalogue* (Watkins Glen, N.Y.: American Life Foundation, 1978); Charles L. Granquist, "Thomas Jefferson's 'Whirligig' Chairs," *Antiques* 109, no. 5 (May 1976): 1056–60.

109. Wye account in James E. Rogers, *A History of Agriculture and Prices in England from 1259 to 1793*, vol. 3 (1866–67), pp. 546–52; Hatfield Priory reference as quoted in *The Oxford English Dictionary*, s. v. *close-stool*; Lindsay Boynton, ed., "The Hardwick Hall Inventory of 1601," and Peter Thornton, "A Short Commentary on the Hardwick Inventory of 1601," in *Furniture History* 7 (1971): 1, 15–17, 32.

110. Estate records of John Jones, 1708, Patrick Gordon, 1736, and Elizabeth Carter, 1744, Philadelphia Register of Wills; Fussell, account book; Nancy A. Goyne (Evans), "Francis Trumble of Philadelphia, Windsor Chair and Cabinetmaker," in *Winterthur Portfolio 1*, ed. Milo M. Naeve (Winterthur, Del.: Winterthur Museum, 1964), p. 228; Schiffer, *Chester County Inventories*, pp. 315–16, 318–20, 325–26.

111. Philip Ludwell, inventory, 1767, as quoted in *Virginia Magazine of History and Biography* 21 (1913) (reprint, New York: Kraus Reprint, 1968), pp. 407–16; William Jevon, inventory, 1767, Lancaster County Historical Society, Lancaster, Pa. (hereafter cited as LCHS); Miller, account book; Alling, account book and daybook.

112. Proud brothers, daybook and ledger; Abner Haven, account book, 1809–18, DCM; Increase Pote, account book, 1824–30, Maine Historical Society, Portland (hereafter cited as MeHS); McDonough, estate records.

113. Gilbert Gaw, bill to Mrs. Elizabeth Fisher, August 16, 1799, DCM; Joseph Robinson, advertisement in *Dauphin Guardian* (Harrisburg, Pa.), May 15, 1809 (reference brought to author's attention by the late William Bowers); Steel, estate records; Miller, account book; Thomas Walter Ward II, inventory book, ca. 1838–45, DCM.

114. Gaines, account book.

115. Proud brothers, daybook and ledger; Landon, account book; Alling, daybook; Wilder, daybook and ledger; Charles Riley, estate records, 1842, Philadelphia Register of Wills (microfilm, DCM).

116. Edward Hazen, *Popular Technology: or, Professions and Trades*, vol. 1 (1846; reprint, Albany: Early American Industries Association, 1981), pp. 104–10; Robert P. Turner, ed., *Lewis Miller, Sketches and Chronicles* (York, Pa.: Historical Society of York County, 1966), p. 57.

117. John Nichols, inventory, 1813, DCM; Hazen, *Popular Technology*, 1:107.

118. William Taylor, estate records, 1832, Suffolk Co., Mass., Registry of Probate (microfilm, DCM); Hazen, *Popular Technology*, 1:110; Proud brothers, daybook and ledger; Silas E. Cheney, daybook, 1807–13, LHS (microfilm, DCM).

119. Baltimore Exchange Hotel, inventory, 1842, Baltimore Exchange Hotel Collection, Maryland Historical Society, Baltimore; W[illiam] Chambers, *Things as They Are in America* (Philadelphia: Lippincott, Grambo, 1854), pp. 93, 188.

120. William, Lord Byron, estate records, n.d., Chancery Masters' Exhibits, C-108, no. 4, PRO; Gordon, estate records.

121. Jedidiah Snowden, bill to John Reynell, October 14, 1754, Harrold E. Gillingham Collection, HSP; Thomas Jervis, estate records, 1761, Philadelphia Register of Wills (microfilm, DCM) (reference courtesy of Arlene Palmer Schwind); Alexander reference in Henry J. Berkley, "A Register of the Cabinet Makers and Allied Trades in Maryland, as Shown by the Newspapers and Directories, 1746 to 1820," *Maryland Historical Magazine* 25, no. 1 (March 1930): 9; Andrew Gautier, advertisement in *New York Gazette; or, Weekly Post Boy* (New York), June 6, 1765; Thomas Shirley, and Sheed and White, advertisements in *South Carolina Gazette*, December 17, 1765, and June 24, 1766, citation file, MESDA; Manigault inventory in Jones, *American Colonial Wealth*, 3:1543.

122. A slat-post chair and an early low-back chair are illustrated in Evans, *American Windsor Chairs*, figs. 3-1, 3-10.

123. The tall, southeastern Pennsylvania chair is illustrated in Evans, *American Windsor Chairs*, fig. 3-11. The settee with a mahogany rail is illustrated in Nancy Goyne Evans, "Striking Accents: Ornamental Hardwoods in the American Windsor," *Maine Antique Digest* (Waldoboro), December 1988, fig. 4.

124. Francis Trumble, bill to Hollingsworth and Rudolph, October 31, 1770, Gillingham Collection, HSP. Francis Trumble, bill to John Cadwalader, July 19, 1771; and William Cox, bill to Gen. John Cadwalader, October 1774; both in Cadwalader Collection, Gen. John Cadwalader, HSP. Lardner inventory in Jones, *American Colonial Wealth*, 1:214–15; bill of lading, brigantine *Charles Town Packet*, May 3, 1774, Bills of Lading of Uriah Woolman, 1772–75, HSP; Francis Trumble, advertisement in *Pennsylvania Gazette* (Philadelphia), December 27, 1775.

125. Shoemaker, Roberts, and Ferguson (Graeme Park) inventories in Thomas Lynch Montgomery, ed., *Pennsylvania Archives*, sixth series (Harrisburg, Pa.: Harrisburg Publishing, 1907), 12:653–54, 658, 710–12, 721, 723–26; Pennsylvania Statehouse references as given in a typescript catalogue of an "Exhibit of Eighteenth-Century Furniture," May 17 to September 30, 1952, organized by the National Park Service for a meeting of the Society of Descendants of the Signers of the Declaration of Independence at Independence National Historical Park, Philadelphia. See also David Stockwell, "Windsors in Independence Hall," *Antiques* 62, no. 3 (September 1952): 214–15.

126. Benjamin Betterton, inventory, 1786, DCM; John Lambert, estate records, 1793, Philadelphia Register of Wills; Anthony Butler (agent for John Penn), receipt book, 1788–99, DCM; William Cox, bill to General Henry Knox, May 19, 1795, Papers of Henry Knox, MeHS; Philadelphia Customhouse Papers, Outward Entries, May 1, 1785–August 31, 1786, HSP; Harrold E. Gillingham, "The Philadelphia Windsor Chair and Its Journeyings," *Pennsylvania Magazine of History and Biography* 55, no. 3 (October 1931): 301–32; Philadelphia Outward Foreign Entries, 1789–1803, including manifest of schooner *Polly*, November 28, 1789, and Outward Coastwise Entries, 1798–99, U.S. Customhouse Records, NA; Philadelphia Outward Coastwise and Foreign Entries, 1791–92, and Outward Foreign Entries, 1799–1801, U.S. Customhouse Records, French Spoliation Claims,

NA; import notice of ship *Clementina, South Carolina Gazette,* June 17, 1784, Prime Cards, WL.

127. Francis Trumble, bill to Cox(e) and Frazer, May 27, 1784, Coxe papers, Tench Coxe Section, HSP. The Taylor and King label is illustrated in William MacPherson Hornor, Jr., *Blue Book: Philadelphia Furniture* (1935; reprint, Washington, D.C.: Highland House, 1977), pl. 500. Manifests of ship *South Carolina*, October 4, 1796, and brig *Maria*, October 26, 1796, Philadelphia Outward Entries, U.S. Customhouse Records, French Spoliation Claims, NA. The Murphy consignments are listed in manifests of the brig *Maria*, July 15, 1797, Philadelphia Outward Coastwise Entries, U.S. Customhouse Records, and the brig *Eliza*, August 9, 1797, Philadelphia Outward Entries, U.S. Customhouse Records, French Spoliation Claims, NA.

128. The Letchworth and Steel settees are illustrated in Santore, *Windsor Style*, 1: figs. 185–86. A low-back, eight-legged settee closely related in its bamboowork to the one illustrated was once in the Philadelphia collection of Howard Reifsnyder. The Fox and Jonestown chairs are illustrated in Evans, *American Windsor Chairs*, figs. 3-101, 3-102.

129. The tall chair from southeastern Pennsylvania and the Frederick County side chair are illustrated in Evans, *American Windsor Chairs*, figs. 3-18, 3-82.

130. The Baltimore Museum's spindle-back bench is illustrated in William Voss Elder III and Jayne E. Stokes, *American Furniture, 1680–1880* (Baltimore, Md.: Baltimore Museum of Art, 1987), pp. 57–58. The daybed is illustrated in *Property from the Collection of the Late Helen Janssen Wetzel*, October 2–4, 1980 (New York: Sotheby Parke-Bernet, 1980), lot 1688.

131. The knuckle-arm settee is illustrated in Charles Santore, *The Windsor Style in America*, vol. 2 (Philadelphia: Running Press, 1987), p. 194. The chair with the barrel-shaped stretcher turnings is illustrated in Evans, *American Windsor Chairs*, fig. 3-9.

132. The comparable Frederick County Windsors are illustrated in Evans, *American Windsor Chairs*, figs. 3-82, 3-90. The Pennsylvania German table is illustrated in Beatrice B. Garvan and Charles F. Hummel, *The Pennsylvania Germans: A Celebration of Their Arts, 1683–1850*, (Philadelphia: Philadelphia Museum of Art, 1982), fig. 96.

133. Another eight-legged settee of this type is illustrated in [Homer Eaton Keyes], "Some Pennsylvania Furniture," *Antiques* 5, no. 5 (May 1924): 224, fig. 5. The smaller settee is illustrated in Santore, *Windsor Style*, 2: fig. 207. Chairs with comparable turnings are illustrated in Evans, *American Windsor Chairs*, figs. 3-63 (side stretchers), 3-80 (bamboo and baluster supports, stretchers).

134. Caleb Cresson, Sr., estate records, 1816, Philadelphia Register of Wills (microfilm, DCM).

135. Cox, bill to Knox. One of Knox's larger Philadelphia settees may be that illustrated in Ruth Davidson, "The League Exhibition," *Antiques* 86, no. 4 (October 1964): 392. It is described as coming from Knox's home in Thomaston, Maine, the house he retired to in 1796 after leaving Philadelphia. John B. Ackley, bill to Zacheus Collins, August 13, 1796; and Zacheus Collins, letter to John C. Heineken, September 8, 1796; both in Collins Papers, LC. Joseph Henzey, bill to Stephen Girard, August 7, 1791, Girard Papers, Girard College, Philadelphia, Pa. (hereafter cited as GC)

(microfilm, American Philosophical Society, Philadelphia, Pa. [hereafter cited as APS]).

136. Settees made by Steel are in the Philadelphia Museum of Art and Independence National Historical Park, Philadelphia. Sampson Barnet, advertisement in *Delaware Gazette* (Wilmington, Del.), October 10, 1789, as quoted in Charles G. Dorman, *Delaware Cabinetmakers and Allied Artisans, 1655–1855* (Wilmington: Historical Society of Delaware, 1960), p. 12.

137. A settee of undulating bow and arms is illustrated in Hornor, *Blue Book,* pl. 481. An armless settee is illustrated in Santore, *Windsor Style*, 2: fig. 215.

138. Andrew Gautier, advertisement in *New-York Gazette* (New York), April 18, 1765; Thomas Ash, advertisement in *Rivington's New-York Gazetteer*, February 17, 1774, as quoted in Rita S. Gottesman, comp., *The Arts and Crafts in New York, 1726–1776* (1938; reprint, New York: Da Capo Press, 1970), p. 110; John Aspinwall (d. 1774), inventory, 1786, DCM; William Rhinelander, estate records, 1785, New York Estates, New York Public Library (hereafter cited as NYPL). Jacob Vanderpool, advertisement in *Town and Country Journal, or the American Advertiser* (New York), December 11, 1783; and Gabriel Leggett, advertisement in *Daily Advertiser*, March 20, 1786; both as quoted in Gottesman, *Arts and Crafts, 1777–99*, pp. 123, 130. Thomas and William Ash, advertisement in *New-York Packet* (New York), October 7, 1784; Timpson and Gillihen, advertisement in *New-York Packet*, July 11, 1785; sailing notice of brig *Rockahock* in *Gazette of the State of Georgia* (Savannah), May 11, 1786, citation file, MESDA; Book of Inward Entries, District of Elizabeth River, Port of Norfolk, 1789, State Library of Virginia, Richmond; manifest of brig *Enterprize*, August 16, 1794, New York Outward Entries, U.S. Customhouse Records, French Spoliation Claims, NA; David Coutant, bill to John Beekman (including Schermerhorn), February 5, 1793, White-Beekman Papers, New-York Historical Society, New York (hereafter cited as NYHS); David Coutant, bill to Robert R. Livingston, April 19, 1788, Robert R. Livingston Papers, NYHS; John DeWitt, advertisements in *New-York Weekly Chronicle* (New York), June 18, 1795, and *New-York Daily Advertiser* (New York), January 2, 1798, as quoted in Gottesman, *Arts and Crafts, 1777–1799*, pp. 115–16.

139. The settee is illustrated in *Caroline H. Bertron Estate*, November 6–7, 1935 (New York: Rains Galleries, 1935), lot 563.

140. Manifest of brig *Rebecca*, December 22, 1789, New Haven, Outward Foreign Entries, U.S. Customhouse Records, French Spoliation Claims, NA; manifest of schooner *Union*, January 17, 1791, Fairfield-Bridgeport, Conn., Outward Foreign Entries, U.S. Customhouse Records, French Spoliation Claims, NA; Chappel and White, advertisement in *Farmer's Journal* (Danbury, Conn.), November 9, 1790, as quoted in David and Mary Lou Thomas, "A Tall Clock by William Chappel, Cabinetmaker of Danbury," *Connecticut Historical Society Bulletin* 31, no. 2 (April 1966): 55; John Wadsworth, bill to Statehouse, June 8, 1796, CHS; John and Horace Wadsworth, advertisement in *American Mercury*, November 7, 1796 (reference courtesy of Nancy E. Richards).

141. Comparable Rhode Island Windsors are illustrated in Evans, *American Windsor Chairs*,

figs. 6-42, 6-43. The members of the Tracy group were Ebenezer, Sr., Ebenezer, Jr., Elijah (son), Stephen (nephew), and Amos Denison Allen (son-in-law). For a discussion of the Tracy family and its work, see Evans, *American Windsor Chairs,* chap. 6, pp. 285–302.

142. The Boston Museum settee is illustrated in Randall, *American Furniture,* fig. 194. The second low-back settee is illustrated in Santore, *Windsor Style,* 2: fig. 210.

143. A documented Tracy Windsor chair with features relating to those in the low-back settee—swelled spindles, chestnut seat, crowned baluster heads—is illustrated in Evans, *American Windsor Chairs,* fig. 6-103, right.

144. The triple-back settee with the white pine seat is illustrated in Nancy Goyne Evans, "Identifying and Understanding Repairs and Structural Problems in Windsor Furniture," in *American Furniture 1994,* ed. Luke Beckerdite (Hanover, N.H.: University Press of New England for the Chipstone Foundation, 1994), p. 17, fig. 20. When Henry Francis du Pont purchased this settee from a coastal Connecticut dealer in 1959, it was said to be of regional origin. Two other examples were in Hartford collections in the 1920s or earlier. One of these (fig. 1-82), which was formerly in the Sykes collection, was exhibited in the Girl Scout Loan Exhibition at the American Art Galleries, New York, in 1929.

145. A short-loop settee is illustrated in Wallace Nutting, *A Windsor Handbook* (1917; 2d ed., Framingham and Boston: Old America Co., n.d.), p. 178. Nutting also introduced a triple-back settee to his reproduction line. His work can be recognized by the New York character of the turnings in the arm posts and the ten legs, and the fanlike bend of the spindles at either side of a center vertical within each arch. Knuckle arms and swelled spindles complete the design. The Nutting reproduction settee is illustrated in Wallace Nutting, *Supreme Edition General Catalogue* (1930; reprint, Exton, Pa.: Schiffer, 1977), fig. 515. Another antique settee is illustrated in an advertisement of John Walton, *Antiques* 108, no. 1 (July 1975): 20.

146. Job Danforth, Sr., ledger, 1788–1818, RIHS; Proud brothers, ledger. Manifests of sloop *Aurora,* July 10, 1790; April 26, May 3, June 5, July 7, 21, and December 9, 1791; April 21, July 6, and September 28, 1792; September 3, 1793; May 21 and August 18, 1794; August 1, 21, and September 14, 1795; all in Newport, R.I., Inward and Outward Entries, U.S. Customhouse Records, FRC-Waltham.

147. The Ford Museum settee is illustrated in Robert Bishop, *The American Chair* (1972; reprint, New York: Bonanza Books, 1983), fig. 278. Another Rhode Island double chair is illustrated in Nutting, *Furniture Treasury,* fig. 1643.

148. Comparable Rhode Island and border Windsors are illustrated in Evans, *American Windsor Chairs,* figs. 6-61 (necked baluster base), 6-163 (bud turning). Another small, Rhode Island settee of high-back form without the bow is illustrated in *American Furniture,* December 3–5, 1931 (New York: National Art Galleries, 1931), lot 449.

149. Ebenezer Stone, advertisement in *Independent Chronicle* (Boston, Mass.), April 13, 1786; manifests of sloop *Hercules* and schooners *Pomona* and *Almira,* June 4, August 3, and September 3, 1799, Philadelphia Outward Coastwise Entries,

U.S. Customhouse Records, NA; William Seaver, advertisement in *Columbian Centinel* (Boston, Mass.), May 29, 1793, and April 20, 1796; manifest of ship *Pattern,* January 10, 1798, Boston-Charlestown, Mass., Outward Entries, U.S. Customhouse Records, French Spoliation Claims, NA; James C. Tuttle, advertisement in *Salem Gazette* (Salem, Mass.), August 19, 1796; Ansel Goodrich, advertisement in *Hampshire Gazette* (Northampton, Mass.), September 16, 1795 (reference courtesy of Susan B. Swan).

150. The Boston cross-stretcher side chair and bow-back armchair are illustrated in Evans, *American Windsor Chairs,* figs. 6-209, 6-215.

151. The settee once belonged to Wallace Nutting and is illustrated in *Furniture Treasury,* fig. 1637; it is also illustrated in Santore, *Windsor Style,* 1: fig. 191. Comparable Windsors are illustrated in Evans, *American Windsor Chairs,* figs. 6-59, 6-141, 6-221 (crest volutes), 6-219 (Tuttle chairs).

152. The Ivy Hill settee is at MESDA.

153. Manifest of ship *Active,* May 25, 1784, Philadelphia Outward Entries, Customhouse Papers, HSP; Chandless, advertisement in *Baltimore Daily Repository* (Baltimore, Md.), January 9, 1791, as quoted in Prime, *Arts and Crafts, 1786–1800,* p. 172; George McCandless and Jacob Small, Jr., estate records, June 1, 1793, and October 24, 1794, Baltimore Co., Md., Inventories (microfilm, DCM). Manifests of schooners *Betsy* and *Patsy* (November 30, 1796), *Rachel* (March 7 and December 14, 1797), *Experiment* (June 2 and August 8, 1798), *Bee* (March 12, 1799), and *Sally* (December 19, 1799); brig *Eleanor* (June 9, 1797); ship *Abigail* (June 16, 1798); sloop *Hercules* (March 18, 1799); and *Thetis* (August 23, 1799); all in Baltimore Outward Entries, U.S. Customhouse Records, French Spoliation Claims, NA.

154. Manifests of sloop *Nancy,* September 12, 1785, and brig *Friendship,* November 6, 1784, Philadelphia Outward Entries, Customhouse Papers, HSP; Robert McKeen, advertisement in *Virginia Gazette, and Petersburg Intelligencer* (Petersburg), September 6, 1793, citation file, MESDA; David Ruth, bill to Peyton Skipwith, November 6, 1797, Peyton Skipwith Papers, Swem Library, College of William and Mary, Williamsburg, Va. (hereafter cited as WM); George Mason, inventory, January 10, 1797, Rockbridge Co., Va., Registry of Probate (reference courtesy of Margaret Beck Pritchard). Vosburgh and Childs, advertisement in *Hall's Wilmington Gazette* (Wilmington, N.C.), February 9, 1797; Hopkins and Charles, advertisement in *City Gazette and Daily Advertiser* (Charleston, S.C.), March 7, 1798; both in citation file, MESDA. Humiston and Stafford, advertisement in *Charleston City Gazette and Advertiser* (Charleston, S.C.), November 29, 1798, as quoted in Prime, *Arts and Crafts, 1786–1800,* p. 184.

155. A serpentine-top settee is illustrated in Patricia E. Kane, *300 Years of American Seating Furniture* (Boston: New York Graphic Society, 1976), fig. 197. A manuscript copy of the Gilbert Gaw label is in the Girard Papers, GC (microfilm, APS).

156. A settee of varied back height is illustrated in Nutting, *Furniture Treasury,* fig. 1640. A curved-plank settee is illustrated in Santore, *Windsor Style,* 2: fig. 218.

157. Comparable Philadelphia and Baltimore fancy Windsors are illustrated in Evans, *American Windsor Chairs,* figs. 3-120, 4-7, 4-12.

158. Estate of Daniel Trotter, household goods taken by Ephraim Haines (son-in-law) at the appraisal, December 31, 1800, DCM; George Halberstadt, estate records, 1812, Philadelphia Register of Wills; Commodore John Barry, inventory, 1803, DCM; John Craig, estate records, 1807–8, Philadelphia Register of Wills.

159. Philadelphia Outward Coastwise Entries, 1800–1811, U.S. Customhouse Records, NA; New Orleans entry, manifest of ship *John,* January 3, 1804, Philadelphia Outward Foreign Entries, U.S. Customhouse Records, NA; Philadelphia Outward Foreign Entries, 1803–10, U.S. Customhouse Records, NA; Girard Papers; Charles C. Robinson, daybook, 1809–25, HSP.

160. Schiffer, *Chester County Inventories,* p. 120; Gilbert Burnett and Joseph Robinson, advertisements in *Pennsylvania Republican* (Harrisburg), November 3, 1812, and January 16, 1813 (notices brought to author's attention by the late William S. Bowers); Edwin R. Mulhern, advertisement in *Klines Gazette* (Carlisle, Pa.), 1806 (reference courtesy of Milton E. Flower).

161. John Karnes, advertisement in *American Citizen and General Advertiser* (New York), October 6, 1801; and William Challon, advertisement in *Mercantile Advertiser* (New York), July 24, 1802; both as quoted in Rita Susswein Gottesman, comp., *The Arts and Crafts in New York, 1800–1804* (New York: New-York Historical Society, 1965), pp. 138, 148. Joseph Vail, inventory, 1805, DCM.

162. James Barron, inventory, 1803, DCM; Rev. John Murray, letter to William Palmer, July 23, 1803, Papers of Rev. John Murray, 1799–1810, NYHS.

163. William Buttre, advertisement in *Longworth's Directory* (1810), n.p.; William Ash I, insolvency record, 1811, Historical Documents Room, Queens College, Flushing, N.Y. At Ash's death in 1815 settees and "Settee Seats" were among the shop materials enumerated in his estate inventory (DCM). New York Outward Entries, 1799–1802, U.S. Customhouse Records, French Spoliation Claims, NA; manifest of sloop *Concord,* August 1, 1800, Newport, R.I., Inward and Outward Entries, U.S. Customhouse Records, FRC-Waltham; G. and F. Penny, advertisement in *Columbian Museum and Savannah Advertiser* (Savannah, Ga.), January 22, 1808, as quoted in Theus, *Savannah Furniture,* p. 89; Thomas Howard, advertisement in *Providence Gazette* (Providence, R.I.), April 3, 1813, as quoted in Wendell D. Garrett, "Providence Cabinetmakers, Chairmakers, Upholsterers, and Allied Craftsmen, 1756–1838," *Antiques* 90, no. 1 (October 1966): 517.

164. Phyllis Kihn, "Captain Solomon Ingraham," *Connecticut Historical Society Bulletin* 29, no. 1 (January 1964): 26; manifest of schooner *Experiment,* November 16, 1805, New London, Conn., Outward Foreign Entries, U.S. Customhouse Records, FRC-Waltham; Thomas and David S. West, advertisement in *Connecticut Gazette,* April 20, 1807; Lee, estate records; Allen, memorandum book; manifest of sloop *Candidate,* October 25, 1817, New London, Conn., Outward Coastwise Entries, U.S. Customhouse Records, FRC-Waltham.

165. Samuel J. Tucke, bill to Francis Dana, July 31, 1802, Dana Papers, MHS; Tilden, lawsuit vs. Seaver; Mabel M. Swan, *Samuel McIntire, Carver, and The Sandersons, Early Salem Cabinet Makers*

(Salem, Mass.: Essex Institute, 1934), p. 28; invoice of cargo for schooner *Patty*, October 26, 1801, Salem, Mass., Customhouse Records, PEM; Jonathan Paddock, estate records, 1810, Nantucket Co., Mass., Registry of Probate.

166. Boynton, ledger, 1811–17; Abel Wilder, advertisement in *New Hampshire Sentinel* (Keene, N.H.), August 7, 1807, Wilder Family Notes; Henry Beck, advertisement in *New Hampshire Gazette* (Portsmouth, N.H.), September 20, 1808, New Hampshire Notes; David Teirs, advertisement in *Upper Canada Gazette* (Toronto), January 23, 1802, as quoted in Shackleton, *Furniture of Old Ontario*, p. 21; Jay Humeston, advertisement in *Nova Scotia Royal Gazette* (Halifax), November 23, 1804, as quoted in George MacLaren, "The Windsor Chair in Nova Scotia," *Antiques* 100, no. 1 (July 1971): 124.

167. Silas Cooper, advertisements in *Columbian Museum and Savannah Advertiser*, December 18, 1801, and *Republican and Savannah Evening Ledger* (Savannah, Ga.), October 31, 1809, and March 3, 1810, citation file, MESDA; Alexander Walker, advertisement in *Virginia Herald* (Fredericksburg), July 13, 1802, and April 26, 1805, citation file, MESDA; John and Hugh Finlay, advertisement in *Federal Gazette and Baltimore Daily Advertiser* (Baltimore, Md.), November 8, 1805, as quoted in William Voss Elder III, *Baltimore Painted Furniture, 1800–1840* (Baltimore: Baltimore Museum of Art, 1972), p. 11. Francis Younker, advertisement in *American and Commercial Daily Advertiser* (Baltimore, Md.), September 12, 1810; George Kearns, advertisement in *Martinsburg Gazette* (Martinsburg, W.Va.), April 5, 1811; Matthew Wilson, advertisement in *Farmer's Repository* (Charles Town, W.Va.), February 12, 1813; all in citation file, MESDA. David Russel, memorandum of an agreement with Isaac Smith, February 4, 1803, Handley Library, Winchester, Va. (reference courtesy of Neville Thompson).

168. Hector Sanford, advertisement in *Scioto Gazette* (Chillicothe, Ohio), December 26, 1805, as quoted in a letter from John R. Grabb to the author, December 3, 1978; Jane E. Sikes, *The Furniture Makers of Cincinnati 1790 to 1849* (Cincinnati: By the author, 1976), pp. 89, 134, 205, 227; William Challen, advertisement in *Kentucky Gazette and General Advertiser* (Lexington), May 9, 1809, citation file, MESDA; Charles McKarahan, advertisement in *Nashville Clarion*, October 5, 1810, as quoted in Beasley, "Tennessee Cabinetmakers and Chairmakers," p. 618.

169. Comparable fancy and Windsor chairs having ornamental medallions are illustrated in Evans, *American Windsor Chairs*, figs. 3-118 (fancy), 3-120, 4-7 (Windsor).

170. Elder, *Baltimore Painted Furniture*, figs. 42–44; Stiles Tuttle Colwill, *Francis Guy, 1760–1820* (Baltimore: Maryland Historical Society, 1981), pp. 75–85.

171. Walters, *Furniture Makers of Indiana*, pp. 31–32; Reverend Ambrose Edson, estate records, 1836, Somers, Conn., Genealogical Section, CSL.

172. The chair with a Keene history is in a private collection. The Powers portrait is illustrated in Little, *Asahel Powers*, fig. 1.

173. Comparable Windsors are illustrated in Evans, *American Windsor Chairs*, figs. 7-35 (stretcher medallion), 7-44 (legs), 7-2 (Providence owner), 7-50 (Taunton chairmaker), 7-7 (Connecticut chair).

174. Comparable chairs are illustrated in Evans, *American Windsor Chairs*, figs. 7-60, 7-61 (Worcester Co.), 8-33 (Nova Scotia).

175. Aaron Boughman, Charles Robinson, Anthony Steel, Thomas Millard, and Benjamin Love, estate records, 1813, 1825, 1817, 1818, and 1821, Philadelphia Register of Wills.

176. Comparable Moon chairs are illustrated in Evans, *American Windsor Chairs*, fig. 3-135.

177. Philadelphia Outward Coastwise and Foreign Entries, 1815–21, U.S. Customhouse Records, NA; J. H. Stevenson and Co., export book, 1822–26, DCM.

178. Alling, ledger, 1815–18; Charles Fredericks, advertisement in *Longworth's American Almanac, New-York Register and City Directory* (New York: David Longworth, 1815), n.p.; John K. Cowperthwaite and William Brown, advertisements in *Longworth's City Directory* (1818), pp. 7, 10; Whitehead Fish, Abraham Brinckerhoff, Lewis Bancel, and John C. Vanden Heuvel, inventories, 1819, 1823, 1828, and 1826, DCM; Carman Smith, advertisement in *The Portico* (Huntington, N.Y.), July 20, 1826, Cabinetmaker File, NYSHA; George C. Jewett, Bates and Johnson, and Davis and Bussey, advertisements in *Albany Directory* (1819), n.p.; Gerrit Visscher, advertisement in *Klinck's Albany Directory* (Albany: E. and E. Hosford, 1822), n.p.

179. Henry Barney, advertisement in *Connecticut Courier* (Bridgeport), April 9, 1823 (reference courtesy of Wendell Hilt); manifest of sloop *Candidate*; Silas Cheney, ledgers; Daniel Munger, advertisement in *Franklin Herald and Public Advertiser* (Greenfield, Mass.), Sept. 28, 1824, as quoted in Peter Rippe, "Daniel Clay of Greenfield" (Master's thesis, University of Delaware, 1962), p. 47; Low and Damon, advertisement in *New-Hampshire Patriot* (Concord), February 6, 1816, as illustrated in Donna-Belle Garvin, James L. Garvin, and John F. Page, *Plain and Elegant, Rich and Common, 1750–1850* (Concord: New Hampshire Historical Society, 1979), p. 149; Joan MacKinnon, *Kingston Cabinetmakers, 1800–1867*, National Museum of Man Mercury Series (Ottawa: National Museums of Canada, 1976), pp. 12, 14; and MacKinnon, *A Checklist of Toronto Cabinet and Chair Makers, 1800–1865*, National Museum of Man Mercury Series (Ottawa: National Museums of Canada, 1975), p. 68.

180. John Underwood, "Household Furniture purchased . . . in 1822," in Robert Underwood, account book, 1795–1804, Private collection (photostat, DCM); John Hand, Jr., bill of freight to John Lloyd, May 3, 1817, John Lloyd Collection, LC. N. Blasdell advertisement in *Alexandria Herald* (Alexandria, Va.), January 3, 1820; Hobday and Barnes, advertisement in *Richmond Enquirer* (Richmond, Va.), October 30, 1816; both in citation file, MESDA. Harrison reference in William M. S. Rasmussen, "Living with Antiques: The Oaks, Richmond, Virginia," *Antiques* 13, no. 5 (May 1978): 1064–65.

181. Joel Brown, advertisement in *North Carolina Star* (Raleigh), March 29, 1822; Grimes and Cooper, advertisement in *Western Carolinean* (Salisbury), February 4, 1822; William Culverhouse, advertisement in *Catawba Journal* (Charlotte, N.C.), October 10, 1826; all as quoted in Craig, *Arts and Crafts*, pp. 197, 202, 205–6, 214, 221.

Northern Warehouse, advertisement in *City Gazette and Commercial Advertiser* (Charleston, S.C.), March 27, 1819, as cited in E. Milby Burton, *Charleston Furniture, 1700–1825* (Charleston, S.C.: Charleston Museum, 1955), p. 9; Davenport inventory, as quoted in Theus, *Savannah Furniture*, pp. 21–22.

182. Samuel Stibbs, advertisement in *Cincinnati Directory* (Cincinnati: Robinson and Fairbank, 1829), n.p.; McSwiney and Barnes, advertisement in *Louisville Public Advertiser* (Louisville, Ky.), March 1, 1820, citation file, MESDA. Sherwood and Dodd, advertisement in *Nashville Whig* (Nashville, Tenn.), January 8, 1823; S. Williams, advertisement in *Nashville Clarion*, January 6, 1818; and James Bridges, advertisement in *Knoxville Register*, August 24, 1819; all as quoted in Beasley, "Tennessee Cabinetmakers," pp. 613–14, 621.

183. A roll-top rocking settee is illustrated in Harlow, "Decorated New England Furniture," p. 866, pl. 18. Bates and Johnson, advertisement in Pearce, *Albany Directory* (1819), n.p. The Johnson roll-top settee is illustrated in John L. Scherer, "Labeled New York Furniture at the New York State Museum, Albany," *Antiques* 119, no. 5 (May 1981): 1125, figs. 19, 19a. Alling, ledger, 1803–53.

184. Holcomb, account book; Samuel Church, advertisement in *Constitution* (Toronto, Canada), July 19, 1836, as illustrated in Mackinnon, *Toronto Cabinet and Chair Makers*, p. 29; William H. Mapes, advertisement in *Rising Sun Journal*, September 29, 1838, as illustrated in Walters, *Furniture Makers of Indiana*, p. 145; Charles van Ravenswaay, *The Anglo-American Cabinetmakers of Missouri, 1800–1850* (St. Louis: Missouri Historical Society, 1958), p. 250; Wilder, daybook and ledger; Peter A. Willard, estate records, 1842–43, Worcester Co., Mass., Registry of Probate; Calvin Stetson, account book, 1843–57, DCM. Erastus Jones, advertisement in *Morning News* (New London, Conn.), March 27, 1845; and George W. Smith, advertisement in *Aurora* (Norwich, Conn.), April 29, 1846 (both references courtesy of Wendell Hilt).

185. Rocking chairs with similar arms are illustrated in Kenney, *Hitchcock Chair*, pp. 198–99. Comparable Windsors are illustrated in Evans, *American Windsor Chairs*, figs. 5-49 (Prince of Wales feathers, ringed spindles), 5-40 (arrow stretchers), 5-45 (spindle disks).

186. An Allwine settee is illustrated in Jane Sikes Hageman, *Ohio Furniture Makers, 1790 to 1845* (Cincinnati: By the author, 1984), p. 83. The Cumberland-spindle settee is illustrated in Dean A. Fales, Jr., *The Furniture of Historic Deerfield* (New York: E. P. Dutton, 1976), fig. 180.

187. Branson and Riley, estate records; Lester Rich, advertisement in *Doylestown Democrat* (Doylestown, Pa.), January 11, 1831 (reference courtesy of Wendell Hilt); Jacob Fillman, advertisement in *Der Advocat* (Sumneytown, Pa.), July 4, 1827 (reference courtesy of Frederick S. Weiser); Yarnal reference in Schiffer, *Chester County Inventories*, p. 120.

188. Helme, book of prices; Joseph Jones, advertisement in *Chester County Democrat* (Downingtown, Pa.), November 23, 1830 (reference courtesy of Wendell Hilt); Joseph Jones, bill to Benjamin Sharpless, May 13, 1842, as quoted in Schiffer, *Furniture of Chester County*, p. 134 (see also pp. 43, 48, 108–10, 127–29, 179, 181, 226–27 for competitors);

William G. Beesley, daybook, 1828–36, Salem County Historical Society, Salem, N.J.

189. Frederick Fox, advertisement in *Berks and Schuylkill Journal* (Reading, Pa.), April 26, 1845; and John F. Schroder, advertisement in *Lancaster Union* (Lancaster, Pa.), February 15, 1842; John Swint, advertisements in *Lancaster Examiner and Herald* (Lancaster, Pa.), April 14, 1847, and December 13, 1848; all in Advertisement File, LCHS. George W. Boyd, estate records, 1863, Dauphin Co., Pa., Register of Wills; William E. Willis, advertisement in *Erie Observer* (Erie, Pa.), April 20, 1833 (reference courtesy of Wendell Hilt).

190. A. and E. Brown, advertisement in *King's Rochester City Directory and Register* (Rochester, N.Y.: Welles and Hayes, 1840), n.p.; Miles Benjamin, ledger, 1821–29, NYSHA; Nathaniel Rose (Rose and Sykes), advertisement in *New-York Enquirer* (New York, country edition), February 2, 1827 (reference courtesy of Wendell Hilt); Anonymous (Philip I. Arcularius, Jr.), advertisement in *Brooklyn Directory for 1832–33* (Brooklyn, N.Y.: William Bigelow, 1832), p. 99; Alling, ledger, 1803–53, and daybook.

191. Daniel Proud, estate records, 1833, Providence, R.I., Registry of Probate; Joel Pratt, Jr., and Son, broadside advertisement, Hartford, Conn., 1840, Ford Museum; T. Deland, bill to Daniel W. Rogers, April 7, 1829, Papers of Daniel W. Rogers, PEM. Bennett and Piggott, advertisement in *New-Bedford* (Mass.) *Mercury,* August 3, 1832; and William Bates and Thomas Allen's New York–style Windsor; both as quoted and illustrated in Elton W. Hall, "New Bedford Furniture," *Antiques* 113, no. 5 (May 1978): 1112, fig. 9, and 1118; Merriam and Holden, bill to H. H. Bigelow, November 25, 1856, DCM.

192. Dewey and Woodworth, advertisement in *Vermont Gazette* (Bennington), November 12, 1827, Bennington Museum, Bennington, Vt.; Henry F. Dewey, account book, 1837–64, Shelburne Museum, Shelburne, Vt. (microfilm, DCM); Wilder, daybook and ledger; Marshall Spring, estate records, 1849, Oxford Co., Maine, Registry of Probate; Samuel Church, advertisement in *Constitution,* July 19, 1836, as illustrated in Mackinnon, *Toronto Cabinet and Chair Makers,* p. 29.

193. Hamilton and Kevan, letter to Humberston Skipwith, May 8, 1832, Peyton Skipwith Papers, WM; Washington G. Henning, advertisement in *Lewisburg Chronicle* (Lewisburg, W. Va.), February 24, 1853 (reference courtesy of Anne C. Golovin).

194. Lee and Skinner, source not given (Cincinnati), May 1, 1822; and Lee, advertisement in *Cincinnati Directory* (1829); both as quoted or illustrated in Sikes, *Furniture Makers,* pp. 141–42; see also pp. 126, 145, 175–76, 189, 205, 207, 217–20, 258–59. Nelson Talcott, daybook, 1839–48, DCM; J. Jones, advertisement in *Western Sun* (Vincennes, Ind.), June 20, 1829, as quoted in Walters, *Furniture Makers of Indiana,* p. 122; Sherwood and Dodd, advertisement in *Nashville Whig,* June 16, 1823, as excerpted in Beasley, "Tennessee Cabinetmakers and Chairmakers," p. 614; John Overton, inventory, 1833, Claybrooke-Overton Collection, Tennessee State Library, Nashville, Tenn. (reference courtesy of Mrs. Lawrence Dortch).

195. White data in Lea, *Ornamented Chair,* p. 64.

196. Comparable Baltimore and related Windsors are illustrated in Evans, *American Windsor Chairs,* pl. 16, fig. 4-17.

197. The Baltimore Museum of Art chairs are illustrated in Elder, *Baltimore Painted Furniture,* p. 82. *London Book of Prices* (1802), pl. 6, no. 10; *Second Supplement to the London Chair-Makers' and Carvers' Book of Prices for Workmanship* (London: T. Sorrell, 1811), pl. 1, no. 7; *The New-York Book of Prices for Manufacturing Cabinet and Chair Work* (New York: J. Seymour, 1817), pl. 6, no. K-3.

198. The sofa is illustrated in Elder, *Baltimore Painted Furniture,* pp. 56–57. Hope, *Household Furniture,* pl. 45.

199. Alling, ledger, 1803–53; Pote, account book.

200. The Hovenden painting is illustrated in "Collectors' Choice: From the Collection of Mr. and Mrs. Lawrence A. Fleischman," *Antiques* 86, no. 5 (November 1964): 575. The Nees Windsor is illustrated in Evans, *American Windsor Chairs,* fig. 3-147.

CHAPTER TWO

Production of Children's Furniture and Miniatures

Children's Furniture

EARLY EVIDENCE OF CHILDREN'S PAINTED SEATING

Through the mid nineteenth century attitudes toward the nurture and status of children were changing. Infant and child mortality remained at high levels. Still, parents were strongly attached to their children, much like parents of today. The loss of an infant son born while he was away from home was a grievous blow to the merchant-magistrate Samuel Sewall of Boston (d. 1730). Cotton Mather, the New England divine (d. 1728), knew the agony of absenting himself from the cradleside of an infant in convulsions to minister to his congregation. At Sabine Hall in the northern neck of Virginia, Colonel Landon Carter recorded an expression of tenderness toward a grandchild in 1770 when he and the child crossed the Rappahannock River by boat: "The wind and tide against, & the boat so small, we were 33 minutes getting opposite to Col. Fauntleroy's; it being very cold, & my little grandson with me, unwilling to freighten him, his first trip by water, we turned into the Col's."[1]

Both parental love and the desire for convenience are expressed in the acquisition of furniture scaled to infant or child size. Cradles, low chairs, and highchairs predominate, but specialized articles were also available. Children's furniture dating before the mid eighteenth century usually was rush-bottomed. John Jones, a Philadelphia merchant who died in 1708, kept a child's chair and "old Cradle" in the house, possibly for the grandchildren. Early records for neighboring Chester County, Pennsylvania, list chairs for children, beginning in 1717. In 1723 in the Joseph Coeburn household at Aston, two children's chairs stood in the parlor, and the household even had a children's room. John Gaines II of Ipswich, Massachusetts, recorded the sale of "little" chairs priced at 3s. beginning in 1726. The item "to bottom a little chair" confirms the general type.[2]

The Philadelphia accounts of Solomon Fussell contain many references to children's rush-bottom seating produced during the 1740s. The usual price was 2s.6d. to 3s., although in 1742 the chairmaker sold a "Rake back" child's chair for 4s.6d. A year later he made one of the several "4 Slat" chairs named in the accounts and in 1748 constructed "2 Brown Childrens Chairs without Armes." Black and "white" chairs are also mentioned; the latter term identifies seating without paint or stain. Among Fussell's customers for children's furniture were a barber and a gunsmith. Other chairmakers who produced children's rush-bottom seating in the prerevolutionary years include Solomon Legare, Jr., of Charleston, South Carolina, and William Barker of Providence, who fabricated a child's "grat" (arm) chair for the merchant John Brown in 1765. When appraisers enumerated the contents of Daniel Jones's Philadelphia shop in 1766, they counted a total of "24 Childrens Chairs" on the premises, all with rush bottoms.[3]

Windsor seating for children was in production by 1759, when the Philadelphia merchant Garrett Meade purchased a dozen Windsor chairs and "one D[itt]o for a child" at 10s. from Francis Trumble. Another "Windsor Chaire for a Child" was acquired by John Cadwalader for his daughter Nancy in 1772 at a cost of 12s. In New York James Beekman recorded a cash payment on October 27, 1762, "for 2 Childrens Green Chairs," although he did not indicate whether they were made locally or imported. Children's Windsor furniture was also carried in the flourishing seaborne trade. Seating arrived in quantity at Charleston, South Carolina, where in 1766 the merchants Sheed and White advertised "childrens dining and low chairs" imported in the brigantine *Philadelphia Packet*. Also in the mid 1760s, Francis Trumble consigned Windsor seating to Tobias Rudolph at Head of Elk (Elkton), Maryland; the Maryland merchant retained a child's chair for family use. One little Windsor and a cradle stood in the Philadelphia parlor of innkeeper John Edwards in 1767. In the postwar period a "Childs Green Arm'd Chair" was recorded among the possessions of the Nantucket widow Dinah Jenkins. Green paint, the prevailing finish on Windsor furniture until the 1780s, often identified plank-seat furniture in written records.[4]

CHILDREN'S LATE EIGHTEENTH-CENTURY "LOW" SEATING

Although the rush-bottom child's chair remained in use after the Revolution, Windsors gradually became more popular. The Proud brothers of Providence continued to make and "bottom" rush-seated "Littel" chairs, as they had before the war, although the price increased from 3s. to 4s.6d. In 1801 they recorded "a Littel Chair wooden Bottmed" at 5s.; by 1803 their standard charge for a "Littel Green Chair" had risen to 7s.6d. Saint George Tucker of Williamsburg, Virginia, acquired Windsor seating for his children from the New York shop of Thomas Ash and William Ash in 1786. Thirty-eight little Windsors were shipped to Charleston from Philadelphia between August 20 and October 1, 1789, and the trade to that city continued during the 1790s. By 1798 children's Windsors were being exported to overseas destinations, such as Surinam. At this date David Ruth of Granville County, North Carolina, had already supplied children's low chairs and highchairs to the Skipwith family at Prestwould plantation in adjacent Mecklenberg County, Virginia. Maryland inventories of the 1790s identify children's Windsors in the Baltimore area. In Philadelphia, the estate of cabinetmaker Daniel Trotter, valued in 1800, contained a "child's windsor chair." By then the local industry was sufficiently well established that chairmakers probably routinely stockpiled parts to frame children's chairs. A shop inventory made after John Lambert's premature death in 1793 itemizes both "Bottoms" and sets of "Sticks" for children's Windsors.[5]

Chairmakers in New England were also producing children's Windsors. In Glastonbury, Connecticut, woodworker Solomon Cole switched from making children's rush-bottom chairs to producing wooden-bottom seating by 1800. Isaac Senter, a leading physician in Newport, Rhode Island, began to replace his household seating in 1786. The addition of sturdy wooden-bottom chairs for the children was a wise move in view of the considerable cost in furniture repair incurred by this family as the children were growing up. The records of Amos Denison Allen in South Windham, Connecticut, document a steady demand for children's Windsors in the late 1790s; the recorded price was 6s. to 7s. Only twice did customers call for a "little Chair Kitchen" at 3s.—that is, a rush-bottom chair. James Chestney probably offered both wooden- and rush-bottom seating for children at Albany in 1797, since the cut illustrating his advertisement includes Windsor, slat, and fiddle-back chairs of adult size.[6]

A rare commentary on the use of painted seating in daily life is found in a letter written at Boston on March 19, 1799, by Reverend John Murray to his friend, the New York chairmaker William Palmer. Palmer's gift of a child's fancy or Windsor chair aroused considerable excitement in the Murray household:

O, my Friend, could you see the extasy my little girl is . . . in, consequent on seeing her little Chair, . . . which but this moment arrived, you would be delighted—her Mama don't act as she does, but she is full as much pleased—They both wish for an opportunity of thanking you for the

Fig. 2-1 Child's high-back Windsor armchair, Rhode Island, 1785–1800. White pine (seat, microanalysis); H. 27¹⁄₁₆″, (seat) 8⅝″, w. (crest) 14⅛″, (arms) 14¼″, (seat) 13½″, D. (seat) 11⅛″. (Museum of Art, Rhode Island School of Design, Providence, gift of Mrs. Henry Vaughan: Photo, Winterthur.)

Fig. 2-2 Child's sack-back Windsor armchair, Philadelphia, 1780–90. H. 28″, (seat) 12⅜″, w. (arms) 16⅞″, (seat) 15⅜″, D. (seat) 11″. (Private collection: Photo, Winterthur.)

prittiest Chair they ever saw. . . . My attention is again drawn to my little girl and her chair—she places it in different directions—she beholds it with wonder—with transport—with love—she comes up to me, and kisses me, was there ever, Papa so beautiful a Chair. Well, said I what shall I say to Mr Palmer—for, after all, it is to him you are obliged—give him thanks, and tell him that I wish I knew anyway in which I would testify my gratitude.[7]

Windsor chairs made for children follow the patterns developed for adult seating, scaled to appropriate size; some examples are more successful adaptations than others. Records almost never differentiate between patterns when itemizing children's Windsors, although they usually distinguish in some way between highchairs for feeding and low chairs for sitting. The rarest child's Windsor is the low-back chair, of which few survive. Children's high-back chairs are also rare, and this pattern has unfortunately become a target for the faker's art in the twentieth century. Among genuine examples is a chair of Rhode Island origin, as identified by the deep V cut under the crest scrolls, the oxbow arm pieces, the large caps in the leg balusters, the conical post tops, and the well-modeled oval seat (fig. 2-1, pl. 1). The proportions are not the best, since the back is out of scale with the base, but the turnings above and below the plank are in accord, and the overall design possesses considerable individuality. One unusual feature is the counterclockwise carving of the crest volutes.[8]

With the introduction of the sack-back pattern and the start of large-scale production in the postrevolutionary years, more children's seating entered the market. Earliest in style is a Philadelphia chair with ball-foot legs (fig. 2-2). In typical Philadelphia fashion, the bow tips are squared and the spindles are noticeably enlarged below the arm rail. The bulbous turning at the base of the posts places the chair in the postwar period. This feature was introduced to selected sack- and fan-back seating during the 1780s, as confirmed by documented chairs. The posts are further drilled at the top to accommodate a restraining rod (figs. 2-17 to 2-19). This chair once had knuckle arm terminals. Another example, with the knuckles intact, is supported on legs ending in tapered feet; the seat is branded by Joseph Henzey. A third Philadelphia sack-back child's chair, marked by Anthony Steel, has full bamboo-style supports.[9]

Fig. 2-3 Child's sack-back Windsor armchair, Rhode Island, 1785–95. White pine (seat); H. 27″, (seat) 11″, W. (arms) 17¼″, (seat) 14½″, D. (seat) 10″. (Peabody Essex Museum, Salem, Mass.: Photo, Winterthur.)

Fig. 2-4 Child's sack-back Windsor armchair, attributed to the Tracy family, eastern Connecticut, 1790–1800. Yellow poplar (seat) with maple and oak (microanalysis); H. 22⅛″, (seat) 9⅞″, W. (arms) 17¼″, (seat) 15⅜″, D. (seat) 11⅝″. (Edgar and Charlotte Sittig collection: Photo, Winterthur.)

Fig. 2-5 Child's sack-back Windsor armchair, New York, 1785–95. Yellow poplar (seat) with maple and oak (microanalysis); H. 25″, (seat) 11⁷⁄₁₆″, W. (arms) 18″, (seat) 14¼″, D. (seat) 11⅜″. (Winterthur 86.3.)

New England sack-back seating is represented in part by a Rhode Island chair having a plank bottom of pronounced triangular form, a type sometimes associated with children's Windsors of the area (fig. 2-3). Further links with the region include the prominent ridge at the center front of the seat; the suggestion of a ledge on the plank, forward of the spindle platform; the pronounced, rounded pads forming the arm terminals; and the prominent caps in the baluster and spool turnings.[10]

Sack-back work from eastern Connecticut and New York City further extends the pattern range (figs. 2-4, 2-5, pl. 2). Both chairs have heavy bows. Typically for each area, one bow has pointed ends, while the other has squared, shoelike tips. The profiles of the turnings and the bulbous spindles contrasted with the tapered ones demonstrate further regional variation. The roundwork of figure 2-4 exhibits features typical of Tracy family production, with some modification of proportions. Also present are other trademarks of this family's work, including round-tipped stretchers; a thick, canted-edge plank; and mitten-type arm terminals. The New York chair (fig. 2-5, pl. 2) reveals its lineage in similar fashion, from the large, robust turnings and oval, rounded-edge seat to the simple arm pads slightly canted at the front tips.[11]

The continuous-bow chair is a classic design in American Windsor-chair making. A remarkable example of this pattern is the deftly crafted child-size seat of figure 2-6. For its small size, the chair has excellent proportions and superb turnings; the extra-embellished spindles and braced back make it remarkable. Published over the years as a Rhode Island chair, this distinctive Windsor has individual elements that are much more akin to New York work: the full-saddled seat with its slightly drooping front corners and the round elements of the legs, arm supports, and medial stretcher. A child's chair of similar pattern, branded by Walter MacBride, closely resembles it in the turnings, seat, and outward belly of the bow above the arm bend. Several adult chairs labeled by the Ash brothers, Thomas I and William I, have vase-turned back spindles similarly accented by small beads in the upper part of the sticks.[12]

Children's fan-back chairs were made in Pennsylvania and in New England. Turnings range from the full baluster to the full bamboo style. Of particular interest is a group of four fan-back chairs in the rare armchair form, ranging in height from 21½ to 29¾ inches. All the chairs were constructed in the region of Rhode Island and southeastern Massachusetts (figs. 2-7 to 2-10). Each of these Windsors is distinctive, yet the greatest distance between any two of the four shops represented probably was less

Fig. 2-6 Child's continuous-bow Windsor armchair, New York, 1790–1800. Yellow poplar (seat, microanalysis) with maple, oak, and other woods; H. 25¼″, (seat) 12⅛″, W. (arms) 15″, (seat) 12½″, D. (seat) 12⅝″. (H. Richard Dietrich, Jr., collection: Photo, Winterthur.)

Fig. 2-7 Child's fan-back Windsor armchair, Nantucket, Mass., 1795–1805. White pine (seat) with maple and oak; H. 28¾″, (seat) 10⅝″, W. (crest) 18⅛″, (arms) 20⅛″, (seat) 13¼″, D. (seat) 10⅜″. (Private collection: Photo, Winterthur.)

Fig. 2-8 Child's fan-back Windsor armchair, Cape Cod, Mass., 1795–1805. White pine (seat, microanalysis); H. 29¾″, (seat) 11¾″, W. (crest) 11¾″, (arms) 21⅛″, (seat) 14⅝″, D. (seat) 12⅜″. (The late Elvyn G. Scott collection: Photo, Winterthur.)

than 100 miles. A Nantucket Windsor (rear view), recovered from an island family, and a Cape Cod chair (front view) are two examples of this group (figs. **2-7**, **2-8**). The features in the Nantucket chair are copied from those in full-size island seating, allowing for individual interpretation. Because the total seat depth is only 14 inches, the craftsman did not have to construct the plank and rear projection in two parts, as he would have for an adult Windsor of this type. The stark simplicity of the Cape Cod chair is a striking contrast. The legs are copies of those in a chair attributed to Samuel Wing of Sandwich, who began his chairmaking career about the mid 1790s. The thick, flat, angular arms are stylistically earlier than those found in the lath-supported arms of figure 2-9.[13]

Further regional variation is seen in figures **2-9** and **2-10.** The first chair is a close copy of an adult-size Windsor of rare design. The full-size and small chairs share similar structures, including lath-supported arms that are possibly unique and squared-shield planks; the smaller seat is made of curled maple, the larger one of white pine. The leg turnings are quite similar, given the differences in length. Almost certainly the crest tips in the child's chair once had small projecting volutes like those in the large Windsor. Some resemblance between figures 2-9 and 2-10 may be noted in the elongated baluster turnings of the back posts. The double-ogee crest of figure 2-10 has a close mate in a chair from the Connecticut–Rhode Island border. Obvious Rhode Island features include the elongated spool turnings of the back posts, the angular forward-scroll arms, the flat-chamfered plank edges, and the thick tapered feet with pointed toes. The absence of stretchers is rare in American work, although a child's settee from the same general region is also without braces (fig. 2-48).[14]

Production of Children's Furniture and Miniatures 147

Fig. 2-9 Child's fan-back Windsor armchair, Rhode Island, 1795–1805. Curled maple (seat) with maple and oak; H. 21½″, (seat) 8″, W. (crest) 11½″, (arms) 14¾″, (seat) 11⅝″, D. (seat) 11½″; crest tips broken off. (Private collection: Photo, Winterthur.)

Fig. 2-10 Child's fan-back Windsor armchair, Rhode Island, 1790–1800. H. 24¼″, (seat) 10⁵⁄₁₆″, W. (crest) 14½″, (arms) 13⅛″, (seat) 11⅞″, D. (seat) 9⅛″. (Private collection: Photo, Winterthur.)

Children's bow-back Windsors made at the end of the eighteenth century show surprising variety, at a time when the adult seat was mass-produced. Examples range from the Middle Atlantic region to New England and include chairs with baluster- and bamboo-turned supports. Two special and rare designs of Philadelphia origin are illustrated in figures **2-11** and **2-12.** The spindle-back chair is documented to the shop of Joseph Henzey and is one of two known examples. The design appears to be an early interpretation of the bow-back Windsor, since baluster leg turnings are almost unknown in Philadelphia work of that pattern. Two other factors support an early date for this chair. One is the bow design, which consists of the lower half of two fan-back posts joined in a continuous arch; the other is an incised inscription cut twice into the plank bottom of a companion chair at Colonial Williamsburg, which reads "I S L / 1787." The slat-back Windsor of figure 2-12 follows an adult pattern associated with the shop of John Letchworth. The design is based upon high-style joined mahogany seating current to the postwar Philadelphia furniture market. This chair may be the only child-size example of this pattern.[15]

A rare interpretation of the bow-back style in children's seating originated in the shop of a Pennsylvania German craftsman (fig. **2-13**). The long, narrow proportions of the seat and back are the reverse of those usually found in adult seating of similar origin. Unmistakable Pennsylvania German characteristics include a bow face with a narrow, centered channel; a flat-chamfered seat back; a dual leg system with ball-foot front legs and tapered back feet; stretchers with slight swellings at the tips; and double-scored baluster turnings, reflecting Delaware Valley rush-bottom work.[16]

Small bow-back Windsors from New England, with and without arms, are shown in figures **2-14** and **2-15.** The armchair, probably of Rhode Island origin, exhibits strong influence from both the adjacent Connecticut border region and New York. The beaded, flat-faced bow without much bulge or a waist is found in all three areas; the thickened spindles and hollow cone turnings of the post bases are common in New York work. The forward scroll arms and the thin, saddled and chamfered forward seat edges are more typical of Rhode Island seating (fig. 2-10). Full-swelled balusters are

Fig. 2-11 Child's bow-back Windsor side chair, Joseph Henzey (brand "I·HENZEY"), Philadelphia, ca. 1787–90. H. 23½″, W. 14½″. (Hagley Museum and Library, Wilmington, Del.)

Fig. 2-12 Child's bow-back Windsor side chair, possibly John Letchworth, Philadelphia, ca. 1796–1802. (Former collection J. Stogdell Stokes.)

Fig. 2-13 Child's bow-back Windsor side chair, region of Lancaster County, Pa., 1790–1805. Yellow poplar (seat) with maple and other woods; H. 27¼″, (seat) 11⅜″, W. (seat) 11″, D. (seat) 12¾″. (Historical Society of York County, York, Pa.: Photo, Winterthur.)

Fig. 2-14 Child's bow-back Windsor armchair, Rhode Island, 1790–1800. Maple and other woods; H. 28¼″, (seat) 13½″, W. (arms) 12¾″, (seat) 12″, D. (seat) 10⅞″. (Private collection: Photo, Winterthur.)

Fig. 2-15 Child's bow-back Windsor side chair, Rhode Island, 1790–1800. Yellow poplar (seat) with maple, hickory, and oak (microanalysis); H. 28″, (seat) 13⅝″, W. (seat) 13⅜″, D. (seat) 13⅝″. (Winterthur 64.823.)

Production of Children's Furniture and Miniatures 149

present in the work of all three areas, although when combined with a bulbous upper turning, as shown, the pattern is more typical of Rhode Island and New York. The narrow, cylindrical spools and broad, thick ring turnings of the legs, common in New York work, may also be noted in coastal New England seating.

The bow-back side chair (fig. 2-15) is more easily placed. The back elements—the bow face, curve, and spindle profile—and the seat shape parallel those of the armchair. The key to identification lies in the spools and rings of the leg turnings. Profiles of comparable broad, compressed form appear in several Rhode Island chairs. Among examples of the small bow-back side chair are others of obvious Rhode Island origin that have balloon-style bows and full rounded turnings in the manner of figure 2-14. A plain side chair supported on bamboo-turned legs braced by cross stretchers probably originated farther north in the Boston area.[17]

CHILDREN'S HIGHCHAIRS THROUGH 1800

The survival of some early turned or wainscot English highchairs (baby chairs) documents the use of this tall form from at least the sixteenth century. Both twist-turned and caned examples are known from the late seventeenth century. John Claudius Loudon described the function of the "child's high chair" in his encyclopedia (1833): "To be used when [the child] first begins to sit at table. There is a bar or stick put across between the arms, to keep the child from falling out, and sometimes there is a footboard. A child in average health is put into such a chair when about twelve or fourteen months old." Eighteenth-century children seem to have behaved much like those of today at mealtime; an early volume on child behavior (1701) admonished young children: "Eat not too fast nor with Greedy Behavior. Eat not vastly but moderately. Make not a noise with thy Tongue, Mouth, Lips, or Breath in Thy Eating and Drinking. Smell not of thy Meat; nor put it to Thy Nose; turn it not the other side upward on Thy Plate."[18]

Only the rare manuscript document describes particular features of the highchair. In June 1771 "a Mahogany Child's Chair wth a Table before it" was shipped to London by Gillows of Lancashire, England. Still, use of the feeding tray seems to have been uncommon until well into the following century. Some American highchairs had restraining bars, as described by Loudon, particularly in the eighteenth century, but the footrest was rare and the feeding tray unknown until well into the nineteenth century. Most footrests in place today were added at a later date.[19]

Rush-bottom highchairs preceded those of Windsor design in American use. The shop accounts of John Gaines II in Ipswich, Massachusetts, record the sale of a "child table chair" in September 1726. A similar chair sold three years later for 5s. Philadelphia chairmaker Solomon Fussell recorded this form on several occasions in 1739; Benjamin Franklin acquired a highchair at the shop in 1743–44, about the time of his daughter Sarah's birth. In Providence, Rhode Island, there were occasional calls at William Barker's shop for a "childs highcheer" in 1754 and later; his price in 1775 was 6s.[20]

The earliest reference to the Windsor highchair dates from June 1766, when the merchants Sheed and White of Charleston, South Carolina, announced the arrival of Windsor furniture from Philadelphia, including "childrens dining and low chairs." Similar Philadelphia merchandise was still available in the city at the end of the century. The Boston "Childs Table Chair" supplied for 8s. to Major General Henry Knox by cabinetmaker Stephen Badlam in October 1784 may have been of Windsor construction in view of the price; Badlam had sold Knox "kitchen Chairs" with rush bottoms at only 3s.8d. apiece a month earlier. Highchairs sold in postwar Providence by the Proud brothers, Daniel and Samuel, appear to have been of Windsor design; the price varied from 7s.2½d. to 9s. One patron was also a customer for a set of six family dining chairs. Merchant Elias Hasket Derby of Salem, Massachusetts, bought "table" and low chairs for children in 1798 from the local craftsman Jedidiah Johnson. Three years later, in December 1801, woodworker Amos Denison Allen of South Windham,

Fig. 2-16 Ralph Earl, *Mrs. William Taylor and Child*, Connecticut, 1790. Oil on canvas; H. 48½″, w. 38″. (Albright-Knox Art Gallery, Buffalo, N.Y.)

Fig. 2-17 Child's high-back Windsor highchair, Philadelphia, 1755–65. Yellow poplar (seat) with maple, ash, and oak (microanalysis); H. 40⅜″, (seat) 23½″, w. (crest) 18⅜″, (arms) 17⅛″, (seat) 16⅛″, D. (seat) 13⁹⁄₁₆″; footrest not original, paint and decoration old but not original. (Winterthur 64.924.)

Connecticut, sold a "high little Chair for child to sit at Table" for 6s.6d. Two related highchairs by the Tracy family are known today (fig. 2-25).[21]

The rising popularity of the highchair and the increasing prominence of Windsor furniture in daily life by 1790 are illustrated in Ralph Earl's portrait of Mrs. William Taylor of New Milford, Connecticut, and her young son, Daniel (fig. 2-16). If purchased in the general area of New Milford, the Taylor highchair could have been made by any of several contemporary western Connecticut craftsmen in the communities of Danbury, Litchfield, and Ridgefield. The sack-back pattern illustrated was only one of several current designs.

The first Windsor highchair design in the American market was the Philadelphia high-back pattern (fig. 2-17), which, with necessary modifications, followed adult seating of prerevolutionary date. More than half a dozen ball-foot examples are known, and most of these have some features in common. The hand of Francis Trumble seems to be represented in the illustrated chair from the Winterthur collection. The design resembles several full-size high-back chairs, one bearing Trumble's brand, in the thin wafers capping the arm-post balusters and in the profile of the double-baluster medial stretcher. The crest with its single-sweep scrolls relates to another high-back chair, which may have originated in Trumble's shop. Variant highchair patterns introduce carved volutes with a short preliminary cut at the base or a medial stretcher of plain, bulbous center. The present highchair is in superb condition, retaining its original feet. It has an outer coat of medium yellow paint, which with the decoration was applied in about the 1820s or 1830s. The footrest is a later addition (and restored), but the arm posts were always drilled to receive a rod, or guard, to confine the child. In a later version, long tapered feet are substituted for the cylinder-and-ball supports, and the undercarriage has a plain, swelled medial stretcher. Other changes include bulbous post tops and turnings of a variant profile.[22]

Fig. 2-18 Child's sack-back Windsor highchair, John B. Ackley (brand "ɪ·ʙ·ᴀᴄᴋʟᴇʏ"), Philadelphia, ca. 1786–95. Yellow poplar (seat) with maple, oak, and hickory; ʜ. 37⅛", (seat) 21⅜", w. (arms) 16¼", (seat) 14⅞", ᴅ. (seat) 10¼"; footrest not original. (Private collection: Photo, Winterthur.)

Fig. 2-19 Child's sack-back Windsor highchair, probably Francis Trumble or Joseph Henzey, Philadelphia, 1780–90. Yellow poplar (seat) with maple, oak, and hickory; ʜ. 35⁷⁄₁₆", (seat) 20⅜", w. (arms) 17¹⁄₁₆", (seat) 15¼"; ᴅ. (seat) 10¼"; medial stretcher probably replaced. (Private collection: Photo, Winterthur.)

Fig. 2-20 Child's sack-back Windsor highchair, Michael Stoner (brand "ᴍ·sᴛᴏɴᴇʀ"), Harrisburg or Lancaster, Pa., ca. 1793–1800. Yellow poplar (seat) with maple, oak, and hickory (microanalysis); ʜ. 33½", (seat) 19¼", w. (arms) 16⅜", (seat) 14¹¹⁄₁₆", ᴅ. (seat) 10⁵⁄₁₆"; upper structure patched. (Winterthur 66.537.)

The sack-back chairs illustrated in figures **2-18** and **2-19** represent Philadelphia work of the early postrevolutionary period. The chair in figure 2-18 is documented to the shop of John B. Ackley; that in figure 2-19 was made by Francis Trumble or Joseph Henzey, as suggested by a comparison of the legs with adult seating. Trumble is more likely to have been the maker, since a virtually identical highchair, which descended in a family of Georgetown, District of Columbia, bears the initials "FT" painted in green on the plank bottom. Although the arm posts of both chairs are pierced to accommodate a rod (the rod shown in figure 2-19 is a modern replacement), the top element in the Ackley chair has been updated to a standard bulbous shape. The same profile is inverted at the post bases in the Trumble chair. The D-shaped planks have rounded edges in place of the earlier flat-chamfered profile. One of the most significant elements of these chairs is the leg design. The support had to be lengthened in the highchair form, and craftsmen developed several approaches to address this need. The chair in figure 2-19 is framed with legs having balusters of medium length, while that in figure 2-18 introduces two patterns, one formed of two short, stacked balusters, the other consisting of a baluster of long length. Stacked balusters were also used in several high-back baby's chairs with knuckle arms made by Joseph Henzey. Which of these patterns is the most successful? Each has merit, but a better solution is illustrated in figure 2-24.

The Pennsylvania German highchair of figure **2-20,** documented to the Harrisburg or Lancaster shop of Michael Stoner, resembles Philadelphia work, with the substitution of an oval plank as befits its late date of ca. 1793–1800. Although there is some restoration to the bow, rail, and arm supports, the rarity of a chair that can be documented to the shop of a Pennsylvania German craftsman offsets that condition. Pennsylvania German mannerisms are evident in the swelled stretcher tips and the flared tops and necked bases of the baluster turnings (fig. 2-13). Other details of Stoner's style include the low, squared bow with blocked tips, the Philadelphia-style knuckle arms, and the hollow cone turnings at the arm-post bases.

Fig. 2-21 Child's sack-back Windsor highchair, Philadelphia, ca. 1785–90. Yellow poplar (seat, microanalysis); H. 34⅞″, (seat) 20¼″, w. (arms) 16″, (seat) 14¼″, D. (seat) 10¾″; footrest not original. (Private collection: Photo, Winterthur.)

Fig. 2-22 Child's sack-back Windsor highchair, John B. Ackley (label), Philadelphia, ca. 1794–1806. Yellow poplar (seat) with maple, oak, and hickory (microanalysis); H. 37⅛″, (seat) 22⅜″, w. (arms) 17¾″, (seat) 14⅞″, D. (seat) 10³⁄₁₆″; footrest not original, outer arm terminals replaced. (Winterthur 65.2036.)

Two Philadelphia sack-back chairs executed in the bamboo style of the late eighteenth century are contrasted in figures **2-21** and **2-22**. Figure 2-21 is the earlier in date and represents the first and most successful flowering of the Windsor bamboo style in Philadelphia. The grooved sections are carefully turned with swells and hollows, and a peculiar cuplike profile is present at each foot and in the side stretchers. The arm posts are deliberately styled to accommodate a rod. Although turned round, the top swells are shaved flat at the side faces. The "cuplike" interpretation of the bamboo turning lasted only a year or two in Philadelphia.

The highchair in figure 2-22 bears the label of John B. Ackley. Comparison with figure 2-21 identifies it as a stylistically later and less imaginative turned product. The arm posts, which are inordinately heavy, would have been more successful if inverted. Comparison with Ackley's earlier highchair (fig. 2-18) shows that the bows and planks in the two tall seats are essentially the same. The label fixed to the seat bottom bears the name and address of the printer Richard Folwell, who occupied the identified premises at 33 Arch Street from 1794 to 1796. During the same years and until 1807 Ackley's shop was in North Front Street.

A provincial interpretation of the bow-back highchair originated in the Pennsylvania-Maryland border region encompassing Adams and Frederick counties (fig. **2-23**). This unusual design, recognized by its distinctive curving arms and drooping, scrolled terminals, relates to other regional seating, some examples of which have family histories (fig. 1-87). The highchair turnings exhibit a transitional state between the full baluster and full bamboo styles; characteristically, the bamboowork is vigorously swelled at the nodules. Arm-post turnings follow those of another area pattern; the side stretchers have swelled ends in the manner of Pennsylvania German work from Lancaster and York counties. An unusual detail is the stamped ornament on the seat platform, which loops around the spindles. It is similar in concept, though not in execution, to platform decoration in several other border chairs. As expected in this inland

Fig. 2-23 Child's bow-back Windsor highchair and detail of punchwork, area of Frederick County, Md., and Adams County, Pa., 1800–1810. Yellow poplar (seat) with maple, oak, and hickory (microanalysis); H. 34⁹/₁₆″, (seat) 20¹³/₁₆″, W. (arms) 17″, (seat) 14⅞″, D. (seat) 11¾″. (Winterthur 54.82.)

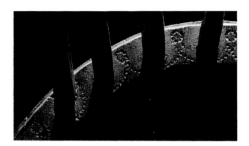

rural location, the basic design dates from the late 1700s, but the actual work falls at the beginning of the 1800s.[23]

Shifting the regional focus, two well-turned and well-proportioned sack-back highchairs of New York and Connecticut origin provide still another solution to the problem of the long leg design in the highchair (figs. **2-24, 2-25**). Much of the extra length is added successfully to the tapered, cylindrical feet. The chairs, which share basic design elements, permit a comparison between New York City work and that produced by the Tracy family in neighboring New London County, Connecticut. Starting at the top, the high forms feature bow tips typical of their regions, the squared foot of New York and the tapered point of New England. Contrasted in the arm rails are the canted-edge, circular pads of New York origin and the mittenlike grips common in eastern Connecticut. The spindles are shaped with either the thickened tapers consistent with New York design or the bulbous swells typical of eastern Connecticut. The oval, rounded-edge New York seat with a centered pommel is more sculptural than the New England plank, which is formed with a flat-canted edge and a forward-pointing projection. The profiles of the legs and stretchers show the rounded swells and narrow, cylindrical spools favored in New York and the slim roundwork and broad, compressed spools typical of Connecticut. Stephen Tracy's chair also includes two features associated with later Tracy family production: double-scored bamboo turnings (under the arms) and a triple-swelled medial stretcher. Another sack-back highchair branded by Stephen's cousin Elijah Tracy has many similar features, although the arm supports are baluster turned and the leg turnings are more bulbous.[24]

The sack-back highchair was one of the most popular eighteenth-century patterns. Further regional diversity is illustrated in two Rhode Island Windsors, probably of Providence origin (fig. **2-26**). Almost identical in upper structure, the chairs demonstrate again how two local craftsmen (or one chairmaker at different times) approached the problem of the long leg design. Starting with the S-post pattern, well known in the

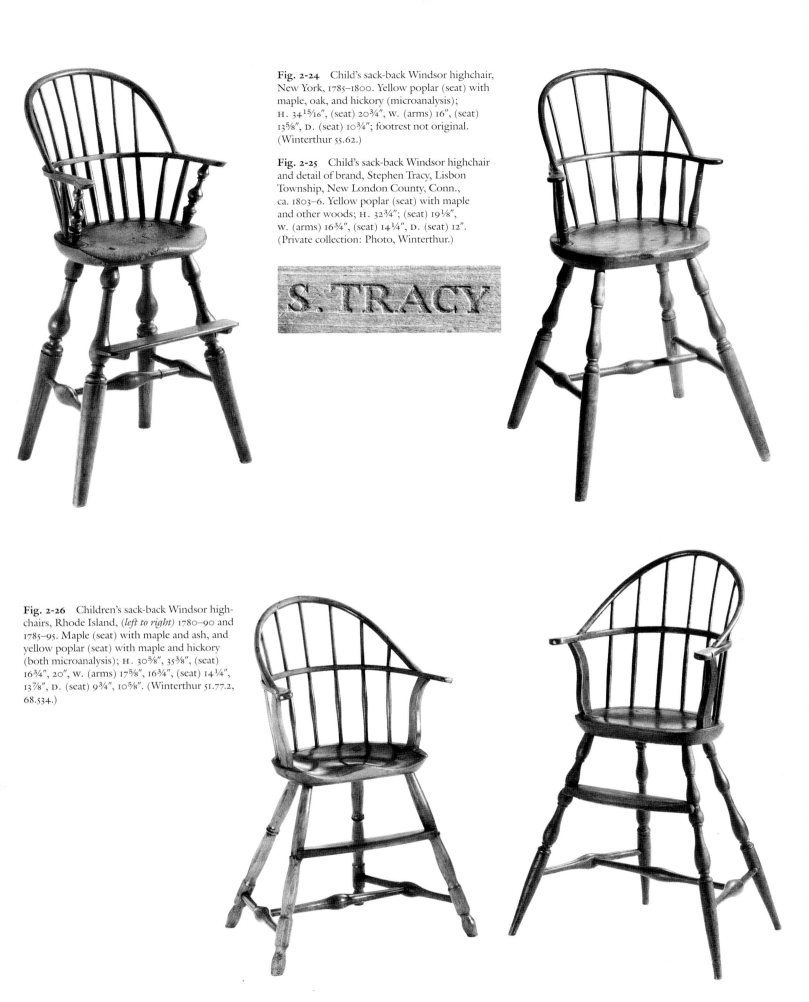

Fig. 2-24 Child's sack-back Windsor highchair, New York, 1785–1800. Yellow poplar (seat) with maple, oak, and hickory (microanalysis); H. 34¹⁵⁄₁₆″, (seat) 20¾″, W. (arms) 16″, (seat) 13⅝″, D. (seat) 10¾″; footrest not original. (Winterthur 55.62.)

Fig. 2-25 Child's sack-back Windsor highchair and detail of brand, Stephen Tracy, Lisbon Township, New London County, Conn., ca. 1803–6. Yellow poplar (seat) with maple and other woods; H. 32¾″; (seat) 19⅛″, W. (arms) 16¾″, (seat) 14¼″, D. (seat) 12″. (Private collection: Photo, Winterthur.)

Fig. 2-26 Children's sack-back Windsor highchairs, Rhode Island, *(left to right)* 1780–90 and 1785–95. Maple (seat) with maple and ash, and yellow poplar (seat) with maple and hickory (both microanalysis); H. 30⅝″, 35⅜″, (seat) 16¾″, 20″, W. (arms) 17⅝″, 16¾″, (seat) 14¼″, 13⅞″, D. (seat) 9¾″, 10⅝″. (Winterthur 51.77.2, 68.534.)

Fig. 2-27 Child's continuous-bow Windsor
highchair, Rhode Island, ca. 1792–1800. Footrest
not original. (Private collection: Photo, George
E. Schoellkopf.)

Fig. 2-28 Child's continuous-bow Windsor
highchair, Connecticut–Rhode Island border
region, 1790–1800. H. 36¾″, (seat) 21⅞″,
W. (arms) 14½″, (seat) 13¾″, D. (seat) 10″;
footrest not original. (Private collection: Photo,
Winterthur.)

postwar furniture market in Rhode Island, the chairmaker(s) socketed similar upper
structures into modified D-shaped planks. The earlier of the two chairs (left) still
retains flat-chamfered seat edges. Below the same plank the turnings are copies or adaptations of the S-post adult prototypes. In designing the upper leg, the chairmaker did
his best with models that did not particularly lend themselves to an aesthetically pleasing solution. The maker of the second chair had an advantage, since regional turned
work of the mid 1780s introduced greater versatility. Using updated baluster turnings
and the "new" Rhode Island tapered-toe foot, the woodworker introduced additional
elements to the front legs at the point of the footrest: a large ball and a second, smaller
baluster, the two separated by a spool. In the back supports, the chairmaker lengthened the balusters and eliminated the ball turning. Both front and back leg patterns
have considerable merit. Although the extra turnings at the front add interest, their
sole purpose may have been to support the footrest, which appears to be original and
to have been framed around the spool turnings during construction. The board retains
traces of the original blue-green paint found on other parts of the chair. The turned
swellings immediately above and below the rest form effective stops, even though the
board has shrunk somewhat. The footrest in the earlier chair may also be original. It is
identical in design and was in place when the chair was sold in the 1929 auction of the
Howard Reifsnyder collection. More than twenty years later the two chairs came
together in the Winterthur collection.[25]

Two continuous-bow highchairs from the Connecticut–Rhode Island border
region permit comparison of work of the same pattern done in the same area but with
different results (figs. **2-27, 2-28**). Critical to the success of the design are the curves of
the bow and the shape of the seat. In figure 2-27 a Rhode Island chairmaker captured
the classic qualities of the best New York and Rhode Island adult prototypes. He
employed to advantage a tall, broad arch; a slight arm lift; a shield-shaped seat shaved
thin at the front edge; and vigorous, well-proportioned turnings. Although the long,

Fig. 2-29 Child's bow-back Windsor highchair, Rhode Island, 1795–1800. White pine (seat) with ash, maple, hickory, and mahogany (arms) (microanalysis); H. 35⅜", (seat) 20⅜", W. (arms) 12¾", (seat) 12¾", D. (seat) 12¾". (Winterthur 68.535.)

Fig. 2-30 Child's bow-back Windsor highchair, Rhode Island, 1800–1805. White pine (seat) with hickory, oak, and walnut (arms) (microanalysis); H. 34", (seat) 20¾", W. (arms) 12¾", (seat) 11⅞", D. (seat) 11". (Winterthur 58.2.1.)

full-swelled balusters are not common in Rhode Island work, they appear in two chairs documented or attributed to Joseph Stone of East Greenwich. The Stone chairs and the highchair also share other elements.[26]

The Connecticut border chair of figure 2-28 lacks the classic touch of figure 2-27, but it has a particular character of its own. Use of the oval plank is uncommon in the continuous-bow pattern. Basic features that link the chair to the border region are the thickened spindles reduced to slim proportions at the base and the collarless baluster tops. The broad, compressed spool and ring turnings compare with those in the Tracy sack-back Windsor (fig. 2-25). The footrests in figures 2-27 and 2-28 appear to be later additions.[27]

The bow-back style was the late eighteenth-century design rival of the sack-back pattern. Two delicate bow-back highchairs (figs. **2-29, 2-30**) are identified as Rhode Island work by their full rounded arches, sawed rectangular-scroll arms, and baluster-turned sticks and tapered toes (fig. 2-29). The comparison illustrates how the bow was effectively combined with a new support structure as Windsor design moved from baluster- to bamboo-turned elements. Plank contours were also updated; the rounded saddle was eliminated in favor of a saucered surface and chamfered edges. A penciled inscription on the seat bottom of the chair in figure 2-30 associates it with five members of the Arnold family, and census records suggest Providence as their place of residence. Another Rhode Island highchair of equally broad leg splay is transitional in design, having three-section bamboowork above long, tapered feet; the work is accented by high-mounted H-plan stretchers.[28]

The last several chair groups described lack any provision for a restraining rod. In New York and New England work, especially, the choice lay between delicacy of design and convenience. A way around the dilemma was to tie the occupant into the seat, using a rag, tape, strap, or similar device. Though seldom mentioned, the practice must have been common. James Wells Champney's painting *Boon Companions* (1879) shows a child confined in this manner. A sixteenth-century Dutch engraving depicts a domestic interior with a child seated before a blazing hearth, tied about the waist with a cloth knotted at the chair back. The child's nurse kneels at one side, and a walker stands nearby.[29]

CHILDREN'S LOW SEATING OF THE EARLY NINETEENTH CENTURY

Nineteenth-century children's chairs are rarely identified by pattern in records dating before 1850. Even seating types are not often explicitly distinguished, although price, internal evidence, and knowledge of a craftsman's activity range can help modern researchers distinguish between rush, Windsor, and fancy seating. These interpretive aids supplemented by a survey of extant seating permit a better understanding of the use of children's Windsors after 1800. The South, Midwest, Middle Atlantic states, New England, and Canada all give evidence of this form.

A small body of material provides insights into the chair trade. In New York City, William Ash signed John Cruger's receipt book in 1803 upon receiving payment for four children's chairs. During the following years "Small Windsor chairs for Children" are mentioned in city records in conjunction with adult seating painted green, yellow, or black. The wide price range of children's low Windsors is recorded in the Philadelphia accounts of Charles C. Robinson: the cheapest chair was 50¢ and the most expensive $1.75. The addition of arms or other structural embellishment to the basic pattern may account for part of the difference, but undoubtedly, the primary factor was painted decoration. When Anthony Steel of Philadelphia died in 1817, appraisers itemized more than four dozen children's Windsors on the shop premises. The records of David Alling of Newark, New Jersey, provide more detail. Included in a consignment of painted seating sent to New Orleans in 1819 were "12 little winsor Childrens Chairs brown & Green" valued at $1.50 apiece. A shipment the following year contained yellow children's chairs. In the 1830s Alling received a child's Windsor for repairs and repainting, and he recorded the sale of several "childrens winsor armed chrs." The two "small" chairs located in the "Spare" bedroom of chairmaker Ebenezer P. Rose at Trenton along with eight full-size green Windsors were likely of stick-and-socket construction. In Schenectady, Thomas Kinsela's shop inventory suggests that he turned and framed both rush- and wooden-bottom seating for children.[30]

Documented activity in New England begins with an 1803 appraisal of Ansel Goodrich's shop in Northampton, Massachusetts, which contained unfinished children's chairs. In an exchange of services several years later, Amos Denison Allen of Windham, Connecticut, supplied a child's chair to the blacksmiths Frink and Chester. At Barkhamstead, chairmaker Eli Wood's estate in 1818 contained parts for "little Chairs," including many dozens of "Standards" (posts), legs, and "Streches." The same year James Gere of Groton supplied Major Stephen B. Allyn, a chairmaker of Norwich, with "stuff" for twelve small chairs. On one occasion Allyn returned a framed child's chair to Gere as part payment for his turning services. More parts for small chairs are recorded in the Boston inventory of Benjamin Bass, who died in 1819.[31]

Records for later years identify seventeen "little winsor" chairs in the Windham, Connecticut, shop of Frederick Allen, son of Amos Denison Allen. Neighboring Worcester County, Massachusetts, was a center of activity from the 1830s on. The inventories of several shops document the production of children's Windsor seating. In 1835 one "Lot of small chair seats" stood in the shop of Gilson Brown in Sterling. Brown had earlier supplied Nathaniel Silsbee with stock for seventy-two chairs of "small" size. Peter Peirce of neighboring Templeton did a sizable trade in chair parts. Appraisers found "1800 p[iece]s little chair stuff" lying in the shop, which they valued at 10¢ the hundred in 1836. At Peter Willard's death, appraisers itemized both finished chairs and sixty-four small Windsors "part finished" at his Sterling property; additional small "stuff" on the premises consisted of legs and seats. Local chairmaker John B. Pratt bought the seats and thirty-one completed chairs, some with arms. A manuscript book of prices for shop work prepared by James C. Helme of Plymouth, Luzerne County, Pennsylvania, records typical prices paid to journeymen in 1838 for making and/or framing chairs. For each child's armchair constructed in a workmanlike manner, the journeymen received 25¢. Ornamenting a dozen children's chairs earned him 75¢. Work that did not measure up to standard was "paid for accordingly."[32]

The export trade carried children's Windsor chairs to many destinations, domestic and foreign, usually as an accompaniment to adult seating. A manifest of private household furnishings shipped to New York from Philadelphia on May 30, 1800, included a lot of "Six Windsor Chairs & one arm Chair [and] Two Childrens Chairs," possibly representing a suite of furniture. The term *small* was often used in relation to child-size chairs. Philadelphia seating bound for Charleston, South Carolina, in 1803 consisted of "six & half dozen Windsor Chairs, seventeen small d[itt]o." Another shipment in 1807 itemized chairs in three sizes—adult's, youth's and children's—the latter two described as "small" and "very small." Charleston was a good market for Philadelphia chairmakers. Typically, the owners of the Northern Warehouse advertised in 1816: "Windsor Chairs, (Philadelphia make) warranted good, of various colors, Children's high and low Chairs." A random sampling of export records describes other shipments of children's Windsors from Philadelphia to Alexandria, Baltimore, Norfolk, Savannah, Martinique, Santiago de Cuba, and Saint Martin.[33]

A low chair for children referred to in records is the type known today as a youth's chair. In the early nineteenth century it was called by various names: a "miss Chair," as recorded by Thomas Safford of Canterbury, Connecticut, in January 1815; a "half chair," as constructed in 1811 by Thomas Boynton at Boston; the "half size Chair" standing in the Boston shop of Benjamin Bass at his death in 1819; or the "Little chair timber ½ high" credited to turner Pliny Allen in the accounts of Nelson Talcott of Portage County, Ohio, in 1840. The term *half-size chair* found favor with many New England chairmakers, although in 1840 Joel Pratt, Jr., and Son of Hartford offered "a great variety of . . . Misses and Children's" chairs "*equal* to *any* to be found elsewhere." Associating these youth's chairs with young girls may indicate that the seats were used principally as sewing chairs.[34]

As for eighteenth-century children's Windsors, styles introduced after 1800 copied adult seating. Earliest in design is a southeastern Pennsylvania armchair from Chester County with a molded, wavy top rod. Baluster-turned arms and bamboo-style legs identify its transitional character. Beneath the seat is the inscription: "From Abm Sharpless / to / Isaac Massey / 1800 / Take good care of this." Sharpless, who was born in 1748, is identified in a 1771 deed as a joiner of Concord Township. There is no evidence linking him with the Windsor-chair-making trade, suggesting that he may have acquired the chair by exchange or purchase. Among turned rod-back forms represented in children's seating are both single- and double-bow square-back chairs, some of the latter embellished with a medallion in the crest. A few side chairs are branded; armchairs are uncommon.[35]

A well-formed medallion-back side chair (fig. 2-31) with some original straw-colored surface paint and decoration visible came to the Winterthur collection from the Arthur J. Sussel sale of 1958. Its proportions are excellent, and the bamboo turnings are of good quality for Delaware Valley work. The balloon-style seat with flat edges, one of several plank patterns used in the early nineteenth century, is a duplicate of a shape found in rush-bottom fancy seating. The dark paint in the grooves seems to be part of the original decorative scheme, although the lines on the cross rods have been touched up or renewed. The medallion, or tablet, decoration represents a second paint coat (pl. 17). One documented chair with a similar crest is branded "w. GILLINGHAM," probably the stamp of William Gillingham of Buckingham Township, Bucks County.

Following the heyday of the rod-back patterns, a few chairmakers introduced narrow, slat-type crests to children's seating. The New England style tends to be plain. Delaware Valley and Pennsylvania work has a projection, or low tablet, at the center top. Other uncommon patterns in children's seating from the 1810s are the winged

Fig. 2-31 Child's square-back Windsor side chair, Delaware Valley, ca. 1802–12. Yellow poplar (seat) with maple, oak, and hickory (microanalysis); H. 28″, (seat) 13⁹⁄₁₆″, W. (crest) 14³⁄₈″, (seat) 14⅛″, D. (seat) 12¾″; paint and decoration partially original. (Winterthur 58.120.5.)

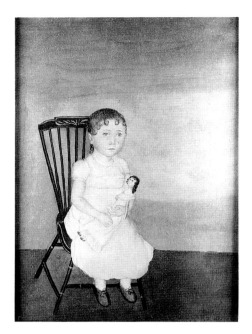

Fig. 2-32 *Eliza Williams,* Roxbury, Mass., ca. 1818. Watercolor on paper; H. 8⅞″, W. 6½″. (Philadelphia Museum of Art, Philadelphia, Pa., gift of Edgar William Garbisch and Bernice Chrysler Garbisch.)

Fig. 2-33 Child's slat-back Windsor side chair and detail of brand, Spring and Haskell, Hiram, Me., 1830–40. White pine (seat) with beech and birch (microanalysis); H. 28⅞″, (seat) 13¾″, W. (crest) 15½″, (seat) 13⅝″, D. (seat) 13¾″. (Winterthur 73.298.)

Fig. 2-34 Child's roll-top Windsor side chair, Pennsylvania, 1830–40. Yellow poplar (seat) with maple; H. 29¾″, (seat) 14½″, W. (crest) 14¾″, (seat) 14⅜″, D. (seat) 13⅝″. (Private collection: Photo, Winterthur.)

tablet of Baltimore origin (fig. 2-38) and the stepped tablet. The stepped tablet was popular in Massachusetts and northern New England. It is represented here in a portrait of Eliza Williams (fig. **2-32**), who with her twin sister, Isabella, was born about 1813 in Roxbury, Massachusetts, near Boston. The sisters are pictured in facing companion portraits seated in similar chairs, each with a doll in her lap. The artist has captured the special qualities of the Boston-style tablet crest: the shallow depth and the low arch along the bottom edge. Even the leafy frond painted across the crest face duplicates in a general way original decoration found occasionally on crests of this pattern.[36]

By far the most common pattern in low seating for children was the chair with a broad (deep) inset slat (fig. **2-33**). Some supporting posts are completely cylindrical; others have shaved faces with or without a back bend. The long spindles usually are shaped in one of three patterns: a plain taper, a taper with a ball turning, or a flat "arrow." The child's armchair became more common beginning with this style. Regional characteristics, family histories, and documentation reveal the broad geographic range of the design. The illustrated chair is a relatively uncommon example of marked children's seating from Maine; it was made by Spring and Haskell of Hiram. Unfortunately, little remains of the original paint, which consisted of a brick red ground embellished with yellow and white banding and white quarter-fans in the crest corners. A dark grained coat was applied later. Variations of the broad-slat chair include a Philadelphia pattern with a centered, hollow-cornered tablet extension, top and bottom, and a Worcester County, Massachusetts, round-arch-slat chair with arrow spindles. An adult-size chair of arched-slat pattern bears the label of Joel Pratt, Jr., of Sterling.[37]

A rare pattern in children's Windsor seating is the roll-top crest (fig. **2-34**), although the same top piece was popular in rush-bottom fancy seating. The illustrated Pennsylvania example is rarer than the New England roll-top Windsor and is almost identical to one of full size labeled by the Philadelphia chairmaker George Turner.[38]

In the 1820s and later, plain rectangular tablets framed above the posts were frequently employed in children's furniture. J. P. Wilder of New Ipswich, New Hampshire, branded a chair with a straight top closely fitted to the post ends. Boston styling

Fig. 2-35 Child's tablet-top Windsor side chair, southern Pennsylvania or Maryland, 1835–45. Yellow poplar (seat); H. 28⅜″, (seat) 15″, W. (crest) 17⅜″, (seat) 13½″, D. (seat) 12⅞″; dark green ground with black, yellow, gilt, red, white, and dark green. (Florence and George Dittmar collection: Photo, Winterthur.)

Fig. 2-36 Child's tablet-top Windsor side chair, John Swint (brand "J.SWINT. / CHAIR MAKER"), Lancaster, Pa., 1845–55. Yellow poplar (seat); H. 22⅝″, (seat) 10¼″, W. (crest) 14¾″, (seat) 12½″, D. (seat) 11¼″; medium light green ground with medium dark green, black, shaded bronze, copper, and gilt. (Harry B. Hartman collection: Photo, Winterthur.)

included hollow corners (fig. 1-39) and ends shaped in arcs (fig. 2-42). The Baltimore rectangular top introduced a substantial overhang. One chair, which originated in Maryland or southern Pennsylvania, exhibits rather extraordinary embellishments to the basic pattern (fig. **2-35,** pl. 18): ringed "horns" in the crest; a shaped and scalloped-edge stay rail; a short, arrow-patterned central spindle; boldly turned posts and legs; and a prominent, ball-turned front stretcher. The dark green ground is decorated with banding, penciling, gilding, and polychrome floral ornament.[39]

Contemporary in design are New England tablet tops of rounded or loaf shape (fig. 2-46) and the Pennsylvania shouldered-crest pattern (fig. **2-36,** pl. 19). The illustrated Lancaster example, stamped by John Swint in small letters on the plank, represents a second stage of the crest design, as identified by the flare of the lower corners. The top piece closely follows a Philadelphia pattern of the mid 1840s. Original paint of medium light green color with penciling, banding, and metallic ornament still bears much of its original varnish overcoat. Later styles introduced a vertical splat, followed by a pierced splat accompanied by a notched crest. After the Civil War the balloon back appeared in children's seating. Another midcentury pattern is the low-back chair with a heavy arm rail and a thick capping piece across the back; the turnings are heavy cylinders, balls, and rings (fig. 2-43).[40]

CHILDREN'S HIGHCHAIRS OF THE EARLY NINETEENTH CENTURY

Nineteenth-century highchairs follow the same designs as children's low seating. In 1800 a Philadelphia shipper sent six "Children Table Chairs" on consignment to Charleston, South Carolina, in one cargo. Eighteen more tall seats, shipped directly by chairmaker James Whitaker, followed in 1803; some probably were fancy furniture with rush bottoms. Charleston import notices consistently list children's high and low chairs from Philadelphia. In New York, chairmaker William Ash in May 1803 supplied the family of John Cruger with a highchair to go with four low chairs purchased at the same time. Ebenezer Knowlton of Boston constructed similar seating; when he died in 1811 "4 high small chairs" stood in the shop. On many occasions during the 1810s the brothers Proud of Providence recorded the sale of "a table Chair for a Child." A record of May 8, 1812, shows that Samuel B. Mumford supplied them with "25 Legs to high Chair 07 Cent" the set. The usual price for a completed chair was $1.25. On one occasion when a chair came into the shop for a new coat of green paint, the refurbishing charge was 25¢. Vermont chairmaker Thomas Boynton employed John Parker to make "childrens dining chs" among other seating forms at the piece rate of 31¢; after painting, Parker striped half a dozen for 24¢.[41]

Chairmakers in rural New York and New Jersey also constructed highchairs. An enumeration of 1815 mentions a highchair supplementing the tables, cradle, and "small" children's chairs in David Miller's kitchen at Chatham Township, Morris County, New Jersey. In 1819 David Alling shipped children's dining chairs from Newark to New Orleans; these were probably fancy seating with rush bottoms, since the valuation was $2.50 apiece. Alling marketed similar seating in Mobile, Alabama, in the 1830s; one chair is described as a "curld scroll armed table chr." In Philadelphia, Windsor-chair maker Charles C. Robinson sold highchairs at prices ranging from $1.25 to $1.75. An October 11, 1813, record reads, "To John Emeric the Baker for Table Chair."[42]

New England activity was brisk in the 1820s. Advertising at Providence in 1824, Rhodes G. Allen offered "Childrens Chairs, high and low." In neighboring Pomfret, Connecticut, Zadock Hutchins had some call for the tall form, since at his death in 1830 there were six such chairs in the shop. Along the Connecticut River at Essex, Elisha Harlow Holmes earlier sold a "Small high chair" for $1.25 to Reverend Mr. Steel. Perhaps it was the fancy one his brother-in-law Frederick Allen constructed for Holmes when he worked there in 1828. Similar furniture was also acquired at auction for resale by business entrepreneurs. Daniel Rogers, Jr., of Gloucester bought fifteen children's dining chairs in 1829 from auctioneer T. Deland at Salem for 52¢ apiece.[43]

Geographic diversity remained characteristic of the highchair market in the 1830s and 1840s. Hartford retailer Philemon Robbins obtained considerable finished stock from suppliers outside the community. Sullivan Hill of Spencer, Massachusetts, was one of the craftsmen who provided highchairs upon occasion. Sales entries in Robbins's accounts mention highchair colors of yellow and "quaker" (gray). At Newark, New Jersey, an unusual entry in David Alling's 1839 accounts for a "table for childs chr" at 83¢ appears to describe a special tray for feeding purposes. Within two decades another innovation, as developed in England, was current. John C. Hubbard advertised in the 1860 Boston directory that he manufactured Astley Cooper chairs for children. Sir Astley Cooper (1768–1841), an eminent English physician, advocated the use of children's tall-legged dining chairs with ramrod-straight backs to encourage correct posture. With the introduction of this theory, children's furniture design had come full circle to the stiff, straight, unyielding seats of the era before the Windsor.[44]

If anything, the single-rod, or cross-bow, style was more popular as a highchair pattern than as a low seat for children. There are many such highchairs, ranging from designs of considerable sophistication to clumsy handiwork. John Lewis Krimmel depicted a single-bow highchair in his sketch of a family Christmas celebration in southeastern Pennsylvania during the 1810s. Considerably fewer highchairs have double bows. The illustrated example is typical of eastern Connecticut work (fig. 2-37). It is a particularly vigorous interpretation, from the nodular bamboowork to the distinctively modeled, angular seat. Complementing the angular plank are exaggerated, projecting crest and arm tips. The front stretcher appears to have served as a footrest upon occasion. Among the patterns that followed in the market, both the narrow slat and the stepped tablet (fig. 2-32) are uncommon in the highchair. A few examples have deep, shaped slats with single or double tablet projections or arched tops. Two of the latter bear the label of Joel Pratt, Jr., of Sterling, Massachusetts. One has plain spindles, while

Fig. 2-37 Child's square-back Windsor high-chair, eastern Connecticut, 1802–12. H. 38½", (seat) 24", W. (crest) 17⅞", (arms) 17½", (seat) 13⅝", D. (seat) 13". (Mr. and Mrs. Donald Ladd collection: Photo, Winterthur.)

Fig. 2-38 Child's slat-back Windsor highchair, Boston, 1825–40. H. 35″, (seat) 21⅝″, W. (crest) 13½″, (arms) 11¾″, (seat) 12″, D. (seat) 11⅞″; medium light mustard ground with black, dark mustard, and reddish brown. (Steven and Helen Kellogg collection: Photo, Winterthur.)

Fig. 2-39 Child's slat-back Windsor highchair, C. Coffin (owner, brand), New York, 1810–20. H. 35¹⁵⁄₁₆″, (seat) 20⅛″; right arm structure replaced. (Harold and Ruth Montgomery Worley collection: Photo, Museum of Early Southern Decorative Arts, Winston-Salem, N.C.)

the other has flat arrow-shaped sticks. At least one Baltimore child's highchair has a winged-tablet top.[45]

The plain slat-back highchair, like the child's low seat, is the pattern that became widespread. The three basic variations are identified by plain, ball, or flat (arrow) spindles. A ball-spindle highchair survives with its original pale yellow paint and decoration almost intact (fig. **2-38**). The fruit-and-leaf motif of the crest establishes a visual focus, and the imaginative use of black penciling defines the late-type turnings, especially in the use of vertical panels in the front legs. The blocklike quality of the seat is tempered by the penciled T-shaped panel on the top surface. Another penciled panel defines the top of the original footrest, which wraps around the inside of the front legs, probably held secure by round tenons. The similarity of the seat plank to that of a Boston writing-arm chair and another highchair (fig. 2-42) and the close relationship of the leaf-and-fruit decoration to compositions used in eastern Massachusetts painted furniture (fig. 1-39) pinpoint the chair's geographic origin. In December 1835 Elbridge Gerry Reed, a chairmaker of Sterling who probably was a supplier of the Boston market, put arms on twenty-four children's "dining Chairs" and added "steps," or footrests, to six of them.[46]

Another highchair in the slat style is framed with spindles in the rare Cumberland pattern (fig. **2-39**) and is likely the product of a New York chairmaker. The double-scored grooves forming a ring near the post bases strengthen this attribution, as does the leg profile, which is close to that of two cross-back New York chairs. The brand "C. COFFIN," probably that of an owner, appears on the plank bottom. Members of the Coffin family were part of a Nantucket group that relocated along the Hudson River and established the town of Hudson. A rare child's low chair with a slat back and Cumberland spindles, although clumsy by comparison, is also doubly scored in the lower posts. The front stretcher is of ball-and-arrow form, a type seen on adult seating from New York.[47]

Fig. 2-40 Child's slat-back, double Windsor highchair, attributed to Daniel Stewart, Farmington, Me., 1820–30. White pine (seat) with birch and maple; H. 33¼″, W. 24⅝″, D. 11¾″; front stretcher missing. (Colonial Williamsburg, Williamsburg, Va.)

Double highchairs for two children or twins are exceedingly rare. The illustrated example is missing its front stretcher, possibly as a result of too many eager climbers, but is otherwise intact in its birch and white pine (seat) construction (fig. **2-40**). The particular combination of woods indicates a northern New England origin; the crest with its deeply cut corners suggests Maine. A top piece of identical form appears in a child's rocking chair (fig. 2-44) labeled by Daniel Stewart (d. 1827) of Farmington. Faintly discernible in the present illustration is the light shaping of the upper plank forming two individual seating places separated by a central arm, an unconscious reversion to mid eighteenth-century "double chair" work (fig. 1-73). The exposed wood surfaces have mottled black and dark red paint with gilt decoration. Because of the chair's breadth, it may have been inconvenient to draw it to the table, in which case the children surely must have been secured in their seats with ties.[48]

During the early nineteenth century the plain, rectangular tablet was popular in Baltimore and in time made its influence felt along the Atlantic coast. A watercolor portrait of Daniel Martin, signed and dated by the Pennsylvania artist Jacob Stauffer in 1830, depicts a child seated in a highchair of this pattern. The subject rests one foot on a cross board attached to the front legs, another rare early instance of the use of this feature. An 1844 watercolor portrait of a child in a highchair, the subject identified as Eli Rothermel, depicts a similar rest at the chair front. A painting by William T. Bartoll of Marblehead, Massachusetts, from the mid 1840s illustrates a child seated in a New England tablet-top highchair. In time, the rectangular overhang gave way to a rounded profile. Two designs dating to midcentury contrast Pennsylvania and New England work (figs. **2-41, 2-42**). The vigorous curves of the Pennsylvania top piece (pl. 20) and the use of fancy turnings alter the basic character of the design, yet the two chairs share several design elements: tapered, cylindrical arms; squared seats terminating in blunt

Fig. 2-41 Child's tablet-top Windsor highchair, Pennsylvania, 1840–55. H. 34⅜″, (seat) 23⅜″, w. (crest) 14″, (arms) 12⅞″, (seat) 12¼″, D. (seat) 12½″; chocolate brown ground with yellow, gilt, coral red, white, and green; footrest missing and possibly not original. (Philip H. Bradley Co.: Photo, Winterthur.)

Fig. 2-42 Child's tablet-top Windsor highchair, Boston, 1845–60. White pine (seat); H. 32¾″, (seat) 21¼″, w. (crest) 12½″, (arms) 11¾″, (seat) 11¾″, D. (seat) 10⅛″; light mustard ground with black, dark green, and gilt. (Museum of Art, Rhode Island School of Design, Providence: Photo, Winterthur.)

front edges; long, cylindrical legs tapered top and bottom (the rear legs in fig. 2-41); and plain, cylindrical stretchers. The New England crest with its arched ends is a Boston design (pl. 21). Both illustrated chairs have original paint. The Boston chair is light mustard color with penciling and gilt decoration. The dark reddish brown surface of the Pennsylvania chair features the naturalistic polychrome floral work popular in the region toward the mid nineteenth century.[49]

Plank-bottom highchairs dating to the third quarter of the nineteenth century feature low backs in endless, subtle variations. The heavy arms form a semicircle or roll over and downward at the front to anchor in the plank. Most have embellished turnings. Factory names, such as S. S. Howe of South Gardner, Massachusetts, and the Jamestown Wood Seat Chair Company of New York State, replace earlier designations. The Shakers developed a contemporary low-back highchair that features a threaded screw permitting adjustment of the seat height.

OTHER SPECIALIZED FURNITURE FOR CHILDREN

Hole Chairs

Just as the close-stool chair contributed to the creature comfort of the adult world in the eighteenth and nineteenth centuries, so the child's "hole" chair was vital household equipment. It remains so today in young families, although renamed the "pottie chair." Construction of these chairs required wooden seats. Some chairs have board bottoms with paneled backs and sides rather than thick planks and socket construction. The "childs Chair & Pan" that stood in the second bedchamber of William Buckley's Philadelphia house in 1759 was probably board-framed. Like the rocking chair, some hole chairs came into being as conversions. Thus, Silas Cheney of Litchfield,

Fig. 2-43 Child's low-back Windsor hole chair, eastern Connecticut or Rhode Island, 1845–65. H. 16⁷⁄₁₆″, (seat) 8⁵⁄₁₆″, w. (arms) 13½″, (seat) 12″, D. (seat) 11″; pale mustard yellow and orange-brown maple-grained ground, old but not original. (Slater Memorial Museum, Norwich Free Academy, Norwich, Conn.: Photo, Winterthur.)

Connecticut, recorded an item in January 1814 "to makeing hole thru Chair." Harry Buckley, the purchaser, had just bought a "Childs Chair" for $1.25, but whether the hole went through the new seat or an old one is unclear. The charge for cutting the hole was 20¢. The earliest reference to new construction of a hole chair that can be identified as a Windsor is found in the order book of Amos Denison Allen of South Windham, Connecticut, who noted in autumn 1799: "Veranus Lathrop a little Chr with hole in the bottom." In Philadelphia, Anthony Steel stocked the hole chair by 1817, at which time "6 Small arm chairs with holes" stood ready for sale. David Alling of Newark, New Jersey, noted the sale of an occasional "childs wood seat chr hole in" from 1829 to 1840 at prices ranging from $1 to $1.25. In Hartford in the mid 1830s Philemon Robbins's charge was only 67¢. The two craftsmen's products may have differed considerably in the painted decoration.[50]

At James C. Helme's shop in Luzerne County, Pennsylvania, a journeyman's pay in 1838 for making a child's chair with a hole in the seat was 30¢. The price was 5¢ more than he was paid for making a child's armchair or highchair because of the extra work required to cut and shape the hole. At about the same date, chairmaker Jacob Felton of Fitzwilliam, New Hampshire, sold half a dozen hole chairs for 28¢ apiece to Anthony Van Doorn, a furniture dealer of Brattleboro, Vermont. These chairs probably were "left in the wood" for Van Doorn's workmen to paint and decorate. Elbridge Gerry Reed framed "8 Little Chairs with hole" at Sterling, Massachusetts, in 1834 for Benjamin Stuart, who probably supplied the prepared stock, since the labor charge per chair was only 8¢. Beyond the Green Mountains in Bennington, Vermont, H. F. Dewey also had an occasional call for this chair at 83¢ apiece. Among the chairmakers of Worcester County, Massachusetts, who supplied a large section of the New England market by the early 1840s, it was common practice to stockpile parts. Thus, appraisers found "71 seats with holes" valued at 3¼¢ apiece at the Sterling shop of Peter A. Willard in 1842. Four years later a local sale of Joseph F. Loring's shop stock disposed of 100 such children's chairs completely framed. Calvin Stetson of Barnstable on Cape Cod was supplied from the Boston market. His accounts with William P. Haley of Boston show regular shipments of children's hole chairs between 1843 and 1848.[51]

Of the Windsor hole chairs for children that survive, the largest number are of late-type patterns. Figure **2-43** is typical and illustrates two descriptions recorded in craftsmen's accounts. In 1841 H. F. Dewey of Bennington, Vermont, noted the sale of both a highchair and a "round back Chair with hole" to Aaron Hubbell. The term *round back* as used here certainly refers to the low style, as nothing else of the period fits the description. A few years earlier David Alling of Newark, New Jersey, identified a child's seat by its finish as "1 small chr with hole pt'd immitation." Chances are the simulated wood was maple, as illustrated. The painter has superbly rendered the "flowers," or grain, common to the stripes and eyes of ornamental maple in shades of light mustard brown. A local gift to the Slater Museum of Norwich, the chair probably represents eastern Connecticut or Rhode Island production.[52]

Rocking Chairs

A dearth of eighteenth-century furniture and references leads to the conclusion that the child's Windsor rocking chair was almost unknown before 1800. There were rush-bottom rocking seats for children in the eighteenth century, as for instance the "Littel Chair with Rockers" priced under $1 and sold by the Proud brothers of Providence in 1790. Conversions probably were made before the turn of the century, and rocker replacements were necessary from time to time. A typical repair was "puting on rockers & bottoming a little Chair." Abner Haven of Framingham, Massachusetts, charged 21¢ for this service in 1810. In 1814 Abner Taylor at his shop in Lee charged the same amount for adding only "a pr. Small chair rockers." Just what type of chair Thomas Safford of Canterbury, Connecticut, identified in a January 1813 record of "making rockers little Chair" is not clear, since he produced kitchen (slat-back), fancy, and Windsor chairs. The 33¢ cost suggests a fancy or Windsor chair, which would have required paint and possibly some decoration. Safford also framed "Little rocking Chairs" and charged prices ranging from $1.17 to $1.34. Chairmakers in many areas were doing rocker replacement work in small chairs by the early 1800s. The cost seems to have been about the same everywhere, as several references from the 1830s attest: 31¢ in the shop of Thomas J. Moyers and Fleming K. Rich of Wythe Court House, Virginia; 33¢ at the Kennebunk, Maine, establishment of Paul Jenkins; 34¢ at Titus Preston's shop in Wallingford, Connecticut.[53]

The earliest evidence of production of children's Windsor rocking chairs is found in two Charleston, South Carolina, newspaper notices of 1806–7 advertising the receipt of Windsor furniture from Philadelphia. Many manuscript references are not as specific about chair type. The "Little Chair with rockers" sold for just under $1 at the Plymouth, New Hampshire, shop of Jacob Merrill, Jr., in 1802 appears to have been a Windsor. Joseph Griswold's little rocking chair priced at about 66¢ in Buckland, Massachusetts, in 1807 could have had either a rush or wooden bottom. The $2 price of the "childs rocking chair" sold in Vermont by Thomas Boynton in 1813 suggests a fancy rush-bottom form, although a fancy Windsor cannot be ruled out. The Proud brothers of Providence, makers of both rush-bottom and Windsor seating, constructed a "Littel Chair with Rockers" in 1819 for $1; later accounts record a "half Grown Rocking Chair," probably a "youth's" chair, at the same price. Circumstantial evidence identifies as Windsors the two children's rocking chairs purchased by Reverend Petingal for $1.50 in 1817 from Silas Cheney of Litchfield, Connecticut, since the clergyman purchased six bamboo Windsors, two sewing chairs, and an adult rocking chair at the same time. The child's rocker was uncommon in any construction. Margaret Schiffer, in her study of Chester County, Pennsylvania, inventories through 1850, found only two specific references to children's rocking chairs, one dated in 1814 and another in the 1830s.[54]

Visual evidence of children's Windsor rockers is provided by a painting done about 1825 (pl. 22). The members of a Pennsylvania family sit on Windsor chairs that make up a suite of furniture. The head of the family occupies an armchair, and the two small daughters have their own little rocking Windsors.

References to children's rocking chairs from the second quarter of the century generally are no more explicit than in the earlier period, although they represent a greater geographic range. William G. Beesley constructed children's rocking chairs at Salem,

Fig. 2-44 Child's slat-back Windsor rocking
chair and detail of label, Daniel Stewart,
Farmington, Me., ca. 1822–27. (Old Sturbridge
Village, Sturbridge, Mass.)

New Jersey, in the late 1820s. David Alling of Newark specifically identified a child's fancy rocker priced at $1.25 in 1838. In Pennsylvania, James Helme's book of journeymen's wages set construction prices for little Windsor rockers, exclusive of materials and painting, at 33¢ to 35¢ in 1838. His retail prices probably ranged from 75¢ to $1. A child's rocker sold in a Boston shop for 62¢ probably was a local product, although J. P. Wilder and Jacob Felton of southern New Hampshire distributed similar products over a broad area. During the 1840s chairmaker and dealer Calvin Stetson of Barnstable, Massachusetts, received children's and "half size Rocking wood seat arms" from his supplier William P. Haley of Boston. The sizes may have duplicated those referred to by Schroder and Widmyer at Lancaster, Pennsylvania, as "children's small and large rocking chairs." Appraisers of Lambert Hitchcock's Connecticut estate itemized the larger seats as "Miss Rocking chairs" in 1852, while Elbridge Gerry Reed had called them "half way rocking chairs" in his accounts for 1835. Prices for children's Windsor rockers ranged from a low of about 62¢ to a high of about $1.50 and overlapped price ranges for both common and fancy rush-bottom rockers, so that price is an uncertain guide to identifying specific construction in general references.[55]

Among extant children's furniture, the first major Windsor style displaying significant evidence of original rocker construction is the slat-back pattern. Contemporary documents suggest, however, that plank-seat rocking chairs were made for children in earlier styles, such as the single-bow, double-bow, and stepped-tablet patterns. The rockers either fit into slotted leg bottoms or are socketed by pointed feet. Within the slat-back group most chairs have plain spindles. Only the rare child's rocker has a ball-centered or arrow-spindle back. One fancy slat-back Windsor rocker has Cumberland spindles and plump bamboo-turned legs carved with a long bundle of fasces, or rods, through the center section. Another chair features three sticklike spindles, each with a small, broad shield at the center. The same motif is varied in the front stretcher. The front legs are fancy-turned. Plate 23, a youth's slat-back rocking chair, has a scroll seat, which is unusual in children's seating dating before the mid nineteenth century. The swell of the bamboo-style legs echoes the uncommon profile of the spindles. The freehand decoraton of the crest has the precision of a stenciled design.

A slat-back child's rocker of somewhat unusual pattern bears the label of Daniel Stewart of Farmington, Maine (fig. 2-44). The deeply hollowed crest is a duplicate of one in a child's double highchair (fig. 2-40). The slat shape had some currency in Maine, as attested by a group of bent-back chairs with broad arrow spindles. Hollow-cornered slats of less extreme interpretation also are found in New Hampshire and Vermont work. The stout lower legs of figure 2-44 lend themselves particularly well to the slotted stretcher attachment. As in many rockers, there never were any side stretchers; the rockers themselves function as front-to-back braces. Stewart died in 1827, which provides a fairly early cutoff date for this example.

Children's rectangular tablet-top rocking chairs appeared next in the style sequence. Angular and hollow corners (fig. 1-39) suggest both Baltimore and Boston influence. Chairs of rounded tablet account for a good share of the children's rocking-chair market from the middle of the century and later. Design influence, divided between Boston and Pennsylvania, was eventually fused in one style. As illustrated in figures 2-45 and 2-46, early round patterns (fig. 1-41) gave way to a generic lunette shape, modified here by a slight flare at the lower corners of figure 2-45 (pl. 24) and by small lunette cutouts along the lower edge of figure 2-46. Forward-scrolling arms are almost always present in the rounded-crest rocking chair, although George W. Kibling of Ashburnham, Massachusetts, and John Meservy of Bangor, Maine, made rockers without arms. The scroll, or "raised," seat undoubtedly added a premium to the price, since the design called for the attachment of extra pieces of shaped wood to the front and back edges of the basic plank. Typically, the rockers in scroll-seat chairs are slotted into the legs. Legs in chairs with flat seat planks generally socket directly into the rockers; the illustrated supports are close in profile to those in a tall, adult-size rocking chair from south-central Pennsylvania (fig. 1-56). Figure 2-45, which was purchased at a farm sale near Quarryville, has a penciled inscription on the seat bottom reading, "J C Strickland / Oxford / Pa." Both Oxford and Quarryville are in southern Chester County near the Maryland border.[56]

Figure 2-46 originated in New England, as indicated by the white pine seat and the front leg and stretcher turnings (fig. 1-45). The naturalistic floral ornament of the crest

Fig. 2-45 Child's tablet-top Windsor rocking chair, southeastern Pennsylvania, 1850–70. Yellow poplar (seat, microanalysis); H. 26¾″, (seat) 11″, W. (crest) 16⅛″, (arms) 15⅜″, (seat) 11½″, D. (seat) 13⅝″; dark and reddish brown grained ground with yellow, gilt, red, and shades of green. (E. S. Wilkins collection: Photo, Winterthur.)

Fig. 2-46 Child's tablet-top Windsor rocking chair, New England, 1845–60. White pine (seat); H. 23⅛″; green ground. (Private collection: Photo, Museum of Early Southern Decorative Arts, Winston-Salem, N.C.)

was an alternative to stenciled decoration. The chair appears to have been a commodity
of the export trade. Painted on the plank bottom are the name and place, "J Morrison /
Petersburg / Va," and the chair has a family history due south of that coastal trading
center in Hertford County, North Carolina. Rounding out children's midcentury rocking patterns is the low, heavy-rail armchair (fig. 2-43). Rockers are attached by either
the socket or slot method. One such low chair bears the stamp of Samuel S. Howe of
South Gardner, Massachusetts.[57]

Writing-arm Chairs

Children's chairs fitted with a writing leaf of original construction appear to have been
unknown before the 1840s. Figure 2-47 probably was made for the schoolroom rather
than the home. The plank bears the brand of Boston chairmaker John C. Hubbard.
New England, and particularly Massachusetts, led the way in an educational awakening
that swept the nation during the second quarter of the nineteenth century. Its central
focus was the concept of popular education. Free schools were established in many metropolitan centers during the 1830s, and the movement soon spread to other, less popu-
lated areas. Horace Mann became chairman of the Massachusetts board of education in
1837 and established the first U.S. teacher-training school at Lexington in 1839. By midcentury, Boston had become a center for the manufacture of school furniture, and many
seats were already being designed with pedestal supports to be bolted to the floor.[58]

Figure 2-47 somewhat predates the pedestal chair, but the low-back pattern was
current well beyond midcentury. Before the common use of single and double desks,
the chair with a small writing leaf—this one left-handed—was more convenient than
the lap as a writing support. A flat surface and two nailholes along the right plank side
(as seated) suggest that the seat once held an attached box or basket. Samuel Wales, Jr.,
illustrated low armchairs in the pedestal style with a side container in the 1850 Boston
directory; the seats are identified as "Wales' Basket Primary Chairs." A note from the
Illustrated London News of August 23, 1851, describing the Great Exhibition, further elu-
cidates the use of this feature:

The most interesting American furniture is included in the display of New England. . . . Here we have a set of the desks and chairs used in the New England common schools. The chairs are a great improvement on the system of benches; each child has his own, with a small wooden side pocket for books on the right hand; in some, space is economized by a single iron leg or pillar, which is screwed to the floor. The smaller chairs, for infants, have four legs, with iron cramps. . . . We commend these school fittings, from their simplicity and cheapness, to the notice of many in the country interested in village education.[59]

Canadian furniture makers Jacques and Hay of Toronto had developed a line of school furniture by 1852, the year they received the local school contract. Boston-based firms probably competed for the commission, but Jacques and Hay were able to supply the furnishings at 20 to 30 percent less than the cost from Boston. The firm's standard single or double student's desk and chair had a slanted writing surface of wood with an open shelf below, the whole attached to iron supports fixed to the floor. Separate chairs with wooden seats and backs had similar metal bases. For "younger children" Jacques and Hay built "a single chair-like seat . . . provided with a small open work iron basket attached to its side, designed to contain the pupil's books, &c."[60]

Settees

Another rare form in children's seating is the settee. Because it is uncommon, over the years the form has been produced with intent to deceive. The illustrated example from the Winterthur collection may be the only extant child's long seat of eighteenth-century date (fig. 2-48). The features are identified with the Connecticut–Rhode Island border region. Basswood, the material of the seat, is found in some Rhode Island Windsors and in chairs originating in several other areas of New England. The most prominent regional characteristic is the crest of squared projecting tip, a top piece that has its counterparts in adult-size fan-back chairs made in the border area, one of which has a

Fig. 2-48 Child's high-back Windsor settee, Connecticut–Rhode Island border region, 1790–1805. Basswood (seat) with maple and hickory (microanalysis); H. 28⅜″, (seat) 10⅛″, W. (crest) 32¼″, (arms) 31¼″, (seat) 28¼″, D. (seat) 9⅞″; right arm support replaced; both arm terminals probably reshaped. (Winterthur 65.1307.)

basswood seat. The second feature associated with border work and with Windsors of northern coastal Connecticut is the collarless articulation between the baluster and upper leg element (fig. 2-28). In fact, the entire leg profile compares well with border work. Occasionally the arm supports of chairs from the border region exhibit slightly different elements than the legs, even though the profiles are comparable, as illustrated. The right arm support is an old replacement; all other parts retain crystals of green pigment beneath at least six later coats of paint. At some point one or both pad-type handgrips probably broke off and the rail tips were shaped in a deep chamfer to compensate for the loss. Like the little chair illustrated in figure 2-10, the settee never had any stretchers.[61]

Contemporary documents contain few references to the child's settee, again suggesting its rarity. As early as 1774 Philadelphia chairmaker William Cox specially constructed a "Grien Settee for Miss Nancy," a young daughter of the well-to-do John Cadwalader. The substantial price of 30s. speaks to the careful work that went into its making. Of either high or low pattern, the small form required careful scaling to size, in both its elements and its overall proportions. A second reference to a child's long seat from the accounts of Silas Cheney in Litchfield, Connecticut, is less clear. In July 1805 the craftsman delivered a "Childs Banch" to Moses Seymore, Jr., and charged him 7s.6d.; it is impossible to know whether the seat represented board or Windsor construction. The use of the term *bench* and comparison of the price with that of the Cox settee would suggest board construction, although the price is still greater than that charged for a child's Windsor chair. An inventory of the estate of New York cabinet- and chairmaker John Martin in 1834 lists a new "Childs Settee" valued at 75¢. That figure could identify a rush-bottom seat or a plain slat-back Windsor. Dating between these two references is a nineteenth-century child's settee of slat-back pattern, which has eight bamboo-turned legs and is about ten inches longer than the illustrated seat.[62]

Cribs and Cradles

The terms *child's crib* and *crib bedstead*, which are found in records from the close of the eighteenth century into the nineteenth century, appear to describe a child's small, framed, rectangular bedstead with corner posts, a row of spindles or narrow vertical slats all around, and capping rails. The spindles are cylindrical or arrow-shaped. Although cribs were offered for sale with Windsor chairs and were made in the same shops, production was mainly a minor sideline. The Philadelphia export trade provides an early record of the crib. Richard Brenan of Charleston, South Carolina, advertised "A Quantity of Windsor Chairs of various colors" and "Childrens Cribs" from Philadelphia on September 12, 1798, and the trade in this commodity to South Carolina continued for some years. Philadelphia shippers sent cribs to Havana in 1800 and to Puerto Rico in 1809. Several southern chairmakers produced the form, including Samuel Parsons and Son of Richmond, who offered "Chairs, Settees, Cribs, Cradles, &c. of any fashion wanted, on short notice" in 1801–2. Listings of cribs and cradles together eliminate the possibility that one term was a synomyn for the other. Henry R. Burden, a Philadelphia chairmaker who relocated to Washington, offered cribs in the capital city in 1815; as late as 1828 William M. Morrison still stocked the form locally. Household inventories originating in Chester County, Pennsylvania, list children's cribs in 1811 and 1823.[63]

Mention of the crib is of late occurence in New England records. Moses Parkhurst of Paxton, Massachusetts, charged a customer $4 for a "crip bedsted" in 1822. A similar reference appears that year in the estate inventory of Stephen B. Allyn of Norwich, Connecticut, and other, later references are also found in Connecticut records. Elisha Harlow Holmes of Essex constructed a cherry crib and another described in his accounts as a "Double crib bedstead" in 1829. Insolvency proceedings that year against David Finch of Bridgeport required a property evaluation, which itemized a crib worth $3. A new pine "cribb" from William Rawson's Killingly shop cost $5 almost a decade later. At Portland, Maine, the turner Increase Pote recorded the delivery of a set of crib legs to a customer in 1828. Probably representative of the general type is the rectangular crib with narrow slat or spindle sides, extended corner posts, and rockers at the bottoms of long legs pictured in the advertisements of furniture makers or dealers.[64]

Use of a receptacle smaller than a crib to support the recumbent form of an infant dates from antiquity when Pharaoh's daughter found the baby Moses in a basket floating in the bulrushes at the river's edge. Rockers or some device to introduce motion to the cradle were current around A.D. 1000; hoods were a later feature. Of parallel interest is the depiction in ecclesiastical art of the stick-and-socket-framed manger as a cradle (fig. 2-49).[65]

By the sixteenth century European physicians recognized the therapeutic benefits of the cradle to encourage sleep, provide exercise, and protect the infant from harm. As late as 1754 the *Dictionary of Arts and Sciences* still emphasized the specialized function of the form rather than its appearance: "a well known machine in which infants are rocked to sleep." The Windsor cradle, which was an American development, appears to have been unknown before the 1780s or 1790s at the earliest, although evidence of the form in other construction is present in American documents and surviving furniture from the seventeenth century and later. A woodcut from the illustrated book *Mother Goose's Melody: or Sonnets for the Cradle* published by Isaiah Thomas in 1794 depicts a mother seated in a bow-back Windsor side chair tending a baby that lies in a woven cradle.[66]

General references to cradles in eighteenth-century records provide insights into production and use. At Leicester, Massachusetts, Robert Crage (Craig) priced his cradles from a modest 6s. to a substantial £3.8.3 in 1758. John Paine recorded the sale of a cradle on Long Island in 1762 and also had some trade in replacing cradle rockers. In prerevolutionary Philadelphia cradles are mentioned occasionally in inventories, along with children's chairs. Francis Trumble, cabinet- and chairmaker, offered "walnut chairs and cradles" for sale at his shop in 1775. Following the war a child's chair and cradle are mentioned in the inventory of John Cornthwaite, a leather tanner of Baltimore County, Maryland. Amos Denison Allen of South Windham, Connecticut, recorded Veranus Lathrop's purchase of a 15s. cradle painted blue on March 13, 1798. The presence of a child in the Lathrop household initiated a series of purchases that continued with a "Little Chair" for 6s. in November and "a little Chr with hole in the bottom" the following October.[67]

Early nineteenth-century references to the cradle extend the geographic range. Sometimes the construction material is identified. The Pennsylvania German cabinetmaker Abraham Overholt of Bucks County made a walnut cradle in 1802. Cherry is recorded in both Chester County, Pennsylvania, and Providence, Rhode Island. Soft woods are identified as pine in Otsego County, New York, and Pomfret, Connecticut; as whitewood in Albany; and as poplar in Chester County, Pennsylvania. Philemon Robbins recorded the sale of a willow cradle at Hartford in 1835, a period when finely woven baskets of this material were popular. A few surface finishes are mentioned. Elisha Harlow Holmes of Essex, Connecticut, stained a cradle in 1827. Paint colors include blue, red, and mahogany. Notes identifying construction or pattern are found from time to time. In 1818 Thomas Safford of Canterbury, Connecticut, referred to "Boards for a Cradle," an indication that the bed was framed with solid sides. A cradle made by Abner Taylor of Lee, Massachusetts, in 1817 had a "top," or hood. Pine cradles available in the store of Thomas W. Ward II in Pomfret, Connecticut, represented three variations of the basic pattern. The most expensive at $4 had a "foot & Head" (hood), another with a foot eliminated the hood, and a third was open at the bottom end (fig. 2-56). Moyers and Rich of Wythe Court House, Virginia, recorded a "swinging Crib" in 1838. As used here the term *crib* possibly was substituted for the word cradle, although by either definition the form is uncommon and the price expensive at $8.[68]

Nineteenth-century references describe Windsor cradle construction directly or by inference. The earliest dates to 1801 when Samuel Parsons and Son of Richmond opened a Windsor-chair-making business to supply chairs, "Settees, Cribs, Cradles, &c. of any fashion wanted." A manifest of goods shipped on the sloop *Polly* from Philadelphia to Edenton, North Carolina, on July 16, 1803, specifically enumerates "Four Windsor

Fig. 2-49 Detail of manuscript illumination. From *The Bedford Hours,* Paris, ca. 1423, Addison Manuscripts, Grenville Library, British Library, London.

Cradles". In the same year chairmaker Joseph Cotts offered "Windsor chairs, settees, and Windsor cradles" for sale at Cincinnati, Ohio. A sheriff's inventory of William Seaver's Boston chair shop in 1804 enumerates finished and unfinished work and many stockpiled furniture parts, among them "3 Cradle Tops." Southern chairmakers Archer and Joel Brown made cribs and cradles at the turn of the century in their shops in Petersburg, Virginia. The 1825 inventory of Philadelphia chairmaker Charles Robinson lists a Windsor cradle among the household effects. Ten cradles from the Delaware River port were also shipped to New Orleans in 1831 on the ship *John Sergeant*. In 1826 Elisha Harlow Holmes of Essex, Connecticut, constructed a "Round end cradle" priced at $2.50. This was probably the Windsor form, since board construction does not lend itself to curved shapes.[69]

Windsor cradles were generally patterned after board-constructed cradles, of which three types prevail: the low box with corner posts and raised end panels; the container with a tall hood at one end; and the low box with head and foot panels heightened and arched slightly, and the sides raised in a low step at the head end. Two Windsor patterns—the bow-back and the rod-back—lend themselves to the hooded design (figs. 2-50 to 2-52). The bow-back is the earlier of the two. A documented example of considerable merit (fig. **2-50**) bears the Philadelphia brand of John Letchworth stamped twice beneath the bottom. Immediately adjacent to one strike is a large, handwritten label, probably of early twentieth-century date, illustrating the kind of tales that frequently grew up around "old" or ancestral artifacts in the late nineteenth century and following:

This cradle was—to the best of my knowledge—made by Indians near Bellefonte for my grandmother, Mary Downing Valentine, about 1822 or 3. She was the wife of George Valentine, ironmaster. She must have shown the Indian a Winsor chair to copy, as the design is very similar to one. Sarah Fox Norris.

The bottom construction is unusual for a Windsor. In place of a plank, a mortised and tenoned frame is boarded in the center. The rockers with scrolled stops are close in design to those in Delaware Valley rush-bottom seating (fig. 1-22, left). One of several framing patterns common in the bow-end cradle appears in the hood. All the patterns

Fig. 2-51 Child's tall Windsor cradle, William Seaver and James Frost (two labels), Boston, ca. 1800–1802. H. 37½″, L. 36″, W. (rockers) 19″, (plank) 36″ by 12⅝″; pale mustard ground with black. (Mrs. Richard E. McDevitt collection: Photo, Winterthur.)

begin with a "chair back" at the head, sometimes balanced by a smaller arch at the foot. In figure 2-50 another chair back, complete with lateral curve, forms the hood arch. The structure is supported on straight side sticks and linked to the foot by long rails bent upward to simulate the side profile of a board-constructed cradle with a hood.

Another bowed hood has a second tall, vertical loop at the arch front (fig. **2-51**). The spindle placement is similar to the previous example: vertical sticks at the sides, horizontal sticks across the top. The side rails are shorter, and the design introduces a ripplelike fall from head to foot that complements the curved styling of the ends yet reduces the side height for easy interior access. The head and foot bows are curved forward at the base and anchored into the plank in the manner of a chair. Like the previous cradle, this one has bow faces and rail tops with crown-molded surfaces similar to those found on chairs of this pattern. Purely Boston styling emerges in the slim, nodular profiles of the spindles with their distinctive base flare and extra swell in the long sticks. Other features associated with high-style Boston Windsor work are the tiny swelled-taper feet and the double, cup-turned swells of the end stretchers. The original rockers, attached to rabbets cut on the inside faces of the feet, are nail-pinned in place. The stamped initials "AHG," which seem to be contemporary with the cradle, are centered on the outside face of the foot rocker. Although not identified, they probably are those of the original owner. The edges of the plank forming the cradle bed are rounded slightly like the back of a chair seat. Covering the exposed wooden surfaces is the original pale straw-color paint with black penciling and a varnish finish.[70]

Among tall American cradles, figure 2-51 is one of the highest. It is documented on the plank bottom with a double, uncut label of the chairmaking firm of William Seaver and James Frost, whose partnership existed only between 1800 and 1803. The date can be further narrowed by the fact that the 57 State Street address on the label was no longer current when the Boston directory of 1803 placed the firm in Battery March Street.

Fig. 2-52 Child's Windsor cradle, eastern Massachusetts or southern New Hampshire, 1800–1815. White pine (plank); H. 28¼″, (plank) 36¾″ by 13½″. (Historic Deerfield, Deerfield, Mass.: Photo, Winterthur.)

Two more pattern alternatives for the bow-style hooded cradle follow the two-bow plan of the Seaver and Frost example. In one case the horizontal spindles extend almost down to plank level; in the other, they terminate the forward bow on heavy side rails that run from head to foot. Below the rails are short, vertical spindles. In a nonhooded version of the bow-end cradle, an arched head is joined to a squared foot through the use of horizontal side rails that form lap joints with the short foot rail. The bed is elevated on bamboo legs and braced in the manner of the Seaver and Frost cradle.

The rod-style cradle hood was also framed in several forms. One pattern supports the high framework on four stout posts and springs low-arched rods between them near the post tops. The spindle arrangement resembles that in the Seaver and Frost cradle; straight side rails are terminated at low foot posts. A similar cradle in the Winterthur collection employs the arched rods of the hood as capping pieces on long spindles that serve as posts and pierce full-length side rails. Two Philadelphia spindle-framed cradles made of mahogany with rockers similar to figure 2-50 have heavy, molded railings around all four sides through which pass the long vertical spindles that support the hood. The hood has a similar molded framework forming a crown, with horizontal spindles running from front to back. Both foot rails arch in a low serpentine curve, and one hood crown follows suit. The second hood forms a low, angular arch. Another cradle hood has a solid, paneled, board roof.[71]

The cradle illustrated in figure **2-52** could just as easily have had a wooden hood as a cloth one. The side wings needed only to be raised to the height of the tall posts and a crown added. As designed, the head end resembles a square-back armchair, and both the head and foot "bow" in lateral curves. Leg bottoms have been rounded in the lathe to produce a soft finish line and then slotted to accommodate unusual head-to-foot rockers. A faint scribe line around each lower leg between the groove and the wooden pin served as a guide to cut the rocker slots. The brace linking the center of the curved rocker boards is bamboo-turned like the rest of the roundwork, and the plank edges are double-beaded in the manner of a chair seat. The collapsible cloth hood at the head of the cradle appears to be original in its fittings and printed brown fabric. The fittings, made of tinned sheet iron, consist of two brackets and two straplike arches. The brack-

Fig. 2-53 Child's Windsor cradle, Rhode Island, 1815–25. White pine (plank, microanalysis); H. 16″, L. 36″. (William E. Lewis collection: Photo, Garth's Auctions, Inc.)

ets are vertical tabs secured to the horizontal member of each wing by two long tangs whose tips are visible. Handmade loop-eye pins connect straps and brackets. A square-end cradle variant has a head and foot angled backward in the manner of a bent-back chair; long side rails slope gently from the high to the low end.[72]

The hoodless pattern with stepped sides was current in Windsor cradle design of the early nineteenth century. The example illustrated in figure **2-53** features Cumberland spindles flattened on both faces. This double-baluster-shaped stick appears in Windsor work originating in New York (fig. 2-39) and Rhode Island. The combination of Cumberland spindles and a white pine plank points to Rhode Island as the most likely place of origin. This notion is reinforced by a feature in another cradle constructed of Cumberland spindles and strengthened by heavy corner posts with ball tops. Although found on Canada's Niagara Peninsula and perhaps even made in that region, the design exhibits the hand of a Rhode Island craftsman: all the spindle tips have tiny tapered cylinders of the type found in prerevolutionary Rhode Island Windsor work. The Cumberland spindle appears to have had its genesis in Rhode Island as an occasional feature before achieving prominence in New York. In the present cradle, gentle curves in the head and adjacent rails complement the spindle profiles. The upper side rails are merely extended arms terminating in Rhode Island–type scrolls. The rocker profile is based on an earlier pattern (fig. 2-50). A date of no earlier than the late 1810s or the 1820s is suggested by the ring turning centered in each heavy post. Another cradle of almost identical armlike upper rail has a "skeletal" framework, supported only by twelve spindles around an open bottom.[73]

A low cradle of stepped head whose design is a cross between fancy and Windsor styling is distinctive among infant's rocking beds (fig. **2-54**). Although the rockers are replacements, they may be copies of the original pattern, since they are of the same profile as those in figure 2-53. Dating evidence is found in the upper side rails of the head whose forward tips curve in sharp bends. Rails of related form appear in a child's wagon (fig. 2-59) with a slat back that suggests a date in the 1820s. The primary and upper rails of the cradle form corner lap joints secured by the penetration of the wedged slats. The upper rail bends terminate in round tenons that pierce the main rail and are held fast by wedges. Each vertical slat pierces the plank with a round tenon wedged from the bottom. Flared blocking at the interior base of each slat strengthens the structure in an area subject to stress during use. Except for the rockers, all exposed surfaces have "old" blue paint. Other low-tiered Windsor cradles generally have plain spindles and heavy corner posts supporting ball-, button-, or egg-shape finials. One also has tiny horizontal finials at the tips of the side rails in the upper tier.

Fig. 2-54 Child's Windsor cradle, Rhode Island or Massachusetts, 1820–30. White pine (plank, microanalysis); H. 15½″, L. 31¾″, w. (head) 15¼″, (rockers) 23⅟₁₆″, (plank) 30″ by 12″; old blue ground (possibly original, except for rockers); rockers replaced. (Mr. and Mrs. Oliver Wolcott Deming collection: Photo, Winterthur.)

Fig. 2-55 Child's Windsor coach, Massachusetts or northern New England, 1825–35. H. 30″, L. 25″, w. (crest) 15¾″, (plank) 22⅜″ by 12¹⁵⁄₁₆″; wine red ground with golden yellow. (Private collection: Photo, Winterthur.)

Fig. 2-56 Child's Windsor cradle, Massachusetts or northern New England, 1825–35. H. 29⅝", L. 40½", W. (head) 19⅝", (rockers) 27⅜", (plank) 39¾" by 15⅜"; dark brown and brick red grained ground with dark green, yellow, and bronze. (Philip H. Bradley Co.: Photo, Winterthur.)

Two highly individual cradles with horizontal slat-style chair backs forming the head panels round out the basic patterns (figs. 2-55, 2-56). Figure **2-55** is rare if not unique in size and the use of casters. The plank is only 22½ inches long, hardly adequate for accommodating both bedding and an infant. The design was probably intended as a kind of baby coach in which the child was placed in a seated or semi-reclining position. Casters permitted gentle motion to soothe the baby, if desired. The wheels also permitted moving the cradle freely about, indoors or out, without having to carry the bed to its new location. Thus, the young child could enjoy the advantages of fresh air with little effort on the part of the mother. Actually, the open design of the Windsor cradle encouraged good air circulation, which was beneficial to the infant and helpful in keeping the bedding fresh. The turned elements and low arch of the slat in figure 2-55 suggest the dating period. The side and end spindles are ball-centered, although the profile is not readily discernible, since the turnings are flattened inside and out. The squared rails coordinate with the turned and squared long stretchers. The slight backward bend of the head and foot and the shaved post faces complete the chairlike quality of the cradle, which retains its original brick red paint and yellow striping and ornament. The rounded plank suggests the shape Elisha Harlow Holmes identified as a "Round end cradle" in 1825.[74]

Almost twice as long as the bed on casters is a cradle constructed with an open foot (fig. **2-56**). Thomas Walter Ward II had pine cradles of this description in stock at his Pomfret, Connecticut, store when the annual inventory was made on January 31, 1840. The reason for the open end is not obvious: both size and workmanship indicate that money was not a factor; as for convenience, the sides of the bed are of standard height. Perhaps the open end was butted against the side of a full-sized bed in the manner of an open-sided crib now identified with northeastern North Carolina. Cylindrical posts with ball finials represent traditional elements in cradle design, although the loaf-top slat probably was reasonably current with the chair market when the cradle was built. A stepped, or tiered, profile is achieved through the use of deep side slats sawed to form. The tiny lunette-shaped cutout, or slot, along the side at the head posts is present in work associated with several New England areas, and the profile of the slat suggests Massachusetts influence. Similar narrow, round-tipped rockers pinned in place appear in rocking chairs of the 1820s and 1830s. The plank probably is made of pine; the flat edge is defined by a dark green painted band. Covering all exposed surfaces are remnants of dark brown and brick red rosewood graining. Yellow penciling fills the bamboo grooves and outlines all the slat edges. Stylized floral forms once were stenciled brightly in bronze on both faces of the side slats and the crest interior. In an open-foot variant, head posts have shaved faces and the legs socket into the rockers; the side rails lack a step.[75]

Go-Carts, Baby Cages, Wagons, and Rocking Horses

Alice Morse Earle wrote in 1899 that "a go-cart or standing-stool was a favorite instrument to teach a child to walk." She noted that some examples had a narrow toy shelf. Depending upon the sophistication of the equipment, the art of the turner, cabinetmaker, or carpenter was represented. The form has a broad base for stability, consisting of three, four, or six sides (fig. 2-57). Where the sides meet, wheels or casters with housings are fitted below the base frame. Turned or squared posts slant upward and inward to support a small square or circular frame at the height of a child's waist. The apparatus was useful both to teach an infant to walk and to keep a child under control once this skill had been mastered. Visual representations of the go-cart are known from about 1435; the illuminated *Book of Hours of Catherine of Cleves* illustrates a domestic scene with the seated Virgin and the infant Jesus at her side standing in an open-framed go-cart on wheels similar to that pictured. A French woodcut of 1482 depicts a child behind a push-type walker, and a seventeenth-century illustration shows a child standing in a conical stationary cage of basketwork, also called a baby tender or pen.[76]

A small rectangular, eighteenth-century American cage of post-and-board construction at Colonial Williamsburg contains a raised floor and an interior seat, creating a pen for playing. Another pen, or cage, combines the arts of the Windsor- and fancy-chair maker with that of the carpenter (fig. 2-58). The Windsor construction is obvious, and knowledge of fancy-chair making is evident in the use of thin, bent strips of wood around the top and bottom, which confine the spindles in much the same manner as the casing around a compass-shaped rush seat. Simple carpentry is represented in the butt construction of the cage back and floor, the seat with its cleat and vertical post, and the play or food box. The paint, which is cream color over white (probably a primer) with gilt penciling, could be original, as no other paint appears on the wood in chipped areas. Further supporting this observation is the date "1819" painted on the reverse of the backboard.[77]

References to this specialized equipment for children appear in American documents of eighteenth- and nineteenth-century date, although they generally do not give particular descriptions. As early as January 22, 1743, Solomon Fussell, a Philadelphia chairmaker, debited a customer's account for "mending one Chair & a goecart." Robert Crage (Craig) of Leicester, Massachusetts, charged Jonathan Pudney 2s.8d. for making "a goe Cart for a Child" on March 14, 1758. The following year he debited an Oxford resident 3s. for a similar apparatus "Sent By his son." Under the date June 27, 1776, the inventory of Jacob Fetter, Sr., in Lancaster, Pennsylvania, itemizes "one Children walking Stool." The rather high evaluation of 7s.6d. probably indicates that the apparatus was more elaborate than most. Other go-carts stood in the Philadelphia shops of John Lambert (d. 1793) and Anthony Steel (d. 1817) at their deaths; appraisers valued the latter example at $1.[78]

Several other Windsor-type baby tenders or walkers were constructed. A stationary example consists of four slanted, cylindrical posts linked by five tiers of cylindrical stretchers, or braces, of diminishing width from bottom to top, the level of mounting staggered slightly between any two adjacent sides. Posts are tapered at the toes and capped by a ball finial at the top (fig. 2-53). The general appearance is that of modified panels for a slat-back chair. Another apparatus is on casters. Stretchers uniting the four bamboo-turned legs are mounted low in box style. A shallow board frame is nailed around the upper legs, and a hinged top with a central circular hole opens to admit a child. A toybox nailed to the front of the frame is an old, but later, addition. Go-carts

Fig. 2-57 Child in go-cart. From Andrew W. Tuer, *Forgotten Children's Books* (London: Leadenhall Press, 1898–99), p. 93. (Winterthur Library.)

Fig. 2-58 Child's Windsor cage, New York or southern New England, ca. 1819. H. 19", (seat) 9⅜", W. (top) 13", D. (top) 19½"; cream ground with gold. (Connecticut Historical Society, Hartford, gift of Charles S. Bissell: Photo, Winterthur.)

Fig. 2-59 Child's Windsor wagon, Massachusetts, possibly Worcester County, 1825–40. White pine (plank); H. 24⅝", L. (body) 28¾", (with tongue) 80¼", W. (at wheels) 26½", (plank) 27⅛" by 11½"; brownish red ground (base structure) and medium dark blue-green ground (plank and body) with black. (Worcester Historical Museum, Worcester, Mass.: Photo, Winterthur.)

similar to that in figure 2-57, except with casters and a circular top frame, continued to be manufactured in England throughout the nineteenth century. John Claudius Loudon illustrates one in his *Encyclopaedia* (1833), and the firm of William Brear and Sons of Addingham, Yorkshire, still produced the form around 1900.[79]

Stick-and-socket construction was occasionally employed in small vehicles built for the conveyance of children. An early representation appears in a portrait of the Josiah Wedgwood family in their English garden or park, painted by George Stubbs in 1780. A small child is seated in a diminutive version of an open riding chair whose small wooden seat of Windsor construction, with a plank bottom, turned legs, and low, Gothic-pattern upper structure, is mounted on a carriage frame. A nineteenth-century American vehicle, probably from Worcester County, Massachusetts, is of wagon form with iron-rimmed wheels (fig. **2-59**). The body is nothing more than a cradle with a slat-type chair back at one end that has shaved-face posts and long ball spindles. The upper side tiers terminate in forward bends, not unlike the side pieces in several cradles (fig. 2-54). Although the double-ogee capping piece at the "foot" recalls an eighteenth-century pattern, its design has a purpose. When the long front pole is in an upright position, it can be steadied in the notch between the two curves.[80]

References to children's wagons are uncommon in early records and probably represent vehicles of simpler construction than that illustrated. Silas Cheney of Litchfield, Connecticut, built a child's wagon in 1803 for the family of Ebenezer Boles. The price was 9s., or $1.50. In Windsor, Vermont, Thomas Boynton repaired a child's wagon in 1822 and a "little Waggon" two decades later. A pen-and-watercolor drawing of the Cowdrey children executed about 1838 at Ithaca, New York, by Henry Walton depicts two small children, hand in hand, standing in front of a large wagon mounted on a spring frame. The body of board construction decorated with ornamental banding corresponds in profile to figure 2-54. A long tongue is upright at the wagon front. An illustrated notice of Wakefield and Howe in a Boston directory of 1856 depicts a small vehicle of stagecoach form; a pole with T-shaped cross piece is at the front.[81]

At the same time that craftsmen were building go-carts and wagons, they were also producing rocking horses for children's amusement and exercise. Before the revolutionary war, cabinetmaker William Savery of Philadelphia billed Joseph Pemberton for "Mending a hobby horse," the forerunner of the rocking horse, which consisted of a stick and horse's head that children pretended to ride. The fabrication of rocking horses perhaps was introduced to the city in 1785 by William Long "from London." In advertising his business, Long advised that rocking horses taught children to ride and gave them a "wholesome and pleasing exercise." The price of a "middle size" rocking horse at a local toy shop was $27 in 1800. Several years later Samuel Coates paid $20 for "a Rocking horse Compleat" and $2 for a "Packing Case" to ship the order to an out-of-town client. At Boston Daniel Rea repainted a child's rocking horse for a local resident in 1791 and charged him 6*s*. By the third quarter of the nineteenth century customers could choose a rocking apparatus that substituted a small chair and a flattened horse's head for the complete equine figure (pl. 25), but the principle of the rocking base remained the same. The animal heads have leather harnesses and real, fabricated, or painted manes. Seated in the small chair behind the head with the rockers in motion, a child could imagine that he was driving his own horse-drawn vehicle. Most extant examples are fitted with a low-back chair of midcentury date or later. Sometimes the open supports beneath the chair are exchanged for a semi-enclosed platform. One horse bears the legend "From Emersons Bazaar, 37 Merrimack St., Haverhill." In another pattern the single animal's head is replaced by two smaller heads mounted as posts on forward extensions of the seat. A glider mechanism is substituted for rockers in still other frames. The illustrated horse is relatively rare in retaining its original painted decoration. The head is white daubed with black and has touches of red at the mouth and nostrils and light purple on the neck. The ears are made of cloth painted black. The chair seat, which appears to be woven, is actually a plank painted in trompe l'oeil canework in colors of straw yellow and black. The rest of the chair and the rocking frame surfaces are painted a pinkish red brick color with black striping.[82]

A fitting postscript to this survey of children's Windsor furniture is a pencil drawing addressing a human dimension that is all too familiar (fig. 2-60). The sketch is one of several made by Mary Sigourney Russell of Connecticut for her husband, Reverend Francis T. Russell, in 1862. The articles of small furniture and toys scattered about the parlor announce the presence of children in the household. With three small boys, mother (Mary) has had a hectic day and has just found a few moments to work on the family mending at her sewing machine. In walks father with an unannounced friend! Clearly delineated in a state of disarray are a child's late Boston-style rocker and a low armchair. Behind them is a cradle drawn with the faintest suggestion of spindles along the sides between ball-top posts.

Miniature Furniture, or Toys

Miniatures attract and fascinate young and old alike. In an illustration from *Rhymes for the Nursery* (Boston, 1837), a mother busy at her sewing sits beside her child at play (fig. 2-61). At the child's feet is a small-scale version of a room interior showing a fireplace wall, a tea table, and chairs. Although this edition of the *Rhymes* dates from 1837, the costumes and furniture are typical of the 1820s or earlier.

Of the several modern terms used for small-scale furniture, *miniature* is a good generic word. The term *craftsman's sample* or *cabinetmaker's sample* is a misnomer in many cases, and the name *doll furniture* seems at times too restrictive. Period references to miniature furniture are almost unknown, so that two records dating to the 1820s and 1830s are of particular interest. When the brig *Hannah* left Philadelphia on July 30, 1821, bound for Santiago, Cuba, she carried 42 fancy chairs, 252 Windsors, and "One Box Toy Chairs." Appraisers who made an inventory of Cyrus Cleaveland's shop in Providence, Rhode Island, in 1837 found among the coconut shells, "Dipper Handles,"

Fig. 2-62 Miniature bow-back Windsor side chair, Connecticut–Rhode Island border region, 1795–1810. Yellow poplar (seat) with maple, ash, and oak (microanalysis); H. 11½″, (seat) 5¼″, W. (seat) 5⅝″, D. (seat) 5¼″; right rear leg replaced and possibly right and medial stretchers. (Winterthur 64.1316.)

Fig. 2-63 Miniature slat-back Windsor side chair, New York or Connecticut, 1815–30. Yellow poplar (seat) with maple and ash (microanalysis); H. 9½″, (seat) 4¹³⁄₁₆″, W. (crest) 4⅞″, (seat) 5½″, D. (seat) 4⅝″. (Winterthur 59.1013.)

and "Dipper Tools" a group of "6 Toy Bedsteads," which they valued at 25¢ apiece. *Toy,* then, is one term that found acceptance in the general period under discussion.[83]

Small replicas of eighteenth-century Windsor chairs are not uncommon, but most are twentieth-century products. All the more remarkable, then, is an 11½-inch toy chair that was so carefully modeled around the turn of the nineteenth century that it can be identified as a product of the Connecticut–Rhode Island border area (fig. **2-62**). Correct for this location are the flat bow face with scratch beads; the raised, blunt-edge seat front; the full, elongated balusters; and the round-tipped stretchers. The craftsman also made some attempt to define the spindle swell common to the region.[84]

Several Windsor patterns current during the first four decades of the nineteenth century are represented in miniature seating. Most probably were made within a decade or so of their stylistic currency. The earliest is a hybrid chair in the Peabody Essex Museum, Salem, Massachusetts, in which a wooden seat and socketed front legs are combined with shaved-face rear posts of fancy construction, forming a continuous unit from crest to toe. The pattern of triple cross rods in the upper and lower back and a crest enhanced by two small, hollow-cornered medallions was current in Boston about 1810. Next in date is a plain, slat-back pattern introduced in New York and New England before the War of 1812 (fig. **2-63**). The design eventually became popular from the South and Midwest to Canada. The presence of a flaring, arc-front seat suggests a Connecticut, New York, or Pennsylvania origin. Another slat-back miniature has a balloon-type seat, as found in figure 2-67, and tiny arrow spindles. Several miniatures feature slats with hollow upper corners, a pattern first manufactured in adult seating in the 1820s (fig. 2-44).[85]

Two diminutive chairs, less than 6 inches high, with arrow spindles and rounded-slat crests, represent in size, quality, and simple design the kind of furniture that became especially popular for nineteenth-century dollhouses (fig. **2-64**). The background of the chairs is far from ordinary, as handwritten tags indicate: "2 doll's chairs made by Thomas Goddard for his great granddaughter Mrs. John P. Peckham (Matilda Allen) when she was about 3 yrs. old, by her great grandfather Thomas Goddard. They are now about 90 yrs. old. (1934)." Thomas Goddard, a cabinetmaker in Newport, Rhode

Island, was in his late seventies when he whittled these chairs in the 1840s for little Matilda. Her grandchild presented them to the Newport Historical Society in 1934.

The roll-top, half-spindle pattern represented in miniature by figure **2-65** was popular from the 1820s. Although the pattern is generally associated with New England fancy-chair making, both rush- and wood-seat chairs were constructed. The miniature, which is completely hand fashioned including the roundwork, bears distinct evidence of New York styling in its combination of a balloon seat with a ball-centered front stretcher and back posts tapered sharply at the base below a ringed band (fig. 2-39). Surface paint is mottled dark brown and brick red with yellow banding and decoration.

The Baltimore tablet-top chair was popular in miniature furniture. The superb turnings of a 10-inch-high example are well-proportioned, detailed replicas of the prototypes, as are the plain back legs set close together at the top (fig. **2-66**). The seat is well modeled. Surfaces are covered with golden mustard yellow paint (now discolored from the varnish) penciled in black; the crest features green and bronze gilt decoration. A rare pair of tablet-top miniatures features a large, shield-shaped back splat (fig. **2-67**) whose profile derives from the arrow spindle. Although the simplicity of the bold turnings suggests rather than duplicates Baltimore roundwork, these elements in combination with the careful proportions and well-executed decoration have produced outstanding examples of the miniature art. A penciled date of 1830 on both chair bottoms may be contemporary. On a dark blue-gray-green ground the decoration is executed principally in golden yellow, although accents of poppy red appear on the crest, splat, and seat front and form the foliage of the back posts and legs.[86]

Most miniature chairs in the tablet-top group have plain, tapered spindles with heavier plain posts, shovel- or balloon-shape seats, and plain, swelled and tapered legs (pl. 26). The left-hand chair of plate 26 has two early features associated with Pennsylvania work of the 1790s: shapely, grooved bamboo legs and a modeled shield-shape seat. The rectangular crest and naturalistic decoration suggest, however, that the miniature was made near the end of its assigned dating period of 1810 to 1830. The balloon seat of the miniature at the right is characteristic of Windsors dating to the 1820s and 1830s. The bold yellow decoration of this chair contrasts effectively with the brownish red surface color. A more unusual design is that of plate 27, its small tablet perched atop three arrow spindles without accompanying end posts. The shovel-shape plank followed the balloon seat in popularity. Blue-green paint and bright stylized decoraton make this a distinctive example.

Fig. 2-65 Miniature roll-top Windsor side chair, New York, 1825–40. H. 12⅞", (seat) 5⅞", W. (crest) 7⅝", (seat) 6¹³⁄₁₆", D. (seat) 7¼"; dark brown and brick red grained ground with yellow; repairs and some restoration. (Mr. and Mrs. Oliver Wolcott Deming collection: Photo, Winterthur.)

Fig. 2-66 Miniature tablet-top Windsor side chair, Baltimore, 1825–40. H. 10", (seat) 5¹⁄₁₆", W. (crest) 6⁷⁄₁₆", (seat) 5¼", D. (seat) 5½"; golden mustard yellow ground with black, bronze, dark gold, and light green; repairs and some restoration. (Steven and Helen Kellogg collection: Photo, Winterthur.)

Fig. 2-67 Miniature tablet-top Windsor side chairs (pair), Baltimore, 1825–40. Yellow poplar (seats); H. 12", (seats) 6⁵⁄₁₆", W. (crests) 9", (seats) 7⅛", D. (seats) 7¼"; dark blue-gray-green ground with yellow and poppy red. (Florence and George Dittmar collection: Photo, Winterthur.)

Miniature work of the third quarter of the century and later focuses on low, round-back, and tablet-top styles (fig. **2-68**). Ball-tipped feet were relatively common in this period. Except for the loaf-top pattern, which is a rounded tablet top, fashions harked back to the eighteenth century, but their nineteenth-century interpretation is unmistakable. Turnings are heavier, stretchers are mounted in box style, seats have blunt edges and few surface contours, and arms are rounded in blunt tips. The naturalistic floral decoration in pastel colors on the crest of the balloon-back chair with spindles is

Fig. 2-68 Miniature low-, balloon-, and bow-back Windsor chairs, Pennsylvania (*left center*) and New England, 1850–80. (*Left to right*) H. 10″, 13⅝″, 16⅝″, 11¾″; grounds of dark brick red, dark brown and dark red graining, orange-coral, and olive green. (Mr. and Mrs. Oliver Wolcott Deming collection: Photo, Winterthur.)

Fig. 2-69 Miniature tablet-top Windsor rocking chair, Maryland or southern Pennsylvania, 1820–35. (New-York Historical Society, New York.)

typical of the late period, along with the lavish use of gilt decoration in Pennsylvania work. Plate 28, a New England miniature that is identical in structural elements to the low-back chair at the left in figure 2-68, retains its original light-colored surface paint and penciled, daubed, and floral decoration. The balloon-back miniature in plate 29 is of simpler design than its Pennsylvania counterpart in figure 2-68 and has a black splat in place of spindles, a common pattern alternative. The brilliant red paint covering the surface of this chair was known in the nineteenth century as coquelicot, or poppy, color.

Rocking chairs and settees are among the special forms found in miniature seating. Few miniature rocking chairs exist. One specimen, shown supporting two nineteenth-century peg dolls, has a Baltimore-inspired tablet top and complementary arrow-shaped spindles (fig. **2-69**). The forward-scroll arms are a holdover from Baltimore-Pennsylvania design of the late eighteenth century, which became popular once again in the nineteenth century. Even the small extension above the crest has a prototype in Baltimore-influenced chairmaking. An elegant miniature settee sold at auction in recent years has an extension of similar profile centered in the crest; also featured are urn-shaped back splats, hollow-cornered rectangular medallions in the front stretchers, and vigorous German-American bamboowork, all reflecting Maryland-Pennsylvania design influence. A subtle touch in the illustrated rocking chair are the feet, which are rounded at the rocker connections.[87]

More miniature settees are known than rocking chairs. A double-seated group has two-section, Pennsylvania-type shouldered crests; slat backs and arrow spindles identify another group. The largest number of miniature settees have rectangular tablet tops and probably originated in southern Pennsylvania and Maryland. One well-preserved example has roundwork and heavy, banded ornament typical of this area (fig. **2-70**). The pale, mustard brown ground is decorated principally in bronze—the fruit compositions, heavy banding, ball-and-ring work—defined by black penciling and accents. Green-daubed leafage and wine red highlights in the bronze compositions are bright additions. The arms are mahogany colored.

Fig. 2-70 Miniature tablet-top Windsor settee, southern Pennsylvania or Maryland, 1830–40. Yellow poplar (seat); H. 10½″, (seat) 4⅞″, W. (crest) 15″, (arms) 14⅛″, (seat) 14″, D. (seat) 4⅞″; pale mustard brown ground with black, bronze, green, wine red, and mahogany color (arms). (Florence and George Dittmar collection: Photo, Winterthur.)

Fig. 2-71 Miniature Windsor settee-cradle, Maryland or southern Pennsylvania, 1850–70. H. 14⅝″, (seat front) 8⅝″, W. (crest) 25¾″, (arms) 25¼″, (seat) 25½″, D. (seat) 7″. (Historical Society of York County, York, Pa.: Photo, Winterthur.)

The provenance of a small, rocking settee-cradle, which stands 14⅝ inches high, is not as certain (fig. **2-71**). Although the unusual tablet-top arm attachment is found in a full-size Baltimore settee (fig. 1-96), the turnings seem closer in character to New England work. The miniature is in a Pennsylvania museum, however, and another small settee owned in the area has related, simpler turnings with back posts scored like the lower part of the rear legs in figure 2-71. The detailing and proportions of the two examples are remarkable. Other settee-cradles tend to be crudely fashioned by comparison.[88]

Notes

1. Peter Gregg Slater, *Children in the New England Mind* (Hamden, Conn.: Archon Books, 1977), pp. 18–22, 29; "Extracts from the Diary of Col. Landon Carter," *William and Mary Quarterly* 13, no. 1 (July 1904): 46.

2. John Jones, estate records, 1708, Philadelphia Register of Wills; Margaret B. Schiffer, *Chester County, Pennsylvania, Inventories, 1684–1850* (Exton, Pa.: Schiffer, 1974), pp. 105, 133, 201, 388; John Gaines II and Thomas Gaines, account book, 1712–62, Joseph Downs Collection of Manuscripts and Printed Ephemera, Winterthur Library (hereafter cited as DCM and WL.)

3. Solomon Fussell, account book, 1738–48, Stephen Collins Papers, Library of Congress (hereafter cited as LC; microfilm, DCM). For Legare, see Harrold E. Gillingham, "The Philadelphia Windsor Chair and Its Journeyings," *Pennsylvania Magazine of History and Biography* 55, no. 3 (October 1931): 302. William Barker, account book, 1763–67, Rhode Island Historical Society, Providence (hereafter cited as RIHS); Daniel Jones, estate records, 1766, Philadelphia Register of Wills.

The word *small* found in reference to chairs should be interpreted with caution, since it does not always refer to children's furniture. The term is also used for adult seating, to identify a side chair in contrast to a *large,* or arm, chair.

4. Trumble references are found in Nancy A. Goyne (Evans), "Francis Trumble of Philadelphia, Windsor Chair and Cabinetmaker," in *Winterthur Portfolio 1,* ed. Milo M. Naeve (Winterthur, Del.: Winterthur Museum, 1964), pp. 228, 230. Francis Trumble, bill to John Cadwalader, May 9, 1772, Cadwalader Papers, Gen. John Cadwalader, Historical Society of Pennsylvania, Philadelphia (hereafter cited as HSP); James Beekman, account book of personal affairs, 1761–96, White-Beekman Papers, New-York Historical Society, New York (hereafter cited as NYHS); Sheed and White, advertisement in *South Carolina Gazette* (Charleston), June 24, 1766 (citation file, Museum of Early Southern Decorative Arts, Winston-Salem, N.C. [hereafter cited as MESDA]); John Edwards, estate records, 1767, Philadelphia Register of Wills (microfilm, DCM); Dinah Jenkins, estate records, 1788, Nantucket County, Mass., Registry of Probate.

5. William, Daniel, and Samuel Proud, ledger, ca. 1770–1825, RIHS; Thomas Ash and William Ash, bill to Saint George Tucker, August 8, 1786, Tucker-Coleman Collection, Swem Library, College of William and Mary, Williamsburg, Va. (hereafter cited as WM). The 1789 shipping records are found in Gillingham, "Philadelphia Windsor Chair," pp. 327–28. Philadelphia Outward Coastwise and Foreign Entries, 1792–98, including manifest of ship *Thomas Chalkley* for Surinam, February 15, 1798, and schooner *Eagle* for Charleston, August 25, 1792, U.S. Customhouse Records, French Spoliation Claims, National Archives, Washington, D.C. (hereafter cited as NA); Philadelphia Outward Coastwise and Foreign Entries, 1792–98, manifest of brig *Fame* for Charleston, June 28, 1794, U.S. Customhouse Records, NA; David Ruth, bill to Peyton Skipwith, November 6, 1797, Peyton Skipwith Papers, WM; John Fisher, William King, and John Bwiney, estate records, 1794 and 1796, Baltimore County, Md., Inventories (microfilm, DCM); Estate of Daniel Trotter,

household goods taken by Ephraim Haines at the appraisal, December 31, 1800, DCM; John Lambert, estate records, 1793, Philadelphia Register of Wills.

6. Solomon Cole, account book, 1794–1809, Connecticut Historical Society, Hartford (hereafter cited as CHS); Joseph K. Ott, "Recent Discoveries among Rhode Island Cabinetmakers and Their Work," *Rhode Island History* 28, no. 1 (February 1969): 8; Amos Denison Allen, memorandum book, 1796–1803, CHS; James Chestney, advertisement in *Albany Chronicle,* April 10, 1797 (reference courtesy of Helen McKearin).

7. Reverend John Murray, letter to William Palmer, July 23, 1803, Papers of Reverend John Murray, 1799–1810, NYHS.

8. Comparable Rhode Island Windsors are illustrated in Nancy Goyne Evans, *American Windsor Chairs* (New York: Hudson Hills, 1996), figs. 6-38 (scrolls), 6-21 (arm pieces), 6-19 (baluster caps), 6-33 (post tops), 6-18 (seat).

9. A sack-back armchair by William Widdifield and a fan-back side chair by John Wire, both with bulbous turnings at the post bases, are illustrated in Evans, *American Windsor Chairs,* figs. 3-40 (*right*), 3-48. The steel chair is illustrated in William MacPherson Hornor, Jr., *Blue Book: Philadelphia Furniture* (1935; reprint, Washington, D.C.: Highland House, 1977), pl. 482.

10. Comparable Rhode Island Windsors are illustrated in Evans, *American Windsor Chairs,* figs. 6-40, 6-43 (seat ledge), 6-31 (arm terminals).

11. Sack-back Windsors by the Tracy family are illustrated in Evans, *American Windsor Chairs,* fig. 6-98.

12. Comparable New York Windsors are illustrated in Evans, *American Windsor Chairs,* figs. 5-12 (overall), 5-17 (Ash brothers). The MacBride chair is privately owned.

13. Comparable Windsors are illustrated in Evans, *American Windsor Chairs,* figs. 6-234 (Nantucket chair), 6-226 (Wing chair).

14. Comparable Windsors are illustrated in Evans, *American Windsor Chairs,* figs. 6-23 (lath-post chair), 6-136 (border chair), 6-43 (spool turnings), 6-72 (scroll arms), 6-42 (plank edges), 6-75 (feet). Figure 2-10 is illustrated in Wallace Nutting, *Furniture Treasury* (1928; reprint, New York: Macmillan, 1966), fig. 2513.

15. Figure 2-12 is illustrated in Nutting, *Furniture Treasury,* fig. 2520. Adult-size, slat-back Windsors and a joined mahogany prototype are illustrated in Evans, *American Windsor Chairs,* figs. 3-53, 3-54.

16. Comparable Windsors are illustrated in Evans, *American Windsor Chairs,* figs. 3-74, 3-75.

17. Comparable Windsors are illustrated in Evans, *American Windsor Chairs,* figs. 6-76, 6-83 (Rhode Island spool-and-ring turnings), 6-209 (Boston cross-stretcher chair).

18. John Claudius Loudon, *An Encyclopaedia of Cottage, Farm, and Villa Architecture and Furniture* (1833; rev. ed., London: Longman, Orme, Brown, Green and Longmans, 1839), p. 1087; *The School of Manners or Rules for Children's Behaviour* (4th ed.; London: Thomas Cockerill, 1701), as quoted in Alice Morse Earle, *Child Life in Colonial Days* (New York: Macmillan, 1899), p. 216.

19. Gillows Papers, Shipping Invoices and Letters, 1744–72, Westminster Public Library, London (microfilm, DCM).

20. Gaines, account book; Fussell, account book; William Barker, account book, 1753–66, RIHS.

21. Sheed and White, advertisement in *South Carolina Gazette;* Matthew and Richard Brenan, advertisement in *Charleston City Gazette and Advertiser* (Charleston, S.C.), December 11, 1799 (Prime Cards, WL); Stephen Badlam, account of General Henry Knox, 1784, Henry Knox Papers, New England Historic Genealogical Society, Boston, Mass. (microfilm, Massachusetts Historical Society, Boston); Proud brothers, ledger; Jedidiah Johnson, bill to Elias Hasket Derby, May 15, 1798, Derby Family Papers, Peabody Essex Museum, Salem, Mass. (hereafter cited as PEM); Allen, memorandum book.

22. The full-size, high-back chairs attributed to Trumble are illustrated in Evans, *American Windsor Chairs,* figs. 3-6, 3-9. Other period examples are illustrated in Charles Santore, *The Windsor Style in America,* vol. 1 (Philadelphia: Running Press, 1981), figs. 222–24. Wallace Nutting manufactured a reproduction chair of this pattern, as illustrated in *Wallace Nutting Supreme Edition General Catalogue* (1930; reprint, Exton, Pa.: Schiffer, 1977), p. 90, fig. 209.

23. Comparable Windsors are illustrated in Evans, *American Windsor Chairs,* figs. 3-88, 3-90 to 3-92.

24. Wallace Nutting reproduced a sack-back highchair with New York turnings and Connecticut swelled spindles, as illustrated in Nutting, *Catalogue,* p. 90, fig. 205.

25. *Howard Reifsnyder Collection,* April 24–27, 1929 (New York: American Art Association, 1929), lot 446. The taller of the two highchairs (fig. 2-26, *right*) was purchased by Henry Francis du Pont in 1928 from a Providence dealer, who probably acquired it in neighboring Wickford.

26. A New York highchair is illustrated in Santore, *Windsor Style,* 1: fig. 226. Wallace Nutting marketed a continuous-bow highchair in the New York style with a broad back and full turnings, to which he added Connecticut-type swelled turnings, as illustrated in Nutting, *Catalogue,* p. 90, fig. 270. The Stone chairs are illustrated in Evans, *American Windsor Chairs,* figs. 6-51, 6-52.

27. Comparable Windsors are illustrated in Evans, *American Windsor Chairs,* figs. 6-139, 6-140 (spindles), 6-168 (*left*), 6-173 (baluster tops).

28. The highchair with the transitional turnings was sold from the Reifsnyder collection in 1929; *Reifsnyder Collection,* lot 443.

29. *Boon Companions* is illustrated in Anita Schorsch, *Images of Childhood* (New York: Mayflower Books, 1979), fig. 67. The Dutch engraving is reproduced in Mario Praz, *An Illustrated History of Furnishing,* trans. William Weaver (New York: George Braziller, [1964]), fig. 64.

30. "A Notebook and a Quest," *Antiques* 32, no. 1 (July 1937): 8–9. Small Windsors are mentioned with adult seating in William Ryder, Captain Joseph Dobell, and Thomas Marston, estate records, 1806, 1811, and 1814, DCM; Michael Stoner, estate records, 1810, Lancaster County, Pa., Register of Wills; Charles C. Robinson, daybook, 1809–25, Philadelphia, HSP; Anthony Steel, estate records, 1817, Philadelphia Register of Wills; David Alling, invoice book, 1819–20, and daybook, 1836–54, New Jersey Historical Society, Newark (hereafter cited as NJHS; microfilm, DCM); Ebenezer P.

Rose, estate records, 1834–36, Archives and History Bureau, New Jersey State Library, Trenton; Thomas Kinsela, estate records, 1822–23, Schenectady County, N.Y., Surrogate Court.

31. Ansel Goodrich, estate records, 1803, Hampshire County, Mass., Registry of Probate; Andrew Frink and Jonathan Chester, ledger, 1806–ca. 1817, Windham Historical Society, Willimantic, Conn.; Eli Wood, estate records, 1818–19, Barkhamstead, Conn., Genealogical Section, Connecticut State Library, Hartford (hereafter cited as CSL); James Gere, ledger, 1809–29, CSL; Benjamin Bass, estate records, 1819, Suffolk Co., Mass., Registry of Probate (microfilm, DCM; document brought to author's attention by Page Talbott).

32. Frederick Allen, estate records, 1830, Windham, Conn., Genealogical Section, CSL; Gilson Brown, Peter Peirce, and Peter A. Willard, estate records, 1833–35, 1836, and 1842–43, Worcester County, Mass., Registry of Probate; James C. Helme, book of prices, 1838, DCM.

33. Manifests of sloop *Friendship* (May 30, 1800), schooner *Rising Sun* (June 25, 1803), and schooner *Juno* (December 4, 1807), Philadelphia Outward Coastwise Entries, U.S. Customhouse Records, NA; Sass and Gready, Northern Warehouse, advertisement in *Courier* (Charleston, S.C.), May 22, 1816; Philadelphia Outward Coastwise (1801–6) and Foreign (1805, 1810, 1820) Entries, U.S. Customhouse Records, NA.

34. Thomas Safford, ledger, 1807–35, CSL; Thomas Boynton, ledger, 1811–17, Dartmouth College, Hanover, N.H. (hereafter cited as DC; microfilm, DCM); Bass, estate records; Nelson Talcott, daybook, 1839–48, DCM; Henry W. Miller, account book, 1827–31, Worcester Historical Museum, Worcester, Mass.; Thomas Needham and Co., bill to Joseph G. Waters, May 24, 1833, Waters Family Papers, PEM; Philemon Robbins, account book, 1833–36, CHS; Calvin Stetson, account book, 1843–57, DCM; Thomas Walter Ward II, inventory book, ca. 1835–45, DCM; broadside advertisement of Joel Pratt, Jr., and Son, Hartford, Conn., 1840, Henry Ford Museum and Greenfield Village, Dearborn, Mich.

35. The Sharpless chair is illustrated in Herbert F. Schiffer and Peter B. Schiffer, *Miniature Antique Furniture* (Wynnewood, Pa.: Livingston, 1972), fig. 90.

36. Baltimore winged-tablet chairs are illustrated in Evans, *American Windsor Chairs,* figs. 4-7, 4-8.

37. An adult-size Philadelphia Windsor and the Pratt chair are illustrated in Evans, *American Windsor Chairs,* figs. 3-127, 7-60.

38. The Turner chair is illustrated in Evans, *American Windsor Chairs,* fig. 3-140.

39. A photograph of the Wilder chair is in Visual Resources Collection, WL (hereafter cited as VRC), no. 73.321.

40. Pennsylvania splat-back, pierced-splat, and balloon-back Windsors are illustrated in Evans, *American Windsor Chairs,* figs. 3-146, 3-147, 3-149.

41. Manifests of schooner *Virginia* (October 23, 1800) and brig *Charleston* (August 3, 1803), Philadelphia Outward Coastwise Entries, U.S. Customhouse Records, NA; "Notebook and Quest," pp. 8–9; Ebenezer Knowlton, estate records, 1811, Suffolk County, Mass., Registry of Probate (microfilm, DCM; document brought to author's attention by Page Talbott); Proud brothers, ledger,

and Daniel and Samuel Proud, daybook and ledger, 1810–34, RIHS; Boynton, ledger.

42. Allen Holcomb, account book, 1809–28, Metropolitan Museum of Art, New York; David Miller, probate records, 1815, DCM; David Alling, account book, 1801–39, ledger, 1803–53, invoice book, and daybook, NJHS (microfilm, DCM); Robinson, daybook.

43. Rhodes Allen, advertisement in *Providence Directory* (Providence, R.I.: Brown and Danforth, 1824), p. 33; Zadock Hutchins, estate records, 1830, Pomfret, Conn., Genealogical Section, CSL; Elisha Harlow Holmes, daybook, 1825–30, CSL; Elisha Harlow Holmes, ledger, 1825–30, CHS; T. Deland, account of Daniel W. Rogers, 1829, Papers of Daniel Rogers, Jr., PEM.

44. Robbins, account book; Alling, ledger; Hubbard in *Boston Directory* (Boston, Mass.: Adams, Sampson, 1860), p. 80.

45. The Krimmel sketchbooks are in DCM. Comparable eastern Connecticut Windsors are illustrated in Evans, *American Windsor Chairs,* figs. 7-7, 7-8. The Pratt highchairs are illustrated in advertisements, as follows: Jane Wilson, *Antiques* 86, no. 3 (September 1964): 243; James Bakker, *Maine Antique Digest* (Waldoboro), April 1981. A photograph of the Baltimore highchair is in photographic files, MESDA, no. 10,692.

46. An eastern Massachusetts Windsor with a similarly shaped seat plank is illustrated in Evans, *American Windsor Chairs,* fig. 7-40. Elbridge Gerry Reed, daybook, 1829–51, Old Sturbridge Village, Sturbridge, Mass. (hereafter cited as OSV).

47. Comparable New York chairs are illustrated in Evans, *American Windsor Chairs,* figs. 5-34, 5-39, 5-40, 5-45. The child's low Windsor with Cumberland spindles is illustrated in *American Antique Sale,* June 5, 1972 (Reading, Pa.: Pennypacker Auction Centre, 1972), lot 413.

48. Another double highchair is pictured in Nutting, *Treasury,* fig. 2544.

49. The Stauffer watercolor is illustrated in *Fine Americana,* January 26–29, 1977 (New York: Sotheby Parke-Bernet, 1977), lot 595. The Rothermel watercolor is illustrated in *James G. Pennypacker Collection,* October 29, 1973 (Reading, Pa.: Pennypacker Auction Centre, 1973), lot 10. The Bartoll canvas is illustrated in Narcissa G. Chamberlain, "William T. Bartoll, Marblehead Painter," *Antiques* 122, no. 5 (November 1982): 1088. A comparable Boston Windsor with arc-style crest ends is illustrated in Evans, *American Windsor Chairs,* fig. 7-40.

50. Buckley child's chair reference, as quoted in Nancy Goyne Evans, "Unsophisticated Furniture Made and Used in Philadelphia and Environs, ca. 1750–1800," in *Country Cabinetwork and Simple City Furniture,* ed. John D. Morse (Charlottesville: University Press of Virginia, 1969), pp. 169–70; Silas Cheney, daybook, 1813–21, Litchfield Historical Society, Litchfield, Conn. (hereafter cited as LHS; microfilm, DCM); Allen, memorandum book; Steel, estate records; Alling, ledger and daybook; Robbins, account book.

51. Helme, book of prices; Jacob Felton, daybook, 1836–38, OSV; Reed, daybook; Henry F. Dewey, account book, 1837–64, Shelburne Museum, Shelburne, Vt. (microfilm, DCM); Willard, estate records; Joseph F. Loring, estate records, 1845, Worcester County, Mass., Registry of Probate; Stetson, account book.

52. Dewey, account book; Alling, daybook.

53. Proud brothers, ledger, 1770–1825; David and Abner Haven, account book, 1785–1830, DCM; Abner Taylor, account book, 1806–32, DCM; Safford, ledger; Thomas J. Moyers and Fleming K. Rich, account book, 1834–40, DCM; Paul Jenkins, daybook, 1836–41, DCM; Titus Preston, ledgers, 1795–1817 and 1811–42, Sterling Library, Yale University, New Haven.

54. Import notices, *Charleston Courier* (Charleston, S.C.), August 11, 1806, and December 31, 1807 (citation file, MESDA); Jacob Merrill, Jr., account book, 1784–1812, Charles S. Parsons, New Hampshire Notes, VRC; Joseph Griswold, account book, 1798–1804, DCM; Boynton, ledger; Proud brothers, daybook and ledger; Cheney, daybook; Schiffer, *Chester County Inventories,* pp. 106, 134.

55. William G. Beesley, daybook, 1828–36, Salem County Historical Society, Salem, N.J.; Alling, daybook; Helme, book of prices; Kittredge and Blakes, bill to Mr. R. B. Bradford, November 21, 1838, DCM; Josiah Prescott Wilder, daybook and ledger, 1837–59, Charles S. Parsons, Wilder Family Notes, VRC; Felton, daybook; Stetson, account book; Schroder and Widmyer, advertisement in *J. H. Bryson's Lancaster Directory for 1843* (Lancaster, Pa.: James H. Bryson, 1843), p. 19; Lambert Hitchcock, estate records, 1852, Unionville, Conn., Genealogical Section, CSL; Reed, daybook.

56. The Kibling chair is at Old Sturbridge Village. The Meservy chair is privately owned.

57. The Howe chair is privately owned.

58. Samuel Eliot Morison and Henry Steele Commager, *The Growth of the American Republic,* vol. 1 (4th ed.; New York: Oxford University Press, 1950), pp. 511–13. Advertisements by William G. Shattuck in *Boston Directory for 1852* (Boston, Mass.: George Adams, 1852), p. 43; Joseph L. Ross in *Boston Directory for 1853* (Boston, Mass.: George Adams, 1853), p. 44; William O. Haskell (of Boston) in *Providence Directory for 1858* (Providence, R.I.: H[ugh] H. Brown, 1858), n.p.

59. Samuel Wales, advertisement in *Directory of the City of Boston* (Boston, Mass.: George Adams, 1850), p. 40; "Clues and Footnotes," *Antiques* 115, no. 5 (May 1979): 1064.

60. Joan Mackinnon, *A Checklist of Toronto Cabinet and Chair Makers, 1800–1865,* National Museum of Man Mercury Series (Ottawa: National Museums of Canada, 1975), p. 68.

61. Comparable border Windsors are illustrated in Evans, *American Windsor Chairs,* figs. 6-147, 6-148 (crest), 6-145 (turnings).

62. Goyne, "Francis Trumble," p. 230; Silas E. Cheney, daybook, 1802–7, LHS (microfilm, DCM); John Martin, estate records, 1834, DCM. The bamboo-turned settee was advertised by Nathan Liverant and Son, *Antiques and the Arts Weekly* (Newtown, Conn.), August 30, 1985.

63. Richard Brenan, advertisement in *Charleston City Gazette and Advertiser,* September 12, 1798 (Prime Cards, WL); import notice, *Charleston Courier,* August 11, 1806 (citation file, MESDA); manifests of brig *Hannah* (November 19, 1800) and schooner *Ranger* (September 1, 1809), Philadelphia Outward Foreign Entries, U.S. Customhouse Records, NA; Samuel Parsons and Son, advertisement in *Virginia Argus* (Richmond), October 20, 1801 (citation file, MESDA); Henry R. Burden and William M. Morrison, advertisement in *Daily National Intelligencer* (Washington, D.C.),

October 12, 1815, and April 14, 1828, as quoted in Anne Castrodale Golovin, "Cabinetmakers and Chairmakers of Washington, D.C., 1791–1840," *Antiques* 107, no. 5 (May 1975): pp. 909, 917; Schiffer, *Chester County Inventories,* p. 114.

64. Moses Parkhurst, account book, 1814–39, OSV; Stephen B. Allyn and David Finch, estate records, 1822 and 1829–30, Norwich and Bridgeport, Conn., Genealogical Section, CSL; Holmes, ledger and daybook; William Rawson, account book, 1835–41, OSV; Increase Pote, account book, 1824–30, Maine Historical Society, Portland. A crib stands before the Cincinnati cabinet warerooms of Barton White, as illustrated in David Henry Shaffer, *Cincinnati, Covington, Newport, and Fulton Directory for 1840* (Cincinnati: J. B. and R. P. Donogh, 1839), facing p. 297.

65. Ellen and Bert Denker, *The Rocking Chair Book* (New York: Mayflower Books, 1979), p. 15. Fifteenth-century cradles are illustrated in Penelope Eames, "Furniture in England, France and the Netherlands from the Twelfth to the Fifteenth Century," *Furniture History* 13 (1977): pls. 34a,b, 35a. Nutting illustrates several hooded examples in *Furniture Treasury,* figs. 1564–67.

66. Denker, *Rocking Chair Book,* p. 15; *Dictionary of Arts and Sciences* (London: W. Owen, 1754), vol. 1, part 2, p. 780. The woodcut is from *Mother Goose's Melody,* as illustrated in Linda Grant DePauw and Conover Hunt, *Remember the Ladies: Women in America, 1750–1815* (New York: Viking, 1976), p. 27.

67. Robert Crage, ledger, 1757–81, OSV; John Paine, account book, 1761–1815, Institute for Colonial Studies, State University of New York at Stony Brook (microcards, DCM); Trumble, advertisement in *Pennsylvania Gazette* (Philadelphia), December 27, 1775, as quoted in Goyne, "Francis Trumble," p. 233; John Cornthwaite, estate records, 1782, Baltimore County, Md., Inventories (microfilm, DCM); Allen, memorandum book.

68. Abraham Overholt, account book, 1790–1833, as transcribed in Alan G. Keyser, Larry M. Neff, and Frederick S. Weiser, trans. and eds., *The Accounts of Two Pennsylvania German Furniture Makers,* Sources and Documents of the Pennsylvania Germans, 3 (Breinigsville, Pa.: Pennsylvania German Society, 1978), p. 12; Margaret Berwind Schiffer, *Furniture and Its Makers of Chester County, Pennsylvania* (Philadelphia: University of Pennsylvania Press, 1966), p. 109; Thomas Howard, Jr., bill to Albert C. Greene, June 19, 1815, A. C. and R. W. Greene Collection, RIHS. Otsego County reference in Holcomb, account book; Pomfret reference in Ward, inventory book; Albany reference in George Merrifield, account book, 1831–47, DCM. The whitewood and poplar references may identify the same wood. Robbins, account book; Holmes, daybook. Blue paint is mentioned in Merrill, account book; red paint is mentioned in Cole, account book; mahogany color is mentioned in Henry Nye, bill to Ebed Hersey, Jr., March 11, 1813, DCM; Safford, ledger; Taylor, account book; Moyers and Rich, account book.

69. Parsons, advertisement in *Virginia Argus;* manifest of sloop *Polly,* July 16, 1803, Philadelphia Outward Coastwise Entries, U.S. Customhouse Records, NA; Jacob Cotts, advertisement in *Western Spy and Hamilton Gazette* (Cincinnati, Ohio), November 30, 1803, as quoted in Jane E. Sikes, *The Furniture Makers of Cincinnati 1790 to 1849*

(Cincinnati: By the author, 1976), p. 89; David Tilden, lawsuit vs. William Seaver, 1804, Colonial Court Records, Social Law Library, Boston, Mass. (reference courtesy of Charles A. Hammond and John T. Kirk); Archer Brown, advertisement in *Petersburg Republican* (Petersburg, Va.), January 22, 1805, and Joel Brown, advertisement in *Virginia Apollo* (Petersburg, Va.), May 30, 1807 (both in citation file, MESDA); Charles Robinson, estate records, 1825, Philadelphia Register of Wills; manifest of ship *John Sergeant,* November 7, 1831, Philadelphia Outward Coastwise Entries, U.S. Customhouse Records, NA; Holmes, daybook.

70. Comparable Boston Windsors are illustrated in Evans, *American Windsor Chairs,* figs. 6-207 (sticks, feet), 6-211, 6-212 (stretchers), 6-200 (seat edges).

71. Mahogany spindle-framed cradles are illustrated in Santore, *Windsor Style,* 1: figs. 255–56.

72. The bent-back cradle is illustrated in Wallace Nutting, *A Windsor Handbook* (1917; 2d ed., Framingham and Boston: Old America, n.d.), p. 113.

73. The cradle found in Canada is illustrated in Philip Shackleton, *The Furniture of Old Ontario* (Toronto: Macmillan, 1973), fig. 234. Comparable Rhode Island Windsors are illustrated in Evans, *American Windsor Chairs,* figs. 6-1, 6-2 (spindle tips), 6-72 (scroll arms). The cradle with "skeletal" framework is illustrated in an advertisement of Herbert Schiffer, *Antiques* 115, no. 6 (June 1979): inside back cover.

74. Holmes, daybook.

75. Ward, inventory book; John Bivins and Forsyth Alexander, *The Regional Arts of the Early South* (Winston-Salem, N.C.: Museum of Early Southern Decorative Arts, 1991), p. 25, fig. 13. Massachusetts Windsors with arched slats in the crest are illustrated in Evans, *American Windsor Chairs,* figs. 7-60, 7-61.

76. Earle, *Child Life,* p. 23; John Plummer, *The Book of Hours of Catherine of Cleves* (New York: Pierpont Morgan Library, 1964), pl. 23; Schorsch, *Images of Childhood,* fig. 11.

77. The Colonial Williamsburg baby cage is illustrated in Barry A. Greenlaw, *New England Furniture at Williamsburg* (Williamsburg, Va.: Colonial Williamsburg Foundation, 1974), fig. 163.

78. Fussell, account book; Crage, ledger; Jacob Fetter, Sr., estate records, 1777, Lancaster County Historical Society, Lancaster, Pa. The Lambert reference is in Hornor, *Blue Book,* p. 311. Steel, estate records.

79. The Loudon and Brear go-carts are illustrated in Christopher Gilbert, *Town and Country Furniture* (Leeds, Eng.: Temple Newsam, 1972), figs. 43, 49.

80. The Stubbs portrait of the Wedgwood family is owned by the Wedgwood Museum Trust; the study photograph is from the Courtauld Institute of Art, London. A wagon of similar body to that illustrated in figure 2-60, except for having a rounded foot and a continuous bent rail, was described as coming "from the Tuttle homestead in Sterling, Mass." when sold at auction by Hap Moore at Biddeford, Me. The wagon is illustrated in *Antiques and the Arts Weekly,* June 24, 1988.

81. Cheney, daybook, 1802–7; Thomas Boynton, ledger, 1817–47, DC (microfilm, DCM). The Walton watercolor is illustrated in *101 American Primitive Water Colors and Pastels* (Washington, D.C.: National Gallery of Art, 1966), fig. 84.

Wakefield and Howe, advertisement in *Boston Directory for 1856* (Boston: George Adams, 1856), p. 18 (advertising section).

82. William Savery, account of Joseph Pemberton, 1774–75, Pemberton Papers, HSP; 1785 advertisement and 1800 toy sale, as quoted in Marshall B. Davidson, ed., *The American Heritage History of American Antiques from the Revolution to the Civil War* (New York: American Heritage Publishing, 1968), p. 379; Margaret Fawdry, *Rocking Horses* (1986; rev. ed., London: Pollock's Toy Theatres, 1989), pp. 67–83, 88–90; John Patton, bill to Samuel Coates, ca. 1807–10, Coates-Reynell Business Papers, HSP; Daniel Rea, daybook, 1789–93, Baker Library, Harvard University, Cambridge, Mass. The Emerson Bazaar horse is illustrated in an advertisement of Bonner's Barn, *Maine Antique Digest,* February 1980.

83. Manifest of brig *Hannah,* July 30, 1821, Philadelphia Outward Foreign Entries, U.S. Customhouse Records, NA; Cyrus Cleaveland, estate records, 1837, Providence, R.I., Registry of Probate.

84. Comparable Windsors are illustrated in Evans, *American Windsor Chairs,* figs. 6-72, 6-111 (bow face), 6-30, 6-104 (seat front), 6-52 (balusters), 6-49, 6-126 (stretchers). The chair was purchased by Henry Francis du Pont in 1944; it was sold previously at the George F. Ives sale, Danbury, Connecticut, in 1924. Advertisement of Ives sale, *Antiques* 5, no. 5 (May 1924): 283.

85. The Boston miniature is illustrated in Sandra Brant and Elissa Cullman, *Small Folk: A Celebration of Childhood in America* (New York: E. P. Dutton, 1980), fig. 296. A full-size, Boston Windsor with triple cross rods in the back is illustrated in Evans, *American Windsor Chairs,* fig. 7-29.

86. Comparable Baltimore Windsors are illustrated in Evans, *American Windsor Chairs,* figs. 4-15, 4-19.

87. The miniature settee is illustrated in Santore, *Windsor Style,* 1: fig. 221. A Baltimore fancy-chair prototype for many features found in the miniature rocking chair and settee is illustrated in Evans, *American Windsor Chairs,* fig. 3-118.

88. Other miniature settees are illustrated in *Small Folk,* figs. 274, 290.

CHAPTER THREE

Production of Stools, Stands, and Miscellaneous Forms

Stools

The *Oxford English Dictionary* defines a stool as "a wooden seat (for one person) without arms or a back; a piece of furniture consisting in its simplest form of a piece of wood for a seat set upon legs, usually three or four in number, to raise it from the ground." Stick stools were common in the daily life of ancient Egypt, and evidence of their continued use can be found in representational and written documents down to modern times. Early written references to stools date to about A.D. 725 and 1000. A carving done in 1284 in a choirstall from Harz, Germany, details a workman's stool. Other low sitting stools are depicted in a pen-and-ink drawing executed in Flanders around 1445.[1]

A low footstool of rectangular top, stick legs, and socket construction depicted in a panel from the Merode Altarpiece (1425–28) demonstrates that through the centuries certain forms changed very little. The design was still current in the nineteenth century, as illustrated in figure 3-7. Randle Holme included both a rectangular- and a round-top socketed stool among the household objects depicted in his *Academy of Armory* (1688). Seventeenth-century paintings from the Low Countries depict stools of various forms (fig. **3-1**). The seated smokers of Adriaen Brouwer's tavern scene seem a contented lot. In the foreground the victim of a practical joke sits on a stick-supported stool and rests a foot upon one made of sawed boards. Board-framed stools were a popular alternative to those of stick-and-socket construction. A seat called a joint stool, introduced during the sixteenth century, used a mortise-and-tenon framing technique. This type of stool remained popular for more than 150 years. The stool with a stuffed or upholstered seat came into limited use only during the latter part of the seventeenth century.[2]

A general chronology of the stool in American life before the revolutionary war emerges from surviving records and other resources. Esther Singleton, writing early in the twentieth century, documented in some detail the extensive use of seating stools, principally the joint stool, in Boston homes of the seventeenth century. Only the rare household had more chairs than stools before 1650, but the situation changed during the next quarter century. In 1652 the household of clergyman John Cotton contained twenty-six chairs, about thirty stools, six forms (benches), and a couch. By 1675 appraisers noted no stools in John Freack's house; his seating comprised forty-five chairs. Sixty-two chairs and six stools stood in John Wensley's house in 1686, and other probate records yield comparable figures. Early Pennsylvania references to the "Joint Stoole" date from around 1700 and include households in both Philadelphia and adjacent Chester County.[3]

A New England reference of 1718 documents a second type of stool with the item "to a cricket for yr mother"; the cricket was also called a footstool. This one was charged to Phillip Fowler by John Gaines II at Ipswich, Massachusetts. Eastern Pennsylvania descriptions enlarge the picture. Mary Garrett's household at Darby con-

Fig. 3-1 Adriaen Brouwer, *The Smokers,* Flanders, 1605–38. Oil on wood panel; H. 18", W. 14⅜". (Michael Friedsam Collection, Metropolitan Museum of Art, New York.)

tained "2 Stools and Two Cussions" in 1742; a year earlier appraisers itemized four green stools in the Philadelphia home of Owen Owen. Solomon Fussell's chairmaking accounts of the 1740s record work on rush-bottom stools. The craftsman bottomed and cased five chairs and a stool in 1742 for Doctor Thomas Graeme of Graeme Park. George Emlen ordered "2 Superfine Rushbottom Stooles" a year later. The 1775 listing of a "high seat" for 3s.4d. in the Providence accounts of the Proud family is an early reference to the tall form. Cabin stools for use aboard ship are mentioned in the mercantile papers of Bostonian (Roxbury) David S. Greenough in 1772. A Windsor stool was first identified in documents only a few years earlier. Mansell, Corbett and Company of Charleston, South Carolina, placed an advertisement on February 16, 1767, that listed "green Windsor chairs and stools" among an assortment of goods imported from London on the ship *Heathcote*. The "2 wooden Stools" recorded in Mary Richards's Baltimore inventory a few years later were probably of American construction.[4]

Stools can be separated into three groups based upon height: footstools, sitting (medium-high) stools, and high stools. Windsor construction is found in all three groups, although specific references are uncommon. Stools are often identified by function or size rather than construction method. Among the early references is the listing of twelve Windsor chairs made in 1782 for Samuel Meredith by Samuel Moon of Fallsington, Bucks County, Pennsylvania, which were accompanied by three stools whose individual price of 3s.9d. suggests similar construction. At neighboring Philadelphia Windsor-chair maker Thomas Mason shipped two dozen chairs and four stools to Charleston, South Carolina, in autumn 1792; an earlier anonymous shipment in 1785 numbered eleven dozen chairs and twenty-four stools. Delaware levy court dockets record a Sussex County purchase of "24 good Windsor stools" on November 11, 1794. Intended as general courtroom furniture, the stools would have been of medium, or sitting, height. During the same decade a pair of "Wooden stools" stood in the public area of Samuel Fraunces's Philadelphia tavern.[5]

In the early nineteenth century appraisers found "18 stool chairs" with wooden bottoms on the shop premises of Windsor-chair maker Nathaniel Brown, an emigrant to Savannah from Philadelphia. John Wall, another Philadelphian, shipped chairs, settees, and stools to that southern community, and competitor James Whitaker consigned similar furniture to a Charleston firm. New York shops were also active. When Joseph Vail died in 1805 appraisers noted a stock of six sets of stool legs. The "two green stools" standing in the Joseph Prentis study at Williamsburg, Virginia, in 1809 in company with a "green stick settee" probably represented New York or Philadelphia export goods.[6]

In 1817 "20 stool feet" were among the thousands of furniture parts stockpiled at Anthony Steel's Philadelphia shop. Joseph Burden shipped new stools and chairs from Philadelphia to the Caribbean in 1821. A rare, explicit New England reference was recorded by True Currier when he sold a "wood Bottomed stool" at Deerfield, New Hampshire, in 1822. Chairmaker David Alling of Newark, New Jersey, stocked a good supply of stools during the 1830s. References run from the general (a "winsor stool") to the specific ("1 high winsor stool painted"). He "stained & varnished" another stool and painted "18 winsor rosewood stools" in imitation of fine wood. Appraisers along the eastern seaboard recorded wooden stools in several locations during the 1830s and later. John Oldham's Baltimore household contained pine stools in 1835. Twenty-five "wood stools" were part of Edward Bulkley's stock surrendered during New Haven insolvency proceedings a few years later. Three Windsor stools made up part of the finished seating at Abraham McDonough's Philadelphia facility in 1852.[7]

FOOTSTOOLS, OR CRICKETS

The terms *footstool* and *cricket* were interchangeable in the seventeenth and eighteenth centuries. Randle Holme described the form in 1688 as "a kind of low footed stool, or Cricket as some call it." Pictorial and literary references describe its use. An eighteenth-century illustration from the *Codex Amiatinus* (Biblioteca Laurenziana, Florence) pictures the prophet Ezra seated on a low benchlike stool, his feet elevated on a low footrest of board construction. His bent knees form a lap to support a manuscript. The footstool also served to raise the feet above the cold, drafty floor, and it was an essential accompaniment to the elevated chair that symbolized authority or social position. Another function is indicated in a volume by William Cartwright titled *The Lady-Errant* published sometime before 1643: "I'l stand upon a Crickit, and there make Fluent Orations to 'em." Such use brings to mind a watercolor folk painting titled *The Wedding* (ca. 1805) in which a minister stands upon a footstool before a matrimonial couple and guests.[8]

In 1736 Nathan Bailey defined a cricket as "a low stool, such as children use to sit upon." Similar use was described by Elizabeth Gaskell in *Mary Barton, A Tale of Manchester Life* (1848): "Mary drew her little cricket out from under the dresser, and sat down at Mrs. Wilson's knees." Alice Morse Earle had further comment. Speaking of a forebear who was a minister, she related that "each morning while he shaved, his little son, five years of age, stood by his dressing-table on a footstool and read Latin to his father." Baroness Hyde de Neuville depicted in watercolor a similar scene of a mother and child at Amsterdam, New York, in May 1808 (fig. **3-2**). By that date Thomas Sheraton had described the low stool used "to rest the foot upon" and provided further details: "These are generally stuffed with hair, and covered with some kind of needle-work. The frame of the stool is sometimes oval, at other times square, or of an octagon shape, with turned legs mostly, as these are lighter than any other. The sizes are various; but the height of the frame, without the stuffing, runs about 6 or 6½ inches, and the length from 9½ to a foot, and from 7 to 8 inches wide."[9]

An early reference to the cricket in America dates to July 1718, when John Gaines II of Ipswich, Massachusetts, charged a customer 2*s.* for making a stool of this description. The construction probably was open framing for rush or else board framing. The next known reference is not until 1784, when Chancellor Livingston bought a stool of low height from John Brower of New York. Soon after, Judge Saint George Tucker of Williamsburg, Virginia, paid freight from New York for merchandise that included "three Crickets." The form achieved broad social acceptance, as seen in the estates of James Galloway, a carpenter-cooper of Baltimore, and Elias Hasket Derby (d. 1799) of Salem, Massachusetts, the premier American merchant of his day. Derby's inventory recorded two crickets valued together at $1.50 in the southeast parlor of the mansion along with mahogany and Windsor chairs; two other crickets worth $2 were located in the southeast chamber, a room furnished with silk-bottom mahogany chairs. Certainly, the cricket painted green by Daniel Rea of Boston for William Bradford in 1800 was of Windsor construction. Just a year later Silas Cheney of Litchfield, Connecticut, sold one of the crickets he made between that date and 1812 for retail at 50¢ or less. The three options in utilitarian stools at this date were open framing for rush, board framing, and stick-and-socket Windsor construction. Cheney's records indicate that mahogany crickets sold for $1.25 or more, and even plain "stuft" crickets cost 83¢.[10]

Low stools continued to be called either crickets or footstools during the early nineteenth century. An 1812 entry in the accounts of Abner Taylor of Lee, Massachusetts, emphasizes the continuing interchangeability of the words: "To a Cricket or foot stool." Taylor's price was 29¢; the price range of the nineteenth-century utilitarian stool was 12¢ to 42¢ (some examples probably were unpainted). Nine "Cricket Stools" used in the household of furniture maker Frederick Allen of Windham, Connecticut, in 1830 were evaluated at 22½¢ apiece. Increase Pote of Portland, Maine, turned cricket legs for as little as 4½¢ in 1824. Thomas Walter Ward II stocked crickets of modest price at his store in Pomfret, Connecticut. Customers could select examples of "Large" size supported on "Turned Legs" or "Plain Legs." Another general group priced at about 50¢ appears to have been divided between wooden seats and open frames for rush. At least one lot of stools listed in the 1819 inventory of Benjamin Bass's Boston shop was specifically identified by appraisers as "11 crickets of wood." At the top of the general market were crickets retailing for 75¢ to $1, and even as high as $4. Several descriptions

Fig. 3-2 Baroness Hyde de Neuville, *Mother and Child*, Amsterdam, N.Y., May 20, 1808. Watercolor on paper; H. 7¼", W. 13⅜". (New-York Historical Society, New York.)

Fig. 3-3 Board-end footstool and detail of brand, Elijah Tracy, Lisbon Township, New London County, Conn., ca. 1789–1802. White pine; H. 6⁵⁄₁₆″, W. 14¹⁄₁₆″, D. 6¼″. (Slater Memorial Museum, Norwich Free Academy, Norwich, Conn.: Photo, Winterthur.)

provide a clearer picture: "Bird eye maple"; "Crickets covered with carpeting"; "cricket frames curl'd maple [and] Carpeting"; "Mahogany Crickets"; crickets covered with "Brussels carpet" or "Hair Cloth"; "Grecian crickets"; and crickets with "mahogany Legs," the tops probably intended for a fabric covering. One unusual stool, possibly a painted one, was priced at $1.50 in 1835 and described by Philemon Robbins in his Hartford accounts as a "Cricket with wheels."[11]

From a practical standpoint, Windsor and board-framed stools were the most serviceable for everyday use, and they have survived in the greatest numbers. Rush-seated stools required frequent attention, especially with hard use, and were less favored. A representative stool of board construction is documented to the shop of Elijah Tracy in Lisbon, Connecticut (fig. 3-3). The stool ends are short rectangular pieces of board sawed in round arches at the bottom to form feet. In framing, these pieces are fitted into open mortise slots cut on the inside surfaces of the long side skirts and nailed twice on the skirt faces at these points. To this sturdy frame the top board is nailed randomly across the ends and length. The maker's stamp is under the top board.

Simple Windsor-type stools with crudely shaped parts undoubtedly are homemade affairs (fig. 3-4). Even the cheapest 12¢ stool listed in some craft accounts would have had uniformly shaved legs, demonstrating the woodworker's familiarity with his tools. Offhand crickets of stick-and-socket construction have oval, round, or rectangular tops, the latter sometimes three-sided at the ends. Legs either socket inside the board or plank or pierce the top surface, held secure by wedges. The handhold crudely cut from the center of the present example permitted convenient carriage from place to place and easy extraction from storage beneath another piece of furniture. The simple design has a timeless quality. The seat, pierced by wedged legs, suggests the terminal date, since internal construction became common in Windsor furniture soon after the turn of the nineteenth century. The use of beech for the top points strongly to a New England origin, possibly the northern regions. Of the dozen or more Windsors in the Winterthur collection containing beech in their construction, all but one have white pine seats; the odd example employs a basswood plank. These materials were used for Windsor construction only in New England. Of the three documented chairs in this group, two are from Maine and one from New Hampshire.

To qualify as footstools, or crickets, low stools should be no more than 10 inches high. Thomas Sheraton suggested 6 to 6½ inches, and many surviving examples stand about 8 inches high. Low stools with baluster-turned legs are rare; among those on the market, many are from a later period. Windsor crickets, unlike taller stools of this con-

Fig. 3-4 Windsor footstool, probably Massachusetts or northern New England, 1790–1820. Beech (top) with oak (microanalysis); H. 7½″, W. 14½″, D. 6¼″. (Winterthur 65.1325.)

Fig. 3-5 Windsor footstool, Rhode Island, ca. 1802–12. Basswood (top) with maple (microanalysis); H. 8″, W. (top) 11¾″, D. (top) 7″. (Private collection: Photo, Winterthur.)

Fig. 3-6 Windsor footstool, probably New England, 1815–30. Maple (microanalysis); H. 8″, W. (top) 11½″, D. (top) 7¼″. (Winterthur 59.1969.)

struction, seem to have become popular only at the beginning of the bamboo period (fig. **3-5**). Even Baroness Hyde de Neuville's sketch of 1808 delineates a bamboo-turned footstool (fig. 3-2). The illustrated cricket is more delicate than its image suggests. Just under 12 inches in length, the plank, or top, is almost 1⅝ inches thick. The edges were once flat at the top, then chamfered, but the center of each long side is now well worn and rounded from use. On the bottom are light, lengthwise plane marks. Maple legs pierce the top surface in tiny tips that are wedged. Slight humps are present at these points because the soft basswood has worn down around the hardwood tips. This low form never had any stretchers. The bamboowork, which has exceptionally well-formed segments, can be compared with the arm supports in a child's highchair from Rhode Island (fig. 2-30). That relationship, coupled with the material and profile of the plank, points to a similar origin for the footstool.[12]

Manuscript references to figured maple stools of any size are uncommon, while references to footstools are rare. Just as often, citations describe a framework for rush or fabric seats. Correct in period for the curled maple example illustrated in figure **3-6** is an April 1817 reference from the accounts of chairmaker Thomas Boynton of Windsor, Vermont: "a Bird eye maple cricket" for 75¢. David Alling's Newark, New Jersey, accounts itemize maple stools in several sizes from the mid to late 1830s, including half a dozen medium to tall "curld counter stools" and "2 wood top curl maple stools" priced at $1.50 each. An insolvency inventory of the Edward Bulkley shop at New

Fig. 3-7 Windsor footstool, northern New England, 1825–40. Basswood (top) with birch (microanalysis); H. 7⅛″, W. (top) 13″, D. (top) 8″; medium yellow ground with reddish brown, dark and light green, white, and black. (Winterthur 67.709.)

Fig. 3-8 Asahel L. Powers, *Charles Mortimer French,* Ludlow, Vt., ca. 1832. Oil on wood panel; H. 36″, W. 21¾″. (New York State Historical Association, Cooperstown.)

Haven, Connecticut, lists "seventeen curled maple stools in the wood," that is, without the finishing stain and varnish coat. Other crickets probably similar to the illustrated stool were recorded by Silas Cheney of Litchfield, Connecticut, in January 1812 and December 1819. Although the craftsman did not specify the wood, it may have been mahogany. On the first date Tapping Reeve, founder of the Litchfield Law School, acquired "2 Crickets stuft & readed legs." On the second date, Charles G. Bennet purchased "2 Crickets turnd legs reded rails." The present example substitutes a solid, finished wood top for an open or stuffed framework. A related cricket in maple with an oval top similarly chamfered along the bottom edge has legs turned to the same pattern without the reeding and rake of this example.[13]

Footstools of rounded and angular top remained popular in the second quarter of the nineteenth century. Among rectangular patterns, the seats are thick, the sides frequently flat and chamfered, and the legs often slender and tapering (fig. **3-7**). Usually there are no stretchers. Some examples retain their original grained, hand-painted, or stenciled decoration. Here, a medium yellow ground has stylish, free-flowing painted floral decoration within a banded frame (pl. 30); similar banding accents the legs. A varnish coat protects all visible surfaces. The combination of a basswood seat and birch legs denotes a northern New England origin. A similar footstool is seen in Asahel Powers's striking portrait of Charles Mortimer French painted about 1832, when the subject was six years of age (fig. **3-8**). The portrait was recovered in Ludlow, Vermont, an area where Powers painted many canvases. The sitter's chair is intended to be of stepped-tablet pattern, although the artist has taken liberties with the profile. The footstool resembles that illustrated in figure 3-7, complete with flat-chamfered plank edges and slim legs; it has grained surfaces. Contemporary terminology identifies this as an "Imitation Stool," which describes the painted ground. A few rectangular crickets have turned legs similar to those in figure 3-6 without the top cylinder; one has a contoured top depressed across the center.[14]

Footstools of round or oval plank display somewhat more variation than those with rectangular tops. Plank edges are straight (fig. **3-9**, *right*), flat and chamfered (fig. 3-9, *center*), rounded, or canted (fig. 3-9, *left*). Some seats have saucered tops; others are domed in imitation of stuffing (fig. 3-9, *left*). Turned legs are seen more frequently in this group than in the previous one; some supports are braced with stretchers. A plain, tapered leg with a long, gradual swell ocasionally marked at its fullest point with a single groove is common (fig. 3-9, *right*). At least two stools in this group are documented. One is branded "A. W. PRATT," the name of a chairmaker who probably worked in northern New England; another is identified with the Canton,

Fig. 3-9 Windsor low stool and footstools, New England, 1825–40. (*Left to right*) H. 6¾", 10⅜", 6¼", W. (top) 12", 14¼", 10⅜", D. (top) 8¾", 10", 7¾". (Mr. and Mrs. Oliver Wolcott Deming collection: Photo, Winterthur.)

Ohio, shop of "W. Stripe" through a stencil. A few special shapes can be noted, such as the lobed, or double-heart, form illustrated; a modified octagonal top is more square than rectangular. Although all three stools illustrated in figure 3-9 may be properly called "low" stools, the one at the center, which measures 10⅜ inches in height, is really too tall to serve comfortably as a footstool and is better suited to function as a low seat.[15]

Low stools of uncommon length were identified as "foot benches" in the nineteenth century (fig. **3-10**). The illustrated example is of late date, judging by the thin top and slim leg profile. References to the form are late as well. Mrs. Isaac Bronson of New York City bought "One pr of Foot Benches" from Albert B. Merrill in spring 1837. Four years later Frederick Starr included this form in an advertisement of cabinet furniture and chairs made at his Rochester shop. Lines and Angur offered the foot bench in New Haven the same year. Among a list of articles purchased in 1851 for Sarah Arnold of Rhode Island from the shop of William H. Lee in New York was a foot bench priced at $1.50. The legs of figure 3-10 are close to those illustrated in figure 3-7, although they are banded by grooved rings rather than paint. The top is not quite as thin as it seems, since there is a broad, shallow chamfer below the flat edges. The mottled dark and reddish brown ground is decorated only with a hollow-cornered, penciled yellow panel around the top bordered on the outside by a medium green band.[16]

Fig. 3-10 Windsor foot bench, New England, probably northern region, 1825–50. H. 10¼", W. (top) 27", D. (top) 7½"; dark brown and reddish brown grained ground with medium green and yellow. (Hitchcock Museum, Riverton, Conn.: Photo, Winterthur.)

Ranging in height from about 9 to 12 inches, low stools served several needs. They provided general seating for children (fig. 2-61), though the form was inadequate for adult seating. Several accounts mention "low stools" specifically. Elisha Harlow Holmes of Essex, Connecticut, varnished a low stool in 1826. Several years later Luke Houghton distinguished between high and low stool production in his shop in Barre, Massachusetts. David Alling's charge for a low stool at Newark, New Jersey, was 50¢, two-fifths the cost of his high Windsor stools. Ten inches was a suitable height for the "milking stool" identified by several craftsmen, including Job E. Townsend, who made milking stools at Newport in 1806. With a price range of 12¢ to 25¢, the form was simple. Holmes's accounts indicate that even purchasers of mahogany bookcases, field bedsteads, and cherry dining tables had need of milking stools. The item came in different qualities, as indicated by Philip Deland in an account of 1844: "To one milking stool nice." Another special use for pairs of low stools was as coffin supports, although folding stools were also used for this purpose. Many furniture makers and upholsterers rented out special equipment for funerals as a business sideline. John Gillingham's Philadelphia inventory of 1794 lists "two Coffin stools"; those of Francis Trumble and George Halberstadt also mention coffin boards. Another of the many miscellaneous uses of the low stool is illustrated in William Sidney Mount's painting of his studio, where a low seat beside the easel serves as a stand to support painting equipment.[17]

Baluster-turned legs were better suited to the low sitting stool than to the cricket, but the support is still rare among low forms. The two seats illustrated in figure **3-11** are choice examples of New England origin. That at the left, executed in pine and maple, employs slim, round shapes closely identified with Rhode Island work. The circular tops of both stools are saucered to provide comfortable, secure seats. The second small stool originated in Boston. The blocked and swelled balusters, rounded collars, thick ball turnings, and swelled and necked feet are characteristics of work documented to that city. The balusters are identical to those of figure 3-15. Use of the bamboo medial stretcher signals a transitional construction dating to around 1800. Samuel J. Tuck of Boston used this feature in the last of a three-chair sequence featuring baluster turnings. Another low Boston stool of simple round seat and full bamboo support structure employs a special swelled side stretcher occasionally found in Boston work.[18]

A few stools have bamboo turnings of early style with three-section legs and H-plan stretchers (fig. **3-12**). Based upon the stylized angular profile, this example appears to

Fig. 3-11 Low Windsor stools, *(left to right)* Rhode Island and Boston, 1785–1800 and ca. 1798–1802. White pine (seats) with maple, and with ash (both, microanalysis); H. 11⁵⁄₁₆″, 10⁹⁄₁₆″, DIAM. (seat) 10⁷⁄₈″, 10⁹⁄₁₆″. (Private collection: Photo, Winterthur; Winterthur 67.1180.)

Fig. 3-12 Low Windsor stool, eastern Connecticut, ca. 1796–1804. H. 8¾", DIAM. (seat) 9³⁄₁₆". (Private collection: Photo, Winterthur.)

Fig. 3-13 Low Windsor stool and detail of brand, Josiah P. Wilder, New Ipswich, N.H., 1835–50. H. 12¼", DIAM. (seat) 10⁷⁄₁₆". (Old Sturbridge Village, Sturbridge, Mass.)

have originated in eastern Connecticut. The work is similar to the bamboo style as interpreted by the Tracy family. Another stool with three-section bamboo legs has rounded, grooved swells. The box stretchers, mounted on a single level, are turned with slim double balusters joined end to end in Rhode Island style, a provenance reinforced by the presence of flat-chamfered seat edges. The low oval stool of figure 3-9 (*center*) illustrates the later bamboo style framed with box stretchers on staggered levels to avoid weakening the supports. Turnings of cylindrical form are typical. The legs are grooved and tapered, top and bottom, to add style.[19]

A round stool of still later date has distinctive fancy work in the form of thick rings in the legs at the stretcher points (fig. **3-13**). Stamped on the bottom is the maker's identification "J. P. WILDER / WARRANTED." The top, made for stuffing, is unfinished. Similar stools marked by Wilder have plain, swelled legs. Although Josiah Prescott Wilder's extant accounts date from 1837 and later, he may have made and marked furniture independently before that time. Daybook entries mention stools from cricket to countinghouse size; in between were plain stools that retailed for about 25¢ apiece. On one occasion a Miss Elisa Bachelder purchased "4 Stools without paint," presumably to finish and decorate them herself. Stools for children at 14¢ apiece are also listed.[20]

MEDIUM-HIGH STOOLS

Medium-high stools, about 15 to 20 inches in height, provided youth and adult seating and were called by various names. A group of "Misses" stools was shipped from the New Jersey port of Perth Amboy in November 1810 to Norfolk, Virginia. Wait Garret of New Hartford, Connecticut, referred to the same size seats as "table stools," and in neighboring Litchfield Silas Cheney sold "6 Stools to Sett on" in 1818. Cheney's seats were priced at more than 80¢ apiece and probably represented fancy or at least fancy Windsor seating. The stool made for Richard W. Greene of Providence, Rhode Island, by the firm of Church and Sweet on January 28, 1824, appears to have been destined for Greene's "shower bath," which the firm had worked on two weeks earlier. A parallel reference to a bathhouse in a context with Windsor furniture appears in eighteenth-century English records. The general use of the term *stool* without further description often identified a seat of medium height.[21]

Although not of Windsor construction, medium-high stools of "curl maple . . . for counter" were part of a large furniture order supplied by David Alling of Newark to the New York firm of J. W. Meeks and Company in September 1833. Later, in 1855, W. D. Rand and Company, operators of the Steam Chair Factory at Louisville, Kentucky, differentiated between counter stools and taller desk stools. The turned work of Alling's seats may have resembled that of the "24 Turkey Leg stools" for rushing itemized in the 1842 sale of Peter Willard's estate at Sterling, Massachusetts. Of chair height, the stool legs had multiring-turned shafts reduced in diameter at the base to terminate in small ball tips. After David Alling's death in the 1850s, appraisers identified large, medium, and small stools among the shop stock. Philadelphia furniture of that date in the estate of chairmaker Abraham McDonough included a "windsor piano stool," a seat that qualifies as medium-high. Two craft accounts of 1858 refer to stool height by actual measurement. J. W. Mason of New York City supplied the steamboat *Keyport* with "5 Doz 18 inch wood stools"; J. P. Wilder of New Ipswich, New Hampshire, stocked "20 inch Stool Legs."[22]

Representational art illustrates the uses of the medium-high stool. Out of doors it was a seat to lounge upon in front of the village tavern, the local store, or a military barracks. A "Pic-Nick" scene at Camden, Maine, probably painted by Jerome B. Thompson about 1850, clearly depicts a medium-high stool standing at the end of a long cloth-covered table. William Sidney Mount's scenes of rural life on Long Island place fiddlers on stools in several genre scenes. In another work Mount drew the interior of a Long Island tavern and store with its six-plate stove and sitting stools. In domestic interiors old men sit on medium-high stools at the hearth smoking their pipes; women used stools around the quilting frame or at the spinning wheel. By the 1840s the stool was well established for dining purposes. A lithograph of *William H. Ladd's Eating House* at Boston shows rows of tables lined with stools seating male patrons. Lewis Miller, the carpenter-chronicler of York, Pennsylvania, depicted stools for family dining. He also sketched the metalworker Frederick Zorchger, whom he termed "A chymist," seated at his shop hearth on a medium-tall stool (fig. **3-14**). In the caption, Miller related an incident that had occurred in 1805: "See his crucible by Science of makeing gold. His composition blew up a full discharge."[23]

Both medium and tall stools were used in shops and stores. Pictorial material illustrates both forms, and manuscript accounts price the seats from approximately 50¢ to $1, again suggesting a difference in size. The records of William Barker of Providence, Rhode Island, describe "a Seet for the Shop" as early as 1753, and similar work followed in 1757 and 1767. Local members of the Proud family made "Shop Chairs" from 1782, and they had calls for repairs as well. Family accounts for 1816 record the sale of a "high Seat for Store" to Benjamin and Charles Dyer for 84¢. In Connecticut Elisha Hawley of Ridgefield and Silas Cheney of Litchfield received occasional requests for "seats for shop." David Alling of Newark, New Jersey, made extensive repairs for the firm of Shugarth and Macknet in 1838, "mending seat & putting new legs & rounds to one shop stool." One wonders why the firm did not simply buy a new stool. At this date Lewis Miller had already sketched the interior of William Spangler's tobacco shop at York, Pennsylvania, showing the working hands seated around a large table on medium-high stools rolling cigars. Tall shop stools are represented in Edward Hazen's published interior of a watchmaker's shop.[24]

Windsor sitting stools of medium height range in date from the late eighteenth to the mid nineteenth century. First is a superb stool of Boston origin (fig. **3-15**) whose baluster and adjacent turnings are identical to those of figure 3-11 (*right*). The feet have been interpreted in the rare long-swelled-taper style of Boston, which drops the spool-and-ring turning in favor of extending the lower leg (fig. 1-84). The T-shaped stretcher is often employed in three-legged stools, although it appears more frequently in nineteenth-century work. The centered swells of the braces hint at the modified blocking that characterizes some Boston Windsor work. The seat is semi-finished, having sharp edges and flat sides. The original horsehair stuffing and linen undercover are still in

Fig. 3-14 Lewis Miller, *Frederick Zorchger, A Chymist*, York, Pa., ca. 1814–25, depicting a scene of 1805. Ink and watercolor on paper. (Historical Society of York County, York, Pa.: Photo, Winterthur.)

place beneath the old, but later, silk cover of the exterior. Another medium-size stool has baluster-turned legs in the New York style. Its modified, contoured oval seat with a pommel front and back for seating either way was made for use by a craftsman.[25]

A well-formed, bamboo-turned stool from the Dominy family of Easthampton, Long Island, may have been used as a shop seat in later years, although it likely was made or acquired for another purpose (fig. 3-16). Under stuffing of late date, the top appears to be finished for use without a covering. The slender bamboo supports with their long swells and hollows relate to work executed along Long Island Sound, and the choice of white pine for the stool top suggests Rhode Island influence. Yellow poplar was the wood of choice for Windsor seat planks in New York City. Long Island, however, was located in a crosscurrent of influences from the west and north, and beyond Brooklyn the chairmaking industry was established late. A bamboo-style stool, of midcentury date, was recovered in Lincolnville, Maine (fig. 3-17). The pine seat consists of two pieces of wood joined off-center. Branded on the plank bottom is the name "ML:INMAN," which could be that of the maker or owner.[26]

Fig. 3-15 Medium-high Windsor stool with stuffed seat, Boston, 1795–1800. Birch (seat, microanalysis); H. 15″, DIAM. (seat without stuffing) 11″. (Ledlie I. Laughlin, Jr., collection: Photo, Winterthur.)

Fig. 3-16 Medium-high Windsor stool, Dominy family (owner, brand "Dominy" in script), Long Island, N.Y., or southeastern coastal New England, 1805–25. White pine (seat) with maple and hickory (microanalysis); H. 16¼″, W. (seat) 14⅜″, D. (seat) 11″; stuffing added later. (Winterthur 57.26.663.)

Fig. 3-17 Medium-high Windsor stool and detail of brand, M. L. Inman, New England, possibly Maine, 1840–60. H. 15¾″, DIAM. (seat) 12⅛″. (M. K. collection: Photo, Winterthur.)

HIGH STOOLS

Tall stools met several needs, but their main function was to accompany a tall desk or writing stand, such as furnished countinghouses and more modest places of business. This use undoubtedly predates its first mention in documents. An early reference to "1 Writing Desk & Stool" is found in the estate inventory of Doctor Archibald McNeill of Saint George's Parish, South Carolina, recorded on July 4, 1774. The followng year Francis Trumble of Philadelphia advertised "chairs and stools for counting-houses." In Baltimore County, Maryland, a writing desk and stool are itemized in the 1784 estate of George Wells. Of particular note is the 1795 inventory of merchant William Beekman of New York, which lists "a green painted square Writing Table wth 3 Stools." When Victor du Pont set up his New York counting room in 1799 to inaugurate a trans-Atlantic business, his purchases included "a Coumpting house Desk" for $30 and "2 Counting house stools" for $4.[27]

Countinghouse seating became a commodity of the lucrative furniture export trade in Philadelphia. A popular market was the prosperous city of Charleston, where Matthew and Richard Brenan retailed Philadelphia countinghouse stools in 1799 along with Windsor chairs, settees, and children's highchairs. The following year the schooner *Virginia* carried similar merchandise to the city. Calls for the tall seat continued at Charleston through 1810, when the seaborne trade began to suffer as relations with Great Britain deteriorated. Through the war years Philadelphia chairmakers relied on supplying the local market as they could. In 1815 Charles C. Robinson recorded the sale of a "Desk Stool" to David Hoopes, an iron merchant. Among New York business-men, Isaac Clason on Broadway and John P. Mumford in Broome Street provided tall stools for their counting rooms.[28]

New England production of the tall seat is recorded in several accounts and adver-tisements. Thomas Boynton of Vermont priced his "high writing stool" at 75¢ in 1814. In Litchfield, Connecticut, in 1821 Silas Cheney recorded an order for a shop sign and "one Seat for writing before Desk" priced at 83¢. Harvey Dresser, who operated an extensive cabinet, furniture, and lumber business at Southbridge, Massachusetts, offered stools from cricket to desk size in 1829. Advertising from his Boston warerooms the following year, Samuel Beal itemized a stock of 1,400 fancy chairs, 1,500 Windsors, and "50 Desk Stools." Of equal magnitude was David Alling's furniture trade at Newark, New Jersey; Alling catered to the export market and bespoke work for local customers rather than to warehouse sales. He made a "desk stool 3 ft high" for one customer in 1830 and sold a "counting house chr" and "cushion for same" to another in 1838. In semi-rural southern New Jersey, the business of William G. Beesley of Salem was considerably more modest, but he too had an occasional call for a countinghouse stool, which he priced from 62½¢ to 75¢. One made for Jacob W. Mulford, Esq., in 1828 reflects Salem's prosperity as a county seat of government.[29]

Cabinetmakers and chairmakers who enjoyed an extensive trade sometimes constructed and retained business furniture for their own use. After Samuel Proud's death at Providence in 1835, appraisers itemized a "Writing Desk & 1 Stule" in his workshop. Valued at more than $2,500, the estate was a sizable one for a craftsman. Philadelphia appraisers found a "Desk and railing, stool & case" in the first story of Abraham McDonough's chair store and manufactory in 1852. A local contemporary, Charles Riley, retailed the countinghouse stool as well as a square-top seat. At half the price of the tall model, the square-top stool appears to have been of medium size but a rather unusual article. By 1855 John B. Robinson, proprietor of Philadelphia's Great Western Chair Manufactory, referred to backless business seating collectively as "Office Stools."[30]

Other records shed further light on terminology and appearance. Valuing the contents of John Lambert's Windsor-chair shop in 1793, appraisers noted the presence of "High stool Feet." The language had changed by 1837, when David Alling of Newark, New Jersey, sold "12 stool legs 2 ft long" to Dod Bassett and Company. The Proud brothers of Providence consistently referred to the tall stool as a "high seat" during the early nineteenth century. Other records mention special seat treatments. In June 1835 Philemon Robbins of Hartford sold a "high stool seat stuffd" for $1.50. Isaac Wright, a chairmaker of the same city, sold a high stool with a hair seat for $1.58. Robbins followed with cane-seat stools priced at $1.25 each in July 1835. Similar seating in curled maple sold for $2 at David Alling's establishment in Newark several years later. Alling also noted the repair of a high Windsor stool, which he repainted "green." His new tall, wood-seat stools, whether painted or "stained & varnished," sold for the substantial price of $1.12½ in 1837–38. Most Windsor high stools made during the early nineteenth century were priced between 67¢ and $1.[31]

Tall stools with early turnings have contoured, sometimes saddled, seats. The earliest, a T-braced, baluster-turned example (fig. 3-18), exhibits a mixture of elements which originated in Philadelphia. This could be the pattern that Francis Trumble advertised in 1775, especially because strong stylistic mannerisms point to Trumble as the maker. The design has its genesis in Windsor work of the 1750s, as indicated by the thick rings above pointed ball feet and the collared swells centered in the stretchers. The seat, though well worn and chipped, is contoured to saddle form with a center-front pommel. A suggestion of flat-chamfered shaping at the edges is again indicative of early design. Trumble's hand seems evident in the collared stretcher swells and the profile of the balusters, both close in form to the back posts of his early fan-back chair. The knoblike turning capping the leg balusters, however, has no exact counterpart in early Windsor-chair making. That feature may be a modification of a swelled stretcher collar.[32]

Two stools from the Connecticut–Rhode Island border region demonstrate the range of local originality (figs. 3-19, 3-20). Independent choices in seat shape, leg splay, and turned elements have produced designs that are different and yet compatible. The Rhode Island character is well captured in figure 3-19 in such elements as the long, pointed foot tapers and elongated spool turnings. Connecticut work appears to have provided the inspiration for the blocked stretcher centers. The oval seat is designed with a pommel, front and back, permitting use in either direction. The sharp crease under the pommels is reminiscent of that in a tall sack-back Rhode Island chair.[33]

Fig. 3-19 High Windsor stool, Rhode Island, 1790–1800. Maple with other woods; H. 20⅞″, W. (seat) 15″, D. (seat) 11⅝″. (Private collection: Photo, Winterthur.)

Fig. 3-20 High Windsor stool, Connecticut–Rhode Island border region, 1790–1800. Basswood (seat) with maple and hickory (microanalysis); H. 24⅝″, W. (seat) 15⅜″, D. (seat) 16⅛″. (Winterthur 59.1820.)

Rhode Island–style baluster and stretcher caps are seen in figure 3-20. The shapely, elongated balusters almost duplicate those found in work of the Connecticut–Rhode Island border. The straight-tapered feet are often seen in Connecticut Windsors. The chairlike, shield-shaped seat is original to the stool. It was never drilled to receive spindles and bears traces of the same early green paint found on the support structure. A split from front to back necessitated its repair long ago with two bracing blocks nailed to the underside. Amos Denison Allen of Windham, Connecticut, may have been referring to such a chair-seated stool in 1802, when he charged a customer 2*s.* for "a high chair without back." The gradual rise of the seat across the front is also typical of work originating in eastern Connecticut and the border region. The material is basswood, which is sometimes found in the seats of chairs from this area. The stool was purchased for the Winterthur collection in 1946 from a dealer in Milford, Connecticut.[34]

The plank of the high stool illustrated in figure **3-21** has been adapted from the curved-edge seat of the high-back chair made in postrevolutionary Philadelphia. The well-contoured bamboowork and H-plan stretchers with a bamboo medial brace suggest a date of around 1800. Basically, the turnings are styled as three-section bamboowork with a typical long central unit. The extra, short section near the top simply extends the legs for the specialized function of the seat. When the section is eliminated, the pattern is that of a Philadelphia chair of the 1790s. The use of either hickory or ash for the legs instead of maple, as found in Philadelphia work, suggests northern New Jersey, where the stool was recovered, as the general region of its construction.[35]

A high point in bamboo design is exemplified in a three-legged tall stool of Moravian origin (fig. **3-22**). Strong and forceful in its interpretation, the roundwork is related to Windsor chairs made in the Moravian community at Salem, North Carolina, in the 1820s. The letters "G D" branded on the stool and chairs signify congregational ownership (Gemein Diacony). The seat covering is not original, and at present it is impossible to determine whether the plank was initially intended to receive a covering. A ring on the seat bottom just inside the edge marks the point where holes were drilled for the legs.[36]

Only slightly later in feature, but actually much later in date, is a four-legged stool braced with double tiers of stretchers (fig. **3-23**). The shapely bamboowork is well conceived, having long units at top and bottom to provide visual and structural height and short sections through the center that serve as suitable anchor points for the double, box-style bracing system. The circular plank, well shaped for its date, has a central depression, rounded top edges, and canted sides. Stamped on the bottom in small serif letters is the brand "J. C. HUBBARD / BOSTON." Identical stools also have a second brand reading "WM. WHITE / BOSTON." Hubbard was in business in Boston from 1826, but White's name first appears in directories only in 1857. Listings through 1862 place the two men at individual addresses, but from 1863 both craftsmen conducted business at 701 Washington Street. There they remained until 1875, when a relocation or street renumbering placed them at No. 885. White was a young man in 1857, as indicated by a directory listing of 1903, which still identifies him as a furniture manufacturer; Hubbard, much older, died in 1877. Although the men shared the same address, their individual directory listings suggest they conducted business both jointly and independently, a notion supported by the use of only one brand on the illustrated stool. There are also shorter stools marked both singly and jointly, as described. In the shorter stools, either the stretcher placement is modified or the bamboowork is reproportioned. Another example by Hubbard modifies the tall pattern illustrated by introducing two more stretchers and a medial cross bar at the point of the upper groove. This brace supports the mechanism for a revolving seat.

A well-splayed high seat with features that seem later than those of the Hubbard and White stool probably dates earlier (fig. **3-24**). The stool has fancy ball and multiple-ring turnings, which first made their appearance in the chair market during the 1820s with the introduction of fancy rush-bottom seating in the so-called "Hitchcock" style. Use of a compressed ball between two flaring cylindrical units in the feet probably springs from a Baltimore foot developed about 1820. Like other Baltimore fancy work, this feature was known in chairmaking centers up and down the coast. The swell at mid leg also has something of the character of Baltimore supports, though executed in

Fig. 3-21 High Windsor stool, probably Delaware Valley, 1795–1810. Maple and other woods; H. 22⅜", W. (seat) 15⅞", D. (seat) 10⁵⁄₁₆". (Historic Deerfield, Inc., Deerfield, Mass.: Photo, Winterthur.)

Fig. 3-22 High Windsor stool and detail of brand, Gemein Diacony (Moravian church ownership), Salem (Winston-Salem), N.C., 1815–30. Yellow poplar (seat) with hickory; H. 29⅝", DIAM. (seat) 14¾"; seat probably not stuffed originally. (Old Salem, Inc., Winston-Salem, N.C.)

Fig. 3-23 High Windsor stool and detail of stamp, John C. Hubbard, Boston, ca. 1855–76. H. 32½", DIAM. (seat) 14". (Private collection: Photo, Winterthur.)

Fig. 3-24 High Windsor stool, southeastern New England, 1835–55. Ash (seat) with maple (microanalysis); H. 31½", W. (seat) 20", D. (seat) 12⅜". (Winterthur 59.2715.)

longer, leaner form. The source of inspiration may be of earlier date, however, since the legs in a chair made just after 1800 by Abraham Shove of Bristol County, Massachusetts, have similar contours. The swells in Shove's chair legs are accompanied by cones at the leg tops, which are marked by double scribe lines forming thin disks that resemble those in figure 3-24. A second chair by Shove has supports of the same profile without the cone tops. By eliminating the multiple-ring turnings, the profile of figure 3-24 also resembles that of the long back posts in a chair from the Connecticut–Rhode Island border. The ash of the stool plank, though unusual, is found occasionally in southeastern New England work. A Rhode Island armchair of the 1790s at the Yale University Art Gallery has such a seat.[37]

TALL CHAIRS (CHAIR-STOOLS)

Simultaneous with the manufacture of tall stools for the counting room and other uses was the production of tall chairs to meet similar needs. Francis Trumble's *Pennsylvania Gazette* notice of 1775 specifically identifies both "chairs and stools for counting-houses," and production of the form continued into the nineteenth century. Thomas Hodgkins, a furniture supplier of Jacob Sanderson at Salem, Massachusetts, debited Sanderson's account in October 1808 for "making two Chare stools and tow [*sic*] foot stools." Thomas Boynton produced a 75¢ "writing Chair" for Shubael Wardner and Company at Windsor, Vermont, in 1816. The "writing Chair" belonging to William Fosbrook, a New York City whitesmith, was itemized with a desk and "nest or set of Drawers" at his death in 1820. Upstate, chairmaker Allen Holcomb of Otsego County recorded the sale of a "high Stool Chair" in December 1822. Henry W. Miller of Worcester, Massachusetts, sold a "Desk Chair" for $1.36 a few years later. The price may be compared with that of his "Desk Stool" at 75¢. H. F. Dewey's "high Chr for desk" sold for $1.50 at Bennington, Vermont, in 1840; by contrast, 50¢ was the price of his high stool. Tall examples of late date include "Steamboat Stools" sold by William Galligan of Buffalo, New York, and pictured in an advertisement of 1846. These stool-chairs have scroll seats and a late Boston-style crest (fig. 1-45).[38]

The earliest chair-stools were merely standard chairs constructed in prevailing patterns and elevated on long legs. A high-back chair represents postrevolutionary construction, and several bow-back seats with and without arms date to the end of the century. An early nineteenth-century example has two crest rods that center a hollow-cornered, square medallion. Each of these seats could be classified as medium-high, and some probably were rendered more comfortable through the use of a low stool to support the feet. Of the few truly "tall" chair-stools of eighteenth-century design, two have bow backs. A particularly fine one follows the classic bow-back styling of Rhode Island developed during the 1790s, probably at Providence (fig. 3-25). Typically, the sawed arms roll forward at the front; the baluster-turned spindles identify the best period work. Coupled with a semifinished seat to receive stuffing, the chair was clearly a top-of-the-line product and probably cost the merchant who bought it a tidy sum. Remnants of the original linen undercover remained on the seat up to the middle of the twentieth century; the rectangular footbar is a late addition. The presence of four swelled stretchers mounted in box style indicates that this 1790s-style chair was actually constructed at the turn of the century, when the box-type bracing system was first adopted in the Windsor. The leg turnings confirm the date, since they represent a late variant pattern rather than styles dating to the early 1790s. Following its service in the countinghouse, this tall chair is said to have been used at the organ in the First Baptist Church of Providence.[39]

Except for an occasional late, revolving tall chair and other seats conceived as stools to which a back was added, chair-stool design of the nineteenth century followed the patterns of the period. Most chair-stools have standard chair parts from the plank upward, and they frequently lack arms. Patterns range from the square-back, double-rod style (fig. 2-37) to the slat-back and tablet-top designs (figs. 2-38, 2-41, 2-42); the sticks are turned or shaped to bamboo, ball, or arrow profiles. John C. Hubbard's name appears on the planks of several tall chair-stools capped by a narrow, rounded-end Boston tablet that first became popular in the 1840s (fig. 2-42).[40]

Stands and Tables

Stands and tables with legs socketed directly into the top without benefit of a joined framework are the most elusive Windsor forms to track in documents because they are never identified as such, and it is often difficult to identify the construction even by inference. The form has roots in the ancient world. A simple stick-and-socket stand dating to the second century A.D. served as a butcher's block. A low table and stool of similar construction are depicted in a monastery carving from the thirteenth century. In a fifteenth-century triptych panel, Robert Campen clearly delineated the through-tenon construction found in many contemporary tables and raised work surfaces of simple form. Dutch genre paintings of later date continued to illustrate the importance of simple stick-and-socket stools and tables in daily life.[41]

With only a few exceptions, turned American tables of true Windsor construction are small in size, having tops that measure less than 20 inches in diameter. For this reason they are more appropriately called stands. As defined by Edward Phillips in his dictionary, first published in 1658, a stand is "a Frame to set a Candle-stick on." The flexibility of the term, even in the late seventeenth century, is indicated in a work by Sir John Chardin: "We set our Candlesticks upon Tables or Stands." In the first and only study devoted to this American Windsor form, published in 1924, Clarence W. Brazer used the term *candlestand*. The six examples known to him had been recovered in southeastern Pennsylvania. A seventh stand in private hands was found in Chester County, and through the years local dealers have owned others. Margaret Schiffer, in

Fig. 3-25 Windsor chair-stool with seat for stuffing, Providence, R.I., 1800–1810. H. 51⅛", W. (arms) 21⅛", (seat) 27½", D. (seat) 17¼"; lower front stretcher reset and probably replaced, upper front stretcher an addition. (Rhode Island Historical Society, Providence.)

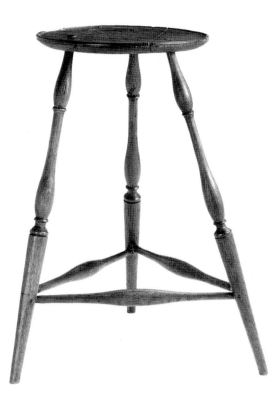

Fig. 3-26 Windsor stand, southeastern Pennsylvania or Delaware Valley, 1780–95. Yellow poplar (top) with maple (microanalysis); H. 26⅜″; Diam. (top) 18″. (Winterthur 64.1525.)

Fig. 3-27 Windsor stand, southeastern Pennsylvania, 1780–95. Oak (top) with hickory and oak (microanalysis); H. 26⅛″; Diam. (top) 13½″. (Winterthur 64.1522.)

her comprehensive study of Chester County inventories through 1850, noted the common local use of painted yellow poplar for stands and small tables, although specific construction is never identified in the documents. Thomas Harris of East Whiteland Township owned a "Blue poplar stand" in 1799; in the following year East Bradford appraisers found a "Poplar Candle stand" in the home of Faithful Stewart. Furniture identified as "One Small green Table" and a "small blue Table" in the Chichester households of Thomas Howell and Samuel Williams in 1753 and 1769 could well have been of stand size. When the material is named, Schiffer found that poplar stands were the most plentiful after those made of walnut and mahogany, and poplar tables were second only to those of walnut. Brazer identified several Windsor stands as having "poplar" tops (*liriodendron tulipifera*). Schiffer further states that between 1750 and 1800 candlestands almost always stood on the first floor, rather than on upper floors, in Chester County homes.[42]

References to small stands in other contemporary records from southeastern Pennsylvania are equally ambiguous about construction, although circumstantial evidence is sometimes helpful. From time to time Windsor seating is mentioned in conjunction with the stand or table, suggesting a relationship between the two. At the sale of printer Christopher Sauer's confiscated Germantown estate in August 1778, John Mace bought a Windsor chair and two "Little" tables. A Baltimore inventory of 1782 lists a "poplar Table" immediately following an entry for five Windsor chairs. Two Chester County inventories of the 1780s itemize in succession Windsor chairs, a walnut tea table, and either a "Candle Stand" or a "painted Table."[43]

Local shipping records provide an opportunity for speculation. On June 19, 1790, when the sloop *Union* left the Delaware River for Norfolk, Virginia, three Windsor chairs and a table were in the cargo. The schooner *Betsey* carried eight Windsor chairs and two tables to New Bern, North Carolina, six years later. New York port records list the shipment of half a dozen Windsors and a table to a consignee at Norfolk in 1787. John Davis of Philadelphia may have been acting as his own middleman in 1800 when he accompanied a consignment of seven dozen Windsor chairs and a table to Richmond. James Whitaker and William Hayden, makers of Windsor and fancy chairs, shipped chairs and tables to southern ports in 1802 and 1803. Hayden's goods also

included stools. Chairmaker John Mere prepared two consignments of furniture for the *South Carolina Packet* in March 1811. One contained "Seven Bundles chairs, Two Settees, Two tables & one box." At Wilmington on the Delaware River, chairmaker Timothy Hansen may have made Windsor stands during the 1790s. A "Painted poplar Candle stand" stood in the "Kitchen parlor" at his death in 1798. The number of framed Windsors and chair parts itemized by appraisers in the shop and garret suggests that Hanson participated in the export chair trade.[44]

Windsor stands and tables known to originate in southeastern Pennsylvania, the Delaware Valley, and the Chesapeake Bay area probably all date from the postrevolutionary period. The several patterns have subtle variations. One small group has a distinctive, long tapered-toe foot (fig. **3-26**), an unusual feature in Windsors from this region, except in isolated cases. Here, the ring turnings are thinner than in other examples. Stand tops, as found in this late eighteenth-century group, are "dished" and edged with turned, folded rims molded on the outside; legs pierce the tops. The illustrated example relates closely in its tapered foot and dished top to one formerly in the J. Stogdell Stokes collection at Philadelphia. The turned maple legs pierce a yellow poplar top. When Henry Francis du Pont acquired the stand in 1927, it was said to have come from "an old Jersey house." As in the Windsor stool, stretchers are inserted at staggered heights to avoid weakening the frame.[45]

In another, slightly larger, group of stands, it is possible to track the transition of a pattern from the baluster to the bamboo style. Representative of the first design is a delicate example made of oak and hickory, with a top diameter of only 13½ inches (fig. **3-27**). Published by Clarence Brazer as the frontispiece to his article on Windsor candlestands, this small stand was recovered in Chester County. Henry Francis du Pont acquired it in 1926. Two related stands whose dished tops have diameters of more than 17 inches also have folded rims molded in a simple pattern and legs that pierce the top surface.

In the next stage, the circular top was altered to a shallow, dished and rimmed board with flat-chamfered edges; the legs socket inside the top (fig. **3-28,** *left*). The slim turnings with long feet and delicately executed "teardrop" swells at the top remain unchanged; the points of entry into the plank are scribed by a circle on the bottom sur-

Fig. 3-29 Windsor stand (or stool), southeastern Pennsylvania at Maryland border, 1820–40. Yellow poplar (top, microanalysis) with maple; H. 23″, DIAM. (top) 14⅞″. (David Hunt Stockwell collection: Photo, Winterthur.)

face. The top is painted in shades of gray in a pattern of splotches and short jagged lines, probably to imitate marble (pl. 31). The stand was recovered south of Oxford in Chester County near the Maryland border. The last table in the series (fig. 3-28, *right*) has a similar top, but the legs have been converted to a restrained three-section bamboo pattern. The stretchers, which are similar to those in the previous two stands, feature a slim, blocked swell centered by a scribed line. The top is made of yellow poplar; the legs are maple.

The tops on another small group of baluster-turned stands from southeastern Pennsylvania are variously pierced through or internally socketed by the legs. The tapered feet of the stands are slightly shortened. The circular tops are about 15 to 16 inches in diameter. A nineteenth-century group of stands comes from the same region. They are of late, utilitarian form and have flat, circular tops with rounded or straight-chamfered sides. The bases have plain cylindrical, ungrooved legs, tapered top and bottom, and a distinguishing T-shaped brace (fig. **3-29**). Typically for this region, the leg profile is influenced by Baltimore-style fancy and Windsor work of the early nineteenth century. Some examples may have done double duty as stands and stools, as suggested by tops that are slightly rounded at the upper edge. Here, a lack of substantial wear on the stretchers supports its designation as a stand.

In a class by itself is a stand, made entirely of walnut, that exhibits pronounced Pennsylvania German characteristics, particularly as identified with the Pennsylvania-Maryland border region comprising Adams and Frederick counties, west of the Susquehanna (fig. **3-30**). The feet are of early inspiration and draw, directly or indirectly, on Philadelphia work, as can be seen in the flare of the connecting spool and the ball shape above it. An exact profile for the disk-top spool and thick ring at mid leg can be found in a fan-back side chair purchased at an estate sale in Frederick County, Maryland. A second feature associated with this general region is the pronounced swell of the stretcher tips, an interpretation seen in a small group of Pennsylvania chairs from the area west of Adams County. The diminutive top has a dished rim; a buttterfly key on the undersurface represents an old crack repair.[46]

An all-maple stand appears to be the lone representative of a regional interpretation from beyond Pennsylvania (fig. **3-31**). Purchased at the estate sale of a collector in

Fig. 3-30 Windsor stand, Pennsylvania-Maryland border at Adams and Frederick counties, 1790–1805. Walnut; H. 25⅛″, DIAM. (top) 11¾″. (Private collection: Photo, Winterthur.)

Fig. 3-31 Windsor stand, Rhode Island, 1790–1800. Maple; H. 27¾″, DIAM. (top) 13″. (Edward and Helen Flanagan collection: Photo, Winterthur.)

Richmond, Virginia, the stand, even if "collected" in that area, could originally have been a product of the export trade. Its basic turned features suggest a Rhode Island origin, as does the all-maple construction. Many prerevolutionary Rhode Island Windsors were constructed entirely of maple. The close-fitting rolled collars at the baluster tops are another regional feature; a similar profile appears in the upper legs of a pair of cross-stretcher chairs. Elements below are of postwar date. The round-top, tapered foot has close mates in two Rhode Island chairs, one of which also provides a near pattern for the spool turning.[47]

The largest stand-table known is one illustrated by Clarence Brazer in 1924 (fig. **3-32**). The top measures 24½ inches in diameter and the height is comparable. The turnings, like those of the stands in figures 3-26 to 3-28, exhibit strong Philadelphia influence and represent either metropolitan or sophisticated rural craftsmanship. The recovery of so many stands in and around Chester County, as opposed to Philadelphia, can be explained in part by the many close family connections between the two areas, particularly among the Quakers. Another factor is the ownership by metropolitan families of farms or summer homes in the county well into the twentieth century. Outmoded and utilitarian furnishings from the city houses were deposited in the country for informal use.[48]

In addition to the Windsor stands already discussed, there is another distinct class of turned table with vertical, baluster-type legs, ball feet, and cylindrical stretchers mounted both low and high. Although they are frequently classed as Windsor furniture, construction of these tables is such that the round or square board top merely rests upon the upper leg cylinders or intervening cleats and is attached by pegs or nails driven in from the top rather than socketed. Thus, these are not truly Windsor tables.

Although stands and small tables of true Windsor construction have not been identified beyond the greater southeastern Pennsylvania area, with one exception (fig. 3-31), documents from a broad area provide evidence of the use of stands with Windsor furniture. At the Nantucket home of Robert Hussey, "2 highback Chairs" stood close to a "Stand" when appraisers evaluated the household in 1795. Again in 1805, at the home of Charles Swain, a miller, appraisers itemized a "large green chair" and a "great Arm d[itt]o" with a stand. When Samuel Douglas made a set of "Dyneing Chairs" for Benajah Case at New Hartford, Connecticut, in 1814, he also constructed a candlestand. At neighboring Litchfield Mrs. Ann Vail purchased six Windsor chairs and a candlestand from Silas Cheney in 1816. Kitchen chairs, Windsor chairs, and a "light stand" were itemized in succession in the evaluation of Andrew Tracy's home in Cornish, New Hampshire, at his death in 1820. He was the father of chairmaker Stephen Tracy, who resided in the area by that date. Returning to Chester County, Pennsylvania, at West Chester, the county seat, there is a record of a "small table" and a "candle stand" at the home of Isaac D. Barnard, who practiced law in the early 1800s. Barnard appears to have used his "Back room down Stairs" as a combination office and dining room. Accompanying his desk was a clock of "Commercial make" and his "Framed Certificate," as well as a framed copy of the Declaration of Independence. A stove and accessories and a carpet on the floor kept the room comfortable. Perhaps of painted form like the eight Windsor chairs that provided seating at the mahogany dining table and the breakfast table were the "small table," worth 50¢, and the "candle Stand," valued at $1.50.[49]

Wheels and Reels

The ancient art of spinning involves twisting fibers of varying length into a continuous thread of some strength. In its simplest form, the process begins by drawing a few fibers from a bunch of fibrous material while twisting the filaments in one direction with the fingers. The continuing finger action produces an unbroken length, and the twist is retained by winding the thread onto a stick. Various methods of hand spinning were employed in ancient cultures, using the drop spindle, or weighted stick, and distaff. The spindle, when whirled, provided the twist. The distaff, a stick with fingers at the top forming a cage, held the unspun fibers and could be anchored in a fixed object or supported under the arm, thus freeing both hands for the work. The hand-turned wheel probably was introduced to spinning between A.D. 500 and 1000. Developed in the Far East, the apparatus was known in western Europe by the fourteenth century. It is illustrated in the illuminated Luttrell Psalter of 1338 from Lincolnshire, England.[50]

By the late fifteenth century the flyer spinning wheel had been developed in Europe. The flyer, a U-shaped piece of wood mounted on the spindle, permitted spinning and winding to be combined in one operation. The small device speeded the work and made more efficient use of the fibrous materials. Two further improvements were a device to regulate tension on the drive belt and the introduction of a treadle to operate the wheel by foot, thus freeing both hands and increasing efficiency.[51]

By the early seventeenth century, spinning-wheel construction probably was a specialty, or at least a profitable sideline, in many European woodworking shops. Jan Joris van Vliet's engraving *The Turner,* executed about 1634, shows a partially completed flax wheel in the foreground. Holland, Flanders, and French Cambrai were already flourishing centers of the linen industry in 1632, when Thomas Wentworth, under Charles I, introduced Dutch-type flax wheels (fig. 3-33) into Ireland to develop the linen industry as a suitable complement to the English wool trade. Before the century ended, the spinning wheel was an important piece of domestic equipment throughout Europe, and in many areas it formed the foundation of a thriving cottage industry. Spinning schools were established as charitable institutions for the instruction of poor girls. Spinning was also a suitable employment at poorhouses and houses of correction. By the early eighteenth century, many cloth mills contained large spinning rooms. Women of all ranks practiced linen spinning, and wheel size and quality reflected the spinner's social status.[52]

EIGHTEENTH-CENTURY AMERICAN EVIDENCE

Alice Morse Earle has written that there was little time for play among early colonial children lest "the old deluder Sathan" carry out his mischievous work. Children had chores to perform morning and evening, and they used spare moments to advantage by spinning and by knitting or weaving tape. This respect for industry continued into the postrevolutionary period. Sometime before 1803 Laura Littleton of Northampton, Massachusetts, wrote to a friend that she was "learning to spin" as a complement to her skills in knitting and sewing. She continued, "My mamma you know is an industrious woman; and though she is anxious to give her children a good education, she is determined that they will all learn how to work."[53]

Home economy was a part of early Philadelphia life. John Jones, a prosperous merchant who died in 1708, had a sizable estate that included a house in Philadelphia and a "plantation," or farm. The city house contained one woolen and four flax spinning wheels. Joseph Saul specialized in chair and spinning-wheel construction locally by the mid 1740s. He specifically identified wool wheels in his book of accounts, which dates from the early 1760s. Wool wheels are larger than flax wheels and lack a treadle mechanism. Margaret Schiffer in her study of inventories from Chester County, Pennsylvania, found that spinning wheels used before 1750 were commonly located somewhere on the first floor of the home; later, such equipment was often relegated to garrets and lofts. Spinning activity is documented after 1742 in the Moravian community at Bethlehem, Pennsylvania, where turners made spinning wheels "in considerable numbers, there being a constant demand for them throughout the surrounding country, and many being needed for the Sisters' House and for the use of the girls in the school in those days of much spinning." New England craft records likewise chronicle wheel equipment production in the early eighteenth century. At Falmouth, Maine, Joseph Emerson, a turner, used a turning lathe and hand tools to fabricate the spinning-wheel parts found by shop appraisers in the 1740s. Thomas Pratt of Malden, Massachusetts, made and mended wheels in the same period.[54]

During the 1760s there was a call for revival of home manufactures on a grand scale, particularly the production of textiles. This was one of several efforts that marked American growth during the next fifty or more years. Its effects can be seen in records that reflect both the survival of an earlier dependence upon household economy and a renewed emphasis on self-sufficiency. Many households engaged in textile production in this period. Delaware Valley inventories identify "big," "large," or "long" wheels, alternative terms for the wool wheel; they also describe "spinning," "small," "linen," and "Dutch" wheels used for spinning flax. A "basket with tow," the coarser fibers of the flax plant, was found in Melchor Meng's Germantown "Loft over the bake & Vinegar house" when he forfeited his estate in 1778. Charles Jolley of Lower Merion owned a "check reel," one of several names applied to a reeling device with a counting mechanism for winding yarn into skeins. Other local households containing spinning equipment represent a range of occupations and social status: farmer, miller, ironmonger, innkeeper, cooper, shopkeeper, printer, merchant, widow, and gentleman. Contemporary newspaper advertisements chronicle the continuing production of new equipment. John Shearman titled himself a turner and spinning-wheel maker, but he also constructed Windsor chairs. Cabinetmaker and chairmaker Francis Trumble turned his attention in this direction on the eve of the Revolution when concern was mounting about the state of American manufactures. Trumble advertised in 1775: "WANTED. Several journeymen spinning-wheel makers [and] 500 setts of stocks and rims for spinning wheels." Clearly, the craftsman had ambitious plans.[55]

Inventories from Chester and Lancaster counties, Pennsylvania, reflect rural life, away from the convenience of city shops. The garret of William Miller's home in New Garden in 1768 contained a range of equipment and materials: a "Big Wheel, Reel & Swifts," "old Spinning [flax] wheels," "Wool," "Wollen Yarn," and "Linnen d[itt]o." At the death of Miller's son thirteen years later, the rural tradition was still in evidence. In the room above the kitchen were three "little" spinning wheels and a "Spooling wheel & Swifts" for reeling yarn. Joshua Hoopes of Westtown owned five wheels in 1769, and others were recorded in homes in Ridley and Birmingham. In the town of Lancaster appraisers listed a "Quantity of Spinning Wheel Stuff" in the woodworking shop of Jacob Fetter, Sr., in June 1777.[56]

Domestic textile production in the South is recorded in a variety of documents. Port of entry books for Oxford, Maryland, note the receipt of five spinning wheels from Rhode Island in 1770. Appraisers who surveyed the Baltimore estate of Jacob Rahm, a spinning-wheel maker, in 1778 itemized a "Spinning wheel not finished," a "dozen Sett spining wheel irons," and a good supply of wood, including hickory, maple, oak, and walnut. On the eve of the Revolution Joshua Eden made "some extraordinary good Spinning-Wheels" at Charleston, South Carolina, and stood ready to make more if "properly encouraged."[57]

In the North, Colonel Philip Schuyler in upstate New York purchased a wheel at Albany in December 1772 for use at his house in Saratoga. A group of inventories from New Haven County, Connecticut, dating two years later lists a variety of equipment, including "Dutch" and "foot" wheels for spinning linen thread, "great" and "large" wheels for producing woolen yarns, and "clock" reels for winding. The owners' occupations varied from farmer, woodworker, and minister to sea captain; one owner was a widow. The shop of Robert Crage (Craig) in Leicester, Massachusetts, was a production center between 1757 and 1777. He sold linen (foot) and woolen (great) wheels, quill wheels for winding, and clock reels for skeining. Prices ranged from 4s. for the reel to 13s.4d. for a flax wheel. Crage also repaired equipment, noting such jobs as "a whurl for a quill wheele" and an "Exeltree & spokes for a woolen wheel." Sometimes Crage identified the raw materials of his trade; for example, he credited Jonas Livermore, Jr., with "a Red oak tree for Little wheele Rims" and Thomas Green with "two white oak plank for fallows [felloes] for wheels." When a Mr. Campbell of Oxford proposed selling some of Crage's wheels, the woodworker agreed to carry them to his house free of charge.[58]

The realities of a pending conflict with Britain affected craftsmen in Charlestown, Massachusetts. Following the debacle at Bunker Hill, the town lay in ruins, and thirty woodworking craftsmen and their apprentices had to seek employment elsewhere. In time, the "refugees" filed claims for their losses. Cabinetmaker Thomas Wood's household belongings, including "One Greate Spinning Wheel & one smaller d[itt]o," were destroyed. The plight of these people and others who faced a similar calamity during the war is expressed by a turner named Debs in his claim for "the Loss that I sustained by being cast away on account of not knowing wherefore to come to." By contrast, it was business as usual at Taunton the following year when Ezekiel Smith sold a woolen wheel to Robert Vickre for 6s.[59]

Activity increased during the postrevolutionary period, particularly because families in many areas were left destitute by the war. Labor and newly formed industrial groups everywhere joined forces to agitate in favor of encouraging and protecting home manufactures. From the city to the country, from the new northern settlements to the West, spinning equipment found a market. Philadelphia upholsterer John Mason sold wheels in 1789. Abraham Overholt, a craftsman of German background, served a rural market at Bedminster in adjacent Bucks County. Selected items from his accounts describe the activity:

Jan. 29, 1791 I made a spinning wheel for Johannes Dinstmann	0..15..0
June 10, 1791 I turned a pulley for a wool wheel for Johannes Meyer	0.. 0 ..2
Oct. 15, 1792 I turned four new spokes in a wool wheel for Henrich Meyer and made two splints for the wheel rim	0.. 1..0
Feb. 15, 1801 I made a poplar table and painted it brown and a clock reel for Sara Gross	0..11 ..3
May 30, 1815 I made a spooling wheel for Joseph Oberholtzer	1..17..6

In Greensburg near Pittsburgh, gateway to the West, Joseph Armstrong, Windsor-chair maker at the sign of the "chair and spinning-wheel," was ever mindful of the potential of this sideline in 1799 when he offered to accommodate the ladies "with an assortment of SPINNING-WHEELS made of the best dry wood."[60]

Outside Pennsylvania similar documents show the extent of the postrevolutionary spinning-wheel trade. At Bottle Hill near Morristown, New Jersey, Thomas Gardner, spinning-wheel maker, advertised for an apprentice. Sampson Barnet of Wilmington, Delaware, proudly advertised spinning wheels "made by a compleat Artist lately arrived from Europe." Wise Grinnell, who sold wheels of his own make at Greenfield, Massachusetts, also had "a number on hand made by Oliver Cone" in 1795. The Canadian market was a good one for local craftsmen, such as Robert Blackwood of Saint John, New Brunswick, and also for American exporters. The schooners *Nancy* and *Sally* and the brig *Hawk* carried wheels from Boston to New Brunswick and Nova Scotia in 1791 and 1795. Spinning equipment was not always acquired for private family use. The minutes of the Corporation of the City of New York for May 12, 1784, record the purchase of spinning wheels for the poorhouse. A particularly lucrative market for some spinning-wheel craftsmen was the southern trade.[61]

Repairs were as important as new work. The Proud brothers of Providence replaced wheel spokes and legs. In neighboring East Greenwich, Captain William Arnold engaged Windsor-chair maker Joseph Stone to make extensive repairs to his quill wheel — a new "whirle," ten spokes, and a new hub. On rural Long Island business was brisk for John Paine at Southold. He wired flyers, made a new "duch" (Dutch) wheel rim, and replaced spokes. Daniel Rea, Jr., of Boston provided another kind of service. In May 1791 he painted a spinning wheel "mehogony Colour" for cabinetmaker Simon Hall.[62]

NINETEENTH-CENTURY ACTIVITY

The trade in spinning equipment seems to have continued brisk during the first several decades of the nineteenth century, especially in rural and newly settled areas. Coarse fabrics were still needed for general home use, whether the thread or yarn was woven in the household or placed in the hands of a professional weaver. The domestic textile industry, which employed the latest European technology, was still in its infancy. Many inventories describe the continuing importance of spinning in the home. The entire cloth-fabricating process is documented in the equipment enumerated in the household of chairmaker Ebenezer Tracy, Sr., in Lisbon, Connecticut, in 1803: five "Wooling Wheels," "3 Linen d[itt]o," and a clock reel. Presumably, these machines were used to process the fifty pounds of flax and three pounds of wool also itemized by appraisers. The operation was carried to completion when household members rewound skeined fibers onto bobbins on the quill wheel preparatory to weaving on the family loom.[63]

Inventories from Chester County, Pennsylvania, frequently identify the household area where spinning was performed and provide insights into the uses of spun fibers. A particularly complete enumeration is that of the Humphrey Marshall household in East Bradford Township. In 1801 the "Long Room up Stairs" contained equipment for producing yarn in sufficiency—"big" wheels, "little" wheels, swifts, and a reel. Spun fibers on hand included "A Quantity of Woolen Yarn & Basket," "29 Dozn Tow Yarn @ 20 Cts," and "Tow Linnen intended for a Carpet." Yard goods of varied pattern and purpose were stored in the room: "fine Linnen home Made @ 67 Cents" the yard; regular and tow (coarse) linen; cotton "Muslin" and cotton and linen mixed; woolen "Drugget," "Worsted Stuff," and "Worsted & Linnen" mixed. There were checks and stripes, some identified as blue, "Table Linnen," and "Bagging." Presumably, the eleven "Blankets" in the room were also woven locally.[64]

The coastal trade in spinning wheels continued into the early nineteenth century, especially to rural locations. The sloop *Willing Lass* out of Philadelphia carried two dozen wheels to Snow Hill, Maryland, in 1802. The next year the sloop *John Upshur* deposited four wheels at Folly Landing, Virginia, in company with "Six windsor chairs." John Huniker, a Philadelphia chairmaker, sent "one box spinning wheels" and chairs to Charleston in August 1811. The wheels were probably assembled there for local sale or for transport up country.[65]

Prices for wheels as advertised at Greensburg, Pennsylvania, and Chillicothe, Ohio, in 1801 were comparable at $3 and $3.20 apiece. Ebenezer P. Rose of Trenton, New Jersey, distributed his wheels to area outlets in Burlington and Rowley's Mills. Some craftsmen, like Robert Whitelaw of Ryegate, Vermont, offered the very latest developments in spinning equipment, such as the "double geared great wheel head" retailed between 1811 and 1813. In neighboring Keene, New Hamsphire, Azel Wilder manufactured patent wheel heads in 1817.[66]

The 1820 census of manufactures, though incomplete, describes the state of domestic spinning, based upon equipment sales. Eastern shops in upstate New York and central Pennsylvania reported extensive wheel and reel production; supplementary information was supplied for Virginia, Georgia, Kentucky, and Indiana. The largest concentrations of activity were reported by the diligent U.S. marshals who took the census in Ohio and Tennessee. Three-fifths of the national fifty-shop sampling were one-man operations; fewer than ten establishments reported two workmen. Larger shops were uncommon, and only six reported having apprentices in training. Information about shop tools is inadequate in some returns, but single-lathe facilities outnumbered those with two (or more) machines by two to one, and no more than three lathes were found in any one shop. A few entries identify the machines as spring pole, foot, and wheel-activated; several were waterpowered. Spinning-wheel prices varied from $2.50 to $5; prices for flax wheels were the highest, followed by cotton, then wool wheels. Reels cost either $1.50 or $2. Annual production figures are reported occasionally. A shop in Seneca Falls, New York, made 25 spinning wheels and 1,000 chairs in one year. A Blount County, Tennessee, establishment produced fifty wheels and twenty-five reels in a year's time. Shops reporting slow trade were outnumbered three to one by those reporting good sales—in decided contrast to the chairmaking industry as a whole, which experienced a setback during this period of recession. Five shops—four in the midwest and one in southwestern Virginia—even reported that business was better than usual. This situation may reflect, in part, the newness of the regions and the continuing dependence of the inhabitants upon home industry. Much of the trade, however, represented a reaction to economic conditions and an attempt to "manage" during the hard times.[67]

In the acquisition of spinning equipment, money frequently never changed hands, either in bad times or good. Families in need of a new wheel often paid for it in services, labor, or barter goods, the typical mediums of exchange in rural and inland areas into the nineteenth century. Michael Kearns (Kerns) of Martinsburg, West Virginia, exchanged new work for "all kinds of country produce at the market price." George Landon of Erie, Pennsylvania, recorded just such an exchange in January 1818 in an agreement with Ebenezer Graham: "He is to have a big wheel Maid by the last of february for wich he is to Give 3½ Bushels of weete or $4:50 in Cash." Special arrangements were made from time to time between wheelwrights and businessmen. On September 20, 1817, a somewhat involved contract was drawn between James P. Stabler, wheelmaker of Sandy Spring, Maryland, and Joshua Stewart and Company, of which Stabler was also one of the proprietors. The terms were as follows:

Witnesseth that I am to make one hundred spinning wheels for which I am allow'd two Dollars and forty cents a piece for selling them to the user—I am to find all materials except bands—What the said Joshua Stewart & Co takes out of the shop [Stabler's] I am to be paid two Doll & forty cents on delivery [to Stewart]—when the wheels are sold I am to keep the whole amount untill two hundred and forty dollars are paid me with 5 cents a piece for what is Sold to the user [by Stabler]—Then the said Stewart & Co is to have all the cash for which the remainder is sold for until the hundred wheels are made.

9 mo 20th 1817   James Stabler

The actual retail price of Stabler's wheels is not given, but the higher the price, the sooner the wheelwright realized his promised $240 and the more profit the company stood to make. For each sale made by Stabler, he received an additional five-cent commission.[68]

Flax Wheels

Two documented flax wheels of eastern Pennsylvania origin amplify form and nomenclature (figs. 3-33, 3-34). The first is a product of the Philadelphia shop of Jonathan Tyson, whose name appears in directories and other records from 1807 to 1818, the last two years in partnership with Daniel Teese (fig. **3-33**). The main structural element of Tyson's wheel, and of similar units, is the rectangular plank, called a table or bench. It sockets the upper and lower structures independently, in much the same manner as a Windsor-chair seat anchors the legs and back as separate units. Two legs support an A-shaped foot treadle, and the long front leg introduces a tilt to the table. Attached to the tip of the free treadle arm by means of a cord or leather thong is a wooden stick called a footman whose upper end attaches to a curved iron secured in one tip of the metal wheel axle. Activating the foot treadle puts the wheel in motion, which in turn provides the power that operates the mechanism mounted at the table front. The wheel is supported on two uprights, or posts, by means of a metal axle, which pierces the center, or nave. From ten to sixteen spokes connect the nave and rim. Near the table front is a low, turned, horizontal cross bar called the mother-of-all, which provides support for two short uprights called the maidens. Between the maidens a metal rod supports a U-shaped flyer, a spoollike bobbin, and a whorl, or pulley. A driving band, or cord, which lies around the outside rim of the wheel and attaches at the front to the whorl, puts the mechanism in motion when the wheel is activated. Forward of the maidens are the tall upright, cross arm, and vertical cage that make up the distaff. The cage holds the prepared flax fibers to be spun into thread. The sausage-shaped handle at the table front is a tension-adjusting device. When turned, a long screw tip inside the table draws the mother-of-all toward or away from the wheel to increase or decrease tension on the driving band.[69]

Although the Tyson wheel (fig. 3-33) is of considerably earlier date than the wheel shown in figure 3-34, it is of later design. Both machines have turnings found in other eastern Pennsylvania work, but, characteristically, the particular combinations vary from wheel to wheel. The Tyson spinning-wheel leg with its plain, incurved central section is a later version of the supports illustrated in figure 3-34; the compressed ring dividing the balusters is missing. The Tyson foot design has advanced from a peg-tipped oval to an onion shape. In a still later version of this leg, the central section is converted to one long swell flanked by bulges, top and bottom. A double bulge of stouter, shorter form sometimes appears in the wheel uprights. Tyson's uprights differ from the usual profiles, although two elements — the short flaring cone and the ball — are repeated at the top of the front leg. The heavy baluster at the base of the uprights may be likened to the upper center leg profile. The spokes within the wheel are typical of a common regional design. The double beads (or bead and vase) are sometimes separated by a small disk. The vertical members located forward in the machine relate to one another through their finials. Other coordinates include the bulbous egg-shaped forms at the base of the distaff cage and in the shafts of the maidens; the truncated cones near the top of the distaff upright and in the cross arm and the wheel supports; the ball turnings of the mother-of-all, wheel posts, and front leg; and the balusters of the distaff arm and wheel posts. The combination of a tapered cylinder and long swell in the distaff upright appears frequently in work of this region. Sometimes the shapes are repeated in the wheel posts.

The Tyson wheel is unusual in being both labeled and branded. The label, which is attached to the table top, now lies beneath a protective sheet of lucite (separated by

Fig. 3-33 Flax-spinning wheel and detail of brand and label, Jonathan Tyson, Philadelphia, ca. 1807–16. Ash (table) with maple and oak (microanalysis); H. 51″, (table) 18″ by 6⅝″. (Winterthur 72.163.)

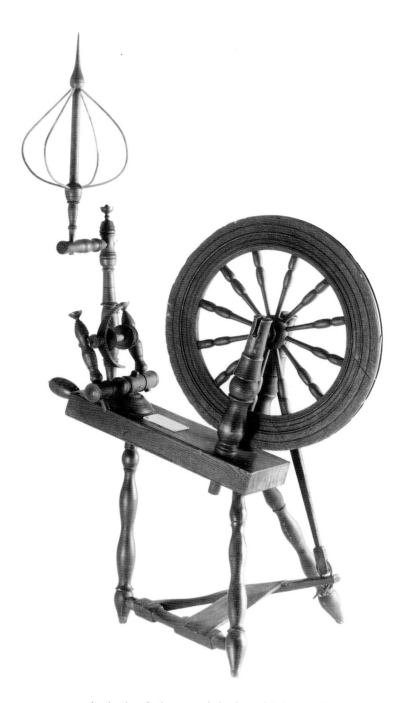

spacers to permit air circulation), and the brand is immediately in front of it. Although discolored and torn at the edges, the label is sufficiently intact to read: "JONATHAN TYSON,/Spinning-Wheel & Chair-Maker,/No. 150, North Front Street,/Between Race and Vine streets, corner/Fearis' court, Philadelphia./N. B. All kinds of work in the above line of/business warranted." The table beneath the label consists of a slab of black ash, although oak was commonly used for the same purpose. All the turnings are maple. In northern New England the turned work was sometimes executed in birch. More often than not, wheel rims were fashioned of oak.

In modern times, the flax wheel has been given many alternative names, with or without justification. It has been called the Irish old or low wheel and the Saxony or Brunswick wheel. Period terms, as already reviewed, include *small, linen,* and *Dutch,* the last a direct reference to the general origin of the apparatus, with its characteristic tilted table and front-to-back orientation.

A second documented flax wheel of eastern Pennsylvania origin (fig. **3-34**) comes from the Berks County shop of Jacob Fox (b. 1788), who like Tyson is known to have made Windsor chairs. Fox's wheel, the later of two documented to his shop, bears the

Fig. 3-34 Flax-spinning wheel and detail of brand, Jacob Fox, Tulpehocken Township, Berks County, Pa., ca. 1839–55. Oak (table); H. 46¾″, (table) 17⅜″ by 6″; luminous orange and black banding. (Chester County Historical Society, West Chester, Pa.: Photo, Winterthur.)

"J. FOX" stamp made by an iron dated "1839," although the design is actually much earlier. The second machine, which is not much different in appearance, bears the earlier "IA: FOX" stamp found on Fox's chairs. Both wheels represent a Pennsylvania style dating earlier than the Tyson wheel. The upper and lower leg in the Fox wheel are almost mirror images. The early-style feet have a well-defined, pegged toe. The heavy center ring midway up the leg became a thin disk before converting to the Tyson-style leg. Differences between Fox's and Tyson's turned treadle arms are basically those of round versus square blocks.

The Fox wheels, which represent general Pennsylvania work, are well coordinated in their turnings. The primary integrating units are the long, swelled elements above the feet, which recur in the wheel posts, the wheel-post braces, the distaff, the maidens, and the wheel spokes, either in upright or inverted form. More subtle relationships are those of the squared reels above the balusters in the wheel posts and distaff upright, the tall pointed finials and ball tops of the maidens and distaff, and the ball-like lower tips of the wheel posts and the tips of the turned treadle arm. Minor differences can be seen in the distaff uprights of Fox's two wheels. Greater variation is found in the wheel spokes. Those in the earlier wheel follow the Tyson pattern, except for introducing a tiny disk between the two bulbous turnings. The sides of the rim are also patterned differently, most noticeably in the introduction here of a bandlike ring edging the inside circumference. The parting of one joint permits commentary on rim construction. The circle consists of four segmental pieces of wood called felloes, which abut one another in diagonal joints secured by internal round tenons. Two tenons are visible through the crack. External pins are clearly visible at each of the joints in Fox's second wheel. Another characteristic of some Delaware Valley wheels that is present here is the use of short, slim, turned braces to lend support to the wheel uprights. The inverted profile approximates Fox's earlier spoke design. Both the Fox wheels are branded on the table end adjacent to the tension device. A bright accent is introduced to the natural wood surfaces of figure 3-34 by bands of luminous orange paint balanced by black penciled lines. The illustrated distaff cage, though not as ornate as Fox's earlier work or as closely coordinated with the other turnings as the Tyson example, probably is original. It is actually a simpler version of the Tyson design and in this form appears on other documented wheels of eastern Pennsylvania origin. When Fox died in 1862 his shop in Tulpehocken Township still contained his tools along with spinning-wheel irons.[70]

John Lewis Krimmel, a Pennsylvania German artist (b. 1789), included studies of the eastern Pennsylvania flax wheel in his sketchbooks (1809–21). A side view clearly delineates turnings comparable to those in the Fox wheels. A disk is centered between two bulbous elements in the spokes. Small braces supporting the wheel uprights anchor in the upper leg rather than in the table, as found in the Fox wheel; similar framing is found in documented Delaware Valley examples. The small, C-curved metal arm of the wheel axle is clearly visible and appears to be attached to the free end of the foot treadle by means of a braided thong. Fox- and Tyson-type spinning wheels influenced flax wheels made well beyond the bounds of eastern Pennsylvania. Turnings in wheels recovered in West Virginia and western Pennsylvania reveal their debt to eastern Pennsylvania work. A later version of the eastern Pennsylvania wheel has bamboo turnings in the legs and in some of the coordinating elements above the table. New England, New York, and Shaker wheels exhibit their own distinctive elements.[71]

A flax-spinning wheel of another form is illustrated in figure 3-35. Depending upon whether structure or function is emphasized, it is called a double-flyer or double-handed wheel. Such wheels are said by some authors to have been made for the use of two persons simultaneously, which could, perhaps, have occured upon occasion. It is more likely, however, that such wheels were made for two-handed spinning by one person. Wheels of this type appear to have been first developed in England, where Thomas Firmin cites their use for the "imployment" of the poor as early as 1677. The idea spread to Ireland and Scotland, where the double-handed wheel was in use at least by the mid eighteenth century. Parallel developments appear to have taken place independently on the Continent and in Scandinavia during the eighteenth century. American double-flyer wheels generally follow a basic pattern first illustrated by Firmin in a publication of 1681. Evidence suggests that their production and use in America was limited to the early decades of the nineteenth century.[72]

Although two-handed wheel turnings often appear early in date, a closer inspection of individual elements suggests otherwise. The tall, double-baluster supports connecting the low platform and upper frame derive from eighteenth-century prototypes, as illustrated in figure 3-34, but with their thick necks and slim bodies, they lack the character of earlier work. Moreover, the profiles are clearly related to the fancy front stretchers in chairs made by Zadock Hutchins at Pomfret, Connecticut, between about 1818 and 1830 and to the Cumberland spindles favored among New York and Newark chairmakers slightly earlier (fig. 2-39). The profile is repeated in the feet. The wheel spokes may be a simpler version of the short ball spindles used in Windsor chairs; multiple banding is substituted at the point of the ball. The scored pattern on the distaff and maidens is much coarser than that found in eighteenth-century work. The finial profiles also date to the nineteenth century, although they are still quite delicate. The

Fig. 3-35 Upright, double-flyer spinning wheel and detail of brand, John Sturdevant, Jr., or John S. Sturdevant, probably New Milford, Conn., 1820–35. Oak (table) with oak, birch, ash, and maple (microanalysis); H. 47⅝″, (lower table) 16″ by 6¼″. (Winterthur 65.554.)

spreading disk with button top supported on a shank (or spool) almost duplicates the finials on some Britannia metal hollowware of the 1820s and later.[73]

An examination of the construction in the upright wheel reveals that each of the two spindle units supported by the maidens has its own vertical tension screw flanking the distaff. The two cords supplying rotation power to the spindles, which carry the flyers and spools, fit into the wheel rim on either side of a center bead and are put in motion simultaneously when the treadle is activated. Treadles usually are of paddle or hornbook form, that is, a broad rectangle with a narrow "handle" at the back attaching to the footman. Here, the wheel is supported within the frame on an upright post, front and back; an alternative type of framing suspends the unit from horizontal members mounted between the corner posts at the midpoint. The distaff arm coordinates in pattern with the four posts; the head, or cage, is a restoration.

Upright wheels have recovery or family histories in New Hampshire, Connecticut, New York, and Pennsylvania, although the latter source may not be valid. The present unit bears the branded name "JOHN / STURDEVANT." at one end of the platform, or table. Records, including population censuses, place men of this name in eastern

Massachusetts, Connecticut, and New York State during the first half of the nineteenth century. The likeliest candidates are John Sturdevant, Jr. (m. 1782, d. 1825), and John Sanford Sturdevant (b. 1798), his son, residents of New Milford in western Connecticut near the New York border. A late nineteenth-century town history identifies the elder Sturdevant as the proprietor of a piece of land and a wheelwright shop in Shepaug Neck given to him by his father. Sturdevant's estate inventory, taken in 1825, describes an active business, detailing a long list of tools appropriate to the trade and the items "Timber for Wheels" and "1 brand or stamp." It seems likely that John Sanford Sturdevant bought his father's branding iron at the sale of his personal property. Strong evidence indicates that John Sanford Sturdevant also followed the woodworking trade, until his death in 1874.[74]

Wool Wheels

The wool wheel is identified by its large size (fig. **3-36**). Its nomenclature is similar to that of the flax wheel. The working apparatus rests upon a long table supported on three legs, generally one at the front and two at the back, though this is occasionally reversed. The wheel of large circumference attaches to a single long, stout support, or post; the wheel nave faces outward, and an axle pin pierces the assemblage. The spokes in many large wheels are plain tapered rods, usually thickened at the rim; the more distinctive wheels have large turned elements at the outer tips, as illustrated. Spinners find that the extra weight of these tips increases the momentum of the turning wheel and lightens the work. Wheel rims vary in width. Broad ones usually are smooth; narrow ones may have a groove, or channel, to guide the driving cord. The cord extends forward to a whorl on the spindle, which is mounted on the faces of two upright maidens supported by a mother-of-all, which in turn is secured on a spindle post. The illustrated spindle head of simple type is put into motion through the direct drive of the wheel; the spindle for winding spun yarn extends beyond the near maiden. Several American devices were developed to improve the wool-spinning head; the most successful was that patented by Amos Minor of Marcellus, New York, in the early nineteenth century. This accelerated head added a small whorl and short cord to the mechanism, thereby increasing the spinning speed and, consequently, the production. Several tension devices are present on wool wheels. The one shown is the sliding-table type, adjusted by loosening the wooden nut and moving the short wood block forward or back, as necessary. Another common type is the wooden pin with a threaded shaft that penetrates the spindle post at a low level and anchors in a small brace at the table front. Tightening the screw increases the forward tilt of the post.[75]

To operate the wool wheel a spinner begins by joining fibers from one end of a small rolled cylinder of carded wool, called a rolag, to a short length of started thread at the tip of the spindle. The wheel is activated with one hand, and while it is in motion the spinner, who is standing, walks backward away from the spindle while manipulating the fiber coming from the rolag with the other hand, drawing it out finely and releasing it gradually to receive a twist for added strength through the action of the turning wheel and spindle. When a few feet have been spun, the spinner reverses the wheel direction and, walking forward, winds the new thread on the spindle. The process, excepting the join, is repeated. A cylindrical stick, or wheel finger, about 7 inches long with a rounded tip, may be used to turn the wheel.[76]

Regional characteristics are even more difficult to establish in the wool wheel than in the flax wheel. The bamboo-turned legs of the illustrated example suggest a southeastern Pennsylvania origin. The stout profile with its rounded nodules and thick depressions relates to late eighteenth-century bamboowork from Maryland. The shape is one that lingered into the nineteenth century in German-American and related work of the eastern Pennsylvania–Maryland border region. The turned parts are particularly well coordinated. Shapes similar to those in the legs are repeated in modified form in the spindle post, wheel post, and maidens. The post bases are also similar, and the profile is repeated in the tips of the wheel spokes.[77]

Fig. 3-36 Wool wheel, southeastern Pennsylvania, 1805–25. Oak (table) with maple and other woods; H. 61½″, (table) 35¾″ by 7⅛″. (Chester County Historical Society, West Chester, Pa.: Photo, Winterthur.)

Reels and Swifts

After preparing a quantity of yarn or thread, the spinner often found it desirable to obtain an accurate measure before cleansing, dyeing, and storing the spun fiber. This called for the use of a reeling device. A skein, the basic unit of measure, equals 560 yards. The simplest measuring and winding tool was a niddy noddy, a hand-operated device with cross arms set at right angles to each other at either end of a short rod. With the yarn end secured to the tip of one cross arm and the connecting shaft held at the center, the niddy noddy was turned and rotated so as to string the yarn around each of the four opposite arm tips consecutively to complete one revolution, which measures approximately two yards. Forty revolutions produce one knot; seven knots equal one skein. The skein of fiber could be left on the niddy noddy under tension for a period of time to remove the kinks and set the twist.

A clock reel provided a more convenient and accurate method of skeining (fig. **3-37**). The vertical model is the most common. Another type of reel employs a longer, benchlike base with the gear box mounted horizontally and the wheel attached at one narrow end. The supporting unit of the upright reel is the platform, or table, set on turned, occasionally shaved, legs. The back corners of the rectangular platform are

Fig. 3-37 Clock reel, southeastern Pennsylvania, 1810–30. Oak (table); H. 36", (table) 13¾" by 6⅞"; luminous orange and black banding. (Judith E. Beattie collection: Photo, Winterthur.)

often cut on the diagonal. Platform edges are plain, beaded, or chip-carved, as shown. The mechanism consists of an upright board, usually plain, sometimes splat-shaped, framed with a box at the top. Some boxes are squared at the bottom, others have shaped extensions at the sides or an arched cutout. Sometimes the edges are chip-carved. A few boxes are open at the front, revealing the internal mechanism. Attached to the front, or occasionally to the side, is a wheel nave containing from four to six radiating, turned or stick-type arms fitted at the tips with short, turned cylindrical cross pieces to support the wound yarn. A turned or slotted handle for convenience in transporting the reel from place to place frequently extends above the box top. Another convenience is the small turned handle (restored in the illustrated example) projecting from one wheel spoke to facilitate rotation. On the box below the wheel nave, an applied paper or painted white circle with numbers constitutes the clock face, or counter. Few reels have survived with the small clock hand used to count the wheel revolutions, and the one in figure 3-37 is a restoration. Inside the box the nave shaft is cut with a thread, or worm, engaging a wooden gear that operates the clock hand and counts the revolutions. Sometimes the gear engages a spring stick mounted on the face of the backboard, causing the mechanism to "click" after a set number of revolutions, thus providing another way to keep track of wound yardage.[78]

The illustrated reel was recovered in southeastern Pennsylvania. Its bright orange and black banding is similar to that on the Jacob Fox flax wheel (fig. 3-34). The delicate feet are reminiscent of supports sometimes found on federal-style card and work tables. The profile also coordinates with the long, wheel-arm balusters and is similar to that of the Fox wheel spokes. The distance around the reel arms is usually two yards; the measure is more precise than that of the niddy noddy. Depending upon the design, the yarn is removed from the reel by slipping it over a cross bar with a slim rounded tip, or partially collapsing one arm to release the tension. Here, by twisting, or loosening, the bulbous element of the upper arm, the tip supporting the cross piece is depressed into a hollow interior. Clock reels predating Windsor construction sometimes have a heavy turned shaft supported on a trestle base. Unusual reels of the nineteenth century are known with a heart-shaped base or an upright board styled in human form. The clock reel was particularly popular in the early nineteenth century, although even as early as 1735 Thomas Pratt of Malden, Massachusetts, repaired a clock reel for Captain Samuel Wait.[79]

The swift followed the reel in order of use. Mounted with skeins, it simplified the process of winding wool into balls for knitting or onto bobbins for weaving. The swift is basically a revolving cage that stands on the floor or is mounted on a table edge. To further facilitate the preparation of bobbins (also called spools or quills) for weaving, the yarn from the swift could be attached directly to a spool mounted in a quill wheel; the revolving mechanism rewrapped the cleaned and dyed yarn in preparation for the final process of cloth making. Early nineteenth-century quill, or quilling, wheels varied in price from $1.36 to $2. The lingering importance of home cloth production is demonstrated in the inventory of woodworker Abraham Shove of Freetown, Bristol County, Massachusetts, made during his lifetime in November 1817. The total value of two spinning wheels, a swift, a quill wheel, and a loom was $12.[80]

Miscellaneous Forms

CHAIRS FOR VEHICLES

Many Windsor-chair-making shops produced seats for horse-drawn vehicles from pre-revolutionary days until well into the 1800s. The riding chair was the first conveyance fitted with a Windsor seat; the wagon used the same seating early in the nineteenth century. The riding chair, also known as a Windsor chair or a Windsor riding chair, was a light, two-wheeled, one-horse vehicle for a single occupant. Certain forms of sulkies qualify as riding chairs. Other terms for the same vehicle are *solo chair, gig,* and *chaise.* The riding chair was first known in England, but the introduction of Windsor construction to the seat was an American innovation (fig. 3-38). The earliest reference to a Windsor riding chair appears in a notice of 1757 from Charleston, South Carolina: "An exceeding neat new solo chair, made in the manner of a *Windsor* chair, the back, rail, and elbows lined with cloth, a box to the seat to take out, the bottom covered with carpet, imported in the *Charming Nancy.*"[81]

Chances are the Charleston vehicle was made in Philadelphia, a center of American coachmaking by the third quarter of the century. Philadelphia vehicles are known to have found a good market in Charleston. The brigantine *Philadelphia Packet* entered the port from the Delaware River in June 1766 carrying a cargo of "102 Windsor Chairs . . . [and] a Riding Chair." Another vehicle is recorded in April 1768 on the schooner *Brouton Island Packet.* A Charleston notice of 1769 advertised "a good second-hand POST-CHAISE, AND A new WINDSOR CHAIR." By 1772 several local coach- and chairmakers were at work, among them George Hewet, who offered "A light WINDSOR CHAIR" for sale. Hewet advised customers that he had "erected a complete and large Range of COACH-HOUSES, for the Reception of Gentlemen's Carriages that may come to be repaired, in Order to prevent their receiving any Injury from the Weather." He further noted that he was prepared to rent coach-house space by the year. Many owners of coaches and chairs had their own facilities, like William Jevon, a prosperous merchant of Lancaster, Pennsylvania, whose premises contained a "Stable with [a] chair house (brick)" before 1767.[82]

Among those who could afford the luxury, the riding chair was a popular vehicle of conveyance for business or pleasure by the 1770s. Prerevolutionary Charleston probate records list riding chairs in many plantation estates; similar vehicles also belonged to a doctor, a clergyman, and a "gentleman." A *Windsor* riding chair is itemized in the estate of planter Thomas Jones, Sr. Merchant Thomas Gilbert of Philadelphia owned a riding chair at his death in 1774; another was in the personal estate of George Kemble, "Livery stable keeper" of the city. A New York notice of April 15, 1771, offered "A neat Windsor Chair to be sold"; available to accompany it was an "extraordinary good Saddle and Chair Horse." Sixteen vehicles were enumerated in 1774 in the Boston estate of Benjamin Coats, probably the proprietor of a livery stable. A "Berlin Coach" received the top valuation at £60; a riding chair held its own among other vehicles at £13.6.8.[83]

Vehicles, like horses, sometimes went astray. William Holiday advertised at Charleston in 1777: "There is a Windsor Chair in my yard: the owner may have it for calling for." The owner of a riding vehicle that was purloined from an alley near Broad and King Streets three years later may not have been so lucky. A description in an advertisement tells what such machines looked like: "STOLEN . . . a solo CHAIR, commonly called a Sulkey, being a Windsor chair, mounted on shafts, the whole painted green, with an iron flip on the aft side." Green appears to have been the popular color for the Windsor riding chair, as it was for the sitting chair into the late eighteenth century. At New York a "green painted Winsor Chair, with harness complete" was offered for sale at the Merchants' Coffee House in November 1780. A Philadelphia notice describes a convenient extra: "TO BE SOLD, A WINDSOR RIDING CHAIR, in good order, the geers almost new; very convenient for travelling, as it is accommodated with a large sliding box with locks."[84]

The export trade revived quickly after the Revolution, and vehicle merchandising along with it. Between 1783 and 1798 Philadelphia riding chairs were shipped to the southern ports of Norfolk, Charleston, and Savannah; another market was Cape François in the West Indies. George Bringhurst, a prominent Philadelphia coachmaker, shipped a Windsor riding chair to Charleston on his own account aboard the ship *Delaware* in March 1792. Jacob Vander Pool of New York began to manufacture sulkies as well as seating furniture, although he may have acquired the carriage work exclusive of the seat from someone else. In the particularly troubled financial situation of postwar Rhode Island, chaisemakers at Providence and Newport were especially active. An occasional riding chair was also shipped from the neighboring port of New London, Connecticut.[85]

Evidence of vehicle repair and new work for the domestic market is scattered among records. In his book of personal accounts James Beekman of New York City noted the purchase of "a Riding Windsor chiar [*sic*] & Harness" under the date August 24, 1785. He kept the vehicle only slightly more than a year before selling it for what he had paid, £5.10.0. Philadelphia coachmakers David and Francis Clark repaired wagons and a Windsor sulky for Samuel Meredith, a city merchant. The sulky required work to the "Boady" in 1789 and "a New felly [felloe] & Spokes in the Wheels." Meredith purchased a new vehicle from Thomas Atkinson on July 31, 1802, for $22 (£6.12.0). Problems arose, and within a month Meredith took the vehicle around to the establishment of George and John Rozell for "staying [the] Shafts with an Iron Stay and two bolts, and mending the Harness." By December Meredith decided to have the sulky painted "two Coats a dark Colour." Wooden repairs to sulkies were recorded by city chairmaker Charles C. Robinson between 1812 and 1818. Several times he replaced the "bottom," or flooring, of a vehicle, but the most common request was for "an arm Chair for a Sulky." The usual price was $2.50. Once Robinson noted, "To puting Back to Sulky Stool" for 75¢. Undoubtedly, this meant that Robinson replaced the upper structure of an armchair (from the "stool" up) because an armless seat in a pitching vehicle would have been dangerous.[86]

Southern artisans began to take an active part in the vehicular trade before the close of the eighteenth century. John Nutt of Wilmington, North Carolina, advertised for an apprentice to "the Cabinet Making and Riding Chair business" in 1788, and other apprentices followed. Nutt's instruction of young men was only too successful, for

Fig. 3-38 Windsor riding chair, Virginia, 1760–80 (vehicle) and ca. 1810–18 (chair). Chair arms restored. (Mount Vernon Ladies' Association of the Union, Mount Vernon, Va.)

within a decade it created trouble, as he indicated in June 1798: "Whereas it has been too much the custom to apply to my negro apprentices to repair riding chairs or other work, which tends to my injury particularly as the materials to complet such jobbs must be purloined from me by said apprentices, Notice is hereby given that I will prosecute any person, under the law against dealing with negroes, who may here as employ any of my apprentices without my permission."[87]

Meanwhile, at their inland location at Fayetteville Thomas and James Beggs formed a partnership in 1793 to build riding and sitting chairs. In Savannah, Georgia, James Anderson II advertised in 1797 that he had "again commenced the chair making Business in Broughton Street . . . where Riding Chairs, Sulkies, etc. will be made in the neatest manner, and on the newest plan." Anderson was not the first vehicle maker in town. Simon Connor had followed the "Wheelwright and Chairmaking Business opposite Mr. Steil's saddler" from as early as 1786. Connor had his ups and downs in business, not the least of which were customers who neglected to pay their bills. After several attempts to collect from Mrs. Dianna Massey for repairs in 1792, Connor wrote in desperation, "Mrs. Diannah . . . the repairs that is done to your chair come to one pound nineteen shillings, sooner than I shall keep you from the use of the Chair, if you will send me Seven Dollars I will give you a rect [receipt], in full if not I shall hire it or charge storidge which is half Dollar per week since I sent you the Bill, which is as little as I can do for the Interest of the Money." The episode appears to have ended well, but four years later Connor's property was one of those partially or totally destroyed by a disastrous fire that consumed part of the town.[88]

After 1800 several craftsmen attempted to establish a sitting- and riding-chair business at Petersburg, Virginia, a tobacco warehousing center. Joel Brown advertised on September 21, 1804: "4 RIDING CHAIRS Well-finished—with harness, or without." Archer Brown and the partners George Dillworth and John Priest placed notices in 1805 and 1806. The local market was soon saturated, and by 1808 Priest had relocated to Nashville, Tennessee.[89]

Little visual evidence of the riding chair remains, in spite of its popularity in its day. A reasonably complete vehicle and seat displayed at Mount Vernon (fig. **3-38**) is a rare survival. It is said to have been owned originally in Virginia by Thomas, sixth Lord

Fairfax, who died in 1781. This information is supported by oral tradition and by the listing of "a chair" and "chair harnesses" in Lord Fairfax's estate inventory filed at Winchester. The chair remained in the family until 1812, when it was sold by a nephew to Major Abraham Davenport of Charles Town, West Virginia. If the original Windsor seat, or a remnant, was still in place when Davenport acquired the vehicle, it probably had a low, possibly a high, back. The present chair dates from about the period of Davenport's purchase. The square back is linked with nineteenth-century design, and the crest is one that had its genesis in Baltimore chairwork. From Major Davenport the historic vehicle passed through the family to the donor. Research conducted at Mount Vernon after the acquisition of the vehicle clearly documents the popularity of the riding chair in Virginia on the eve of the Revolution. Vehicles were recorded as taxable property. At least eighty-five riding chairs existed in Elizabeth City County alone in 1775. George Washington owned a riding chair at this date.[90]

Before the nineteenth century, few documents describe single and double sitting chairs used to convert a "business" wagon to a "pleasure" vehicle. After 1800 such references are common. Both rush-bottom and Windsor seating was used for this purpose. Some seats probably were fastened to the wagon bed with ironwork, but many appear to have been removable, permitting the vehicle to serve a dual function. Wait Garret of New Hartford, Connecticut, specifically listed wagon chairs and wagon chairs "with Legs" in his accounts of the 1810s. The weight of the sitter reasonably secured the seat, particularly if the chair was double and occupied by two persons. Armchairs appear to have been more common for this purpose than side chairs. Prices of 7s. and less certainly refer to rush-bottom work; those over 10s. imply Windsor construction. Contemporary records employ the terms *wagon chair* (the most common term) and *wagon seat*. Production of these items was widespread.[91]

An early reference to the wagon chair appears in the accounts of Solomon Cole of Glastonbury, Connecticut, who charged a customer 32s. to make "2 chairs for waggon" in 1801. The wording is ambiguous, so it is unclear whether Cole made two individual seats or one double one. Thomas Boynton of Windsor, Vermont, noted on August 12, 1815, that he had finished painting "a double chair for a waggon." Harris Beckwith of Northampton, Massachusetts, built a wagon chair priced at 16s. in 1803. The Proud brothers in Providence, Rhode Island, priced similar seating from $2 to $2.50 (12s. to 15s.).[92]

The accounts of Wait Garret in New Hartford, Connecticut, indicate that customers for wagon seating could choose various options. During a nine-month period in 1813–14, one individual purchased new chairs priced at $1.25, $1.50, and $2 apiece. Another customer acquired an elegant "Waggon Chair with Velvet Cushions" for slightly more than $5. General Salem Towne of Charlton, Massachusetts, probably spent his money more wisely when fitting his wagon seat with a "Bellows Top" that opened accordion-fashion to protect the sitter(s) from sun or rain. The work was executed for $10.50 by John Ballard of Framingham in 1817. About that time Lambert Hitchcock advertised from western Connecticut that he made and sold wagon chairs of "an approved pattern." James Chestney of Albany offered "Windsor Waggon Chairs and Settees."[93]

Repairs to wagon chairs often provide more explicit information than accounts for new chairs. At Bennington, Vermont, H. F. Dewey repaired and "matt[ed]" (that is, provided a rush seat for) a wagon chair. The two wagon seats "bottomed" by Allen Holcomb at New Lisbon, New York, about 1820 were also rush-seated. About a year later Holcomb repaired a Windsor "wageon Chair with 9 new sticks at /6[pence] pr stick," for a total charge of 56¢. He later turned "24 Cumberlent [Cumberland] Spindle for Wageon Chairs" at 1¢ apiece for a customer who apparently was constructing new seats. Other craftsmen noted similar repairs. George Landon of Erie, Pennsylvania, turned "12 rods for waggeon Chair"; in Groton, Connecticut, woodworker James Gere supplied a customer with "thirty Bannisters for Waggen seats." Alexander Low's charge for turning "32 rungs for a wagon seet found wood" at Freehold, New Jersey, was 13s.

4*d*. Any number of double, rush-bottom wagon seats exist today, but the Windsor used for the same purpose is almost unknown. A few Windsor settees with blocked feet may have been intended for such a purpose, but other visual evidence is lacking.[94]

FAN CHAIRS

Several decades ago Charles B. Wood III focused attention on the fan chair when he discussed its invention by one John Cram, a maker of musical instruments. Interest in the chair appears to have been stimulated when Charles Willson Peale, the artist and naturalist, sent a drawing and explanation of its mechanism (fig. 3-39) to the famed Philadelphia doctor Benjamin Rush on July 31, 1786. Peale thought that the "health of the sedentary," like the comfort of the healthy, could be improved by the use of the fan chair. The movement of the fan provided a cooling breeze and helped ward off flies in a society where window screens were virtually unknown. To better accomplish the latter objective "some cuttings of papers," or streamers, could be "attached to the fan," according to Peale. Charles Wood writes that "Doctor Rush must have been favorably impressed" with the chair, since he presented the letter and drawing to members of the American Philosophical Society at their meeting on August 18.[95]

The chair Peale drew in his delineation of the fan mechanism is a Philadelphia high-back Windsor. Extant fan chairs also employ the sack-back (fig. 3-40) and bow-back patterns. The Windsor was well suited to this construction, since the H-type brace connecting the legs provided good clearance for the treadle apparatus, and the wooden plank was a suitable anchor for the heavy superstructure. Cram appears to have met with initial encouragement in the production of his mechanical chair. Manasseh Cutler noted in his *Journals* under the date July 13, 1787, a "great armed chair, with . . . a large fan placed over it" in the possession of Benjamin Franklin. Cutler described the aging stateman's use of the chair: "He fans himself, keeps off flies, etc, while he sits reading, with only a small motion of his foot." George Washington seems to have been another of Cram's patrons. Noted among the general's personal expenses on August 8, 1787, while he was in Philadelphia to attend the Constitutional Convention, is the item "By a fan chair," which cost £1.16.6. Although there is no proof that either Franklin or Washington purchased their fan chairs from Cram, the dates and circumstantial evidence are convincing. Other, less ambitious mechanical chairs have turned up in the South, perhaps inspired by Washington's fan chair. Several rush-bottom, slat-back side chairs have fly whisks mounted on the horizontal arm of a simple pole attached at the base to an apparatus to produce motion.[96]

A fan chair of Philadelphia origin (fig. 3-40) was owned by the physician Dr. Eneas Munson, Sr. (1734–1826), of New Haven, Connecticut. How the doctor came to acquire the chair, either first- or secondhand, is unknown. The Philadelphia characteristics are unmistakable, however. Conformity with other Philadelphia sack-back work may be noted at such points as the squared bow tips, arm supports, seat front, leg tops, medial stretcher, and knuckle arms. If Munson received the chair direct from Cram or through an agent, it would have been a simple matter to ship it by water in two containers or packages. Between the date of Peale's drawing and construction of Munson's chair, the inventor made a change in the foot-treadle design. The first device, as rendered by the artist, worked on a simple seesaw principle: the cross rod between the front legs functioned as a fulcrum for the centered foot lever. The Munson chair uses the treadle pattern of the flax-spinning wheel (figs. 3-33, 3-34), and the same treadle

Fig. 3-39 Drawing of John Cram's fan chair and explanation, Charles Willson Peale, Philadelphia, 1786. (American Philosophical Society, Philadelphia.)

Fig. 3-40 Windsor fan chair, Philadelphia, ca. 1787–90. H. (apparatus) 77¼", (chair) 40⅜", (fan) 21¾" by 16"; fan, dark brown with gilt feathers shaded and veined in brown. (New Haven Colony Historical Society, New Haven: Photo, Winterthur.)

mechanism is present in a second fan chair at Mount Vernon. The fulcrum for the A-frame treadle consists of pins that socket into the front leg pieces and the treadle arms. The divided design permitted the sitter to assume a more comfortable posture and to set the treadle in motion with either foot. Tack-studded surfaces provided a good foot grip and reduced wear and tear on the wooden parts. The apparatus supporting the fan attaches to the seat bottom and chair back.

While the fan of the Munson chair is made of hard leather decorated to resemble gilded feathers, the fan of the Mount Vernon chair is pasteboard, as in the original specifications. The principle of activating the fan in either chair is not unlike putting a spinning wheel in motion. The long pole, attached at the bottom to the back of the treadle and at the top to a pulley located behind the fan arm, is simply a longer version of the footman found in the spinning wheel. Leather thongs once linked the pulley and pole arm, permitting back-and-forth movement of the fan. Cram, the inventor, is said to have left Philadelphia and resettled in Virginia, where he manufactured spinning wheels. He is listed in Philadelphia records from the first directory of 1785 through 1789, but his name does not appear in the second city directory of 1791.[97]

The bow-back Windsor supporting Cram's fan apparatus in the Mount Vernon fan chair has been identified as a Long Island chair, but more likely it originated in Rhode Island. Although the flat, tenoned arms with their rounded, horizontal front grips and shapely turned posts have much the character of New York work, the same turnings and related arms appear in Rhode Island construction. In addition, the designs of the D-shaped seat and the legs are peculiar to Rhode Island chairmaking. Both derive from English prototypes. A pair of chairs with closely related leg turnings, but more English than American in overall appearance, is said to have been owned by Samuel Huntington, governor of Connecticut, whose residence at Norwich was close to the Rhode Island border and accessible to the coast. The chairs are identical to two once owned by William Floyd of Mastic, Long Island, which explains the former attribution of the fan chair. Long Island trade at the period of the fan chair's manufacture was focused on New England, and during the British occupation of Long Island in the Revolution, the Floyd family fled to Connecticut. William Floyd later reported to the Connecticut Assembly that he had lost "the Greatest part of [his] Household furniture," which would have necessitated his buying new or secondhand furniture, some of it certainly in Connecticut.[98]

WASHSTANDS

One of the most unusual forms in Windsor furniture is the tall washstand pictured in figure 3-41, one of two known. The origin of the stands can be identified through the turnings, especially the exaggerated, rounded terminals of the leg tops and the post and spindle bases. This vigorous interpretation of bamboowork is rather rare, although it is found in some chairs made by James Chapman Tuttle of Salem, Massachusetts. Similar turned work appears in a long, stepped-tablet settee constructed with three stretchers across the front, each centered by a rectangular medallion identical to that in the stand; the S-scroll arm supports of the settee are an exaggerated type found in Boston work. A short, contoured-back, Windsor side chair attributed to Samuel Gragg of Boston (fig. 1-37) has a similar, though not identical, medallion in the front stretcher. A subtle, stylish touch in the leg turnings of the washstand is the compressed bulbous shape at the tips forming small feet. All the turned work sockets directly into its adjacent board. The box forming the stand table consists of five boards. The tall back and sides are dovetailed at the corners and attached to the sides of the stand top with nails. The narrow lip across the front is also nailed on. The crest pattern and function of the stand suggest that the small brass knobs projecting from the ends of the top piece were part of the original scheme; they form hangers for towels.[99]

The decoration of the stand is intact and consists of two types of embellishment, turned work and painted work. The first type of ornament, which is subtle, consists of

Fig. 3-41 Windsor washstand, probably Salem, Mass., 1800–1810. H. 53″, W. 31″, D. 17″; mustard yellow ground with wine red. (Photo, Three Ravens.)

eight small, applied bosses: two on the crest face at the tips, two at the lower front box corners, and four marking the upper scrolls of the box sides. Mustard yellow paint covers the exposed surfaces; the decorative accents consist of penciled grooves, dotted bands, and narrow oval loops executed in wine red. Similar decoration in brown and apricot on a light mustard yellow ground appears on a double-bow, square-back chair with Boston-Salem characteristics, which may have been made in Maine. Related decoration, consisting of dotted bands and loops, ornaments a set of Maine side chairs labeled by Daniel Stewart of Farmington. The same chairs provide further evidence of Boston-inspired styling in their crest profiles.

The rarity of the tall Windsor washstand can be explained in several ways. Production was limited geographically. Salem, the probable place of origin, had only a modest coastal trade, being overshadowed by neighboring Boston, although some stands may have been shipped overseas in the Sanderson brothers' furniture export trade. At home, the form apparently did not catch on, probably due to size, cost, and competition from board-framed painted stands with a greater surface area for ornamentation.

Notes

1. John Plummer, *The Book of Hours of Catherine of Cleves* (New York: Pierpont Morgan Library, 1964), pl. 20. The ancient Egyptian, Harz, and Flemish stools are illustrated in Nancy Goyne Evans, *American Windsor Chairs* (New York: Hudson Hills, 1996), figs. 1-1, 1-3, 1-9.

2. The Merode and Holme stools are illustrated in Evans, *American Windsor Chairs,* figs. 1-4, 1-8. Randall Holme, *The Academy of Armory; or, A Storehouse of Armory and Blazon* (1688), vol. 2 (London: Roxburghe Club, 1905), bk. 3, chap. 14, p. 15. An upholstered stool is illustrated in *World Furniture,* ed. Helena Hayward (New York: McGraw Hill, 1965), fig. 314.

3. Esther Singleton, *The Furniture of Our Forefathers* (Garden City, N.Y.: Doubleday, Page, 1913), pp. 191–93; William MacPherson Hornor, Jr., *Blue Book: Philadelphia Furniture* (1935; reprint, Washington, D.C.: Highland House, 1977), p. 297; John Jones, estate records, 1708, Philadelphia Register of Wills; Margaret B. Schiffer, *Chester County, Pennsylvania, Inventories, 1684–1850* (Exton, Pa.: Schiffer, 1974), pp. 124, 142, 298.

4. John Gaines II and Thomas Gaines, account book, 1712–62, Joseph Downs Collection of Manuscripts and Printed Ephemera, Winterthur Library (hereafter cited as DCM and WL); Schiffer, *Chester County Inventories,* p. 124; Owen Owen, estate records, 1741, Philadelphia Register of Wills (reference courtesy of Wendy Kaplan); Solomon Fussell, account book, 1738–48, Stephen Collins Papers, Library of Congress, Washington, D.C.; William, Daniel, and Samuel Proud, ledger, 1770–1825, Rhode Island Historical Society, Providence (hereafter cited as RIHS); Alexander Edward, account of Grant Webster, 1772–93, Greenough Papers, Massachusetts Historical Society, Boston; Mansell, Corbett and Co., advertisement in supplement to *South Carolina Gazette* (Charleston), February 16, 1767 (reference courtesy of Susan B. Swan); Mary Richards, estate records, 1773, Baltimore County, Md., Inventories (microfilm, DCM).

5. Samuel Moon, bill to Samuel Meredith, March 3, 1786, Clymer-Meredith-Read Papers, Samuel Meredith Accounts, New York Public Library, New York (hereafter cited as NYPL); manifest of sloop *Samuel,* October 11, 1792, Philadelphia Outward Entries, U.S. Customhouse Records, French Spoliation Claims, National Archives, Washington, D.C. (hereafter cited as NA); cargo of the *Helena,* October 4, 1785, as quoted in Harrold E. Gillingham, "The Philadelphia Windsor Chair and Its Journeyings," *Pennsylvania Magazine of History and Biography* 55, no. 3 (October 1931): 325; levy court docket, Sussex County, Del., November 11, 1794, State of Delaware, Division of Historical and Cultural Affairs (hereafter cited as DDHCA; reference courtesy of Ann Baker Horsey); Samuel Fraunces, estate records, 1795, Philadelphia Register of Wills.

6. Nathaniel Brown, inventory, 1803, as quoted in Mrs. Charlton M. Theus, *Savannah Furniture* (n.p.: By the author, ca. 1967), p. 48; manifests of brig *Eliza and Sarah* (March 24, 1804) and schooner *Fox* (November 25, 1803), Philadelphia Outward Coastwise Entries, U.S. Customhouse Records, NA; Joseph Prentis, inventory, 1809, Prentis Papers, Swem Library, College of William and Mary, Williamsburg, Va. (hereafter cited as WM).

7. Anthony Steel, estate records, 1817, Philadelphia Register of Wills; manifest of brig *Morgiana,* May 2, 1821, Philadelphia Outward Foreign Entries, U.S. Customhouse Records, NA; True Currier, account book, 1815–38, DCM; David Alling, ledger, 1803–53, and daybook, 1836–54, New Jersey Historical Society, Newark (hereafter cited as NJHS; microfilm, DCM); John Oldham, estate records, 1835, Baltimore County, Md., Inventories (microfilm, DCM); Edward Bulkley, assignment of estate, 1839, New Haven, Genealogical Section, Connecticut State Library, Hartford (hereafter cited as CSL); Abraham McDonough, estate records, 1852, Philadelphia Register of Wills.

8. Holme and Cartwright references in *Oxford English Dictionary,* s.v. "cricket." The prophet Ezra is pictured in Hayward, *World Furniture,* pp. 32 and facing. *The Wedding* is illustrated in *101 American Primitive Water Colors and Pastels* (Washington, D.C.: National Gallery of Art, 1966), fig. 14.

9. Bailey, *Dictionarium Britannicum,* as quoted in John Gloag, *A Short Dictionary of Furniture* (London: George Allen and Unwin, 1969), p. 274; Alice Morse Earle, *Child Life in Colonial Days* (New York: Macmillan, 1899), p. 184; Thomas Sheraton, *Cabinet Dictionary,* vol. 2 (1803; reprint, New York: Praeger, 1970), pp. 212–13.

10. Gaines, account book; John Brower, bill to Robert R. Livingston, January 12, 1784, Robert R. Livingston Papers, New-York Historical Society, New York (hereafter cited as NYHS); John Carter, bill to Saint George Tucker, July 18, 1790, Tucker-Coleman Collection, WM; James Galloway, estate records, 1793, Baltimore County, Md., Inventories (microfilm, DCM); Elias Hasket Derby, estate records, 1799–1805, Essex County, Mass., Registry of Probate; Daniel Rea, daybook, 1789–1802, Baker Library, Harvard University, Cambridge, Mass. (hereafter cited as BL); Silas E. Cheney, ledger, 1799–1817, and daybook, 1807–13, Litchfield Historical Society, Litchfield, Conn. (hereafter cited as LHS; microfilm, DCM).

11. Abner Taylor, account book, 1806–32, DCM; Frederick Allen, estate records, 1830, Windham, Conn., Genealogical Section, CSL; Increase Pote, account book, 1824–30, Maine Historical Society, Portland; Thomas Walter Ward II, inventory book, ca. 1835–45, DCM; Benjamin Bass, estate records, 1819, Suffolk County, Mass., Registry of Probate (microfilm, DCM); Thomas Boynton, ledger, 1811–17, Dartmouth College, Hanover, N.H. (microfilm, DCM); Philemon Robbins, account book, 1833–36, Connecticut Historical Society, Hartford (hereafter cited as CHS); Elton W. Hall, "New Bedford Furniture," *Antiques* 113, no. 5 (May 1978): 1120; Elisha Harlow Holmes, daybook, 1825–30, CSL; Reverend Ambrose Edson, estate records, 1836, Somers, Conn., Genealogical Section, CSL; Paul Jenkins, daybook, 1836–41, DCM.

12. Wallace Nutting reproduced footstools in the 1920s and 1930s in a variety of patterns, some now lacking their original identification. Tops are oval, round, or "ogee"-shaped (a rectangular form with serpentine sides all around). Planks are reasonably deep and usually flattened just below the top surface, then rounded below. The shape is frequently that of a thumb tip viewed horizontally in profile, that is, gently rounded and tapering toward the upper edge. Nutting made baluster- and bamboo-turned legs, with and without stretchers. His baluster footstools are typical in having the baluster socketed into the top. Below that element, spool, ring, and foot turnings are copies of New York profiles. Nutting's bamboo turnings are exaggerated, punctuated by sharp creases at the "swells." The Virginia Craftsmen also produced a small stool in the 1920s with stretchers and turnings comparable to those used by Nutting, although the spool elements are somewhat larger. The top is oval and deep with flat, canted edges. Other long, low stools with oval tops about 1 inch thick, seen occasionally in the market today, appear to have been made at a later date than their design indicates. The thin board top is atypical of period shop work. Wallace Nutting, *Supreme Edition General Catalogue* (1930; reprint, Exton, Pa.: Schiffer, 1977), p. 25; Virginia Craftsmen advertisement, *Antiques* 13, no. 1 (June 1928): 464.

13. Boynton, ledger; Alling, daybook; Bulkley, assignment of estate; Cheney, daybook, and Silas E. Cheney, ledger, 1817–22, LHS (microfilm, DCM).

14. Charles Riley, estate records, 1842, Philadelphia Register of Wills (microfilm, DCM).

15. The Pratt footstool is privately owned. The Stripe footstool is illustrated in "The Old Northwest Territory: Furniture and Interiors," *Antiques* 87, no. 3 (March 1965): 314.

16. Albert B. Merrill, bill to Mrs. Isaac Bronson, April 8, 1837, Bronson Papers, NYPL; Frederick Starr, advertisement in *King's Rochester City Directory and Register 1841* (Rochester, N.Y.: Welles and Hayes, 1841), n.p.; Lines and Augur, advertisement in *Daily Palladium* (New Haven, Conn.), February 29, 1841 (reference courtesy of Wendell Hilt); memorandum book containing "List of articles purchased for Sarah R. Arnold," December 1851, Solomon Drowne Papers, Arnold Family, John Hay Library, Brown University, Providence, R.I.

17. Elisha Harlow Holmes, ledger, 1825–30, CHS; Luke Houghton, ledger B, 1824–51, Barre Historical Society, Barre, Mass., (microfilm, DCM); Alling, daybook; Job Townsend, ledger, 1794–1802, Newport Historical Society, Newport, R.I. (microfilm, DCM); Philip Deland, account book, 1812–46, Old Sturbridge Village, Sturbridge, Mass. (hereafter cited as OSV); John Gillingham, inventory, 1794, Philadelphia Register of Wills (photostat, DCM); Francis Trumble and George Halberstadt, estate records, 1798 and 1812, Philadelphia Register of Wills. The Mount painting is illustrated in Frank H. Goodyear, Jr., "American Paintings at the Pennsylvania Academy," *Antiques* 121, no. 3 (March 1982): 699, pl. 7.

18. Prototypes for the baluster shapes in figure 3-11 *(left),* the turned features in figure 3-11 *(right),* and the Boston swelled side stretcher are illustrated in Evans, *American Windsor Chairs,* figs. 6-59, 6-202, 6-203, 6-211, 6-212.

19. An angular-bamboo-turned chair documented to a Tracy family member is illustrated in Evans, *American Windsor Chairs,* fig. 7-6. The Rhode Island stool with double-baluster stretchers is in a private collection.

20. Josiah Prescott Wilder, daybook and ledger, 1837–59, Charles S. Parsons, Wilder Family Notes, Visual Resources Collection, WL (hereafter cited as VRC).

21. Manifest of schooner *Commerce* (November 8, 1810), Perth Amboy, N.J., Inward and Outward Entries, U.S. Customhouse Records, NA; Wait Garrett, account book, 1810–58, CSL; Silas Cheney, daybook, 1813–21, LHS (microfilm, DCM); Church and Sweet, account of Richard W. Greene, 1824, A. C. and R. W. Greene Collection, RIHS. The English reference is discussed in Evans, *American Windsor Chairs*, pp. 20–21.

22. David Alling, account book, 1801–39, NJHS; W. D. Rand, advertisement in *Louisville Directory and Annual Business Advertiser* (Louisville, Ky.: W. Lee White, 1855), p. 210. A turkey-leg chair is illustrated in Evans, *American Windsor Chairs*, fig. 7-22. Peter A. Willard, estate records, 1842–43, Worcester County, Mass., Registry of Probate; David Alling, estate records, 1855, Archives and History Bureau, New Jersey State Library, Trenton; McDonough, estate records; J. W. Mason, bill to steamboat *Keyport*, July 3, 1858, DCM; Wilder, daybook and ledger.

23. *The Pic-Nick* is illustrated in *American Paintings in the Museum of Fine Arts, Boston*, vol. 2 (Boston: Museum of Fine Arts, 1969), fig. 224. Alfred Frankenstein, *William Sidney Mount* (New York: Harry N. Abrams, 1975), figs. 1, 16, 166. *Ladd's Eating House* is illustrated in Marshall B. Davidson, *Life in America*, vol. 2 (Boston: Houghton Mifflin, 1951), p. 138; Robert P. Turner, ed., *Lewis Miller: Sketches and Chronicles* (York, Pa.: Historical Society of York County, 1966), pp. 57 (top), 95 (top, left).

24. William Barker, account books, 1750–72, 1753–66, RIHS; Proud brothers, ledger, and Daniel and Samuel Proud, daybook and ledger, 1810–34, RIHS; Elisha Hawley, account book, 1781–1800, CHS; Cheney, daybook, 1813–21; Alling, daybook; *Lewis Miller*, p. 57 (bottom, right); Edward Hazen, *Popular Technology: or, Professions and Trades*, vol. 2 (1846; reprint, Albany: Early American Industries Association, 1981), p. 213.

25. The New York–style stool is in a private collection.

26. Although the Inman surname is not common in Maine census records, it appears there more regularly than in New Hampshire. The only candidate is M. Inman, a resident of Old Town, Penobscot County, in 1850. It is impossible to draw any conclusions from these data.

27. Alice Hanson Jones, *American Colonial Wealth*, vol. 3 (New York: Arno Press, 1977), p. 1541; Francis Trumble, advertisement in *Pennsylvania Gazette* (Philadelphia), December 27, 1775; George Wells, estate records, 1784, Baltimore County, Md., Inventories (microfilm, DCM); William Beekman, inventory, 1795, DCM; Longwood Manuscripts, Victor du Pont Accounts, Hagley Museum and Library, Wilmington, Del.

28. Matthew and Richard Brenan, advertisement in *Charleston City Gazette and Advertiser* (Charleston, S.C.), December 11, 1799 (Prime Cards, WL); manifest of schooner *Virginia*, October 23, 1800, Philadelphia Outward Coastwise Entries, U.S. Customhouse Records, NA; Charles C. Robinson, daybook, 1809–25, Historical Society of Pennsylvania, Philadelphia; Isaac Clason and John P. Mumford, estate records, ca. 1815 and 1820, DCM.

29. Boynton, ledger; Cheney, daybook, 1813–21; Harvey Dresser, advertisement in *Windham County Advertiser* (Brooklyn, Conn.), February 30, 1830 (reference courtesy of Wendell Hilt); Samuel Beal, advertisement in *Daily Evening Transcript* (Boston), July 24, 1830; Alling, ledger and daybook; William G. Beesley, daybook, 1828–36, Salem County Historical Society, Salem, N.J.

30. Samuel Proud, inventory, 1835, as quoted in William Mitchell Pillsbury, "The Providence Furniture Making Trade, 1772–1834" (Master's thesis, University of Delaware, 1975), p. 120; McDonough and Riley, estate records; John B. Robinson, billhead, printed 1850–55, inscribed 1855, DCM.

31. John Lambert, estate records, 1793, Philadelphia Register of Wills; Alling, ledger, 1803–53, and daybook; Proud brothers, account books; Robbins, account book; Isaac Wright, account book, 1834–37, CSL.

32. Trumble's early fan-back chair is illustrated in Evans, *American Windsor Chairs*, fig. 3-45.

33. Comparable Rhode Island and Connecticut Windsors are illustrated in Evans, *American Windsor Chairs*, figs. 6-18, 6-53 (feet), 6-59 (spool turnings), 6-81 (pommel crease), figs. 6-99, 6-174 (stretchers).

34. Comparable Connecticut and border chairs are illustrated in Evans, *American Windsor Chairs*, figs. 6-104 (seat rise), 6-148 (balusters), 6-165, 6-172 (feet). Amos Denison Allen, memorandum book, 1796–1803, CHS.

35. Comparable Philadelphia Windsors are illustrated in Evans, *American Windsor Chairs*, figs. 3-24, 3-25 (seat edge), 3-55, *left*, 3-112 (legs).

36. A comparable Moravian Windsor is illustrated in Evans, *American Windsor Chairs*, fig. 8-20.

37. The Hitchcock-style, Baltimore, Shove, and border chairs are illustrated in Evans, *American Windsor Chairs*, figs. 7-22, 4-18, 6-223, 7-51, 6-155.

38. Trumble, advertisement in *Pennsylvania Gazette* (Philadelphia); Thomas Hodgkins, account of Jacob Sanderson, 1808–9, as quoted in Mabel M. Swan, *Samuel McIntire, Carver, and the Sandersons, Early Salem Cabinet Makers* (Salem, Mass.: Essex Institute, 1934), pp. 22–23; Boynton, ledger; William Fosbrook, estate records, 1820, DCM; Allen Holcomb, account book, 1809–28, Metropolitan Museum of Art, New York; Henry W. Miller, account book, 1827–31, Worcester Historical Museum, Worcester, Mass.; Henry F. Dewey, account book, 1837–64, Shelburne Museum, Shelburne, Vt. (microfilm, DCM); William Galligan in *J.F. Kimball and Co.'s Eastern, Western, and Southern Business Directory* (Cincinnati and New York: J. F. Kimball, 1846), p. 300.

39. A bow-back chair-stool is illustrated in Wallace Nutting, *A Windsor Handbook* (1917; 2d ed., Framingham and Boston: Old America, n.d.), p. 187.

40. A Hubbard chair-stool is illustrated in Henry J. Harlow, "Signed and Labeled New England Furniture," *Antiques* 116, no. 4 (October 1979): 879.

41. The butcher's block, monastery carving, and Campen panel are illustrated in Evans, *American Windsor Chairs*, figs. 1-2, 1-3, 1-4.

42. Edward Phillips, *The New World of English Words, or, a General Dictionary* (1658; 6th ed. by John Kersey, Eng., 1706), and John Chardin, *The Coronation of the Present King of Persia, Solyman the Third* (trans. 1686), both as quoted in the *Oxford English Dictionary*, s.v. "stand." Clarence W. Brazer, "Rare Windsor Candlestands," *Antiques* 6, no. 4 (October 1924): 190–94; Schiffer, *Chester County Inventories*, pp. 122–25, 129, 332.

43. Christopher Sauer, "Sale of . . . Goods & Chattles," 1778, as quoted in *Pennsylvania Archives*, ed. Thomas Lynch Montgomery, 6th series, vol. 12 (Harrisburg, Pa.: Harrisburg Publishing, 1907), p. 902; John Cornthwait, estate records, 1782, Baltimore County, Md., Inventories (microfilm, DCM); Schiffer, *Chester County Inventories*, pp. 325, 328.

44. Manifest of sloop *Union* (June 19, 1790), Philadelphia Outward Coastwise Entries, U.S. Customhouse Records, NA; manifest of schooner *Betsey* (April 21, 1796), Philadelphia Outward Entries, U.S. Customhouse Records, French Spoliation Claims, NA; manifest of sloop *Little Tom* (November 18, 1797), New York Outward Coastwise Entries, U.S. Customhouse Records, French Spoliation Claims, NA; manifests of sloop *Jersey Blue* (April 18, 1800), schooners *Success* (May 29, 1802) and *Sally* (July 9, 1803), and ship *South Carolina Packet* (May 9, 1811), Philadelphia Outward Coastwise Entries, U.S. Customhouse Records, NA; Timothy Hanson, inventory, 1798, DDHCA.

45. The table from the Stokes collection is illustrated in Charles Santore, *The Windsor Style in America*, vol. 1 (Philadelphia: Running Press, 1981), fig. 252.

46. The comparable Pennsylvania and Maryland Windsors are illustrated in Evans, *American Windsor Chairs*, figs. 3-2, 3-3, 3-82, 3-92, 3-93.

47. The comparable Rhode Island Windsors are illustrated in Evans, *American Windsor Chairs*, figs. 6-2 (rolled collars), 6-43, 6-125 (round-top feet).

48. The table was formerly in the collection of Louis Guerineau Myers (see Nutting, *Handbook*, pp. 190–91). Myers purchased the table in Baltimore "from a man who had acquired it from an itinerant country dealer," period parlance for the modern "picker."

49. Robert Hussey and Charles Swain, estate records, 1795 and 1805, Nantucket County, Mass., Registry of Probate; Samuel Douglas and Son, account book, 1810–58, CSL; Cheney, ledger, 1799–1817; Andrew Tracy, estate records, 1820–22, Cheshire County, N.H., Registry of Probate; Schiffer, *Chester County Inventories*, pp. 349–50.

50. Patricia Baines, *Spinning Wheels, Spinners, and Spinning* (London: Batsford, 1977), pp. 15, 44–45, 54–55; Dorothy K. Macdonald, *Fibres, Spindles and Spinning-Wheels* (2d ed.; Toronto: Royal Ontario Museum, 1950), pp. 20–21, 28–29; Marion L. Channing, *The Textile Tools of Colonial Homes* (Marion, Mass.: By the author, 1969), pp. 16–17; Rudolf P. Hommel, "More about Spinning Wheels," Early American Industries Association *Chronicle* 2, no. 22 (December 1942): 190–91; G. Bernard Hughes, "Evolution of the Spinning Wheel," *Country Life* 126, no. 3275 (December 10, 1959): 1164, 1166.

51. Baines, *Spinning Wheels*, pp. 82–87, 91–92; Hughes, "Evolution of the Spinning Wheel," p. 1164.

52. The van Vliet engraving is illustrated in Evans, *American Windsor Chairs*, fig. 1-10. Baines, *Spinning Wheels*, pp. 57, 90, 121, 178–79.

53. Earle, *Child Life*, pp. 305–7; Littleton, as quoted in Monica Kiefer, *American Children through Their Books* (Philadelphia: University of Pennsylvania Press, 1948), pp. 149–50.

54. Jones, estate records; Joseph Saul, account book, 1761–62, private collection (photostat, DCM); Schiffer, *Chester County Inventories*, p. 226; Joseph Mortimer Levering, *A History of Bethlehem, Pennsylvania, 1741–1892* (Bethlehem, Pa.: Tunis Publishing, 1903), pp. 388–89; Joseph Emerson, inventory, 1745, Worcester County, Mass., Registry of Probate (photostat, DCM); Thomas Pratt, account book, 1730–68, DCM.

55. Jones, *American Colonial Wealth*, 1:137, 171, 209, 283, 300; Montgomery, *Pennsylvania Archives*, 6th series, 12:648, 700, 712, 726, 900; Mary Attmore and Anna Barbara Bensel, estate records, 1776 and 1773, Philadelphia Register of Wills (microfilm, DCM); John Shearman, advertisement in *Pennsylvania Journal* (Philadelphia), October 3, 1765 (Prime Cards, WL); Trumble, advertisement in *Pennsylvania Gazette* (Philadelphia).

56. William Miller I and William Miller II, inventories, 1768 and 1781, Chester County, Pa., Register of Wills (photostats, DCM); Schiffer, *Chester County Inventories*, pp. 318–22, 328–30; Jacob Fetter, Sr., estate records, 1777, Lancaster County Historical Society, Lancaster, Pa. (hereafter cited as LCHS).

57. Oxford Port of Entry Account Books, vol. for 1759–73, Inward Entries, Maryland Historical Society, Baltimore (hereafter cited as MdHS); Jacob Rahm, estate records, 1778, Baltimore County, Md., Inventories (microfilm, DCM); Joshua Eden, advertisement in *South Carolina Gazette* (Charleston), November 7, 1775, as quoted in Alfred Coxe Prime, comp., *The Arts and Crafts in Philadelphia, Maryland, and South Carolina, 1721–1785* (Philadelphia: Walpole Society, 1929), p. 165.

58. Alexander Chesnut, bill to Col. Philip Schuyler, December 5, 1772, Schuyler Papers, NYPL; Jones, *American Colonial Wealth*, 2:507, 521, 530, 534, 570, 576; Robert Crage, ledger, 1757–81, OSV.

59. Mabel M. Swan, "Furnituremakers of Charlestown," *Antiques* 46, no. 4 (October 1944): 203–6; Ezekiel Smith, account book, 1773–1831, DCM.

60. John Mason, advertisement in *Pennsylvania Packet* (Philadelphia), December 23, 1789, as quoted in Alfred Coxe Prime, *The Arts and Crafts in Philadelphia, Maryland, and South Carolina, 1786–1800* (Topsfield, Mass.: Walpole Society, 1932), p. 226; Alan G. Keyser, Larry M. Neff, and Frederick S. Weiser, *The Accounts of Two Pennsylvania German Furniture Makers*, Sources and Documents of the Pennsylvania Germans, 3 (Breinigsville, Pa.: Pennsylvania German Society, 1978), pp. 3, 4, 7, 12, 15; Joseph Armstrong, advertisement in *Farmers Register* (Greensburg, Pa.), August 2, 1799 (reference courtesy of Marilyn M. White).

61. Thomas Gardner, advertisement in *New-Jersey Journal* (Elizabeth Town), August 26, 1789 (reference courtesy of Susan B. Swan); Sampson Barnet, advertisement in *Delaware Gazette* (Wilmington), October 10, 1789, as quoted in Charles G. Dorman, *Delaware Cabinetmakers and Allied Artisans, 1655–1855* (Wilmington: Historical Society of Delaware, 1960), p. 12; Wise Grinnell, advertisement in *Greenfield Gazette* (Greenfield, Mass.), January 1, 1795, advertisement file, Historic Deerfield, Deerfield, Mass.; Robert Blackwood, advertisement in *Royal Gazette* (St. John, N.B.), 1796, as

noted in Huia G. Ryder, *Antique Furniture by New Brunswick Craftsmen* (Toronto: Ryerson Press, 1965), p. 18; manifests of schooners *Nancy* (August 16, 1791) and *Sally* (June 9, 1795), and brig *Hawk* (September 13, 1791), Boston Outward Entries, U.S. Customhouse Records, French Spoliation Claims, NA; *Minutes of the Common Council of the City of New York, 1784–1831* (New York: By the city, 1917), vol. 1, p. 34.

62. Proud brothers, account books; Joseph Stone, bill to Capt. William Arnold, July 17, 1790, Greene Collection; John Paine, account book, 1761–1815, Institute for Colonial Studies, State University of New York at Stony Brook (microcards, DCM); Daniel Rea, daybook, 1789–93, BL.

63. Ebenezer Tracy, Sr., estate records, 1803, Lisbon Township, New London Co., Conn., Genealogical Section, CSL.

64. Schiffer, *Chester County Inventories*, pp. 333–35.

65. Manifests of sloops *Willing Lass* (April 29, 1802) and *John Upshur* (June 27, 1803), and ship *Pennsylvania* (August 15, 1811), Philadelphia Outward Coastwise Entries, U.S. Customhouse Records, NA.

66. Joseph Armstrong, advertisement in *Farmers Register* (Greensburg, Pa.), August 22, 1801 (reference courtesy of Marilyn M. White); Joseph Hopkins, advertisement in *Scioto Gazette* (Chillicothe, Ohio), December 12, 1801 (reference courtesy of John R. Grabb); Ebenezer P. Rose, advertisement in *Trenton Federalist* (Trenton, N.J.), November 30, 1807 (reference courtesy of James R. Seibert); Robert Whitelaw, ledger, 1804–31, Vermont Historical Society, Montpelier; Azel Wilder, advertisement in *New Hampshire Sentinel* (Keene), September 17, 1817 (Charles S. Parsons, New Hampshire Notes, VRC).

67. Records of the 1820 Census of Manufactures, NA (microfilm, DCM).

68. Michael Kearns, advertisement in *Berkeley and Jefferson Intelligencer* (Martinsburg, W. Va.), August 12, 1808 (citation file, Museum of Early Southern Decorative Arts, Winston-Salem, N.C. [hereafter cited as MESDA]); George Landon, account book, 1813–32, DCM; James P. Stabler, contract with Joshua Stewart and Co., September 20, 1817, Stabler Family Account Books, vol. 2, 1817–20, MdHS.

69. Spinning-wheel nomenclature is given in Baines, *Spinning Wheels*, p. 71; and David A. Pennington and Michael B. Taylor, *American Spinning Wheels* (Sabbathday Lake, Me.: Shaker Press, 1975), p. 5.

70. Jacob Fox, estate records, 1862, Berks County, Pa., Register of Wills (reference courtesy of Lester Breininger).

71. The Krimmel sketchbooks are at Winterthur, DCM.

72. Baines, *Spinning Wheels*, pp. 149–58, including the Firmin information; Pennington and Taylor, *American Spinning Wheels*, pp. 35–42.

73. The Hutchins and ball-spindle chairs are illustrated in Evans, *American Windsor Chairs*, figs. 7-12, 7-49.

74. Samuel Orcutt, *History of the Towns of New Milford and Bridgewater, Connecticut, 1703–1882* (Hartford: Case, Lockwood and Brainard, 1882), pp. 440–41; John Sturdevant, Jr., and John S. Sturdevant, estate records, 1825–26 and 1874, and vital records, Genealogical Section, CSL.

75. Pennington and Taylor, *American Spinning Wheels*, pp. 4, 53–62; Channing, *Textile Tools of Colonial Homes*, pp. 17–19.

76. Baines, *Spinning Wheels*, pp. 198–201.

77. Comparable Maryland and Pennsylvania Windsors are illustrated in Evans, *American Windsor Chairs*, figs. 3-123, 4-2, 4-9.

78. Channing, *Textile Tools of Colonial Homes*, pp. 27–30; Baines, *Spinning Wheels*, pp. 106–9.

79. Pratt, account book.

80. Channing, *Textile Tools of Colonial Homes*, pp. 31–37; Pennington and Taylor, *American Spinning Wheels*, pp. 88–90; Abraham Shove, guardianship inventory of real and personal property, 1817, Bristol County, Mass., Registry of Probate.

81. Riding-chair notice, *South Carolina Gazette*, January 13, 1757 (reference courtesy of Susan B. Swan).

82. Manifests of brig *Philadelphia Packet* (June 5, 1766), and schooner *Brouton Island Packet* (April 14, 1768, from Charleston), Shipping Returns: Charleston, S.C. (1746–67) and East Florida (1765–69), Colonial Office, Public Record Office, London; riding-chair notice, *South Carolina Gazette* (Charleston), February 2, 1769 (reference courtesy of Susan B. Swan); George Hewet, advertisements in *South Carolina Gazette*, August 20, 1772, and February 22, 1773 (references courtesy of Susan B. Swan); William Jevon, inventory, 1767, LCHS.

83. Jones, *Colonial American Wealth*, 1:135–37, 147; 2:561–67, 907–9; 3:1505, 1518–20, 1528–32, 1539–41, 1574–75, 1585, 1598, 1606–8; New York notice, *New-York Gazette, and Weekly Mercury*, April 15, 1771, as quoted in Rita Susswein Gottesman, comp., *The Arts and Crafts in New York, 1726–1776* (New York: New-York Historical Society, 1938), p. 125.

84. Vehicle notices, *South Carolina and American General Gazette* (Charleston), November 20, 1777, and December 20, 1780; vehicle sales, *New York Gazette and the Weekly Mercury*, November 13, 1780, and *Pennsylvania Packet* (Philadelphia), August 5, 1779.

85. Gillingham, "Philadelphia Windsor Chair," pp. 318, 325, 329–30; manifests of brigs *Charleston* (December 12, 1789) and *Alfred* (June 3, 1790), and sloop *Jane* (August 20, 1798), Philadelphia Outward Entries, U.S. Customhouse Records, NA; manifests of ship *Delaware* (October 1, 1791, March 27, 1792), Philadelphia Outward Entries, U.S. Customhouse Records, French Spoliation Claims, NA. Vehicle notices in *Charleston Morning Post* (Charleston, S.C.), January 22, 1787; *Charleston City Gazette and Advertiser*, January 1, 1794, and May 14, 1798; and *South Carolina Gazette* (Charleston), June 15, 1797 (all in Prime Cards, WL). Jacob Vander Pool, advertisement in *Town and Country Journal, or the American Advertiser* (New York), December 11, 1783, as quoted in Rita Susswein Gottesman, *The Arts and Crafts in New York, 1777–1799* (New York: New-York Historical Society, 1954), p. 130; Joseph K. Ott, "Exports of Furniture, Chaises, and Other Wooden Forms from Providence and Newport, 1783–1795," *Antiques* 107, no. 1 (January 1975): 135–41; Ott, "Rhode Island Furniture Exports, 1783–1800, Including Information on Chaises, Buildings, Other Woodenware and Trade Practices," *Rhode Island History* 36, no. 1 (February 1977): 2–13; manifest of brig *Sally* (September 2, 1794), New London Outward Entries,

U.S. Customhouse Records, French Spoliation Claims, NA.

86. James Beekman, account book of personal affairs, 1761–96, White-Beekman Papers, NYHS. David Clark and Francis Clark, George Rozell and John Rozell, accounts of Samuel Meredith, 1789 and 1802–4; and Thomas Atkinson, receipt to Samuel Meredith, July 31, 1802; all in Clymer-Meredith-Read Papers. Robinson, daybook.

87. John Nutt, advertisement in *Wilmington Centinel and General Advertiser* (Wilmington, N.C.), July 23, 1788, and notice in *Hall's Wilmington Gazette* (Wilmington, N.C.), June 21, 1798 (citation file, MESDA).

88. Thomas and James Beggs, advertisement in *Fayetteville Gazette* (Fayetteville, N.C.), January 3, 1793, as quoted in James H. Craig, *The Arts and Crafts in North Carolina, 1699–1840* (Winston-Salem: Old Salem for the Museum of Early Southern Decorative Arts, 1965), pp. 148–49. James Beggs, alone, took apprentices in 1799 and 1800, as recorded in Craig, *Arts and Crafts,* pp. 157–58. James Anderson, advertisement in *Georgia Gazette* (Savannah), September 2, 1797; Simon Connor, advertisements in *Gazette of the State of Georgia* (Savannah), January 12, 1786, and March 22, 1799, and note to Mrs. Massey; all as quoted in Theus, *Savannah Furniture,* pp. 44–45, 49–50.

89. Joel Brown, and Dillworth and Priest, advertisements in *Petersburg Intelligencer* (Petersburg,

Va.), September 21, 1804, and July 11, 1806; and Archer Brown, and Joel Brown, advertisements in *Petersburg Republican,* January 22, 1805, and October 20, 1806 (all in citation file, MESDA).

90. Information about the Fairfax riding chair comes from *The Mount Vernon Ladies Association of the Union Annual Report, 1953* (Mount Vernon, Va., 1954), pp. 44–46. Chairs with crest pieces of the same or variant patterns are illustrated in Evans, *American Windsor Chairs,* figs. 3-153, 4-7, 4-9.

91. Garret, account book. A double wagon chair with a slat back is illustrated in Wallace Nutting, *Furniture Treasury* (1928; reprint, New York: Macmillan, 1966), fig. 1735.

92. Solomon Cole, account book, 1794–1809, CHS; Boynton, ledger; Harris Beckwith, ledger, 1803–7, Forbes Library, Northampton, Mass. (document brought to author's attention by Leigh Keno); Proud brothers, ledger, 1779–1825.

93. Garret, account book; John Ballard, bill to Gen. Salem Towne, June 5, 1817, Salem Towne Papers, OSV; Lambert Hitchcock, advertisement in *Courant* (Hartford, Conn.), March 18, 1822, as illustrated in John Tarrant Kenney, *The Hitchcock Chair* (New York: Clarkson N. Potter, 1971), p. 55; Chestney advertisement in B[arton] Pearce, *Albany Directory for 1820* (Albany: E. and E. Hosford, 1820), n.p.

94. Dewey, account book; Holcomb, account book; Landon, account book; James Gere, ledger,

1809–29, CSL; Alexander Low, account book, 1784–1826, Monmouth County Historical Association, Freehold, N.J.; Ada Hemstreet, "Ancestral Rumble Seats," *Antiques* 19, no. 6 (June 1931): 464–65; Ralph and Terry Kovel, *American Country Furniture, 1780–1875* (New York: Crown, 1965), p. 108.

95. Charles B. Wood III, "Mr. Cram's Fan Chair," *Antiques* 89, no. 2 (February 1966): 262–64.

96. The Cutler and Washington quotations and an illustration of a rush-bottom mechanical chair are found in Wood, "Mr. Cram's Fan Chair."

97. Wood, "Mr. Cram's Fan Chair," p. 264.

98. The Mount Vernon chair is illustrated in Santore, *Windsor Style,* 1: fig. 177. Comparable New York and Rhode Island chairs are illustrated in Evans, *American Windsor Chairs,* figs. 5-19, 6-91 (arms), 6-2 (seat, legs), 6-97 (a Huntington chair). Floyd family background is found in Dean F. Failey, *Long Island Is My Nation* (Setauket, N.Y.: Society for the Preservation of Long Island Antiquities, 1976), pp. 68–71.

99. The second washstand is owned by the Society for the Preservation of New England Antiquities, Sleeper-McCann House ("Beauport"), Gloucester, Mass. The Tuttle chairs are illustrated in Evans, *American Windsor Chairs,* figs. 7-43, 7-44. The settee is illustrated in *Americana,* April 27, 29–30, 1977 (New York: Sotheby Park-Bernet, 1977), lot 914.

Summary

The diverse forms of Windsor furniture discussed and illustrated in this volume are closely linked in several ways. Stick-and-socket construction is the common denominator, and many furniture parts are shared between forms.

The principal unit of construction in all the furniture discussed here is the wooden plank, whether it forms a seat (chairs, settees, stools), bed (cradles, wagon), or table (stands, spinning wheels, reels). This slab of wood anchors both the bases and upper parts of all standard and specialized forms, although the upper and lower structures are independent. Turned legs and posts—baluster-style in the eighteenth century and bamboo-style in the nineteenth—and shaved or turned spindles are also common to most forms. Cradles frequently are legless, and stools lack spindles. Spinning-wheel spokes are spindlelike in profile. Other elements common to Windsor construction—stretchers, arms and arm rails, and crest pieces—are present in a majority of forms. Several specialized features also serve more than one form. Rockers appear on chairs, settees, and children's chairs and cradles. Wheels provide moving power both for travel, as in the invalid's chair, the child's wagon, and the riding chair, and for spinning and winding. Storage compartments of box form are present in many writing-arm chairs; they are also part of the upright washstand and some riding chairs. The child's highchair and the countinghouse stool share a tall form.

Windsor furniture was a familiar element in American daily life following the Revolutionary War. Durable construction, bright surface colors, and modest prices all helped ensure its widespread popularity. Householders and public officials alike found that Windsor furniture served their furnishing needs and fulfilled the dictates of fashion. Chairmakers introduced the Windsor side chair at this time and began to produce sets, and even suites, of Windsor furniture. They made specialized forms in increasing numbers and variety. Probate inventories document the widespread use of Windsor furniture and offer insight into the presence and use of specialized Windsor forms in American households.

Writing chairs are rarely identified by specific construction type, but circumstantial evidence points to the Windsor in many instances. For example, writing chairs were found in households in eastern Connecticut belonging to John Avery, Jr. (d. 1815), a silversmith and clockmaker who was a customer of Ebenezer Tracy, Sr., and to Dr. Samuel Lee (d. 1815), a patron of Tracy's son-in-law Amos Denison Allen. In Philadelphia, chairmaker John B. Ackley (d. 1827) owned a similar chair valued at $1.50.[1]

The Windsor rocking chair was only moderately popular until the 1820s, when it became all the rage. Dr. Lee owned a rocking chair that was painted green. Many rockers were supplied with cushions, like those belonging to John Richards (d. 1829), shopkeeper of Boston, and Isaac Wright (d. 1838), piano manufacturer of Hartford, Connecticut. Richards also owned a nurse chair painted a dark color, and Wright possessed two "wood seat sewing chairs," which he placed in his "Keeping," or sitting, room. A Boston rocker is itemized among the household furnishings of James

Kain (d. 1838), owner of a marble yard in New York City. Reverend Ambrose Edson (d. 1836) of Somers, Connecticut, counted a rare rocking settee among his household possessions.[2]

Stationary settees were more usual than the rocking variety. John C. Vanden Heuval (d. 1826), a merchant of New York City, furnished his country house at Bloomingdale with a "large green settee" and four smaller ones. Thirteen green chairs completed what may have been a suite of furniture. Settees fitted with a cushion seem to have been popular among furniture makers. Daniel Proud (d. 1833) of Providence, Rhode Island, placed one in his "South Parlor." William Gillingham (d. 1850) of Buckingham Township, Bucks County, Pennsylvania, placed his in a similar spot.[3]

An upstairs chamber, or bedroom, was home to "2 Small Windsor chairs for Children" in the New York city residence of Thomas Marston (d. 1814). More highly specialized children's furniture includes a highchair in the household of Reverend Edson and a Windsor cradle for family use in the home of Charles C. Robinson (d. 1825), a Windsor-chair maker of Philadelphia. Lambert Hitchcock (d. 1852), the well-known Connecticut furniture manufacturer, placed a child's rocking chair in his dining room in company with adult-size rocking chairs and standard Windsor and fancy seating. The parlor was the location of a "½ Sise," or youth's, chair in John Richards's home in Boston. His rocking chair and nurse chair were in the same room.[4]

The use of crickets was common in the early nineteenth century. Daniel Proud of Providence had a pair in his "North Parlour," and the front room in the Isaac Wright home at Hartford also had two. Reverend Edson had a cricket covered with haircloth. Estate appraisers in Philadelphia identified furniture maker George Halberstadt's cricket as a footstool in 1812. Some years earlier a high seat described as a "Compting house Stool" was in the possession of Thomas West (d. 1795), a storekeeper and upholsterer of New York City. In Providence, Samuel Proud (d. 1835) used a "Stule" at his "Writing Desk." At a total valuation of 25¢, both pieces of furniture must have been simple in form.[5]

Spinning equipment is relatively common in inventories. Three estates probated on Nantucket Island, Massachusetts, between 1788 and 1799 list wheels and reels. In Westhampton, Massachusetts, the equipment of Justin Parsons (d. 1807), a chairmaker, is described specifically as a "Dutch wheel" (flax) and a "great Wheel" (wool). James Grant, a farmer of Norfolk, Connecticut, owned comparable equipment supplemented by a reel, swift, and loom. Grant's "Large wheel" was fitted with a "head," perhaps one of the early nineteenth-century patented types designed to accelerate the wool-spinning process.[6]

Standard Windsor seating—the side chairs and armchairs that made up most Windsor production—existed alongside most of the specialized household furniture described here. Sometimes standard Windsors were identified merely as green chairs, the common color of the Windsor until the postrevolutionary years, or as dining chairs, reflecting the principal function of the Windsor side chair after its introduction. Some postwar chairs were painted yellow, others black; by the early nineteenth century, some were "figured," or decorated. Windsor chairs in the household of Thomas West had "Stufft" seats. The exact locations of Windsor chairs are given in many inventories. Virtually every area of the home is listed: the parlor (also the keeping room), the dining room (or dining parlor), the kitchen, the entry (hall), the chambers (bedrooms), the piazza (porch or veranda), storage areas, and the workshop. Several affluent householders owned country seats, which they furnished with Windsors. The ubiquitous Windsor chair was part of the fabric of American life from the birth of the nation until the mid nineteenth century.[7]

Notes

1. John Avery, Jr., estate records, 1815, Preston, Conn., and Dr. Samuel Lee, estate records, 1815, Windham, Conn., Genealogical Section, Connecticut State Library, Hartford (hereafter cited as CSL); John B. Ackley, estate records, 1827–28, Philadelphia Register of Wills.

2. Lee, estate records; John Richards, estate records, 1829, Suffolk County, Mass., Registry of Probate (microfilm, Joseph Downs Collection of Manuscripts and Printed Ephemera, Winterthur Library [hereafter cited as DCM]); Isaac Wright, estate records, 1838, Hartford, Conn., and Reverend Ambrose Edson, estate records, 1836, Somers, Conn., CSL; James Kain, estate records, 1838, New York City, DCM.

3. John C. Vanden Heuval, inventory, 1826, New York City, DCM; Daniel Proud, estate records, 1833, City of Providence, Registry of Probate; William Gillingham, estate records, 1850, Bucks County, Pa., Registry of Probate.

4. Thomas Marston, inventory, 1814, New York City, DCM; Edson and Richards, estate records; Charles C. Robinson, estate records, 1825–26, Philadelphia Register of Wills; Lambert Hitchcock, estate records, 1852, Farmington, Conn., CSL.

5. Daniel Proud, Wright, and Edson, estate records; George Halberstadt, estate records, 1812, Philadelphia Register of Wills; Thomas West, inventory, 1795, New York City, DCM; Samuel Proud, estate records, 1835, City of Providence, Registry of Probate.

6. Dinah Jenkins (1788), John Ramsdell (1790), and Robert Gardner (1799), estate records, Nantucket County, Mass., Registry of Probate; Justin Parsons, estate records, 1807, Hampshire County, Mass., Registry of Probate; James Grant, estate records, 1826, Norfolk, Conn., CSL.

7. John Aspinwall (1774–86), James Barron (1803), and Captain Joseph Dobell (1811), inventories, New York City, DCM; Marston, Vanden Heuval, and West inventories; Avery, Edson, Gillingham, Hitchcock, Jenkins, Kain, Lee, Daniel Proud, Samuel Proud, Ramsdell, Richards, Robinson, and Wright, estate records.

Select Bibliography

Books

Baines, Patricia. *Spinning Wheels, Spinners, and Spinning*. London: B. T. Batsford, 1977.

Beard, Mary R., ed. *America through Women's Eyes*. New York: Greenwood Press, 1969.

Bishop, Robert. *The American Chair*. 1972. Reprint. New York: Bonanza, 1983.

Brant, Sandra, and Elissa Cullman. *Small Folk: A Celebration of Childhood in America*. New York: E. P. Dutton, 1980.

Burton, E. Milby. *Charleston Furniture, 1700–1825*. Charleston, S.C.: Charleston Museum, 1955.

Channing, Marion L. *The Textile Tools of Colonial Homes*. Marion, Mass.: By the author, 1969.

Colwill, Stiles Tuttle. *Francis Guy, 1760–1820*. Exhibition catalogue. Baltimore, Md.: Maryland Historical Society, 1981.

Craig, James H. *The Arts and Crafts in North Carolina, 1699–1840*. Winston-Salem, N.C.: Old Salem, 1965.

Denker, Ellen, and Bert Denker. *The Rocking Chair Book*. New York: Mayflower Books, 1979.

Dorman, Charles G. *Delaware Cabinetmakers and Allied Artisans, 1655–1855*. Wilmington: Historical Society of Delaware, 1960.

Dyer, Walter A., and Esther Stevens Fraser. *The Rocking-Chair: An American Institution*. New York: Century, 1928.

Earle, Alice Morse. *Child Life in Colonial Days*. New York: Macmillan, 1899.

Elder, William Voss, III. *Baltimore Painted Furniture, 1800–1840*. Exhibition catalogue. Baltimore: Baltimore Museum of Art, 1972.

Evans, Nancy Goyne. *American Windsor Chairs*. New York: Hudson Hills, 1996.

Failey, Dean F. *Long Island Is My Nation*. Exhibition catalogue. Setauket, N.Y.: Society for the Preservation of Long Island Antiquities, 1976.

Fales, Dean A., Jr. *American Painted Furniture, 1660–1880*. New York: E. P. Dutton, 1972.

———. *The Furniture of Historic Deerfield*. New York: E. P. Dutton, 1976.

Fawdry, Margaret. *Rocking Horses*. 1986. Rev. ed. London: Pollock's Toy Theatres, 1989.

Garvan, Beatrice B., and Charles F. Hummel. *The Pennsylvania Germans: A Celebration of Their Arts, 1683–1850*. Exhibition catalogue. Philadelphia: Philadelphia Museum of Art, 1982.

Garvin, Donna-Belle, James L. Garvin, and John F. Page. *Plain and Elegant, Rich and Common: Documented New Hampshire Furniture, 1750–1850*. Exhibition catalogue. Concord: New Hampshire Historical Society, 1979.

Gilbert, Christopher. *Town and Country Furniture*. Exhibition catalogue. Leeds, Yorkshire: Temple Newsam, 1972.

Gloag, John. *A Short Dictionary of Furniture*. London: George Allen and Unwin, 1969.

Gottesman, Rita Susswein, comp. *The Arts and Crafts in New York, 1726–1776*. New York: New-York Historical Society, 1938.

———, comp. *The Arts and Crafts in New York, 1777–1799*. New York: New-York Historical Society, 1954.

———, comp. *The Arts and Crafts in New York, 1800–1804*. New York: New-York Historical Society, 1965.

Greenlaw, Barry A. *New England Furniture at Williamsburg*. Williamsburg, Va.: Colonial Williamsburg Foundation, 1974.

Hageman, Jane Sikes. *Ohio Furniture Makers*. Cincinnati: By the author, 1984.

Hayward, Helena, ed. *World Furniture*. New York: McGraw-Hill, 1965.

Hazen, Edward. *Popular Technology: or, Professions and Trades*. Vol. 1. 1846. Reprint. Albany: Early American Industries Association, 1981.

Hemenway, Abby Maria, ed. *Vermont Historical Gazetteer*. Vol. 1. Burlington, Vt.: A. M. Hemenway, 1868–91.

Hepplewhite, [George]. *The Cabinet-Maker and Upholsterer's Guide*. 1794. Reprint of 3d ed. New York: Dover, 1969.

Hope, Thomas. *Household Furniture and Interior Decoration*. 1807. Reprint. New York: Dover, 1971.

Hornor, William MacPherson, Jr. *Blue Book: Philadelphia Furniture*. 1935. Reprint. Washington, D.C.: Highland House, 1977.

Hummel, Charles F. *With Hammer in Hand: The Dominy Craftsmen of East Hampton, New York*. Charlottesville: University Press of Virginia, 1968.

Jobe, Brock, ed. *Portsmouth Furniture: Masterworks from the New Hampshire Seacoast*. Boston: Society for the Preservation of New England Antiquities, 1993.

Jones, Alice Hanson. *American Colonial Wealth*. 3 vols. New York: Arno Press, 1977.

Kane, Patricia E. *300 Years of American Seating Furniture*. Boston: New York Graphic Society, 1976.

Kenney, John Tarrant. *The Hitchcock Chair*. New York: Clarkson N. Potter, 1971.

Keyser, Alan G., Larry M. Neff, and Frederick S. Weiser, trans. and ed. *The Accounts of Two Pennsylvania German Furniture Makers*. Sources and Documents of the Pennsylvania Germans, vol. 3. Breinigsville, Pa.: Pennsylvlania German Society, 1978.

Kovel, Ralph, and Terry Kovel. *American Country Furniture, 1780–1875*. New York: Crown, 1965.

Lea, Zilla Rider, ed. *The Ornamented Chair*. Rutland, Vt.: Charles E. Tuttle, 1960.

Little, Nina Fletcher. *Asahel Powers, Painter of Vermont Faces*. Exhibition catalogue. Williamsburg, Va.: Colonial Williamsburg Foundation, 1973.

The London Chair-Makers' and Carvers' Book of Prices for Workmanship. London: T. Sorrell, 1802.

Loudon, John Claudius. *An Encyclopaedia of Cottage, Farm, and Villa Architecture and Furniture*. 1833. Rev. ed. London: Longman, Orne, Brown, Green, and Longmans, 1839.

Macdonald, Dorothy K. *Fibres, Spindles, and Spinning-Wheels*. 2d ed. Toronto: Royal Ontario Museum, 1950.

Mackinnon, Joan. *A Checklist of Toronto Cabinet and Chair Makers, 1800–1865*. National Museum of Man Mercury Series. Ottawa: National Museums of Canada, 1975.

——. *Kingston Cabinetmakers, 1800–1867.* National Museum of Man Mercury Series. Ottawa: National Museums of Canada, 1976.

Miller, Edgar G., Jr. *American Antique Furniture.* Vol. 1. 1937. Reprint. New York: Dover, 1966.

Montgomery, Charles F. *American Furniture: The Federal Period.* New York: Viking, 1966.

Montgomery, Thomas Lynch, ed. *Pennsylvania Archives.* Vol. 12, sixth series. Harrisburg, Pa.: Harrisburg Publishing, 1907.

The New-York Book of Prices for Manufacturing Cabinet and Chair Work. New York: J. Seymour, 1817.

Nutting, Wallace. *Furniture Treasury.* 2 vols. 1928. Reprint. New York: Macmillan, 1966.

——. *Supreme Edition General Catalogue.* 1930. Reprint. Exton, Pa.: Schiffer, 1977.

——. *A Windsor Handbook.* 1917. Reprint. Framingham and Boston: Old America, n.d.

101 American Primitive Water Colors and Pastels. Exhibition catalogue. Washington, D.C.: National Gallery of Art, 1966.

Page, John F. *Litchfield County Furniture.* Exhibition catalogue. New York: Deerfield Books, 1962.

Pennington, David A., and Michael B. Taylor. *American Spinning Wheels.* Sabbathday Lake, Me.: Shaker Press, 1975.

Plummer, John. *The Book of Hours of Catherine of Cleves.* New York: Pierpont Morgan Library, 1964.

Prime, Alfred Coxe, comp. *The Arts and Crafts in Philadelphia, Maryland, and South Carolina, 1721–1785.* Philadelphia: Walpole Society, 1929.

——, comp. *The Arts and Crafts in Philadelphia, Maryland, and South Carolina, 1786–1800.* Topsfield, Mass.: Walpole Society, 1932.

Randall, Richard H., Jr. *American Furniture in the Museum of Fine Arts, Boston.* Boston: Museum of Fine Arts, 1965.

Ryder, Huia G. *Antique Furniture by New Brunswick Craftsmen.* Toronto: Ryerson Press, 1965.

Santore, Charles. *The Windsor Style in America.* 2 vols. Philadelphia: Running Press, 1981, 1987.

Scherer, John L. *New York Furniture at the New York State Museum.* Alexandria, Va.: Highland House, 1984.

Schiffer, Herbert F., and Peter B. Schiffer. *Miniature Antique Furniture.* Wynnwood, Pa.: Livingston, 1972.

Schiffer, Margaret B. *Chester County, Pennsylvania, Inventories, 1684–1850.* Exton, Pa.: Schiffer, 1974.

——. *Furniture and Its Makers of Chester County, Pennsylvania.* Philadelphia: University of Pennsylvania Press, 1966.

Schorsch, Anita. *Images of Childhood.* New York: Mayflower Books, 1979.

Second Supplement to the London Chair-Makers' and Carvers' Book of Prices for Workmanship. London: T. Sorrell, 1811.

Shackleton, Philip. *Furniture of Old Ontario.* Toronto: Macmillan of Canada, 1973.

Sheraton, Thomas. *Cabinet Dictionary.* 2 vols. 1803. Reprint. New York: Praeger, 1970

——. *The Cabinet-Maker and Upholsterer's Drawing Book.* 1793. Reprint. New York: Dover, 1972.

Sikes, Jane E. *The Furniture Makers of Cincinnati, 1790 to 1849.* Cincinnati: By the author, 1976.

Singleton, Esther. *The Furniture of Our Forefathers.* Garden City, N.Y.: Doubleday, Page, 1913.

Smith, George. *A Collection of Designs for Household Furniture and Interior Decoration.* 1808. Reprint. New York: Praeger, 1970.

Supplement to the London Chair-Makers' and Carvers' Book of Prices for Workmanship. London: T. Sorrell, 1808.

Swan, Mabel M. *Samuel McIntire, Carver, and the Sandersons, Early Salem Cabinet Makers.* Salem, Mass.: Essex Institute, 1934.

Theus, Mrs. Charlton M. *Savannah Furniture, 1735–1825.* N.p.: By the author, ca. 1967.

Turner, Robert P., ed. *Lewis Miller, Sketches and Chronicles.* York, Pa.: Historical Society of York County, 1966.

van Ravenswaay, Charles. *The Anglo-American Cabinetmakers of Missouri, 1800–1850.* St. Louis: Missouri Historical Society, 1958.

Walters, Betty Lawson. *Furniture Makers of Indiana, 1793 to 1850.* Indianapolis: Indiana Historical Society, 1972.

Articles

Beasley, Ellen. "Tennessee Cabinetmakers and Chairmakers through 1840." *Antiques* 100, no. 4 (October 1971): 612–21.

Boynton, Lindsay, ed. "The Hardwick Hall Inventory of 1601." *Furniture History* 7 (1971): 1–14, 23–40.

Brazer, Clarence W. "Rare Windsor Candlestands." *Antiques* 6, no. 4 (October 1924): 190–94.

Chase, Ada R. "Ebenezer Tracy, Connecticut Cabinetmaker." *Antiques* 30, no. 6 (December 1936): 266–69.

Dyer, Walter A. "The Boston Rocker." *Antiques* 13, no. 5 (May 1928): 389–92.

Evans, Nancy Goyne. "Unsophisticated Furniture Made and Used in Philadelphia and Environs, ca. 1750–1800." In *Country Cabinetwork and Simple City Furniture,* ed. John D. Morse, pp. 151–203. Charlottesville: University Press of Virginia, 1969.

Fraser, Esther Stevens. "The American Rocking-Chair." *Antiques* 13, no. 2 (February 1928): 115–18.

Gaines, Edith. "The Rocking Chair in America." *Antiques* 99, no. 2 (February 1971): 238–40.

Gillingham, Harrold E. "The Philadelphia Windsor Chair and Its Journeyings." *Pennsylvania Magazine of History and Biography* 55, no. 3 (October 1931): 301–32.

Golovin, Anne Castrodale. "Cabinetmakers and Chairmakers of Washington, D.C., 1791–1840." *Antiques* 107, no. 5 (May 1975): 898–922.

Goyne (Evans), Nancy A. "Francis Trumble of Philadelphia: Windsor Chair and Cabinetmaker." In *Winterthur Portfolio 1,* ed. Milo M. Naeve, pp. 221–41. Winterthur, Del.: Winterthur Museum, 1964.

Granquist, Charles L. "Thomas Jefferson's 'Whirligig' Chairs." *Antiques* 109, no. 5 (May 1976): 1056–60.

Hall, Elton W. "New Bedford Furniture." *Antiques* 113, no. 5 (May 1978): 1105–27.

Harlow, Henry J. "Decorated New England Furniture." *Antiques* 116, no. 4 (October 1979): 860–71.

Hemstreet, Ada. "Ancestral Rumble Seats." *Antiques* 19, no. 6 (June 1931): 464–65.

Hommel, Rudolf P. "More about Spinning Wheels." Early American Industries Association *Chronicle* 2, no. 22 (December 1942): 190–91.

Hughes, G. Bernard. "Evolution of the Spinning Wheel." *Country Life* 126, no. 3275 (December 10, 1959): 1164, 1166.

Kane, Patricia E. "Samuel Gragg: His Bentwood Fancy Chairs." *Yale University Art Gallery Bulletin* 33, no. 2 (Autumn 1971): 27–37.

Kornhauser, Elizabeth Mankin. "Ralph Earl as an Itinerant Artist: Pattern of Patronage." In *Itinerancy in New England and New York,* Dublin Seminar for New England Folk Life: Annual Proceedings, 1984, ed. Peter Benes, pp. 172–89. Boston: Boston University, 1986.

Luther, Clair F. "Anent the Rocking-Chair." *Antiques* 13, no. 5 (May 1928): 409.

Ott, Joseph K. "Recent Discoveries among Rhode Island Cabinetmakers and Their Work." *Rhode Island History* 28 (February 1969): 3–25.

Raley, Robert L. "Interior Designs by Benjamin Henry Latrobe for the President's House." *Antiques* 75, no. 6 (June 1959): 568–71.

Robinson, Olive Crittenden. "A Convertible Boston Rocker." *American Collector* 11, no. 8 (September 1942): 12–13.

Roth, Rodris. "Nineteenth-Century American Patent Furniture." In David A. Hanks, *Innovative Furniture in America from 1800 to the Present,* pp. 23–46. Exhibition catalogue. New York: Horizon Press, 1981.

Stockwell, David. "Windsors in Independence Hall." *Antiques* 62, no. 3 (September 1952): 214–15.

Stokes, J. Stogdell. "The American Windsor Chair." *Pennsylvania Museum Bulletin* 21, no. 98 (December 1925): 46–58.

Swan, Mabel M. "Furnituremakers of Charlestown." *Antiques* 46, no. 4 (October 1944): 203–6.

Thornton, Peter. "A Short Commentary on the Hardwick Inventory of 1601." *Furniture History* 7 (1971): 15–22.

Wood, Charles B., III. "Mr. Cram's Fan Chair." *Antiques* 89, no. 2 (February 1966): 262–64.

Journals of Travel and Social and Economic Commentary

Barck, Dorothy C., ed. *Letters from John Pintard to His Daughter, Eliza Noel Pintard Davidson, 1816–1833*. 4 vols. New York: New-York Historical Society, 1940.

Chambers, W[illiam]. *Things as They Are in America*. Philadelphia: Lippincott, Grambo, 1854.

Channing, George G. *Early Recollections of Newport, R.I., from the Year 1793 to 1811*. Newport, R.I.: A. J. Ward, Charles E. Hammett, Jr., 1868.

Emery, Sarah Anna. *Reminiscences of a Nonagenarian*. Newburyport, Mass.: William H. Huse, 1879.

"Extracts from the Diary of Col. Landon Carter." *William and Mary Quarterly* 13, no. 1 (July 1904): 45–53.

Martineau, Harriet. *Retrospect of Western Travel*. 2 vols. London: Saunders and Otley, 1838.

Trollope, Frances M. *Domestic Manners of the Americans*. 2 vols. London: Whittaker, Treacher, 1832.

Unpublished Works

Jarvis, Edward. "Traditions and Reminiscences of Concord, Massachusetts, . . . 1779 to 1878." Concord Free Public Library, Concord, Mass.

National Park Service. "Exhibit of Eighteenth-Century Furniture." Exhibition catalogue, Independence National Historical Park, Philadelphia, 1952.

Pillsbury, William Mitchell. "The Providence Furniture Making Trade, 1772–1834." Master's thesis, University of Delaware, 1975.

Rippe, Peter. "Daniel Clay of Greenfield." Master's thesis, University of Delaware, 1962.

Manuscripts

Manuscripts in private and public archives have been the most important sources of written information in the preparation of this work. The number of documents consulted is large and includes account books of woodworkers and other craftsmen; individual bills, receipts, and accounts; family business and household records; letters and letter books; probate and land records; census and vital records; court and apprenticeship records; and shipping and export papers. For brevity, the depositories whose holdings have been used are listed here in lieu of the documents, which are identified in the notes. The abbreviations are those used in the notes.

PRIVATE DEPOSITORIES

American Philosophical Society, Philadelphia (APS); Baker Library, Harvard University, Cambridge, Mass. (BL); Barre Historical Society, Barre, Mass. (Barre); Colonial Court Records, Social Law Library, Boston (SLL); Connecticut Historical Society, Hartford (CHS); Dartmouth College, Hanover, N.H. (DC); Girard College, Philadelphia (GC); Hagley Museum and Library, Wilmington, Del. (HML); Hay Library, Brown University, Providence, R.I. (HLB); Henry Ford Museum and Greenfield Village, Dearborn, Mich. (Ford Museum); Historic Deerfield, Deerfield, Mass. (HD); Historical Documents Collection, Queens College, Flushing, N.Y. (QC); Historical Society of Pennsylvania, Philadelphia (HSP); Institute for Colonial Studies, State University of New York, Stony Brook (SUNY); Lancaster County Historical Society, Lancaster, Pa. (LCHS); Litchfield Historical Society, Litchfield, Conn. (LHS); Maine Historical Society, Portland (MeHS); Maryland Historical Society, Baltimore (MdHS); Massachusetts Historical Society, Boston (MHS); Metropolitan Museum of Art, New York City (MMA); Monmouth County Historical Association, Freehold, N.J. (MCHA); Museum of Early Southern Decorative Arts, Winston-Salem, N.C. (MESDA); Mystic Seaport Museum, Mystic, Conn. (MSM); New England Historic Genealogical Society, Boston (NEHGS); New Jersey Historical Society, Newark (NJHS); Newport Historical Society, Newport, R.I. (NHS); New-York Historical Society, New York City (NYHS); New York State Historical Association, Cooperstown (NYSHA); Old Sturbridge Village, Sturbridge, Mass. (OSV); Peabody Essex Museum, Salem, Mass. (PEM); Rhode Island Historical Society, Providence (RIHS); Salem County Historical Society, Salem, N.J. (SCHS); Shelburne Museum, Shelburne, Vt. (SM); Sterling Memorial Library, Yale University, New Haven (Yale); Swem Library, College of William and Mary, Williamsburg, Va. (WM); Vermont Historical Society, Montpelier (VHS); Windham Historical Society, Willimantic, Conn. (WHS); Winterthur Library, Winterthur, Del. (WL), including the Joseph Downs Collection of Manuscripts and Printed Ephemera (DCM) and the Visual Resources Collection (VRC); Worcester Historical Museum, Worcester, Mass. (WHM).

PUBLIC DEPOSITORIES

County Courthouses and City/Town Halls
Baltimore Co., Baltimore, Md.; Berks Co., Reading, Pa.: Bristol Co., Taunton, Mass.; Cheshire Co., Keene, N.H.; Chittenden Co., Burlington, Vt.; Dauphin Co., Harrisburg, Pa.; Essex Co., Salem, Mass.; Hampshire Co., Northampton, Mass.; Hillsborough Co., Nashua, N.H.; Lancaster Co., Lancaster, Pa.; Nantucket Co., Nantucket, Mass.; Oxford Co., South Paris, Me.; Philadelphia Co. and Philadelphia City Hall, Philadelphia; Providence City Hall, Providence, R.I.; Rockbridge Co., Lexington, Va.; Schenectady Co., Schenectady, N.Y.; Suffolk Co., Boston; Worcester Co., Worcester, Mass.

Federal Archives and Libraries
Federal Archives and Records Center, Waltham, Mass. (FRC-Waltham); Library of Congress, Washington, D.C. (LC); National Archives, Washington, D.C. (NA); U.S. Patent Office, Washington, D.C. (PO).

State Archives, Libraries, and Other Facilities
Connecticut State Library, Hartford (CSL); State of Delaware, Division of Historical and Cultural Affairs, Dover (DDHCA); Archives and History Bureau, New Jersey State Library, Trenton (NJSL); New York State Library, Albany (NYSL); Rhode Island State Archives, Providence (RISA); Tennessee State Library, Nashville (TSL); State of Vermont, Division of Vital Records, Montpelier (VVR); State Library of Virginia, Richmond (SLV).

Local Libraries
Concord Free Public Library, Concord, Mass. (CFPL); Forbes Library, Northampton, Mass. (FL); Handley Library, Winchester, Va. (HLW); New York Public Library, New York City (NYPL).

FOREIGN DEPOSITORIES

Public Record Office, London (PRO); Westminster Public Library, London (WPL).

Newspapers

Some of the newspapers listed here reflect the ongoing publication of single serials at different periods or under different publishers with varying titles. Complete chronologies for many of these newspapers are given in Clarence S. Brigham, *History and Bibliography of American Newspapers, 1690–1820*, 2 vols. (Worcester, Mass.: American Antiquarian Society, 1947).

CONNECTICUT

American Mercury (Hartford); *Antiques and the Arts Weekly* (Newtown); *Aurora* (Norwich); *Connecticut Courier* (Bridgeport); *Connecticut Gazette* (New London); *Courant* (Hartford); *Daily Palladium* (New Haven); *Farmer's Journal* (Danbury); *Morning News* (New London); *New Haven Palladium* (New Haven); *Windham County Advertiser* (Brooklyn).

DELAWARE

Delaware Gazette (Wilmington).

DISTRICT OF COLUMBIA

Daily National Intelligencer (Washington).

GEORGIA

Columbian Museum and Savannah Advertiser (Savannah); *Gazette of the State of Georgia* (Savannah); *Georgia Gazette* (Savannah); *Republican and Savannah Evening Ledger* (Savannah).

INDIANA

Indiana Journal (Indianapolis); *Rising Sun Journal* (Rising Sun); *Western Sun* (Vincennes).

KENTUCKY

Kentucky Gazette and General Advertiser (Lexington); *Louisville Public Advertiser* (Louisville).

MAINE

Maine Antique Digest (Waldoboro).

MARYLAND

American and Commercial Daily Advertiser (Baltimore); *Baltimore Daily Repository* (Baltimore); *Federal Gazette and Baltimore Daily Advertiser* (Baltimore).

MASSACHUSETTS

Boston Gazette (Boston); *Columbian Centinel* (Boston); *Daily Evening Transcript* (Boston); *Franklin Herald and Public Advertiser* (Franklin); *Greenfield Gazette* (Greenfield); *Hampshire Gazette* (Northampton); *Independent Chronicle* (Boston); *New-Bedford Mercury* (New Bedford); *Salem Gazette* (Salem).

NEW HAMPSHIRE

Dover Gazette (Dover); *New Hampshire Gazette* (Portsmouth); *New Hampshire Patriot* (Concord); *New Hampshire Sentinel* (Keene).

NEW JERSEY

New-Jersey Journal (Elizabeth Town); *Trenton Federalist* (Trenton).

NEW YORK

New York City
American Citizen and General Advertiser; Daily Advertiser; Mercantile Advertiser; New-York Daily Advertiser; New-York Enquirer; New-York Gazette; New-York Gazette and Weekly Mercury; New-York Packet; New-York Weekly Chronicle; Rivington's New-York Gazetteer; Town and Country Journal, or the American Advertiser.

Other
Albany Chronicle (Albany); *The Portico* (Huntington).

NORTH CAROLINA

Catawba Journal (Charlotte); *Fayetteville Gazette* (Fayetteville); *Hall's Wilmington Gazette* (Wilmington); *North-Carolina Star* (Raleigh); *Western Carolinian* (Salisbury); *Wilmington Centinel, and General Advertiser* (Wilmington).

OHIO

Scioto Gazette (Chillicothe); *Western Spy and Hamilton Gazette* (Cincinnati).

PENNSYLVANIA

Berks and Schuylkill Journal (Reading); *Chester County Democrat* (Downington); *Dauphin Guardian* (Harrisburg); *Der Advocat* (Sumneytown); *Doylestown Democrat* (Doylestown); *Erie Observer* (Erie); *Farmers Register* (Greensburg); *Kline's Gazette* (Carlisle); *Lancaster Union* (Lancaster); *Lancaster Examiner and Herald* (Lancaster); *Mercantile Register or Business Man's Guide* (Philadelphia); *Pennsylvania Gazette* (Philadelphia); *Pennsylvania Journal* (Philadelphia); *Pennsylvania Packet* (Philadelphia); *Pennsylvania Republican* (Harrisburg); *Village Record* (West Chester).

RHODE ISLAND

Providence Gazette (Providence).

SOUTH CAROLINA

Charleston
Charleston City Gazette and Advertiser; Charleston Courier; Charleston Morning Post; City Gazette and Daily Advertiser; Courier; South-Carolina Gazette; South-Carolina and American General Gazette.

TENNESSEE

Knoxville Register (Knoxville); *Nashville Clarion* (Nashville); *Nashville Gazette* (Nashville); *Nashville National Banner* (Nashville); *Nashville Whig* (Nashville).

VERMONT

Northern Galaxy (Middlebury); *Vermont Gazette* (Bennington).

VIRGINIA

Alexandria Herald (Alexandria); *Petersburg Intelligencer* (Petersburg); *Petersburg Republican* (Petersburg); *Phenix* (Staunton); *Richmond Enquirer* (Richmond); *Virginia Apollo* (Petersburg); *Virginia Argus* (Richmond); *Virginia Gazette, and Petersburg Intelligencer* (Petersburg); *Virginia Herald* (Fredericksburg).

WEST VIRGINIA

Berkeley and Jefferson Intelligencer (Martinsburg); *Farmer's Repository* (Charles Town); *Lewisburg Chronicle* (Lewisburg); *Martinsburg Gazette* (Martinsburg).

CANADA

Constitution (Toronto); *Nova Scotia Royal Gazette* (Halifax); *Royal Gazette* (St. John); *Upper Canada Gazette* (Toronto).

Directories

City/town directories published from the late eighteenth century through 1850 (and later) are helpful in identifying many of the branded, stenciled, and handwritten names found on Windsor furniture and also in tracking migratory routes of artisans. Besides names, the volumes provide addresses and usually occupations. Few communities were sufficiently large or prosperous before the early nineteenth century, however, to support the publication of annual directories listing local residents. Only Charleston, Philadelphia, New York, and Boston produced directories before 1790; Baltimore and Hartford published initial volumes during the 1790s. Several dozen communities followed suit in the first half of the nineteenth century. The following directories are those that proved useful in writing this work.

Albany (1819, 1820, 1822); Boston (1850, 1852, 1853, 1856, 1860); Brooklyn, N.Y. (1832, 1835); Cincinnati (1829, 1840); Dover, N.H. (1830); *J. F. Kimball and Co.'s Eastern, Western, and Southern Business Directory* (Cincinnati, 1846); Lancaster, Pa. (1843); Louisville, Ky. (1855); New York City (1810, 1815, 1818); Providence, R.I. (1824, 1858); Rochester, N.Y. (1840); Utica, N.Y. (1843); Wilmington, Del. (1845).

Visual Resources

Decorative Arts Photographic Collection (DAPC) and Visual Resources Collection (VRC), Winterthur Library, Winterthur, Del.

Index